T0350731

ŪSD

Karolinum Press / Institute of Contemporary History

Petr Roubal

Spartakiads

The Politics of Physical Culture in Communist Czechoslovakia

VÁCLAV HAVEL SERIES

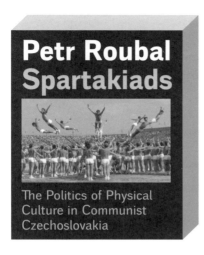

Petr Roubal
Spartakiads

The Politics of Physical
Culture in Communist
Czechoslovakia

KAROLINUM PRESS / INSTITUTE OF CONTEMPORARY HISTORY

KAROLINUM PRESS is a publishing department of Charles University
Ovocný trh 560/5, 116 36 Prague 1, Czech Republic
www.karolinum.cz

Originally published in Czech as *Československé spartakiády*, Prague:
Academia, 2016
Czech edition reviewed by Michal Kopeček (Institute of Contemporary History,
Prague), Muriel Blaive (Institute for the Study of Totalitarian Regimes, Prague)

Text © Petr Roubal, 2019
Translation © Dan Morgan, 2019
Photos © Václav Chochola – heirs, ČTK, ČTK/Pavel Khol, Zdeněk Lhoták,
Národní muzeum, Pavel Štecha – heirs, 2019
Cover photo ČTK (Performance of the army at the 1985 Czechoslovak
Spartakiad)

Cover and graphic design by /3.dílna/
Set and printed in the Czech Republic by Karolinum Press
First English edition

Cataloging-in-Publication Data is available from the National Library of the
Czech Republic

ISBN 978-80-246-3851-5 (Karolinum)
ISBN 978-80-7285-235-2 (Institute of Contemporary History)
ISBN 978-80-246-4366-3 (pdf)

CONTENTS

ACKNOWLEDGEMENTS

The publication of this book would not have been possible without the support of a number of institutions, colleagues and friends. First and foremost, I would like to thank the Central European University in Budapest for their support. Without the advice and help of my supervisor, István Rév, my research would have undoubtedly remained captive to a Manichean view of the communist past. I would also like to mention the help of others on the Central European University faculty, particularly that of Jiří Musil and Marsha Siefert who generously shared their experiences with me. From a cultural-anthropological perspective, I am most grateful to my mentors from the University of Cambridge, Paul Connerton and Nikolai Ssorin-Chaikov. No less important was the assistance of the late Henning Eichberg who helped me discover the cultural and political history of the collective movement. Hana Havelková and Libora Oates-Indruchová expanded my limited view of the subject's gender implications. Martin Franc led me to superb resources on everyday life and consumption during the Spartakiads. Also, significantly contributing to my work were the comments and suggestions made by Adéla Gjuričová, Michal Kopeček, Vítězslav Sommer and Tomáš Zahradníček, colleagues from the Institute of Contemporary History. Discussions with Horst Bredekamp, Muriel Blaive and Maja Brkljačić during the early phase of research were also enlightening. Blanka Chocholová and Marek Chochola, who willingly searched the family archive of Václav Chochola and provided his unique photographs, also deserve my gratitude.

Research for this book was supported by the Grant Agency of the Czech Republic (GPP410/11/P779), the translation by the Editorial Board of the Academy of Sciences of the Czech Republic. The English version of the book was for the most part edited during a research fellowship at Imre Kertesz Kolleg in Jena.

PREFACE

The concrete structure of the largest stadium in the world sits on a hill in Prague. Every five years from 1955 to 1985, two hundred thousand spectators, including prominent guests such as Tristan Tzara, Fernand Leger, Raul Castro, and Juan Antonio Samaranch, would watch from the stands an enormous mass spectacle unrivaled in magnitude the world over. The actors in this theater were gymnasts whose synchronized movements were meant to create the new language of a new society and provide an answer to the fundamental question of state socialism: What is a socialist people and what is their will?

All six of these spectacles known as "Spartakiads" took up only a few days over the course of the forty years of communist reign, yet we can hardly overstate their significance. Spartakiads were the most important communist ritual that best captured and literally embodied the new regime's ambition to create a new person and new society – the objective here was nothing less than the embodiment of communism. In 1955, renowned Czech poet Vítězslav Nezval celebrated Spartakiads as a prefiguration of the future communist society: "If a thousand people can on a single command, / a thousand, upon a thousand people, who don't know each other,/ don't know each others' names, don't know, didn't know each other, / if they can on a single command create a garden patch, / there's no reason, sister, there's no reason, brother, / there's no reason to despair, my friend, my comrade, / over that which gave us our most challenging tomorrow."[1] The vast funding that the party and state administration was willing to spend on this venture (between a half billion and one billion Czechoslovak crowns of that period for a single Spartakiad) attests to the importance that they attributed to

---

[1] Nezval, Vítězslav: "Sborový zpěv". *Nový život*, 1955, vol. 7, n. 9, pp. 893–896.

it. Spartakiads were also ambitious art projects bringing together, in a real *Gesamtkunstwerk* spirit, a broad range of artistic spheres: from music and choreography, to film and architecture, to design and literature (along with the aforementioned poet Nezval, other renowned figures taking part in Spartakiad projects included painter and illustrator Karel Svolinský, architect Jiří Kroha, dancer Milča Mayerová, writers Ota Pavel and Arnošt Lustig, and cinematographer Jan Špáta).

Spartakiads impacted society's everyday life in a way that no other political ritual, such as elections (voting dates were actually postponed due to Spartakiads) or May Day parades, could compare. Throughout the school year leading up to a Spartakiad performance, a million participants from the ages of twenty months to eighty years would train several times a week, and in Prague schools the school year would end early to accommodate Spartakiads. Scarce goods could be bought in Prague when Spartakiads were being held, though such goods would then understandably be even more difficult to find elsewhere and at other times. Spartakiads rhythmically arranged the lives of many Czechoslovaks, as attested to by the writer Ladislav Fuks who viewed Spartakiads as "milestones of sorts" people who "counted their own lives in terms of Spartakiad years, […] wondering if they'd live to see the next Spartakiad or even the one after that."[2] People were humming Spartakiad musical hits such as *Poupata* (Buds) for years after the event had ended. They dreamed about Spartakiads, many friendships and romances began at Spartakiads, and even more than one life was conceived there (though not to the extent that the urban myth claimed) and, though rarely, people died there.[3]

It is not the aim of this study to cover all themes opened by the Spartakiads. Instead, four fundamental questions will be examined: Where did Spartakiads as a cultural and political phenomenon

2   Fuks, Ladislav: "O spartakiádě trochu jinak". *Rudé právo*, vol. 60, 2. 7. 1980, p. 5.
3   Dryje, František: "Sen o spartakiádě, 26. 8. 80". *Analogon*, 1996, vol. 8, n. 16, p. 44.

emerge from? What was their core message, or what was being said through Spartakiads? How were their logistics organized? How did the public react to the Spartakiads? The answers to these questions form the individual chapters of this book with the exception of the second question, whose response requires two separate chapters since Spartakiads symbolized one thing for people in the 1950s and something else for people after the Prague Spring of 1968.

The predecessors of Spartakiads, the German *Turnfests* followed by the Sokol *Slets* (in Czech a *sokol* is a falcon and a *slet* is a gathering of falcons), played a crucial role in depicting the imagined community of the German or Czech nation, understood as organic communities (*Volk*). The image of aligned rows of thousands of gymnasts, which we first encounter in German cities in the 1860s, was to compensate for the lack of uniform and deeply rooted national institutions. The further development of mass gymnastic performances, which soon became one of the primary means of political representation regardless of national or political borders, supports the notion that the human body is an ideological variable.[4] Thomas Garrigue Masaryk, who later became the first Czechoslovak president, scoffed at members of the Czech Sokol community for their flag-waving Slavism that he felt slavishly imitated the German Turners. That they did so under the leadership of "Sudeten" Germans Miroslav Tyrš and Jindřich Fügner was yet another point of ridicule. Yet the imitation did not end there. In the hopes of forging "synchronized Slavism" the Czech Sokols spread Turner gymnastics to other Slavic countries. Towards the close of the 19th century, social democrats also seized upon synchronized exercises: instead of the collective body of the nation, its participants displayed class solidarity. Following split in the workers' sports movement, communist participants also embodied the revolutionary aspirations of the proletariat at the first Spartakiad in 1921. The image of the synchronized movement

---

4   Hoberman, John M.: *Sport and Political Ideology.* University of Texas, Austin 1984, p. 53.

of male (and since the early 20th century also female) bodies evoked several fundamental political themes that were crucial for both nationalist and leftist movements: the subordination of individual will to collectivity, the aestheticizing of discipline (if it is beautiful, it must also be good), collective will, commitment to defense, faith in the rationalization of society and progress (for instance, the communists adopted Tyrš's motto: "Forward! Not one step back! (*Kupředu, zpátky ni krok!*)."

The synchronized movements of the participants represented a visual political strategy by which a mass of human bodies creates the image of the nation's or people's single collective political body. The Turner and Sokol adherents certainly were not the first to make use of this impressive metaphor. The title page for Hobbes's *Leviathan* published in 1651 shows a crowned sovereign, whose body consists of a dense mass of individuals of both sexes, towering over the landscape. Having directly contributed to the creation of this image, Hobbes visualized here his social contract theory.[5] The individuals depicted are renouncing the right to live their solitary, miserable, nasty, cruel and short lives in an everyone-for-themselves war, and are forming a single collective political body of the state – a Leviathan. Since the mid-17th century when this political metaphor first appeared, the theme of the transformation of a mass of individuals into a single symbolic body has been incorporated into the repertoire of modern political regimes with a gradual shift in emphasis from the concept of the state to the concept of the nation and people. Spartakiad's representation of the communist proletariat was part of this tradition, but also significantly changed it. The communist "working people", that is to say, had the Janus face of an "obedient sovereign": The people were understandably the highest authority in a people's democracy ("all power belongs to the people"), but

---

5   Cf. Bredekamp, Horst: *Thomas Hobbes Der Leviathan. Das Urbild des modernen Staates und seine Gegenbilder. 1651–2001.* Akademie Verlag, Berlin 2003.

the decision of to whom, when and why was that of the communist party adhering to Marxist laws of historical development.[6] This theory held that the people themselves are not capable of thinking and acting; the people only know (as in the popular phrase "our people know well") and they express what is on their mind through publicly articulated consent with the party's policies. The image of a perfectly disciplined mass of Spartakiad participants, apparently not taking orders from anyone, managed to capture this antithetical nature of the communist people as an "obedient sovereign" much better than other political rituals. *Obrana lidu*, the daily of the Czechoslovak army, wrote that this was how Spartakiads were to demonstrate that the people of Czechoslovakia "stand unwaveringly behind the Communist Party, behind their National Front government, that they enjoy carrying out their bold and elaborate plans."[7]

The means by which Spartakiads embodied the working people radically changed over the course of communist rule. The first Spartakiad in 1955 presented in its various mass gymnastic pieces the people as a perfect mechanism composed of distinct social and professional groups with a clearly defined task. Participants assumed the symbolic form of workers, farmers or proletarian intelligentsia and only together did they provide a complete testimony about the socialist people. All easily interchangeable symbolic elements formed distinctly defined components of the total mechanism "in our enormous socialist workshop."[8] The symbolism of the mechanism was explicitly developed by the most successful performance of the first Spartakiad entitled *A New Shift Begins*, at the end of which the participants formed with their bodies the image of several huge turning cogwheels. In contrast to previous Sokol practices, the body and its movements were also subordinate to this mechanical logic.

---

6   Fidelius, Petr: *Řeč komunistické moci.* Triáda, Prague 1998. The people thus resemble the fish from Emir Kusturica's film *Arizona Dream.* The people don't think, the people know.

7   "Krása i zbraň". *Obrana lidu,* vol. 14, 2. 7. 1955, p. 1.

8   "Květiny bílé po cestě…". *Rudé právo,* vol. 35, 3. 7. 1955, p. 2.

The participants' bodies were materials for the creation of various words and symbols; their movement was then intended to depict a wide range of work activities.

In contrast to this, later Spartakiads, especially the three that fell within the "normalization" period, i.e. the consolidation period that followed the Soviet led intervention against the Prague Spring in 1968 and lasted till 1989, largely returned to the Sokol representation of the people as an organism.[9] The symbolic elements were no longer mechanically arranged one after another, but the symbolism of the individual compositions – a happy childhood, the beauty of a woman's body, male courage – together created a firm and self-enveloped "organic" whole. If the symbol of the first Spartakiad consisted of a gear made up of the participants' bodies, the Spartakiads during the normalization period were best encapsulated by parents (mothers) performing mass gymnastic routines with three- to six-year-old children that referred to the "unchanging" world of the nature and family. The mass choreography was also altered: instead of symbols and letters, the participants used their bodies to create simple abstract compositions of regular geometrical formations (one of the creators of the cancelled 1990 Spartakiad even suggested using Piet Mondrian's abstract paintings for the choreography).[10]

These changes did not merely lead to a simple return to the Sokol tradition; the creators and sponsors of normalization Spartakiads also attempted to find the lowest common denominator between the ruling power and the public at large and to eliminate all disruptive elements (e.g. the traditional Soviet flag disappeared from Spartakiads during normalization). It essentially consisted of a strange

9   For a general discussion of the term "normalization" in Eastern Europe see Fulbrook, Mary. "The Concept of "Normalisation" and the GDR in Comparative Perspective." In: Mary Fulbrook (ed.): *Power and Society in the GDR, 1961–1979. The "Normalisation of Rule"?* Berghahn Books, New York, Oxford 2009.
10   Belšan, Pavel: "Choreografie a funkce náčiní, nářadí a režijních prostředků ve skladbách ČSS". In: *Sborník ze semináře FTVS UK Praha k problematice hromadných vystoupení Československé spartakiády.* Metasport, Ostrava 1986, p. 56.

type of dialogue in which the side holding all the power tried to find symbols and meanings acceptable for the ritual's consumers. The prevailing view among scholars is that the communist rituals gradually became stale and turned into tedious duty. As explored in the fourth chapter, the Spartakiads' development instead went in the opposite direction, becoming an effective and consensual ritual. Yet their success also raises the question of whether they could still be considered a *communist* ritual.

Considering the scale and complexity of the Spartakiads, another question that arises is how such a spectacle could have been organized by the notoriously inefficient communist bureaucracy. The explanation is not overly complex: despite the assurance of the journal *Literární noviny* that Spartakiads were "not merely an altered form of the Sokol Slets," they were in fact just that.[11] In terms of organization, the Slets and Spartakiads shared a continuity that might even be considered smooth. Spartakiads were held at the Sokol Slet stadium built in 1926 and which more or less remained unchanged from the time of the final Sokol Slet until the 1970s. They followed up on the Sokol routines of simple physical exercises and the organizational network of Sokol clubs. Most importantly much of their success is owed to the professional expertise of former Sokol officials and authors of the mass gymnastic routines for the Slets, whose agenda gradually took over the specialized discourse on mass gymnastics. These individuals saw in state socialism the chance to implement the old slogan "Every Czech a Sokol!" (*Co Čech, to sokol*) through funding and political support that the new regime provided, while another part of the same Sokol subculture was serving long prison terms or seeking a new identity abroad in exile. Though the Communist Party gained a political ritual that legitimized their totalitarian ambitions, it came at the price that it provided or directly created a considerable autonomous space for former Sokol members to decide not

---

11 Frýd, Norbert: "Jsme bohatší". *Literární noviny*, 1955, vol. 4, n. 28, p. 1.

only highly specialized matters, but also those of a conceptual nature. In addition to the involvement of former Sokol members, the almost absurd generosity of state institutions was responsible for the success of Spartakiads, which became part of the "moral economy" of state socialism, a kind of symbolic exchange of gifts between the Party and the people, whereby less lofty aspects such as financial calculations were disregarded. As the authors Ota Pavel and Arnošt Lustig wrote in 1965, the Spartakiad was "a gift to the republic to commemorate its twentieth anniversary and also a gift by the republic to all of its children."[12]

The general public's reaction to Spartakiads was characterized by a broad pallet of attitudes – from open resistance of those trying to prevent Spartakiads or ridiculing them (e.g., the famous animated filmmaker Jan Švankmajer combined Spartakiad photographs with illustrations from the books of the Marquis de Sade) to enthusiastic acceptance mainly by former Sokol members and their descendents. The most common reaction by far was the attempt to "use" Spartakiads to consume everything that the regime offered in its efforts to organize a successful ritual. Perhaps we could best describe this approach in employing the term *Eigensinn*, or obstinate willfulness, which describes a tactic of the oppressed. Such people tolerate the strategy of the ruling power to the extent that is necessary, but also pursue their own objectives as far as the ruling power allows.[13] Though the party was able, with the help of Sokol specialists, to

12 Lustig, Arnošt – Ota, Pavel: "Úvod, k němuž jsme nechtěli hledat název". In: Vladimír Dobrovodský (ed.): *III. celostátní spartakiáda 1965*. Sportovní a turistické nakladatelství, Prague 1966, unpagin.

13 Alf Lüdtke came up with this term and originally used it to describe the power relations in Prussia in the first half of the 19th century, though he also applied it in his later works to Nazism and communism.. See Lüdtke, Alf: "The Role of State Violence in the Period of Transition to Industrial Capitalism. The Example of Prussia from 1815 to 1848". *Social History*, 1979, vol. 4, n. 2, pp. 175–221; Lüdtke, Alf: *Eigen-Sinn. Fabrikalltag, Arbeitererfahrungen und Politik vom Kaiserreich bis in den Faschismus*. Ergebnisse, Hamburg 1993; Lüdtke, Alf: "'… den Menschen vergessen'? – oder: Das Maß der Sicherheit. Arbeiterverhalten der 1950er Jahre im Blick von MfS, SED, FDGB und staatlichen Leitungen". In: Alf Lüdtke – Peter Becker (eds.): *Akten, Eingaben,*

create a picture of a perfectly "legible and obedient" mass on the field of Strahov Stadium, outside the stadium gates it could only helplessly watch as society appropriated Spartakiads and adapted them to its needs.

In this light, the Spartakiad example backs the theories of Malte Rolf, Karen Petrone and other scholars on Soviet rituals. In their view, Soviet rituals were usually not just boring ceremonies that viewers merely had to endure, but instead resembled folk celebrations or even, as Malte Rolf characterized them, *a rausch* or "a collective frenzy."[14] Soviet society integrated them into its everyday life; the rituals gave structure to the collective memory, experience and expectations along similar lines. There thus occurred a kind of self-sovietization, i.e. an adaptation to the new Soviet worldview with its specific perception of time and space. Society could understand the rituals as meaningful, could actively take part in them and remember and look forward to them, but this did not at all mean that it also assumed the official standards of behavior or the official discourse. Instead, these regime-organized rituals formed a frame that society filled with its own festivity, often based on traditional, religious models. Yet these various forms of adaptation, appropriation and hybridization of a socialistic ritual did not at all weaken, but strengthened them. Their adaptation to society's needs ensured that these official cultural practices penetrated the people's lives.[15]

Nevertheless, Spartakiads occupy a somewhat specific place in terms of society's involvement in socialist rituals. On the one hand it may seem that they created a very insignificant space for

Schaufenster – Die DDR und ihre Texte. Erkundungen zu Herrschaft und Alltag. Akademie Verlag, Berlin 1997, pp. 189–222.

14 Rolf, Malte: *Das sowjetische Massenfest.* Hamburger Edition, Hamburg 2006, p. 243; See also Klimó, Árpád – Rolf, Malte: "Rausch und Diktatur". *Zeitschrift für Geschichtswissenschaft*, 2003, vol. 51, n. 10, pp. 877–895.

15 Binns, Christopher A. P.: "The Changing Face of Power. Revolution and Accommodation in the Development of the Soviet Ceremonial System I., II.". *Man (New Series)*, 1979, vol. 14, n. 4, pp. 585–606; 1980, vol. 15, n. 1, pp. 170–187.

negotiations and non-conformist views. Each gymnast had his precisely defined space and predefined task; his movement could be analyzed and even retroactively corrected. It was a case of either performing the task or failing to: the participant either stood on his mark and performed correctly or he didn't. In fact, the opposite was true. Spartakiads required extensive preparations of relatively stable social groups with their own social dynamics, including rehearsals in Prague that would last several days. Unlike the May Day parades, there was much space outside the performance itself for autonomous forms of celebrations. It could even be said that, more than a hybridization of a ritual, what occurred was a carnival-like inversion of values, as Mikhail Mikhailovich Bakhtin refers to it.[16] The conduct of participants before and after the actual performance could be described as anything but the picture-perfect discipline that the participants' bodies displayed during the mass gymnastic routines. In contrast to other socialist rituals, we also find a certain difference in terms of content. The symbolism of the Spartakiads focused much more than, say, the May Day parades on the human body with its semantic ambivalence and multivalence, which (along with the Sokol connotations) allowed the participants to interpret the ritual how they wished. Spartakiad symbolism enabled the involvement of many people who would have otherwise rejected the communist ritual. Yet this kind of inclusive ritual was the very objective of the political powers.

It should be pointed out here that this study is not a comparison of the Czechoslovak Spartakiad within the broader context of the ritual practices of Eastern Bloc countries. We would find throughout the Eastern Bloc a very similar picture of the synchronization of gymnasts and their use as a specific political medium. From a comparative perspective, perhaps the most interesting would be the Soviet, East German, and Yugoslavia mass-gymnastic performances

16 Bakhtin, Mikhail M.: *Rabelais and His World.* Indiana UP, Bloomington 1984.

which, like Spartakiads, made use of the fact that, unlike other symbols such as flags and emblems, the human body could much better represent the trans-national, or in the case of East Germany, the "semi-national" collective.

In Soviet Moscow, mass gymnastic displays already began appearing in the 1920s as part of the program of a broad range of parades on Red Square. During a short intermission of a procession or directly while they were marching, athletes would use their bodies to create various words or symbols, or would present the individual types of sports in a creative manner, as attested to by the superb photographs of Alexander Rodchenko.[17]

These performances, significantly influenced by the strong Russian and Soviet tradition of circus acrobatics, largely appeared in Soviet stadiums only after the Second World War and mainly as opening and final ceremonies of the All-Union sporting events. It was also here shortly after the war that a specific genre of mass choreography in the form of "living signs" composed of spectators in the stands was conceived. As described by Mikhail D. Segal, a leading theoretician of Soviet athletic rituals, this practice originally developed as a reaction to the specific practical problem that spectators in a stadium, unlike those in the stands on Red Square, dressed arbitrarily according to their own taste, thereby "disturbing the overall color composition."[18] There was then just a small step from the attempt at having spectators wear the same color to having them form words and symbols. Organizers of the East German mass gymnastic performances in Leipzig, which otherwise followed up on the tradition of the Turnfests, copied and even improved this

---

17   Cf. Lavrentiev, Aleksandr Nikolajevich: *Alexander Rodchenko. Fotografii.* Planeta, Moscow 1987.
18   Segal, Mikhail D.: *Fizkulturnoie prazdniki i zrelishcha.* Fizkul'tura i sport, Moscow 1977, pp. 20–21; See Edelman, Robert: *Serious fun. A history of spectator sports in the USSR.* Oxford University Press, New York 1993. We come across simple messages spelled out by the spectators' bodies even earlier in stadiums of fascist Italy and Nazi Germany.

Soviet practice in a newly built stadium with a capacity of 100,000 people.[19]

Following several weeks of practice, twelve thousand spectators-cum-participants in the eastern stands of Leipzig Stadium used different colored paper signs to create rapidly changing words and symbols. Of all the Eastern Bloc rituals, the Leipzig Turnfests most resembled in character the Czechoslovak Spartakiads. Yet the Leipzig mass gymnastic festivals did not play such an important role in the East German political system, which is clear from the fact that they were held in Leipzig and irregularly. East Germany's world-class sports in particular and its major international success assumed the role there of "embodying" the national community.

Yugoslavian mass gymnastic performances were linked to the strong Sokol tradition in the individual republics. The most important events were held at the Yugoslavian People's Army Stadium as part of the annual celebrations of Youth Day (*Dan mladosti*) on May 25th, which also celebrated the birthday of Josip Broz Tito.[20] The cult of youth was directly wedded here with the cult of the leader, even after Tito's death. A celebration of the leader, even if dead, as the primary motif of Youth Day, represents the main difference when compared to the Czechoslovak Spartakiads, whose objective was to present the people as the highest authority and were implicitly defined against the cult of the leader.

Although this book does not have overly extensive theoretical ambitions, it is not completely void of theory. It has been rather heavily inspired by Clifford Geertz's understanding of rituals as elaborate discussions on the nature of power, which makes this power

19 Rodekamp, Volker (ed.): *Sport: Schau. Deutsche Turnfeste 1860–2002.* Stadtgeschichtliches Museum Leipzig, Leipzig 2002; Johnson, Molly Wilkinson: *Training Socialist Citizens. Sports and the State in East Germany.* Brill Academic Publishers, Leiden 2008.
20 Grigorov, Dimitar: "'Druže Tito, mi ti se kunemo.' Ritual and Political Power in Yugoslavia. Tito's Birthday Celebrations (1945–1987)". In: Joaquim Carvalho (ed.): *Religion, Ritual and Mythology. Aspects of Identity Formation in Europe.* Pisa University Press, Pisa 2006, pp. 275–292.

tangible and effective.[21] In this light, ritual does not merely serve as a political tool rendering ideological principles accessible to the masses, possibly covering the contradiction between ideology and social reality, but also creates its own autonomous political realm. This independence of the ritual from the political power leads to the perceived effect in which, as Geertz described it, the ritual does not serve the political power, but the power serves the ritual.[22] The symbolism of the ritual can be viewed as a text whose comprehension does not depend on a revelation of the hidden intentions of the ritual's sponsors. It is enough just to read it, or possibly translate or decipher it. Just as we do not need to see into the head of the ritual's sponsors, it is also not imperative for us to know what took place in the private worlds of individuals for the sake of creating legitimacy: what is important is the display (in this case it is physical) of consent in the public sphere. This book also draws on cultural anthropology's view of the human body as a key symbol that, owing to its symmetry and multivocality, can be a metaphor for the entire political community.[23] Ownership of the body itself is part of the very foundation of liberal political theory and forms the individual's autonomy that Canetti poetically expressed by comparing it to a windmill keeping everyone else at bay.[24] Mass gymnastic performances deliberately and explicitly attack the autonomy of an individual's body, creating an aesthetic and political shock through this denial of corporeality.

21 Geertz, Clifford: *Negara. The Theatre State in Nineteenth-Century Bali*. Princeton University Press, Princeton 1983, p. 102 and 124. See Bell, Catherine: *Ritual. Perspectives and Dimensions*. Oxford University Press, Oxford 2009, p. 129.

22 Geertz, C.: *Negara*, p. 13. In his analysis of the symbolic policy of the later Roman Empire, which he explicitly compares to the practices of state socialism, Paul Veyne similarly opposes a functionalist understanding of rituals when he writes that the emperors "did not provide *euergesiai* in order to gain and maintain power, but because they had it." Veyne, Paul: *Bread and Circuses. Historical Sociology and Political Pluralism*. Penguin Books, London 1992, p. 261.

23 Douglas, Mary: *Purity and Danger. An Analysis of Concepts of Pollution and Taboo*. Routledge & Kegan Paul, London 1978; Turner, Victor W.: *The Forest of Symbols. Aspects of Ndembu Ritual*. Cornell University Press, Ithaca 1967.

24 Canetti, Elias: *Crowds and Power*. The Viking Press, New York 1962, p. 17.

Finally, it should be noted that this study does not perceive the communist regime as totalitarian. Should this term appear here, it is describing the notion of some historical players rather than social reality. The dystopian visions of Hannah Arendt's totalitarianism aptly characterize the ambitions of communist leaders (at least for the first half of the 1950s) who undoubtedly wanted to achieve total control over society, or at least create such an impression (e.g., through the image of perfectly aligned rows of Spartakiad participants). The concept of totalitarianism as a description of social reality is inapplicable, as several decades of revisionist historiography of state socialism has already shown.[25] Society under communism may have been "communist," but it certainly remained a society in the sense that it continued to be made up of a complex of contradictory social interests and groups, from which each created its own "communism," i.e. its own *modus vivendi* with the dictatorial power of the communist party, often at the expense of other social groups.

25 See for instance Fitzpatrick, Sheila (ed.): *Stalinism. New Directions.* Routledge, London 1999; Jarausch, Konrad (ed.): *Dictatorship as Experience. Toward a Socio-Cultural History of the GDR.* Berghahn Books, New York – Oxford 1999.

A Genealogy
of the Spartakiads

The idea behind the communist mass gymnastic performances stems from 19th-century nationalist movements that aspired to forge the image of a perfect national community unified under a single will. Yet as a specific form of interaction between the human body and political power, their genealogy stretches back further, all the way to the disciplinary projects of (early) modern times whose objective was – as Michel Foucault describes them – the subordination of the body and its more efficient economic use. In addition to other physical displays such as working, hygiene, eating or sex, sports and physical exercises were also subordinated to this "political economy of the body." Two disciplinary techniques are essential for the genealogy of Spartakiads: political anatomy and social geometry. Foucault defines political anatomy as the way political power subjects the human body to a detailed inspection and manipulation, in which it is "examined, disassembled and reassembled" in order to gain the utmost control over it.[26] Society is then exposed to one other discipline that could be called "social geometry". This redraws traditional or random social bonds and replaces them with the regular distribution of bodies in a perfectly arranged grid. The disciplinary power, in Foucault's words, "manufactures" individuals: it "'trains' the moving, confused, useless multitudes of bodies and forces them into a multiplicity of individual elements – small separated cells, organic autonomies, of genetic identities and continuities, combinatory segments." Both techniques are instruments of power and science through which the body and society are studied as well as controlled. Visibility and a clear arrangement make up a key aspect of the disciplinary project: human bodies are exposed to the gaze of power, whether real or alleged, through which they become "perfectly legible".[27]

---

26 Foucault, Michel: *Discipline and Punish: The Birth of the Prison.* Knopf Doubleday, New York, p. 170.
27 Ibid, p. 145.

Of all the disciplinary techniques of this early modern project, mass gymnastic exercises were derived more than anything else from military drills as refined over the centuries. These drills gradually created a specific understanding of the body as perfect parts of a killing machine. The methods applied in this death production predated American Frederick Taylor's "scientific management" by nearly three hundred years.[28] Control over human movement was achieved by reducing it to a few dozen acts that were precisely defined and described (or drawn) in military manuals. This political anatomy, through which the body and weapon were united, was supplemented by a social geometry in which a uniform time (using drumbeats) and a uniform space (the regular arrangement of bodies on the exercising grounds and ideally also on the battlefield) was created. The military manuals were usually a military secret, and as such were printed in very few copies: the exact movements had to be "inscribed" or, rather, "copied" directly into the bodies of the military recruits.[29]

As Ulrich Bröckling has shown, under absolute monarchy the battles were won by the militaries that managed to best maintain control over their troops. This is why military manuals focused such little attention on the accuracy of shooting and more on shortening the interval between salvos and the synchronization of shots so that it would sound as much as possible like a single shot (for instance, in his military manual from the early 17th century Johann Jacobi von Wallhausen did not list "aiming" among the 32 movements that a soldier should make between his individual shots).[30] After the first shot, the soldiers were anyway shrouded in thick smoke and they

28 Doorn, Jacques van: "Militärische und industrielle Organisation". In: Joachim Matthes (ed.): *Soziologie und Gesellschaft in den Niederlanden*. Neuwied, Berlin 1965, pp. 276–300.

29 In the case of Prussia, there also occurred a direct "physical" connection with the political center since the Prussian King Frederick William I and his son Frederick William II personally wrote the military manuals. Cf. Bröckling, Ulrich: *Disziplin. Soziologie und Geschichte militärischer Gehorsamsproduktion*. Wilhelm Fink Verlag, München 1997.

30 Wallhausen, Johann Jacobi von: *Kriegskunst zu Fuss*. Oppenheim 1615.

would lose sight of the enemy line. Of high importance was the visibility of their own troops dressed in colorful uniforms so that they resembled "ornate birds" and could be controlled.[31] The objective of military drills during early modern times was not so much the subjugation of the enemy as the subjugation of the body of a side's own troops. This was less about killing technology and more about getting-killed technology.

The affinity between the production of a healthy body in gymnastic exercises and the production of death in military drills was also noticed by Horkheimer and Adorno in their *Dialectics of Enlightenment*: "Those who extolled the body in Germany, the gymnasts and outdoor sports enthusiasts, always had an intimate affinity to killing, as nature lovers have to hunting. They see the body as a mobile mechanism, with its hinged links, the flesh upholstering the skeleton. They manipulate the body, actuating the limbs as if they were already severed. The Jewish tradition instills an aversion to measuring human beings with a yardstick, because the dead are measured – for the coffin."[32]

---

31 Frie, Ewald: "Militärische Massenrituale". In: Michael Krüger (ed.): *Der deutsche Sport auf dem Weg in die Moderne. Carl Diem und seine Zeit.* LIT, Berlin 2009, p. 64. Bröckling wrote that absolute monarchies waged war as a strategic game and relied on the fact that the generals on the other side would observe the same rules that – since they shared the same social-economic organization – they had to observe. If the military of absolute monarchies clashed with a different socio-economic organization and different "political technology of the body" such as in the Battle of Valmy, perfect control over the bodies of their own units was not enough to win.
32 Adorno, Theodor W. – Horkheimer, Max: *Dialectic of Enlightenment: Philosophic Fragments*, edited by Gunzelin Shmid Noerr, translated by Edmund Jephcott. Stanford University Press, Stanford 2002, p. 216.

IDEOLOGY OF THE ORGANICISM AND BEGINNINGS OF THE MASS GYMNASTIC PERFORMANCES

The 19th-century nationalist gymnastic movements were the immediate predecessors of communist mass gymnastic performances in Central and Eastern Europe, a fact that the communist organizers never tired of stressing. They often arose as a reaction to a military defeat.[33] Military failures in the Napoleonic Wars led part of the Prussian elite to try to reform military and civilian institutions. The "nationally awakened" intelligentsia, which absorbed universalistic intellectual stimuli of the Enlightenment and French Revolution, including a new view of the "natural" human body and its movements, became involved in the reforms. It also assumed, as George Mosse pointed out, an enlightened theory of the people and the revolutionary practice of political rituals that were to "embody" this theory and provide tangible proof of a *volonté générale*.[34] Yet in the spirit of Romanticism it adapted these stimuli to the needs of a new national community (the *Volk*), i.e. a spiritual, rather than a political union based on, in the words of Isaiah Berlin, an "ideology of organicism."[35] In the absence of a united state and its institutions, national endeavors were aimed at creating the image of a united national organism – tending to its roots in the national past understood as the past of the "tribe" and not the past of institutions,

---

33 In addition to the Prussian or German Turner movement, this also applies for the competing Swedish Ling's gymnastic system that reacted to the loss of Finland, or for the Danish movement, which was a response to the later defeat to Prussia. Cf. Ljunggren, Jens: "The Masculine Road through Modernity. Ling Gymnastics and Male Socialization in Nineteenth-Century Sweden". In: James A. Mangan (ed.): *Making European Masculinities. Sport, Europe, Gender*. Routledge, London 2013, pp. 86–111; Eichberg, Henning: "Body culture and democratic nationalism. 'Popular gymnastics' in nineteenth-century Denmark". *The International Journal of the History of Sport*, 1995, vol. 12, n. 2, pp. 108–124.

34 Mosse, George L.: *The Nationalisation of the Masses. Political Symbolism and Mass Movements in Germany from the Napoleonic Wars through the Third Reich*. Cornell University Press, New York 1975, p. 2.

35 Berlin, Isaiah: *Der Nationalismus*. Hain, Bodenheim 1990.

overseeing its growth (not limited by state borders) and protecting it and immunizing it from "foreign" influences and from a seemingly endless line of national enemies.

The Prussian educator Friedrich Ludwig Jahn took up the strategically important task of democratizing gymnastics, which until then had been practiced almost exclusively only in aristocratic circles.[36] In terms of temperament – he was always disheveled and repeatedly expelled from his studies due to debts and acts of violence – Jahn was an unlikely founder of a movement that a few decades later was to produce images of perfect discipline.[37] The fruits of his intellectual labors were also undisciplined: his unsystematic and unoriginal writings, particularly the book entitled *Deutches Volkstum*, were filled with outbursts of hatred against all enemies of the German nation, such as Poles, French, priests, nobles and, above all, Jews. In Jahn's view, all of these people constituted a threat to the purity of the German people: "The purer the nation, the better; the more mixed, the worse [...] Inferior nations and inferior languages must disappear or be exterminated."[38] Marriage to a foreigner was, in Jahn's eyes, "the mere copulation of animals" and a betrayal of one's country.[39] Elsewhere he states that the German people need a war to realize their own essence and that a wilderness zone guarded by

36   In terms of gymnastics development, the Turner exercises did not represent any significant innovation – they predominantly consisted of an adaptation of health-science and pedagogical experiments of so-called philanthropists, particularly of Gutsmuths. They did, however, transform exercising into a political tool meant to create an able-bodied national community and, at the time of the Napoleonic reign, enhance the morale and physical capabilities of German men.

37   Jahn had long, ungroomed hair, a beard down to his chest, and his relationship to cleanliness was such that his contemporaries, in viewing his muddy boots, asked "whether that was part of his normal appearance or if he had deliberately attempted to soil them as much as possible, just as others tried so hard to keep them tidy." Eisenberg, Christiane: "Charismatic National Leader Turnvater Jahn". *The International Journal of the History of Sport*, 1996, vol. 13, n. 1, p. 22.

38   Quoted from Weber, Wolfgang – Black, Paula: "Muscular Anschluss. German Bodies and Austrian Imitators". In: James A. Mangan (ed.): *Superman supreme. Fascist body as political icon – global fascism*. Frank Cass, London 2000, p. 63.

39   Ueberhorst, Horst: *Friedrich Ludwig Jahn and His Time: 1778–1852*. Moos, Munich 1982, p. 114.

hungry wolves and bears needed to be created on the borders of the future unified Germany (which was to include, in addition to Austria, also Denmark and the Netherlands).[40] In his radicalism and charisma, Jahn attracted the awakening nationalist movement that was gaining particular momentum at German universities; he also had a considerable knack for acquiring funding from the Prussian throne for both himself and his supporters.[41]

Jahn began systematic "patriotic exercises" with Berlin students on specially prepared training grounds of the Prussian army outside the city walls in 1811. These events, which were soon attended by hundreds of students, became a popular spectacle for Berlin society and inspired the establishment of many other Turner clubs in Prussia and later in other German states as well. Turner exercises became a fixed part of the curriculum of Prussian schools; Jahn and many of his students held important posts in the school system and in other state institutions. Yet the rapid spreading of the Turner movement did not last long. After Turner member Karl L. Sand stabbed to death the conservative playwright August von Kotzebue (two years earlier at a gathering in Wartburg, Turner students had burned his writings), Turner clubs and later gymnastic exercises as such were banned. Jahn and many other trainers then spent a number of years in prison.[42]

After his release from prison, Jahn no longer wielded much influence on the Turner movement, which following the defeat of the revolution in 1848 was taken strongly in tow by the Prussian military. However, his legacy fundamentally formed in several regards the movement's further development. As a self-taught linguist, Jahn

---

40 Ibid.
41 Eisenberg, Ch.: "Charismatic National Leader".
42 In 1848, many radical-liberal Turners took part in the revolution and, following its defeat, emigrated to the USA where they played an important role in the development of sports and civic society. Cf. Ueberhorst, Horst: *Turner unterm Sternenbanner. Der Kampf der deutsch-amerikanischen Turner für Einheit, Freiheit und soziale Gerechtigkeit 1848 bis 1918.* Heinz Moos Verlag, Munich 1978.

created special German gymnastic terminology and even came up with the very term *turner*, derived from *torner* in the mistaken belief that it was an old Germanic word meaning "warrior." Jahn and his colleagues then formed from that root dozens of terms such as *Turnplatz*, *Turnverein*, *Turnlehrer* and *Turnerkreuz* (the symbol of the Turner movement consisted of four letters "F" arranged in a cross shape[43]). Turner members then created their own lingo, *Turnsprache*, whose perfection was the responsibility of a special group of experts, the *Turnkünstlerrat*. The compilation of new gymnastic terminology was motivated partly by linguistic purism, which had become an obsession for Jahn, and partly by an attempt to conceal the aristocratic, or courtly origin of many of the new favorite exercises, such as balancing or exercises on pommel horses. The original terminology also gave the impression of a new and exclusive society. The democratic addressing of a person with *Du* instead of *Sie*, the introduction of the informal greeting *Heil* and the simple uniform attire made of unbleached linen were all directed toward the same goal, i.e. the creation of a "horizontal community."

Jahn also founded the tradition of public gymnastic performances by Turner members, the *Turnfests*, even though these festivals hardly resembled the "classic" Turnfests of the latter third of the 19th century. One glaring difference was the complete absence of military drills, which Jahn greatly opposed (the French occupying forces at that time would not have appreciated it either).[44]

Jahn considered the festivals to be a "human necessity" where ideas materialized and were experienced.[45] Unlike the rowdy and chaotic festivals of student *Burschenschaft* fraternities, the Turnfests

---

43 The four "Fs" referred to Jahn's motto: *Frisch, fromm, fröhlich, frei!* (Healthily, devoutly, happily, freely!).
44 See for instance Elias, Norbert: *The Germans*. Polity Press, Cambridge 1994, p. 89.
45 Jahn, Friedrich Ludwig: *Deutsches Volkstum*. Niemann, Lübeck 1810, p. 337; quoted from Nolte, Claire E.: *The Sokol in the Czech Lands to 1914. Training for the Nation*. Palgrave Macmillan, New York 2002, p. 15.

were to be a meaningful ritual, "a means of unification that eliminates differences in faith, differences of geographic and class origin and creates a model of common German life."[46] Turnfests were also intended to present the new movement to the public, to gain political support for it and to convince at least part of the public to join the exercises. It was for this reason that Jahn devoted much attention to choosing the place to hold the festivals: they needed to be easily accessible and to provide the spectators with a good view of the exercise grounds. Yet perhaps Jahn's greatest legacy was his own myth as the founder or father of gymnastics (*Turnvater*), to whom almost all the German gymnastic movements and all political regimes turned for decades as a source of inspiration.

---

46 Jahn, Friedrich Ludwig: *Die Briefe Friedrich Ludwig Jahns.* Ed. Wolfgang Meyer. Verlag Paul Eberhardt, Leipzig 1913, p. 488–489; quoted from Nolte, C. E.: *The Sokol in the Czech Lands to 1914*, p. 15.

A PHYSICAL *SONDERWEG* AND THE POST-1848 TURNER MOVEMENT

The defeat of the liberal revolution of 1848 and the unification of Germany as orchestrated by "pre-modern" (east) Prussian elites sent German policy on a "special path" through modernity, for which the term *Sonderweg* came into use.[47] Setting out on a similarly special path – if we allow that a "normal path" exists – was the gymnastics movement. Gymnastics (the term "sport" was almost a slur) was not for one's individual benefit or enjoyment, but was intended to be a national duty, carried out with a clear, usually military purpose, collectively and without a competitive element. The liberal nationalistic radicalism of Jahn (he died in 1852) and his students faded away after 1848 and was replaced by loyalty to the Prussian ruling elite, by the militarization of the movement, support of imperial policy and conservative values. What had not changed was the ideological foundation that lay in the *Volk* concept. Yet towards the end of the 19th century, an emphasis placed on the organic unity of the national community paradoxically led to a permanent split in the gymnastics movement.

Turner gymnastics, which during the period of Jahn's influence were more of a competitive nature with an emphasis on individual performance, also underwent a transformation. The form of the Turner gymnastic practices, as we know it from later Turnfests, Sokol Slets and ultimately communist Spartakiads, was created by molding Jahn's gymnastics to the needs of physical education in schools. German trainer and teacher Adolph Spiess is mainly credited with this adaptation. In working with school children while in exile in Switzerland, Spiess realized that Jahn's system was not suited for this purpose since it required a special space, complex

---

47 See Kocka, Jürgen: "German History before Hitler. The Debate about the German 'Sonderweg'". *Journal of Contemporary History*, 1988, vol. 23, n. 1, pp. 3–16.

equipment and individual attention to the gymnasts. By eliminating the equipment and the more difficult exercises, Spiess came up with the *Freiübungen* (calisthenics) in the 1830s. These were exercises that did not require equipment and that could be carried out in any space, enabling an entire class to exercise as a collective with all the children making the same movements simultaneously. Spiess also introduced the *Ordnungsübungen* (marching exercises) by which participants were easily arranged, strict order was maintained and which, according to Spiess, was to resemble military discipline.[48] As a singing instructor, Spiess also strove to make the exercises rhythmic, and even composed simple scores for physical education. Pehr Henrik Ling's Swedish physical education system also took a similar route. Ling too made do without equipment, but went much further in regulating and controlling the participants' movements, with the precision of the exercises taking precedence over performance.[49]

Calisthenics were soon adopted by the Turner movement, primarily as a way to cope with the prohibition of exercising outdoors. Turners began to build richly adorned gymnasiums (*Turnhallen*) that held not only an importance for gymnastics, but also became the cultural and spiritual centers of the movement. One of the architects described them as "sanctuaries," in which a man "removes his hat and a woman holds her tongue."[50] Strict discipline needed to be ensured in the limited space of the gymnasiums to prevent collisions between the gymnasts. Moving into covered spaces meant that exercising no longer depended on the weather or time of day, and thus enabled the involvement of workers, who gradually outnumbered all other participants. Yet in democratizing the exercises, the attempt at achieving the participants' perfect discipline also intensified. Marching exercises were increasingly introduced along with

---

48 Nolte, C. E.: *The Sokol in the Czech Lands to 1914*, p. 16.
49 Ljunggren, J.: *The Masculine Road through Modernity*.
50 Mosse, G. L.: *The Nationalisation of the Masses*, quoted from Nolte, C. E.: *The Sokol in the Czech Lands to 1914*, p. 18.

the calisthenics, and in time it was difficult to distinguish Turner gymnastics from military drills.

The nature of the Turnfests, which continued to be the primary means of displaying the movement, also changed. Instead of focusing on displaying the exceptional performances of individuals, they now concentrated on the perfect discipline of the participants.[51] It is in the Turnfests of the early 1860s that we first come across the image of the synchronized movement of thousands of men, dressed in the same outfit, performing simple calisthenics to create, in the words of the organizers, a *tüchtige, kompakte Masse* (an efficient, compact mass).[52] The most important of these Germany-wide Turnfests, held in Leipzig in 1863 to commemorate the fiftieth anniversary of the defeat of Napoleon, saw the participation of some twenty thousand Turners, of which eight thousand performed the same calisthenics for tens of thousands of spectators. At the time the Turner movement had roughly 170,000 members and nearly two thousand clubs. After overcoming a crisis in the 1870s, Turnfests of a similar size were usually held in five year cycles in different German cities that vied for the chance to organize the event. In time, mass calisthenics became the festivals' main program at the expense of other parts of the program.[53] As the Turner movement rapidly expanded

---

51 For the Turnfests, see e.g. Krüger, Michael: "Turnfeste als politische Massenrituale des 19. und frühen 20. Jahrhunderts". In: Michael Krüger (ed.): *Der deutsche Sport auf dem Weg in die Moderne. Carl Diem und seine Zeit.* LIT, Berlin 2009, pp. 75–91; Rodekamp, V. (ed.): *Sport: Schau;* Düding, Dieter – Friedemann, Peter – Münch, Paul (eds.): *Öffentliche Festkultur. Politische Feste in Deutschland von der Aufklärung bis zum Ersten Weltkrieg.* Rowohlt Hamburg 1988; Neumann, Herbert: *Deutsche Turnfeste. Spiegelbild der deutschen Turnbewegung.* Limpert, Wiesbaden 1987; Pfister, Gertrud: "Militarismus in der kollektiven Symbolik der Deutschen Turnerschaft am Beispiel des Leipziger Turnfestes 1913". In: Heinrich Becker (ed.): *Sport im Spannungsfeld von Krieg und Frieden.* DVS, Clausthal-Zellerfeld 1985, pp. 64–79.
52 Quoted from Krüger, Michael: "Die Bedeutung der Deutschen Turnfeste des Reichsgründungsjahrzehnts für die kulturelle Nationsbildung in Deutschland". *Sozial- und Zeitgeschichte des Sports,* 1995, vol. 9, n. 1, p. 10. The first photographs of Turnfests come from the 1861 Berlin Turnfest; the first film footage from the 1908 Frankfurt Turnfest. See Rodekamp, V. (ed.): *Sport: Schau.*
53 Krüger, M.: "Turnfeste als politische Massenrituale des 19. und frühen 20. Jahrhunderts".

in the early 20th century, the number of Turnfest participants multiplied several times over. In 1913, in Leipzig (to commemorate the hundredth anniversary of the Battle of Leipzig) over sixty thousand Turners took part in the exercises.

The exercises themselves at the Turnfests bore a broad range of meanings. The synchronized movement of the gymnasts from all the German states (*aller deutschen Stämme*) and their uniform dress evoked, above all, the image of a country united in the same movement. The effect of such exercises becomes apparent if, for instance, we take into account that soldiers of the German Imperial Army did not wear matching attire, since their uniforms represented the various German states.[54] Following the completion of Germany's political unification, the Turnfests expressed the desire for a broader "spiritual" unification of the entire German nation regardless of state borders. The active participation of Turner clubs from the Austrian and Czech lands was among the factors that served this purpose. The unified movement of gymnasts and their visual uniformity was also proof of the Turner aspiration to not only transcend state borders, but also social classes and political parties, and to represent the German nation in its entirety. Furthermore, Turnfests showed a Germany that was militarily strong and prepared to go beyond the mere *Realpolitik* of Otto von Bismarck. At the Leipzig Turnfest in 1913, where 17,000 Turners performed synchronized calisthenics, Ferdinand Goetz, a key figure of the Turner movement, declared: "We demonstrated that we are a united nation that is strong enough to dictate its laws to the world."[55]

Turnfests successfully managed the dual role of awakening national passions and controlling them, while expressing collective national

54 Frie, E.: "Militärische Massenrituale", p. 64.
55 Hartmann, Grit: "Drei Hepp-hepps und drei Hurras. Turnfeste in Leipzig 1863–1987". In: Grit Hartmann – Cornelia Jeske – Daniel Sturm (eds.): *Stadiongeschichten 1863–2012. Leipzig zwischen Turnfest, Traumarena und Olympia*. Forum Verlag, Leipzig 2002, p. 74.

sentiment and steering them in the right direction.[56] The geometrical crowds of the Turnfests implicitly referred to their alter ego, to the potential "other crowds" of revolutions and social turmoil that were lurking in the shadows. These festivals also represented a visual political utopia of sorts: they did not present Germany as it was, but how it could be if the Turner ideal was successful implemented. That the Turnfests communicated visually through the symbolism of the body and its movement played an important role, enabling them to overcome the limitations of other forms of national communication, such as the written word, and to evoke strong emotions not unlike a religious experience. The exercises for the Turner members, who not only envisaged their imaginary community, but also physically experienced it, was an even stronger experience. It is in this light that Henning Eichberg points out the connection of all three meanings of the word "movement" in these exercises: political movement, physical movement, and emotional movement.[57]

By performing their synchronized calisthenics at Turnfests, the Turners were not only demonstrating their Germanhood, they were demonstrating their masculinity. Women did not perform at Turnfests until right before the First World War at the Leipzig Turnfest in 1913.[58] As George Mosse and others have noticed, Turner exercises represented a kind of response to the basic dilemma of male identity of the second half of the 19th century.[59] The ideal man was to be passionate and disciplined, rational and spiritual, civilized and

---

56 Krüger, M.: "Die Bedeutung der Deutschen Turnfeste", p. 17.
57 Eichberg, Henning: *Bodily Democracy. Towards a Philosophy of Sport for All.* Routledge, London 2011. Turnfests served a number of practical functions necessary for the development of the entire movement. Of particular importance was that it cultivated the physical culture since it allowed for comparisons and unification of gymnastic practices of the many Turner clubs.
58 Pfister, Gertrud: "Frauen bei deutschen Turnfesten. Zum Wandel der Geschlechterordnung in der Turnbewegung". *Sportwissenschaft*, 2000, vol. 30, n. 2, pp. 156–179. Women's performances had appeared at previous Turnfests, but these always consisted of smaller groups generally made up of the clubs of the host city.
59 Mosse, George L.: *The Image of Man. The Creation of Modern Masculinity.* Oxford University Press, Oxford 1996, p. 6. See e.g. Ljunggren, J.: *The Masculine Road through Modernity*, p. 90.

primitive. He was to be the equal of the historical heroic models of the Teutonic warriors (the Vikings were the model for the Swedish gymnasts and the Hussites for the Sokols) and also a member of modern bourgeois society. Voluntary discipline, the cultivation of the body in precise accordance with the given rules and the synchronization of movement with other men creating the image of a single national body – all at least seemingly spanned the antithetical demands placed on male identity of the 19th century.[60]

However, Germany was not unified by the exercises of Turner men in matching uniforms, but by the brutal effectiveness of the Prussian military and political machine. The Turner movement (since 1868 under the umbrella of the *Deutsche Turnerschaft*) thus lost its primary *raison d'être*.[61] Beginning in the 1880s, the Turners also had to deal with new competition in the form of sports imported mainly from England that became, especially for the youth of the middle and upper classes, much more attractive than gymnastic exercises and military drills. In absolute terms, the Turner movement continued to grow. With more than one and a half million members – even though a considerable number of them belonged to the category of non-exercising members (*Maulturner*) – it was on the eve of the First World War the largest sports organization in the world and also a key part of German civic society. Nevertheless, the

60 Mosse placed the Turnerschaft among other exclusively male collectives (*Männerbunde*), in which the subliminal homoerotic is wedded with the desire for sexual purity. The ethos of masculinity is then a way how to transform this sexual tension into moral and political categories. See also Eisenberg, Ch.: "Charismatic National Leader", p. 22. Yet the virtue of the Turners probably did not deviate from that of the average male at that time. According to testimony of one participant of the 1908 Turnfest in Frankfurt, the "roads leading to the brothels were so full that you couldn't even safely walk down them. When one Turner left a brothel, three more would enter. They ultimately had to lock the door; many of the men remained standing in a line outside." Quoted from Krüger, Arnd: "There Goes This Art of Manliness. Naturism and Racial Hygiene in Germany". *Journal of Sport History*, 1991, vol. 18, n. 1, p. 155.
61 The fulfilment of one of the basic requirement of the Turners also altered the situation, i.e. the introduction of physical education at schools (for boys) in the early 1860s, which further undermined the exclusivity of the Turner movement.

relative importance of the Turners was on the decline. The Turners responded to the loss of their dominant position by embracing conservative and even chauvinistic values and upholding the cult of the emperor – support for Bismarck's foreign policies and oppression aimed against the left in Germany.[62]

The shift toward the right led to the splintering of Germany's physical education movement along political, ethnic and gymnastic lines. At the end of the century their previous support for anti-socialist measures led to a separation of working-class Turners (*Arbeiterturnerbund*), who, though radically differing from nationalistic Turners in their political views, shared their larger right-wing rival's support for the ritualization and militarization of physical education as well as their opposition to sports. At the same time, there was dissension regarding newly introduced sports, and it created irreconcilable tension between sports, especially soccer, and gymnastics, which then accompanied physical education for decades in Central Europe.

Further splintering, this time along ethnic lines, paradoxically did not occur because the German Turners were overly chauvinistic, but because they were not chauvinistic enough. In 1887, the Austrian gymnastic clubs, based on the von Schönerer model, began introducing into their statutes the "Aryan paragraph" that was intended to ensure "purely German" exercises.[63] Gradually the entire organization of Austrian Turners (the so-called XV Region) was "aryanized" in this way. The opposition of the Germany-wide Turner organization, the *Deutsche Turnerschaft*, to this process, which in Goetze's view only led the Turners astray from their main task

---

62 Yet the relationships between the empire and the Turners were not entirely harmonious. The Turners continued to view themselves as the expression of the nation's will, existing above the state and its realpolitik. On the other hand, the ruling aristocratic elite looked upon the Turner movement, made up mainly of the lower and middle class, with scorn.

63 See Šinkovský, Roman: "Vývoj XV. turnerského kraje Deutschösterreich v letech 1886–1904. Přeměna liberálního tělocvičného svazu v antisemitskou organizaci". *Česká kinantropologie*, 2005, vol. 9, n. 1, pp. 101–110.

(i.e. the struggle "against the common enemy – the unified Slavs,")[64] and the dispute over what to do with clubs refusing the Aryan paragraph eventually led to the Austrian Turner organization becoming independent.

In response to this discrimination, but also under the influence of Zionism and of the *Muskeljudentum* idea, many Jewish gymnasts joined their own *Jüdische Turnerschaft*.[65] Its founders included prominent athletes such as Alfred Flatow, a repeat Olympic champion in gymnastics who later died at the Theresienstadt concentration camp.

64 Ibid, p. 107.
65 See e.g., Eisen, George: "Zionism, Nationalism and the Emergence of the Jüdische Turnerschaft". *Leo Baeck Institute Yearbook,* 1983, vol. 28, n. 1, pp. 247–262.

THE TURNERS AND THE THIRD REICH

Following the First World War the *Deutsche Turnerschaft* remained firmly on the right of the political spectrum (though formally maintaining all along the status of a non-partisan organization that transcended class), actively opposing the Treaty of Versailles and striving for the integration of all Turners regardless of state borders. Rather than moving toward Nazism, the German Turners gravitated toward the conservative right, just as their primary objective remained their concerns for the nation, not for race (a much stronger affinity between Nazism and the Turner movement was evident in Austria and the Sudetenland).[66] Even though the number of Turner members stagnated during the period following the First World War, two Turnfests during the Weimar Republic (Munich in 1923 and Cologne in 1928) eclipsed their predecessors both in terms of the number of active participants (250,000 and 300,000, respectively) and in the difficulty and complexity of the performed exercises.

The ambivalent relationship of the Turners to the new regime (and vice versa) became apparent soon after the Nazi takeover. The *Deutsche Turnerschaft* reacted to the new political situation with changes in its leadership: Nazi Party member Edmund Neuendorff, who in the 1920s had urged the Turners to preserve the purity of Nordic blood, became its leader.[67] Another regular Turnfest, this time in Stuttgart, had been coincidentally planned for late July 1933

---

66   The main slogan of the Austrian Turner association was "Rassenreinheit, Volkseinheit und Geistesfreiheit" (racial purity, national unity and intellectual freedom) and its members actively took part in, among other things, the July 1934 putsch. In addition to it, however, there was also a strong social-democratic and Christian-social Turner movement. See Janke, Pia: *Politische Massenfestspiele in Österreich zwischen 1918 und 1938*. Böhlau Verlag, Wien 2010, pp. 223–346. Pro vývoj turnerského hnutí v Československu See Burian, Michal: *Sudetoněmecké nacionalistické tělovýchovné organizace a československý stát v letech 1918 až 1938*. Karolinum, Prague 2012; Luh, Andreas: *Der Deutsche Turnverband in der Ersten Tschechoslowakischen Republik. Vom völkischen Vereinsbetrieb zur volkspolitischen Bewegung*. Verlag Oldenbourg, München 2006.

67   Ueberhorst, H.: *Friedrich Ludwig Jahn and His Time*, p. 77.

and needed to be modified to fit the needs of the new regime.[68] Even though it could only be partially changed (a Turnfest's preparation took several years), the new leadership of the *Deutsche Turnerschaft* made use of it to express its loyalty to Adolf Hitler. Neuendorff announced at that time that an army of Turners stood prepared *Seite an Seite, Schulter an Schulter* (side by side, shoulder by shoulder) with the SA and Stahlhelm to march towards the greater German future.[69] He also took the opportunity to declare his opposition to sports, which he believed did not create the proper feeling of brotherhood, unlike calisthenics, which took on a new meaning in the Third Reich: "When we speak of the Turner brotherhood, we mean German socialism. This is the new national-socialist thinking that currently prevails throughout the *Deutsche Turnerschaft.*"[70]

Yet the pandering of Turners to the Nazi regime received only a lukewarm reception. Although Hitler praised the Turnfest as a "festival of German strength," he shortly afterwards forced the German Turner association to disband "out of a feeling of responsibility for National Socialism."[71] The tension between Nazism and the Turners arose from two fundamental problems: First of all, as a totalitarian project National Socialism could not allow a massive organization with millions of participants and its own totalitarian-spirited program of transforming German society to autonomously exist by its side. Secondly, the Nazi leadership did not have a clear sports policy. In Hitler's view, the nation's health did not so much depend on hygiene and physical education, but on racial hygiene. Though in its anti-intellectualism Hitler appreciated the importance of gymnastics

---

68 For a detailed study of Nazi Turnfests, see Lissinna, Hartmut E.: *Nationale Sportfeste im nationalsozialistischen Deutschland*. Palatium Verlag, Mannheim 1997.

69 Krüger, M.: "Turnfeste als politische Massenrituale des 19. und frühen 20. Jahrhunderts", p. 86.

70 Neuendorff, Edmund: "Die Deutsche Turnerschaft, ihr Wesen und Wollen". In: *Führer und Turnfestordnung zum 15. Deutschen Turnfest Stuttgart 1933*. Union, Stuttgart 1933, p. 8.

71 Cf. Hajo, Bernett: *Der Weg des Sports in die nationalsozialistische Diktatur*. Hofmann, Schorndorf 1983.

in school education, it was clear from his passion for boxing and its "aggressive spirit" where he stood in the conflict between the Turners and sportsmen.[72] Many Nazi sports leaders, such as Carl Diem, the organizer of the 1936 Olympic Games in Berlin, and *Reichssportführer* Hans von Tschammer und Osten, opposed calisthenics and especially mass gymnastic performances, which they saw as "constrained drills."[73] In contrast, Alfred Baeumler, whom sports historian John Hoberman considers "the only Nazi sports theoretician worthy of attention," defended Turner exercises. The Turner exercise grounds (*Turnplatz*) was for him a physical and symbolic expression of German community, and as a public educational institution he believed that the Turner association deserved to occupy a position in the "center of culture and of the state."[74]

The Turnfest in Wroclaw (Breslau) in July 1938 was already entirely in the hands of the Nazi state. Despite its reliance on traditional Turner membership and the Turner organizational apparatus, its aesthetical facets strongly resembled the Nazi party rallies in Nuremberg (e.g., the use of floodlights to create a vertical space above the stadium). The Turnfest, which took place under the slogan *Vor uns liegt Deutchland, In uns marschiert Deutschland, Und hinter uns kommt Deutschland* (Germany lies before us, Germany marches in us, Germany is coming behind us), was clearly intended to express support for Hitler's aggression abroad.[75] Among the foreign guest participants, most of the attention by far went to the delegation of seventeen thousand Sudeten Germans headed by their

72 Hitler, Adolf: *Mein Kampf.* Zentralverlag der NSDAP, München 1942, p. 454.
73 *Richtlinien für die Leibeserziehung in Jungenschulen.* Weidmannsche Verlagsbuchhandlung, Berlin 1937, pp. 7–8; quoted from Mosse, George L.: *Nazi Culture. Intellectual, Cultural and Social Life in the Third Reich.* University of Wisconsin Press, Madison 2003, p. 282.
74 Hoberman, J.: *Sport and Political Ideology,* p. 78; Baeumler, Alfred: 'Sinn und Aufbau der deutschen Leibesübungen'. In: Baeumler, Alfred (ed.): *Männerbund und Wissenschaft.* Junker und Dünnhaupt Verlag, Berlin 1934, p. 58; quoted from Magdalinski, Tara: "Beyond Hitler. Alfred Baeumler, Ideology and Physical Education in the Third Reich". *Sporting Traditions,* 1995, vol. 11, n. 2, p. 68.
75 *Schlesische Illustrierte Zeitung,* vol. 12, n. 31, 31. 7. 1938.

1. A poster for the 1938 Turnfest in Breslau (Wrocław) (National Museum).

"leader" Konrad Henlein.[76] Another Turnfest was to be held five years later in 1943, this time in Leipzig at the intensively constructed Adolf Hitler Sportfeld designed by Werner March (who had also designed the Olympic Stadium in Berlin).[77] Yet this Turnfest never took place due to the unfavorable turn in the war.[78]

Despite all efforts by the Turners, they were unable to use the Turnfests (precisely due to their deeply rooted tradition) to express the dynamics of the new Nazi regime and its totalitarian ambition. This task fell to the Nazi party rallies in Nuremberg, which, although they greatly borrowed from the mass choreography and organizational practices of the Turnfests, fundamentally differed in content not only from the Turnfests, but also from the later communist Spartakiads. The main theme of this mass spectacle was the interaction between the omnipotent, hypnotic leader and the malleable mass of members belonging to Nazi organizations. The choreography of the Nuremberg masses (quite poor indeed when compared to the Turnfests or Spartakiads), Speer's architecture and the film representation in Leni Reifenstahl's *Triumph of the Will* were subordinate to this main idea: a completely new understanding of the people, which arose from the will of the leader and whose main objective was to serve the leader. This is well documented by a photograph published in 1935 in a book about the preparations of the aforementioned film and which shows Riefenstahl, Speer and Hitler preparing for the Nuremberg rallies.[79] Hitler is shown in the photograph using strips

76 Cf. Burian, M.: *Sudetoněmecké nacionalistické tělovýchovné organizace*, pp. 301–304.
77 Cf. Nabert, Thomas: "Stadionpläne – von der Grosskampfbahn am Völkerschlachtdenkmal zum Adolf-Hitler-Sportfeld". In: Thomas Nabert – Nannette Jackowski – Wolf-Dietrich Rost (eds.): *Sportforum Leipzig. Geschichte und Zukunft*. Pro Leipzig, Leipzig 2004, pp. 76–77. Hartmann, Grit: "Der verleugnete Architekt. Die Planungen des Werner March". In: Hartmann, G. – Jeske, C. – Sturm, D. (eds.): *Stadiongeschichten 1863–2012*, pp. 21–38; Schmidt, Thomas: *Werner March. Architekt des Olympia-Stadions: 1894–1976*. Birkhäuser, Basel – Berlin 1992.
78 Nevertheless, part of the built complex and its overall concept later served the East German Turnfests that were already being held regularly in Leipzig and had retained the Nazi modification of the name – the *Turn- und Sportfest*.
79 Riefenstahl, Leni: *Hinter den Kulissen des Reichsparteitag-Films*. Eher, München 1935, p. 31.

of paper, each of which represents several thousand SA troops, to create the mass choreography for the Nuremberg rally. Such a representation of a political leader as the creator of the malleable crowd is inconceivable within the context of Turnfests and certainly not in the case of communist Spartakiads which were, as we will later see, to depict the will of a "spontaneous" self-molding people.

In her famous essay *Fascinating Fascism*, Susan Sontag pointed out that the interaction between the leader and mass at the Nuremberg rallies took the form of a carefully orchestrated sadomasochistic orgy: "The Fascist dramaturgy centers on the orgiastic transactions between mighty forces and their puppets, uniformly garbed and shown in ever swelling numbers. [...] it glorifies surrender, it exalts mindlessness, it glamorizes death."[80]

Sontag believes the role of the leader in the Nuremberg rallies was understood as "sexual mastery of the 'feminine' masses, as rape. The expression of the crowds in Triumph of the Will is one of ecstasy. The leader makes the crowd come."[81] The Nuremberg rallies were a culmination of the described development of the German Turners' choreography of the masses, but in their "leader principle" they were also its negation.

---

80 Sontag, Susan, *Under the Sign of Saturn*. Vintage Books, New York 1991, p. 91. See also Thamer, Hans-Ulrich: "The Orchestration of the National Community. The Nuremberg Party Rallies of the NSDAP". In: Gunter Berghaus (ed.): *Fascism and Theatre. Comparative Studies on the Aesthetics and Politics of Performance in Europe 1925–1945*. Berghahn, Oxford 1996, pp. 172–190.
81 Sontag, S., *Under the Sign of Saturn*, p. 102.

THE POLITICAL AESTHETICS OF TYRŠ'S PROJECT

Prevalent throughout all German-speaking countries, Turner gymnastics also strongly influenced Germany's non-German speaking neighbors: Belgium, Denmark and, particularly, Bohemia.[82] The Turner movement then spread from Bohemia to other Slavic countries with the notable exception of Russia, where the direct impact of instructors of Turner's system played a primary role. The speed and facility by which the Turner *habitus* of gymnastics was copied follows a more general trend of imitating national movements in Central and Eastern Europe that (despite attempts at making them distinct

2. A team of Prague Sokol Gymnastic Trainers at the 1st All-Sokol Slet in 1882. The photograph documents Miroslav Tyrš's effort to conform physically to the ideal of Greek statues – seated in the middle he clenches the dumbbell to show his muscles. (National Museum).

---

82   For a general overview of Sokol's history see in particular Claire Nolte's work cited below.

from one another) were based on the same cultural repertoire. Once a nationalization model was created, it was easy to make it – in the words of Benedict Anderson – "available for pirating."[83]

Moreover, the penetration of the gymnastics system into different linguistic regions was facilitated by the non-linguistic nature of this form of culture: there was no need to translate gymnastics, it could be directly copied. The "universal" language of the body and its movements enabled it to rapidly spread, following the political liberalization of the 1860s, to all the major towns of the Slavic lands.[84] The cultural transfer of the Turner *habitus*, as also demonstrated by Tyrš's example, was mostly carried out "physically" through the practical experience of future instructors in instructor-training institutions. The fact that most of these gymnastics movements had a strong anti-German barb, and at best considered the German Turners to be their rival, did nothing to prevent the rapid spread of Turner gymnastics.

That Turner and Slavic Sokol gymnastics were so similar meant that Sokol members needed to be all the more distinct in their appearance. The Prague Sokol uniform design therefore became one of the dominant issues of the movement's earliest phase, while the nature of the exercises was not even really discussed.[85] Designed by

83 Anderson, Benedict: *Imagined Communities. Reflections on the Origin and Spread of Nationalism*. Verso, London 1993, p. 81.
84 As Marcel Mauss pointed out, the language of the body and movement, as well as the practical techniques of the body are culturally and historically conditioned (he gives as an example his own experience from the First World War when he witnessed that eight thousand spades had to be replaced because the British soldiers were unable to use the French tools). Mauss, Marcel: "Les techniques du corps". *Journal de Psychologie*, 1936, vol. 32, n. 3–4, pp. 271–293.
85 *Sokol* magazine was in 1873 so inundated with suggestions of how to change the Sokol uniform that Tyrš had to postpone for several issues the publication of his work *Gymnastics from an Aesthetic Perspective* that the magazine was publishing in installments in order to free space for this discussion. See Domorázek, Karel: "Po stopách díla". In: Miroslav Tyrš: *Tělocvik v ohledu esthetickém*. Karel Novák, Prague 1926, p. 91.

the renowned artist Josef Mánes,[86] the uniform was composed of, in addition to Garibaldi-like red shirts, a broad range of components of supposed Slavic origin, with "German" features such as buttons and button holes scrupulously avoided.

Near the end of the 19th century Tomáš G. Masaryk had poked fun at Sokol for its dependence on the German model, illustrating the "beer-hall patriotism" of the Young Czech Party: "with such Slav and Czech patriotism it is no wonder... that they drew from Germans ideas and national institutions. Sokol can serve as the best example of this: a purely German concept transferred by an ethnic German to us and decked out with national eclecticisms."[87] Yet Masaryk's characterization was not wholly accurate since Sokol did in fact differ from the Turners in several regards. One prominent difference was that Sokol was created fifty years after the Turner clubs, i.e. in a completely different developmental phase of the gymnastics culture. Sokol adopted Turner gymnastics in its highly disciplined, militarized and also decidedly non-revolutionary phase with its already encoded resistance to sports. The central ideological motive of the Turners – i.e. the unification of all German-speaking people into a single cultural community, if not directly into a single state – did not play a dominant role with the Sokols, whose main motive was to solidify a national community in the struggle against a stronger German opponent. Sokol also had to deal with the fulfillment of its own program, i.e. with political independence and redefining the sense and purpose of the gymnastics movements rooted in it, much

---

86   Yet Mánes described his designs as "Turner (turnéřský) uniform.", See Waic, Marek: *Byli jsme a budem*. Agentura Leman, Prague 2012, pp. 22–23. Though the outfit expressed the appropriate geopolitical identity of those wearing it, exercising in it (as Tyrš himself complained) was difficult. Tyrš also did not care for the "the fabric's light color on which every little beer spill was visible." See Tyrš, M.: *Tělocvik v ohledu esthetickém*, p. 25. Moreover, the outfit was too expensive: twenty years after Sokol was founded not even a third of the members owned one. Nolte, C. E.: *The Sokol in the Czech Lands to 1914*, p. 79.

87   Masaryk, Tomáš Garrigue: *Česká otázka – Naše nynější krize – Jan Hus*. Ústav T. G. Masaryka, Prague 2000, p. 88. Quoted from Nolte, C. E.: *The Sokol in the Czech Lands to 1914*, pp. 182–183 (translation modified).

later than the Turners. Finally, a fundamental difference can be found in the roles of Jahn and Tyrš in forming the programs of both movements, despite the fact that both held in their mythologies the same position of founding fathers.[88] Lacking Jahn's charisma, Tyrš made up for it with his systematic thinking and (pseudo-) scientific approach. Unlike Jahn, he was a true ideologist who equipped his movement with a basic theoretical canon.[89]

Masaryk was right in claiming that Sokol's founder Miroslav Tyrš, like his foremost colleague Jindřich Fügner, came from a purely German, Sudeten milieu.[90] Though they had their roots in a different social setting, Czechification meant the chance for social ascension and social prestige for both of these young German-speaking men. In Tyrš's case, this was also an existential matter.[91] As Vladimír Macura has pointed out, converting to a Czech national sentiment offered the opportunity to help create a completely new "world," even if it was only a "Czech world."[92] Both also Czechified their names for the needs of their new roles. Fügner only changed his first name from Heinrich to Jindřich, but Tyrš's name underwent the following gradual modifications: Friedrich Tirsch, Friedrich Tirš, Bedřich Tyrš and, finally, Miroslav Tyrš.[93]

---

88 The cult of Tyrš was mostly tended to by Tyrš's wife Renáta, Jindřich Fügner's daughter, whom Tyrš married when she was seventeen years of age and who survived him by more than fifty years. Cf. Tyršová, Renáta: *Miroslav Tyrš, jeho osobnost a dílo. Podle zápisků, korespondence, rukopisné pozůstalosti a mých vzpomínek.* Český čtenář, Prague 1932.

89 On Tyrš's ideological role see cf. Grebeníčková, Růžena: *Tělo a tělesnost v novověkém myšlení.* Prostor, Prague 1997.

90 Fügner's parents were from the towns of Litoměřice and Broumov; Tyrš's parents were from the towns of Kralupy u Chomutova and Boreč by Lovosice.

91 Cf. Waic, Marek (ed.): *Tělovýchova a sport ve službách české národní emancipace.* Karolinum, Prague 2013, p. 19.

92 Macura, Vladimír: *Masarykovy boty.* Pražská imaginace, Prague 1993, p. 12.

93 Tyrš was very thorough in his "Czechification;" he renamed his father from Vinzenz to Vítězslav and his gymnastics teacher from Schmidt to Šmid. See Jandásek, Ladislav: *Dr. Miroslav Tyrš.* Moravský legionář, Brno 1924, p. 9; Macura considered name changes to be an essential initiation ritual needed to enter an exclusive patriotic community. See Macura, Vladimír: *Znamení zrodu. České národní obrození jako kulturní typ.* H&H, Jinočany 1995, p. 122.

As a graduate and instructor of private physical education institutions, Tyrš held the exceptional position of an "intellectual gymnast" among Prague's young nationalists – both among the young Czech politicians not involved in the gymnastics movement, who were present at the birth of the Sokol movement, and among ideologically and often even nationally "unconscious" gymnasts, who were dazzled by his intellectual prowess. Tyrš's writings, particularly the programmatic tract *Náš úkol, směr a cíl* (Our Task, Direction and Objective), like his two works on *Základový tělocvik* (Basic Gymnastics) and *Tělocvik v ohledu esthetickém* (Gymnastics from an Aesthetical Perspective) acquired for many years the unchallenged status of a professional and ideological canon. Despite later revisions, these writings remained an essential referential frame for leading figures of the Sokol movement and later also for post-war communist gymnastics.

Our Task, Direction and Objective, which Tyrš mostly prepared during his rehabilitation in Switzerland following a nervous breakdown, was created under the influence of the French defeat in 1870.[94] It is a strange mix of social Darwinism, the Czech tradition of political thinking, references to antiquity and Feuerbach's and Schopenhauer's philosophies.[95] Tyrš's ideas on the Sokol program were based on collectivism – voluntary discipline and submission of the individual to the interests of the whole. The proper Sokol was, in Tyrš's view, one for whom the "individual is nothing and the whole everything."[96] Collective gymnastics were then not only intended to transform the Sokol community, but also the entire "Czecho-Slav" nation. Even though the motto "Every Czech a Sokol!" was used somewhat later and in a different context,[97] he was already argu-

---

94 Nolte, C. E.: *The Sokol in the Czech Lands to 1914*, p. 91.

95 With his work on Schopenhauer, which remained in manuscript form, Tyrš unsuccessfully tried to receive a degree at the Prague university.

96 Tyrš, Miroslav: *Náš úkol, směr a cíl*. Vzlet, Prague 1992, p. 5.

97 Tyrš, M.: *Tělocvik v ohledu esthetickém*, p. 18.

ing here that the Sokol endeavors could not possibly be considered complete until "every Czech was also a Sokol."[98] It was in this sense that Sokol was to supposedly differ from all other associations: while it still was not required that everyone be a member of a chorus, industrial or scientific club, the Sokol movement meant the "physical and partly moral education and refinement of the entire Czecho-Slav nation, its instruction aimed at strength, bravery, nobility and increased defensive power." It was therefore important to eliminate the boundary between the audience and gymnasts, "in time, all the spectators must not disappear, but take turns entering from the stands to the athletic field and for some years long to train there."[99] The Sokol therefore was not intended to be an unachievable model, but a good example for the whole nation to follow.[100] Tyrš referred to Feuerbach's statement, which was then often attributed to Tyrš himself: "Whatever the people do not know, nobody knows! Whatever the people still haven't learned, nobody has learned! Whatever has not happened to the people has not happened to anyone!"[101] The roots of Tyrš's later motto about Sokol being above party affiliation can also be found here: "This thing of ours is not for political parties, but for the entire nation."

Tyrš believed that Sokol was preparing Bohemia for nothing less than a merciless and eternal fight for survival among nations in which "that which is no longer fit to live will submit and perish."[102] In the spirit of social Darwinism, Tyrš equated natural laws with historical laws and natural species with national entities, yet did not deduce from these parallels the logical conclusion about the extinction of small and weak nations. Instead, in his "voluntarist-ethical

---

98   Tyrš, M.: *Náš úkol, směr a cíl*, p. 7.
99   Ibid, p. 8.
100   Ibid, p. 13.
101   See for instance Mucha, Vilém: *Dějiny dělnické tělovýchovy v Československu*. Olympia, Prague 1975, p. 15; or *Lví silou. Pocta a dík Sokolstvu*. Nakladatelské družstvo Máje, Prague 1948, p. 166.
102   Tyrš, M.: *Náš úkol, směr a cíl*, p. 9.

understanding of Darwinism," he adapted evolutionary doctrine to the needs of small nations.[103] Sokol publicist Venceslav Havlíček believed that Tyrš "Czechified Darwin for us" in employing a unique modification of Schopenhauer's voluntarism.[104] Large and small nations were in Tyrš's view susceptible to natural inner deterioration if they stagnated in their development. ("Where there is stagnation, there is death.") He therefore warned against the vice of complacency and urged Sokols to strive for continuous improvement ("Forward, not one step back!"[105]), even though this was to be done at a "safe and prudent speed."[106] Yet Tyrš also believed that if the nation developed "in the sun of good, truth and general progress," it would be an invincible power and "invulnerable as a sunbeam." Tyrš assigned Sokol the task of keeping the nation in motion, in "allround good spirits," but also to prepare for a real fight. "A weapon in every fist!" Tyrš roused the Sokols at the conclusion of his treatise: "Whoever plans on defending his nation in times of war must stand guard against all menace that creeps into life in times of peace; he shall use his flaming sword to crush and pulverize the vampires and bats on every field."[107]

As the first Czech art critic, Tyrš placed great emphasis on the aesthetical side of gymnastics and systematically explored in his treatise *Tělocvik v ohledu esthetickém* (Gymnastics from an Aesthetical Perspective) to what extent "our gymnastics is, at its peak, truly

103   Hermann, Tomáš: "Antropologie, evoluční teorie, život národa". In: Taťána Petrasová – Pavla Machalíková (eds.): *Tělo a tělesnost v české kultuře 19. století.* Academia, Prague 2010, pp. 15–26.
104   Havlíček, Věnceslav: *Tyršovy snahy vojenské – Tyrš či Hanuš? – Vliv Darwinovy nauky na Tyrše.* Československá obec sokolská, Prague 1923, p. 61.
105   Ibid, p. 4.
106   Tyrš, M.: *Náš úkol, směr a cíl*, p. 3. This call by Tyrš was not merely an empty proclamation, it also had a real impact on the Sokol's further development. Indeed, it legitimized (Tyrš's) attempts to modernize the gymnastics system and also set the general tone for Sokol publications, which, in addition to self-glorification, also had to show a certain degree of self-criticism.
107   Ibid, p. 14.

3. A study by Josef Mánes for an illustration of the forged Dvůr Králové Manuscript. The model for this nude was Miroslav Tyrš. Pencil drawing ca. 1858.

an art."[108] Tyrš's pioneering program of aestheticising gymnastics was the aspect in which the Sokols probably most differed from the German Turners. He was well aware of this fact and repeatedly emphasized it. "We prefer leaving the primitive crudeness to others," he wrote in 1873. "Everything we do should be adapted to a sense of beauty."[109] The "primitiveness" of the German Turners was apparently evident during their festivals where one could see "unbelievable things," such as "running from lines and even chaos during the ceremonial parades when people left to get beverages served from windows and doors, senseless disharmony during the calisthenics and round dances, a lack of fluidity during complex exercises and even the public exercise (!) of walking on one's hands *with shoes on the hands*. It can be said that in our country a sense for ceremony is developed enough that something like this would never happen."[110] Tyrš urged that the otherwise deplorable "national vanity" be turned into a positive force and contribute to the restoration of the "beauty contests" of antiquity. Thus the Czech Sokol did not necessarily have to be stronger than the German Turner, but it did have to be more beautiful.

Tyrš felt the link between art and gymnastics lay in Greek sculpture as the unsurpassed pinnacle of the plastic arts. Yet without gymnastics Greek sculpture would never have achieved its perfection, "since it was gymnastics that forever ennobled Greek bodies, and it was the gymnasiums that forever provided artists with the beautiful models for their works."[111] In Tyrš's view, gymnastics of his day was to reverse this process and "to model" the Sokol man,

---

108 Ibid, p. 10. Cf. also Krejčí, Jaroslav: *Miroslav Tyrš. Filozof, pedagog a estetik českého tělocviku.* Index, Köln 1986, pp. 123–129.

109 Tyrš, M.: *Tělocvik v ohledu esthetickém,* p. 5.

110 Ibid, p. 75. This feeling of aesthetic exclusivity was also shared by later Sokol leaders. For instance, Augustin Očenášek stated in 1926 that "the requirement for beauty" is that by which the "Sokol movement fundamentally differs from movements brought to us from the West, wildly striving for the highest possible performance of the man-machine." Očenášek, Augustin: "Doslov". In: M. Tyrš: *Tělocvik v ohledu esthetickém,* p. 102.

111 Tyrš, M.: *Tělocvik v ohledu esthetickém,* p. 9.

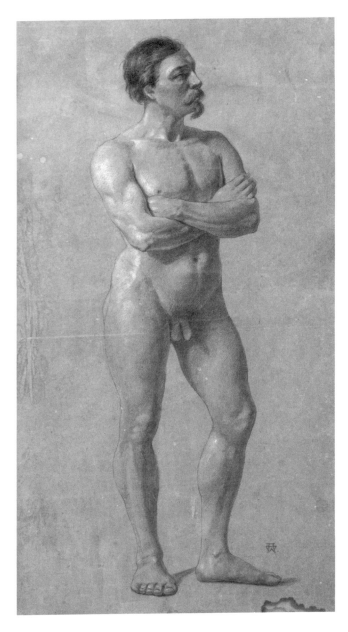

4. Nude of Tyrš
by Antonín Waldhauser
(1835–1913).

through exercises, into the form of a Greek sculpture. It was for this reason that he had denounced the one-sidedness of the Turner exercises that created a figure that did not resemble classical sculptures of antiquity and exposed the gymnast to the threat of "becoming a broad-shouldered yet bird-legged and hunched gymnast."[112] He set an example and tried to mold his own body into a work of art, which he ultimately accomplished.[113] His naked body, both *en face* and *en perdu*, was used several times as a model for artwork. The most well known is Tyrš's nude for Mánes's illustrations of manuscripts, which combined in concentrated form the cult of antiquity, the understanding of masculinity at that time, the political function of gymnastics and the national mythology.[114] Greek sculptures, whose replicas Tyrš believed should stand in every Sokol gymnasium, represented not only the aesthetical, but also the moral ideal. Then, in the sense of the Greek concept of *kalokagathia*, which brings together physical beauty and mental goodness ("a healthy soul in a healthy body"), he presented the refinement of the body as a moral imperative. Yet just as George Moss showed, the acceptance of the normative physical ideal of antiquity and its connection with the moral ideal had its dramatic consequences for those who differed in physiognomic traits from the Greek ideal.[115] Like many other intellectuals of the 19th century, Tyrš did not explicitly think through the consequences of a classical cult of beauty that implies that physical dissimilarity is a moral threat and that the purity of the (white) race becomes a moral obligation since the mixing of races can lead to a deviation away from the aesthetic-moral ideal.[116]

---

[112] Quoted from Marek, Jaroslav: "Vývoj a obsah tělovýchovné činnosti Sokola v letech 1862–1871". *Acta Universitatis Carolinae, Gymnica*, 1967, vol. 2, n. 2, p. 95.
[113] Cf. Sak, R.: *Miroslav Tyrš*, p. 59.
[114] Zich, Otakar: *Sokolstvo s hlediska estetického*. Československá obec sokolská, Prague 1920.
[115] Mosse, G. L.: *The Image of Man*, p. 56–76.
[116] The (male) body of antiquity served for Tyrš as a kind of aesthetic metaphor by which he formed his general aesthetic criteria. The laws that he found in sculptures of antiquity were to be applied in the arrangement of exercise spaces and in the positioning of bodies for exercises.

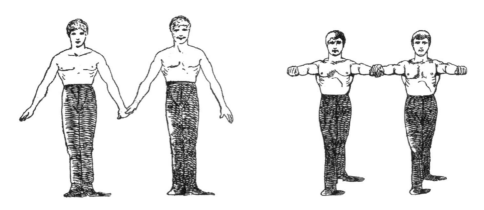

5. Tyrš's own illustration to his article on the first Sokol Slet published in *Sokol* magazine in 1882.

The beauty of gymnastics consisted of, in Tyrš's view, the absolute control over one's body and its movements, and he therefore insisted that the "body be completely under control, so that each movement is made precisely and characteristically, while still appearing unforced."[117] In contrast, the novice gymnast is unable to rid himself of "involuntary" movements: "he twitches, kicks, jerks and flings; in short, he puts all his effort into having the exercise turn out as badly as possible, offensive to the eyes."[118] Tyrš therefore recommended that the gymnasts mainly focus on simple exercises that they could perfect without too much difficulty. He insisted that even advanced gymnasts take part in mastering simple exercises for at least part of the training, the so-called "aesthetical quarter hour."[119] We once again see that the aesthetics of movement was more important for Tyrš than the physical performance. In this belief he was referring to the era's broader understanding of beauty as order and discipline;

---

117 Tyrš, M.: *Tělocvik v ohledu esthetickém*, pp. 13.
118 Ibid.
119 Ibid, p. 17.

beauty that e.g. Friedrich Schiller believed had the ability to free the individual from passion.[120] For Tyrš, therefore, beauty meant discipline, yet the opposite was also true: discipline was beauty. The gymnastic drill was to transform the cluster of gymnasts into an image of aesthetic quality through an elaborate system of rules for distributing the bodies on the exercise grounds and their mutual relations. Tyrš formulated the first basic principles of mass gymnastic compositions by which "human figures were to be used to draw regular geometrical shapes on the ground."[121] The emphasis placed on working out the aesthetical principles and their practical implementation shows to what extent the aestheticization of gymnastics became for him a way to deal with the larger and more experienced Turner rival, or even to surpass it. This successful tactic was also adopted by Sokol and Spartakiad officials in later years.

120   Mosse, G. L.: *The Nationalisation of the Masses*, pp. 25–28.
121   Tyrš, M.: *Tělocvik v ohledu esthetickém*, p. 56. See also Stehlíková, Eva: "Obřadní a divadelní prvky v sokolském hnutí". In: *Divadlo v české kultuře 19. století*. Národní galerie, Prague 1985, pp. 164–165.

SOKOL SLETS PRIOR TO THE FIRST WORLD WAR

Tyrš equipped Sokol with an ideological program, gymnastics terminology and an organizational base. Nevertheless, Sokol would not become a mass movement until nearly two decades after Tyrš's tragic and mysterious death in the Tyrolean Alps in 1884. At that time Sokol was still vying with competing firemen clubs, had fewer than three thousand men in its ranks and only a few Sokol gymnastics halls (training usually took place in the rented spaces of inns or schools). Sokol's real expansion occurred in the early 20th century. While in 1900 there were still fewer than seven thousand gymnasts, the period before the First World War saw a significant annual rise in active membership, and in 1913 the number of Sokols reached one hundred thousand, with most of the active members being junior gymnasts.[122] The swelling of the Sokol ranks is also well apparent in the increased number of Sokol gymnastics halls: 1898–55; 1905–102; 1910–126.[123] It was therefore only with the onset of the 20th century that Sokol entered the everyday life of Czech society (and to a much lesser extent in Moravia), gradually becoming the most important Czech association, with its Slets evolving into major social events. This was largely owing to the new generation of Sokol leaders who were recruited from the group of Tyrš's pupils – especially Josef Scheiner and Jindřich Vaníček.

One of driving forces of Sokol's growth was its constant rivalry with the German Turners, and especially Turners in the Czech lands. In the beginning, the Turner movement spread much faster among the German-speaking population of the Kingdom of Bohemia, and even after Sokol's later development the number of Czech- and

---

[122] The unification of the Bohemian and Moravian organizations and the inclusion of members of female members of the women's divisions also contributed to growth. Formaly the junior Sokols were not members of the movement.

[123] For Sokol gymnastic halls, see Švácha, Rostislav (ed.): *Naprej! Česká sportovní architektura 1567–2012*. Prostor – architektura, interiér, design, Prague 2012.

German-speaking gymnasts and clubs remained more or less even in the Czech lands.[124] Also playing an important role in Sokol's expansion was the Czechification of city councils, particularly in Prague, which became important sponsors of the Czech-speaking gymnastics movement.[125] Prague had come under the complete control of Czech administration by the end of the 1880s and supported Sokol's development in various ways: The city council had in fact donated land for the building of gymnastics halls (and stadiums for the Slets), and generously contributed to the preparation of Slets and provided a considerable amount to the fund to support Sokol's expansion into "endangered areas," i.e. regions with a German-speaking majority.[126] The Czech-speaking Prague bourgeoisie viewed it as a way to have Prague join the ranks of the European metropolises. For instance, in 1910 before the Sokols departed for the international competitions in London, the mayor appealed to their leader: "Mayor Dr. Groš requests that Dr. Scheiner encourage Sokol to set aside all modesty on this occasion and to try to attain for itself and for Prague the greatest possible glory and especially to request that the king receive the Czech delegation since this will be written about all over the world."[127] Sokol was well aware of the key support of Prague City Hall (half of which consisted of Sokol members) and, beginning with the second Sokol Slet in 1891, a ceremonial tribute to "Golden Prague" was included on the agenda of this ritual. The symbiosis between Sokol and Prague was symbolically rendered by Alfons Mucha

124   See Waic, Mar ek (ed.): *Německé tělovýchovné a sportovní spolky v českých zemích a Československu.* Karolinum, Prague 2008.

125   Cf. Nolte, Claire. "Celebrating Slavic Prague: Festivals and the Urban Environment," *Bohemia: Zeitschrift für Geschichte und Kultur der böhmischen Länder,* vol. 52 (2012), n. 1, pp. 37–54.

126   Pokludová, Andrea – Svatošová, Hana: "Turneři, sokolové a obecní samospráva. Opava, Olomouc, Praha". In: T. Petrasová – P. Machalíková (eds.): *Tělo a tělesnost v české kultuře 19. století,* p. 59–69. The communist historiography too maintained this term; for instance the standard textbook of history of sport spoke about "ethnically endangered areas". See Kössl, J. – Krátký, F. – Marek, J.: *Dějiny tělesné výchovy II.,* p. 9.

127   Quoted from Pokludová, A. – Svatošová, H.: "Turneři, sokolové a obecní samospráva", p. 69.

in his poster for the 1912 Slet in which the figure of Slavia holds in her left hand Prague's coat of arms (see fig. I). In terms of its rivalry with the German Turners, controlling Prague was crucial since it enabled the Sokols to organize its Slets in the capital. In contrast, the German minority, lacking a definitive center, had to make do with touring Turnfests in smaller outlying towns of the Czech Kingdom. Both Turnfests and Slets were such challenging events regarding their logistics and funding that they could hardly be organized against the will of local officials.

The Sokol Slets served the same role as the German Turnfests. Their aim was to present to the public what exactly the Sokol gymnastics entailed, to showcase the force and aspirations of the movement and to forge the image of a perfect national community that the public at large was to imitate. Karel Hlaváček, a symbolist poet wrote "We marched through the streets to settle the scores/ to show the people what we want and where we are heading / so that they would see what was revived in our arteries, / what is asleep in their veins, what we are igniting."[128] Yet the Slets also held an important internal role. Like the Turnfests, they helped integrate the individual regional parts of the movement, which, in the Czech case, was further intensified by the unwillingness of Austrian officials to permit an umbrella Sokol organization. They also established a gymnastics canon by which the individual units were governed. The similarity of the Slets and Turnfests is no coincidence: Sokols actually sent out "spies" to Turnfests who would then report in detail on these events in the Sokol press.[129]

Sokol Slets as unrivaled mass spectacles only came into being in the early 20th century. Slets of the 19th century were performed by

128 Hlaváček, Karel: "Když jsme táhli ulicemi...". In: Jan Hiller (ed.): *Památník VII. sletu všesokolského v Praze 1920.* Československá obec sokolská, Prague 1923, p. 25. For Hlaváček's later frustration with the Sokol's moderation see Nolte, C. E.: The Sokol in the Czech Lands to 1914, p. 126.
129 Waic, Marek: "Rej těl v rytmu vlastenectví. Sokolské slety 1882–1938". In: T. Petrasová – P. Machalíková (eds.): *Tělo a tělesnost v české kultuře 19. století,* pp. 51–58.

gymnasts in the hundreds rather than thousands, and often stood in the shadows of other national celebrations.[130] The first Sokol Slet in 1882, which took place on Střelecký Island in the Vltava River at the center of Prague, was still led by Miroslav Tyrš. By banging a metal disk with a wooden stick and counting out loud he kept rhythm for seven hundred Sokols, while some two thousand spectators in provisionally built stands watched them.[131] Despite the modest size of this action, Tyrš established here the main elements of the Slet and later Spartakiad ritual, which had also been taken from the ceremony model of the German gymnastics movement. This included the welcoming of guests (especially those from abroad) at train stations, a festive parade through the city, a commemoration ceremony at the tomb of the founder (and later of the founders), an accompanying cultural program (usually at the National Theatre) and gymnastic performances that culminated with synchronized calisthenics by Sokol men. The self-celebratory role of these events is already evident in the very first Slet, which was to commemorate the twentieth anniversary of the founding of the Sokol movement and to bring to a head the previous ten public Sokol gymnastic events (the first of which had taken place in 1862). The three ensuing Slets, of which two (in 1891 and 1895) were held as part of broader national celebrations – of the Jubilee Exhibition and Ethnographic Exhibition, demonstrated the gradual increase in gymnast membership as well as in the organizational skills of Sokol officials (for instance, at the first Slet they ran out of beer on the exercising grounds).[132] It is not until the two Slets preceding the war (in 1907 and 1912) that the

---

130   Later, it was the other way around. For instance, a monument to František Palacký was unveiled on the occasion of the 1912 Slet; the cornerstone to the Jan Žižka monument was laid on Vítkov Hill in Prague on the occasion of the 1920 Slet.
131   Šourek, Otakar: "Slety a umění hudební". In: *Deset sletů. Přednášky z mimořádné vzdělávací školy Československé obce sokolské o první desítce všesokolských sletů ve dnech 17. a 18. ledna 1948.* Nakladatelství Československé obce sokolské, Prague 1948, p. 35.
132   Waic, M.: "Rej těl v rytmu vlastenectví", p. 52.

events can be considered major social and political rituals.[133] Both of these Slets were prepared several years in advance. A competition was announced to compose both the gymnastic routines and the musical accompaniment with the winning entries further modified by members of the Slet technical committee. Already among these members were representatives of the new generation of gymnasts headed by Augustin Očenášek, who was inspired by the latest gymnastic trends and rejected the rigidity of Tyrš's calisthenics. These officials also oversaw the proper training method in regularly presenting calisthenics to the leaders of the individual Sokol clubs, "so that these leaders would then just as tenaciously drill their gymnasts."[134] Descriptions of the routines would also appear a year in advance in the Sokol press and an extensive promotional campaign would precede the Slet. For instance, prior to the 5th All-Sokol Slet of 1907, half a million Slet-themed postcards designed by Mikoláš Aleš were sold, and the following year an Alfons Mucha-designed poster publicized the event.[135] Both Slets were held on Letná Plain, where new event grounds were built for each Slet with considerable funding and practical assistance from Prague municipality.[136] In their scope, these proto-stadiums already resembled the architectural framework of later Slets during the First Republic and of communist Spartakiads. The event grounds for the 1907 Slet, covering some eleven hectares of Letná Plain, provided a performance space of 26,000 m² and stands for 50,000 spectators, which were filled five times over the course of the Slet. These numbers doubled for the following Slet. The performance space alone for the 6th All-Sokol

133 For more on the Slets, see in particular the commemorative publications: *Památník V. sletu všesokolského v Praze 1907.* Československá obec sokolská, Prague 1908; *Památník sletu slovanského Sokolstva roku 1912 v Praze.* Československá obec sokolská, Prague 1912. A good survey of the slets can also be found in Kozáková, Zlata: *Sokolské slety 1882–1948.* Orbis, Prague 1994.
134 Quoted from Kozáková, Z.: *Sokolské slety 1882–1948*, p. 15.
135 Mucha also designed the poster for the Marathon scene at the 1912 Slet and a poster for the 1926 Slet.
136 All Slets were held on Letná Plain from 1895 to 1920.

6. Rehearsal of the ceremonial scene "Marathon" for the VI. All-Sokol Slet in 1912 on Letná Plain.

Slet of 1912, where 10,624 cobblestones were used as place-markers, covered over 50,000 m², which is merely 20% smaller than that of the later Strahov Stadium, the biggest stadium in the world.[137]

A new part of the program for both of these Slets consisted of the "Slet scenes," featuring an enormous mass theater for the masses on the exercise grounds with hundreds of Sokol "actors." Spectators of the 1907 Slet witnessed a performance of *The Chess Tournament*, which depicted the victory of Žižka's Hussite troops over Sigismund in 1422. The performance area was designed as a chessboard with the individual squares occupied by various types of soldiers. The piece consisted of a prologue (Žižka lining up his troops against Sigismund), two main parts (the start of the fighting and the crucial battle) and the final victory scene. The following Slet included a performance of the Slet piece *Marathon* showing Athenian warriors preparing to fight the Persians. The performance, in which 1,500 Sokol members took part, was an explicit reference to Tyrš's understanding of the gymnastic practices and aesthetics of antiquity as a model worthy of emulation (and thus implicitly rejecting the Turner model).

137   Havlíček, Věnceslav: *Sokolské slety.* Sfinx, Bohumil Janda, Prague 1948, p. 25.

7. Men taking the field at the 6th All-Sokol Slet in 1912 on Letná Plain (National Museum).

The Slets also played an important role in Sokol's Slavic politics, i.e. in "gymnastic geopolitics" of sorts whose objective was to create, if not Slav unity, then at least an image of "synchronized Slavdom." This especially applies to the final pre-war Slet of 1912, which was intended to include all Slavic Sokols. Russia aside, Czech Sokols stood at the inception of physical education in all Slavic countries and took great care to cultivate contacts and build Sokol organization in these countries.[138] Sokol sent out its trainers to lead newly established Sokol clubs in various countries, as well as large delegations

---

138 A noteworthy exception was Slovakia where there was not a single Sokol club until the end of the First World War. The main reason for this was the resistance of Austrian-Hungarian authorities, though it was also due to a lack of interest by the Czech Sokols. As Nolte points out, we do not find in Tyrš's writings a single mention of Slovaks, whom one Sokol journalist described in 1907 as alcoholics, backward villagers and religious fanatics (though Karel Vaníček came to their defense by claiming wrongly that most of them were Lutherans). The American-Slovak Sokol or "native" individuals such as Andrej Hlinka in 1907 represented Slovakia at Sokol Slets. Nolte, C. E.: *The Sokol in the Czech Lands to 1914*, p. 161.

to Sokol Slets held there (e.g., the delegation of 365 Czech gymnasts outnumbered the 215 Slovenian and 60 Croatian Sokols at the Slovenian Sokol Slet in Ljubljana in 1904).[139] The visits by Slavic Sokols to each other's Slets served to solidify contacts, facilitate the sharing of gymnastics know-how and were a way to create a symbolic defense against the force of the expanding Deutsche Turnerschaft. Appearing at the "pan-Slav" Slet of 1912, over which a four-meter-tall sculpture of Slavia on a twenty-meter tall pylon loomed, was an array of Slavic guests, including female trainers of the St. Petersburg Sokol with snowballs, several hundred Serbs and Croatians with oars, American Slovaks with shepherd crooks and Bulgarians in national costumes. Many of them performed calisthenics along with the Czech Sokols to demonstrate the "physical" unity of Slavic nations. Yet the attempt to create a unified Slavic Sokol ran up against the animosities of the individual national movements: the Polish Sokol boycotted events that the Russians were invited to (the 1912 Slet), and also resisted the involvement of Ruthenians, while the Croatian and Serbian Sokols blocked participation of the Muslim Sokol from Mostar, and, as the Balkan Wars progressed, tensions rose between the Serbian and Bulgarian gymnasts, and so on.[140]

---

139 Nolte, Claire E.: "All For One! One For All! The Federation of Slavic Sokols and the Failure of Neo-Slavism". In: Pieter M. Judson – Marsha L. Rozenblit (eds.): *Constructing Nationalities in East Central Europe*. Berghahn Press, New York 2005, pp. 126–140.
140 The gymnastic geopolitics of the Sokols toward France was similarly unsuccessful. Since the late 1880s the Czech Sokol had formed strong ties to L'Union des sociétés de gymnastique de France, yet this organization was bound to the extreme edge of the French political spectrum. The French consul, who chose to leave Prague when Slets were held to avoid encountering these extremists, commented on this relationship: "The nationalists quickly won over all Slavic Czechs with an assortment of taunts, secret promises and anti-Semitism. They needed to show that they have support in Europe, and they found it in Bohemia." Nolte, C. E.: *The Sokol in the Czech Lands to 1914*, p. 120. On the other hand, the Belgian Gymnastics Federation also took part in the Czech Sokol with its leader Cupérus explicitly comparing the Czech struggle with Austria to the Flemish struggle with Francophone dominance. Cf. Tolleneer, Jan: "The dual meaning of ‚Fatherland' and Catholic gymnasts in Belgium, 1892–1914". *International Journal of the History of Sport*, 1995, vol. 8, n. 12, p. 103.

SEGREGATION AS EMANCIPATION

As in the case of the Turnfests, the Sokols also demonstrated their masculinity at the Slets, and in doing so showcased the physical strength of a nation ready to protect its interests. The synchronized movement of several hundred (and later thousand) male bodies became a metaphor for a unified, pure (morally and ethnically) and militant national community. The absence of the female body was not in this context merely proof of the existing patriarchal order, but was also a formative element in the narrative of these performances. The masculinity of the Slet performances was constantly being emphasized and amplified in various ways: the men struck tense poses in their exercises, performed topless, their movements were brusque and resembled military drills. As Claire E. Nolte has pointed out, women in the Sokol movement were relegated to a secondary position, such as the organization of public collections or helping out at the festivals of various Sokol clubs.[141] This is also attested to by Tyrš's speech from 1865: "We come to you, graceful ladies and maidens, who adorn these rooms in good company. It is your silent though powerful influence that controls men's hearts. There is no all-embracing, all-consuming patriotism unless instilled by mother's words, and woe to the nation where the efforts of men are not appreciated by their wives."[142] In the spirit of "natural selection" of social Darwinism, Tyrš encouraged the same women, "to dare not fall in love with someone who is not a Sokol member."[143]

For many years, Sokol leaders considered the involvement of women in gymnastics as a threat to their health and reputation, but

---

141 Nolte, Claire E.: "Every Czech a Sokol! Feminism and Nationalism in the Czech Sokol Movement". *Austrian History Yearbook*, 1993, vol. 24, n. 24, pp. 79–100.

142 Tyrš, Miroslav: "Řeč o veřejném cvičení Sokola Pražského dne 26. března 1865". In: Josef Scheiner (ed.): *Úvahy a řeči Dr. Miroslava Tyrše*. Nákladem tělocvičné jednoty Sokol, Prague 1894, p. 29.

143 Ibid; Cf. Havlíček, V.: *Tyršovy snahy vojenské – Tyrš či Hanuš? – Vliv Darwinovy nauky na Tyrše*, p. 61.

also to the movement's integrity. The presence of women in public exercises challenged the self-proclaimed role of Sokol as a "national army." As late as the 1890s, i.e. at a time when there were already dozens of women's divisions where women could – though separated from men – exercise, the leading Sokol ideologue Karel Vaníček (brother of gymnastics director or *náčelník* Jindřich Vaníček) defined the masculine ideal as the opposite of the insufficient female body: "[…] you won't see a languid fleshiness, or a pale thinness, like we find with female bodies, languishing in the shade, on which sweat appears right away."[144]

Yet Sokol gymnastics also possessed a certain emancipative potential. The attempt to represent the nation's body solely with male bodies and masculine symbolism could not be maintained for long, as Sokol did not only adopt the role of a "national army," but aspired to represent the nation in all of its aspects. Furthermore, the gymnastic exercises of the non-competitive variety that Sokol embraced disrupted the "one-sex model" of competitive sports in which it could be visibly demonstrated that men were physically, morally and biologically superior to women (it was intended to be clearly evident on the sports fields that men and women are completely different creatures).[145]

In contrast, calisthenics did not entail any gender hierarchy. The female body was just as capable as its male counterpart at the synchronization and perfect mastery of simple movements. In fact, external features such as a distinct costume or choreography were needed to tell the difference between the men and women exercising. Lastly, as Libuše Heczková noticed, even Tyrš's "incorporeal" ideal

---

144 Vaníček, Karel: *Sokolstvo, jeho směr a cíl.* Edv. Grégr, Prague 1891, p. 25; quoted from Randák, Jan – Nečasová, Denisa: "Genderové aspekty konstrukce reálného a symbolického těla". In: T. Petrasová – P. Machalíková (eds.): *Tělo a tělesnost v české kultuře 19. století*, p. 144.
145 See Messner, Michael A.: "Sports and Male Domination. The Female Athlete as Contested Ideological Terrain". In: Michael A. Messner – Donald F. Sabo (eds.): *Sport, men and the gender order. Critical Feminist Perspectives.* Human Kinetics Books, Champagne, Il. 1990, pp. 31–44.

of physicality had gender implications. In his view, the perfect body was that of an "eternal" ancient Greek sculpture, in a completely whitened and colorless form uncontaminated with desire. Czech literary historian Arne Novák called this kind of "incorporeal" view

8. Exercises by female members of the Žižkov Sokol at Rieger Gardens in June 1914.
This František Drtikol photograph shows female gymnasts exercising barefooted and scantily clad. The exercises led by Emanuel Siblík were carried out in the early morning hours, as ordered by town officials, so that they would not cause a public nuisance (National Museum).

"Daltonism," or color blindness, though Heczková feels that this is not necessarily a shortcoming, but rather a different way of viewing the human body led by the perfection of form, and understands it as an expression of a perfect order. Daltonism let a woman's body be understood not as a sexual, but as an aesthetical object.[146] The requirement that the male and female body become, in the nation's interest, a kind of casting of the perfect ancient Greek model, did not imply any "natural" gender hierarchy.

Women were first allowed to perform at the 1901 Slet, but it was not until the 1912 Slet that they took over full responsibility for their performance, i.e. for its choreography and rehearsal.[147] Their performance was intended to be an embodiment of the principle of "femininity in female endeavour" (*ženskost v díle ženském*) of Tyrš's pupil and first female trainer Kleméňa Hanušová.[148] The gymnastic performance, for which were solely female trainers responsible, was to emphasize the "otherness" of the female body and its movements. This was also reflected in the participants' costumes which were praised for "enhancing the slenderness and grace of the female figure and adding charm and fineness to their movements."[149] Later Sokol gymnastics director Milada Malá emphasized in her instructions to the women's performance at the Sokol Slet of 1912 the difference between the men's and women's performance:

During the training and performance both the instructors and gymnasts should keep in mind that these are exercises for women, mostly figural or dance-like, providing the chance to develop as much as possible the grace and suppleness of female movements. The power, vigor and solidity,

146 Heczková, Libuše: "Tělo v pohybu. Národní sokolské tělo od daltonismu k rytmice". In: T. Petrasová – P. Machalíková (eds.): *Tělo a tělesnost v české kultuře 19. století*, pp. 157–166.

147 Provazníková, Marie: "Vývoj sletových společných cvičení žen". In: *Deset sletů*, pp. 43.

148 Novotná, Viléma: "Ženské složky v ZRTV". In: Jarmila Kostková (ed.): *Svaz základní a rekreační tělesné výchovy*. Česká asociace Sport pro všechny, Prague 2005, p. 85.

149 Očenášek, Augustin (ed.): *Památník sletu slovanského Sokolstva roku 1912 v Praze*. Česká obec sokolská, Prague 1912, p. 135.

so appealing in the men's performance, have no place here. Yet this does not mean that precision of movements and the correctness of positions do not apply.[150]

It is significant that although Malá emphasized the gender differences, she also insisted that discipline be maintained regardless of the sex. The women's performance was noticed by the German sports press which closely followed the Slet. Depending on their political orientation, they either praised women's emancipation in Sokol and presented it as a model to be followed by German gymnastics (the social-democratic *Arbeiter-turnzeitung*) or merely recorded their surprise that "in fact there was peace and order, which one usually doesn't expect from women" (the nationalistic *Deutschösterreich-ische Turnzeitung*).[151]

Owing to the active involvement of leading figures of the women's movement, an enduring model of women's participation at mass gymnastics performances was established at the 1912 Slet. This model, which we can call "segregation as emancipation" was the only one that the Sokol leadership and, in particular, the conservative male members would tolerate. Ultimately, women were allowed to exercise together with men, providing that their routines looked different and were composed of different exercises. While prior to the First World War this model can be considered a kind of subversive strategy by the young female Sokol trainers and officials against the men's objections, in the post-war period this model was not only tolerated, but directly supported by Sokol's male leaders.

---

150   Ibid, p. 198.
151   Ibid, p. 389.

THE MYSTERY OF DEMOCRACY – SLETS DURING THE FIRST REPUBLIC

Sokol entered Czechoslovakia's First Republic in the completely different and uncustomary role of a state-forming element. Like the German Turnershaft, it had to deal with the fact that its political aspirations were fulfilled, though it could not take most of the credit for this.[152] During the first days and weeks of the new country, Sokol played a major part in maintaining order, overseeing the transition of power and creating at least a semblance of state authority, especially in Slovakia. Sokol president (*starosta*) Josef Scheiner was even appointed by the National Committee as the supreme administrator of the Czechoslovak military shortly after the country had gained its independence. Vavro Šrobár, minister for administration of Slovakia, recalled the role of the Sokols in controlling Slovakia: "The Sokols prevented a strike, manned the trains and formed a lined lane from the train station to the county hall to add gloss, confidence and pride to the Czechoslovak people in hostile Prešpurk and protected the small knot of the Slovak government."[153] Yet as state authority stabilized it was soon evident that Sokol's ambition to play an active political role, to become the nation's central educational institution and its military, would not come to fruition. Some Sokol leaders found it difficult to reconcile themselves with this fall

---

[152] Sokol's contribution to the creation of the Republic was not insignificant. Sokol President Scheiner was imprisoned briefly as a member of the Czechoslovak resistance organization called Maffia and supported Masaryk financially (In *Talks with TGM* Masaryk recalled that in discussions before he went into exile, Scheiner was the only one who showed any practical thinking when he posed the question of financing activities abroad). See Čapek, Karel: *Hovory s T. G. Masarykem*. Československý spisovatel, Prague 1990, p. 115. Many predominantly expatriate Sokol members joined the Czechoslovak Legions where, in addition to fighting for independence, they devoted themselves to a thoroughly Sokol lifestyle including public exercises such as the time in Irkutsk Siberia as documented in *Společná cvičení pro veřejné vystoupení části I. divize v Irkutsku v měsíci červnu 1919*. S.n., s.l.

[153] Quoted from Waic, Marek et al.: *Sokol v české společnosti 1862 až 1938*. Univerzita Karlova, Fakulta tělesné výchovy a sportu, Prague 1997, p. 111.

from glory. For instance, Scheiner's relegation to the nominal post of "general inspector of the Czechoslovak military" was commented on by General Pellé to Marshal Foch: "Beneš told me in Paris that it's a sinecure. Scheiner doesn't seem to have taken it that way: he's very active and interferes with the ministry's work."[154]

However, Sokol did not become just another of the many First Republic clubs. Its role did not lie in the practical realization of executive power, but in the representation of the Czechoslovak nation and its will. A symbiotic relationship was formed between Sokol and the state in which the gymnastics organization performed an important representational role for the young country and, in return, received material support and, above all, certain protection of its exclusive position among Czech clubs, especially those geared towards physical education. If we speak of nations as *imagined communities* then we can refer to states as *imagined institutions* that cannot work without creating in the minds of its people an image of itself. This is particularly apparent in the case of newly created small secular Central European countries whose elites strive hard to cultivate the imagination of its people, to forge a "myth of the state" by "inventing traditions," constructing monuments or forming a new ritual framework. A typical feature of these endeavors was the state's aspiration to present itself as something more than a state, i.e. as a spiritual and aesthetical entity and not merely a mechanical bureaucratic institution. Unlike the many unsuccessful attempts at such self-representation (one such failure was a pseudo-sacral monument on Vítkov Hill in Prague), Sokol could offer the Czechoslovak state in its Slets the image of itself as an institution that was enduring (and even timeless thanks to the organic metaphors), dynamic, spiritual and beautiful.

---

154 Quoted from Waic, Marek: "Sokol Josef Scheiner". *Střed. Časopis pro mezioborová studia*, 2011, mimořádné číslo: Muži října 1918, p. 89.

An especially strong bond was formed between Sokol and the Castle, i.e. the power base around the president. Masaryk had previously during the war reassessed his critical view of Sokol and openly acknowledged its importance for creating and maintaining the new state.[155] In addition to many personal ties, the two institutions were linked by an understanding of their own political role as nonpartisan institutions standing above "mere" party interests and selflessly caring for the welfare of the people and the state. For both the Castle and Sokol, being non-partisan was not only an ideological position, it was also a strategy for survival at a time of increasingly articulated group and party interests. Sokol's identification with Czechoslovak ideology (if not with practical politics) prevented the stronger shift to the right evident in the case of the Deutsche Turnerschaft. This is attested to by the failure of the extreme right's campaign "Every Sokol a fascist," which tried to utilize the 1926 Slet to assert fascism in Czechoslovakia.[156] Czech politician Karel Kramář appealed to the Sokol at that time not to confine itself to its clubs, but to become "the driving force of our nationalism" and "an even more ideal, more beautiful organization than Italian fascism," which, despite its flaws, "had filled the nation with a passionate love for Italy" and had performed "a great service in the Italian public and state life," such as "order in the national economy, in finances, in public works, especially in railways, ridding Italy of all communist threats."[157] Despite similar courtship from the far-right, Sokol remained loyal to the Castle and even expelled fascists from their ranks.[158]

---

155   Masaryk admitted: "I underestimated the Sokol's foreign activities, but when I was abroad during the war I found out that often the only thing that people knew about us was that we have the Sokol which organizes Slets." Krejčí, Antonín: *Dr. Josef Scheiner*, Brno 1932, p. 22; quoted from Waic, M.: "Sokol Josef Scheiner", p. 85.

156   Roček, A.: *Analýza vývoje turnerské tělovýchovy v českých zemích a Československu 1810–1965*, vol. 2, p. 60.

157   Kramář, Karel: "Sokolům!". *Národní listy*, vol. 66, 4. 7. 1926, p. 1.

158   According to the Guidelines to the Resolution of the 7th Congress of the Czechoslovak Sokol community, "Communists, populists (i.e. clericals) and fascists were banned from being members of Sokol clubs." *Sokolský vzdělavatel*, 1936, vol. 8, n. 10, p. 63.

9. More than thirty thousand men performing a piece entitled the "An Oath to the Republic" at the 10th Slet at Strahov Stadium in 1938 (National Museum).

Sokol Slets thus became an embodiment of the "idea" of Czecho-slovakia and its symbolism was *state-ified*. The regular presence of Masaryk and later Beneš at Slet grounds as well as the Sokol trib-ute to the president at Prague Castle became standard parts of the Slets. The military or even Little Entente troops newly represent-ed themselves there with performances. Symbolically depicting the fulfillment of national aspiration were Slet scenes such as the con-struction of the Statue of Liberty at the 1920 Slet, a performance of *Where Is My Home* at the following Slet in 1926 that was to express the "profound affection and love of the Czechoslovak man for his beautiful homeland"[159] or the mass theater of five thousand Sokol participants entitled *Tyrš's Dream* at the 1932 Slet.

159 Quoted from Kozáková, Z.: *Sokolské slety 1882–1948*, p. 29.

In the case of the final First Republic Slet in 1938, there was nearly a complete merging of the state and Sokol. "The people paid tribute to the people," wrote Karel Čapek of the Slet parade in 1938, "the nation celebrated itself."[160] The perfect organization of the mass of Sokol gymnasts was a metaphor for the advancement of the Czechoslovak state system. Čapek justified the loss of individuality in the mass spectacle of the Sokol Slet through the creation of a wholly new human species: "There was a need to make the people into this beautifully organized mass to show man's new beauty both in body and spirit. It's a credit to the Czechoslovak and Sokol democracy that it created and supremely developed the beauty of a mass person."[161] One of the leading foreign guests of the 1938 Slet, PEN Club president Jules Romains, viewed it in a similar spirit, describing the Slet to be "something religious, a worshipping of freedom, the mystery of democracy."[162]

160 Čapek, Karel: "Cesta květů a slávy". *Lidové noviny*, vol. 46, 7. 7. 1938 (morning edition), p. 1.
161 Čapek, Karel: "Den slávy". In: Vendelín Josef Krýsa (ed.): *X. všesokolský slet*. Vlastním nákladem, Prague 1938, pp. 72–73. Čapek also described Slet events here as "the rolling movement of gigantic centipedes; there's something even insect-like about it in its terrible abundance and strangeness."
162 Romains, Jules: "Krok svobody". *Lidové noviny*, vol. 46, 3. 7. 1938, p. 1.

STRAHOV STADIUM

The construction of Strahov Stadium, which in its size is unparalleled in the world, became a physical expression of the symbiosis of Sokol and the state. Historically speaking, I think that two developmental types of the modern stadium can be defined as distinctive architectural genres: the sports stadium and the ritual stadium.[163] The modern sports stadium evolved from an interaction between the ancient Greek model and structures designed for urban entertainment, whose architecture was subordinate to the commercial aspect. With these stadiums there was also more of an attempt to create what Eichberg called "achievement space."[164] This was a standardized and later globalized space that enabled the performances of elite athletes to be precisely measured and compared to tenths of a second. In contrast, the ritual stadium has a different genealogy and different logic. Though also drawing from the traditions of classical antiquity, its genealogy is linked to a political celebration of the French Revolution. Eichberg considered the expansive structure on the Champs de Mars designed to celebrate the first anniversary of the revolution on July 14, 1790 to be the first permanent modern stadium.[165] The aim of this stadium – unlike a sports stadium whose

---

163 On the stadium's historical development see for instance Bale, John: "The Spatial Development of the Modern Stadium". *International Review for the Sociology of Sport*, 1993, vol. 28, n. 2–3, pp. 121–133; Verspohl, Franz-Joachim: *Stadionbauten von der Antike bis zur Gegenwart. Regie und Selbsterfahrung der Massen.* Anabas-Verlag, Giessen 1976. This distinction between sports and ritual stadiums corresponds to the antithesis that Claude Lévi-Strausse described between a competitive game and a social ritual. Owing to its unpredicatable interaction of strategies, chance and skill, the original uniformity and symmetry of the players breaks down and the result is the antithesis between victory and defeat. The opposite occurs during a social ritual: the original disunion and asymmetry of the participants changes into unity and symmetry and all participants end up on the winning side. Lévi-Strauss, Claude: *The savage mind.* Weidenfeld & Nicholson, London 1972, p. 32.

164 Eichberg, Henning: *Body Cultures. Essays on Sport, Space and Identity.* Routledge, London – New York 1998.

165 Eichberg, Henning: "Stadium, Pyramid, Labyrinth. Eye and Body on the Move". In: John Bale – Olof Moen (eds.): *The Stadium and the City.* Keele University Press, Staffordshire 1995. According to Mona Ozouf's description, the ceremony was commenced by a massive procession,

objective was to show performances of the physical elite – was to enable a crowd to experience and see itself as "the people." In addition to Speer's Nuremberg designs, an interesting example of a ritual stadium is Le Corbusier's unrealized project the "National Center for Celebration for 100,000 Participants" from 1936–37. His plan shows a stadium opened at one side to the landscape and supported by a single pillar with numerous formations of people marching on the field.[166] This stadium clearly was not designed for 100,000 spectators, as, for instance, Jeffrey Schnapp claims, but for 100,000 active participants, meaning for the performance of an enormous active mass on the stadium's field.[167] Strahov stadium, even if its maximum capacity was "only" thirty thousand gymnasts, falls into the same category of stadiums, whose aim was not to display the perfect bodies of individuals, but to present the perfect "geometrical organization of a mass of humans." (Karel Čapek)[168]

followed by four to six hundred thousand spectators watching political and religious rituals, after which there were samples of competitive games. Ozouf Mona: *Festivals and the French Revolution*. Harvard University Press, Cambridge Ma. 1988.

166   Le Corbusier – Jeanneret, Pierre: *Oeuvre Complète, 1934–1938*. Girsberger, Zurich 1939, p. 90. Cf. Cohen, Jean-Louis: "Le Corbusier's and Pierre Jeanneret's 1936 Stadium for The People's Front". *Arqtexto*, 2010, vol. 10, n. 17, pp. 6–15.

167   Schnapp, Jeffrey T.: *Staging Fascism. 18 BL and the Theater of Masses for Masses*. Stanford University Press, Stanford 1996, p. 39. Le Corbusier described the stadium's function as such: "Un tel 'Centre' ouvre aux animateurs des possibilités grandioses de création jusqu'ici inconnues: discours, théâtre, gymnique, musique, danse, mise en scene, participation d'une masse de 100,000, groupée, mise dans l'unité, par l'architecture. ("Such a center opens to the organizers unprecedented grandiose possibilities for creation: public speeches, theater performances, gymnastic, musical, dance and stage performances, the participation of a mass of people one hundred thousand in number, arranged and united by the architecture.") Le Corbusier – Jeanneret P.: Oeuvre Complete, p. 90. Werner March's Olympic Stadium in Berlin can serve as an example of a compromise between a ritual and sports stadium. In front of the stadium itself, March designed a ritual space (Maifeld), where marches of Nazi organizations and the exercises of the Turners (captured e.g. in Riefenstahl's film *Olympia*), while the stadium itself was where international sports events took place. The Leipzig sports complex also designed by March has the same arrangement. Another unique feature of March's stadium is a bell tower intended to indicate the spiritual aspirations of these functional, modern edifices.

168   Čapek, K.: "Den slávy", pp. 72–73. The Strahov Stadium was also a ritual stadium in the sense that its construction process fully corresponded with the six-year and later five-year cycle of the Sokol Slets and Spartakiads.

Sokols had already chosen before the First World War Strahov Hill as the place for its future Slets. In 1913, their main architect Ludvík Čížek (chief building councilor for Prague and trainer for Prague's Sokol) drafted a plan for the use of this space that had previously served first as a quarry and later as a military training ground. This plan was partially necessitated by the fact that the Slet grounds on Letná Plain, where the festivals were held from 1895 to 1920, were threatened by the urbanistic plans to link Letná and the Old Town.[169]

Prague's dynamically developing landscape simply lacked available large space owned by the city that would provide sufficient room for the movement of tens of thousands of gymnasts and some two hundred thousand spectators. Yet in terms of accessibility, Strahov Hill was not an ideal solution and presented for all organizers of future Slets and Spartakiads a considerable logistics conundrum.[170] After the First World War, during which an extensive training system for military trenches and shelters was built on the hill, the City of Prague purchased the necessary land and, at the state's expense, began the vast ground work less than a year before the second postwar Sokol Slet in 1926. The Ministry of Public Works had nearly 50 hectares of the land modified and over four hundred thousand cubic meters of earth (including 90,000 cubic meters of rock) dug out and removed. A thousand wagons of cinder and nearly the same amount of sand was imported, spread and flattened with a roller pulled by a team of horses. Besides the embankment grandstands, the stadium

169   Cf. Čížek, Ludvík: "Sletiště VII. sletu všesokolského v Praze na Letné". J. Hiller (ed.): *Památník VII. sletu všesokolského v Praze 1920*, pp. 59–82.
170   The choice of Strahov as the future location of the Slet grounds was therefore primarily based on practical reasons; there later appeared in the Sokol narrative the attempt to justify this choice as part of the Czech historical narrative. While the western edge of the White Mountain Plain at the Hvězda Summer Palace was linked to the defeat in 1620, the eastern edge of the same geomorphologic formation was to form the "victorious" Strahov Slet grounds. The etymology of Strahov was similarly used to see it as "guarding the castle and Prague." Cf. Havlíček, V.: *Sokolské slety*, p. 65.

10. The construction of one of the corner entrances to Strahov Stadium in preparation for the 9th All-Sokol Slet of 1932.

itself and other necessary buildings for the 1926 Slet were still made completely out of wood. The exercise grounds, which would henceforth remain basically unchanged, represented the largest exercise field in the world with its dimensions of 310 x 202 meters.

In 1930 the Ministry of Public Health announced a competition for a definitive design of the Strahov area. First place was awarded to Alois Dryák, a renowned architect and president of the art department of the Czechoslovak Sokol Community, who, among other things, was involved in designing the monuments to František Palacký and St. Wenceslas (including his "travelling" model immortalized in the travelogue of Jerome K. Jerome) with a classicizing adaptation of Čížek's orginal design.[171] Second place went to the

---

171 Jerome, Jerome K.: *Three Men in a Boat and Three Men on the Bummel.* Oxford University Press, Oxfford 2008, pp. 252–256.

functionalist architects Ferdinand Balcárek and Karel Kopp, who took over the project following Dryák's death in 1932 and modified it in a functionalist spirit. However, for the 9th All-Sokol Slet of 1932 only the middle part of the west grandstands with box seats for government officials was built of reinforced concrete, the rest were made of makeshift wood. The importance that the state attributed to the Slets is attested to by the fact that the Strahov Stadium was one of few public projects not halted by the government during the Great Depression.[172] A system of underground speakers was also created at that time to broadcast live music and the commands directly to the participants on the field.[173] This technology brought an end to the unique choreographic element, a kind of "human wave" in which the sound and movement spread out gradually from the orchestra toward the remote ends of the field. Before the use of speakers, the interval between the moment a single note of music or command was heard by the first and last participant was nearly two thirds of a second. Also required for the music's reproduction was the construction of a large music hall 20 x 10 x 8 meters in which all walls, the floor and ceiling were covered with sound muting panels and thick-glassed windows set in rubber to prevent vibrations. The orchestra conductor had a direct view of the field and of the platform for the gymnastics directors. For the Slet of

---

172 Waic, M.: "Rej těl v rytmu vlastenectví", p. 56.

173 This system was used for the duration of the mass exercise performances. One hundred and twelve underground radio speakers were placed in circular concrete wells with a diameter of 3.8 meters and a depth of 8 meters covered by metal lids that also served as drainage pits. After each Spartakiad the speakers were removed and the wells were covered so that field could be used for soccer and other sports. See Archiv České obce sokolské (further AČOS), f. Československá spartakiáda 1975, Závěrečné zasedání Ústředního štábu ČSS 1975, 18. 9. 1975, Podklady, Využití Spartakiádního stadionu po spartakiádě 1975 (Jan Raboch), 8. 7. 1975. After its renewal in 1990, the Czech Sokol Community took over most of the documents of the former Spartakiad staff, meaning roughly 100 meters of uncatalogued archive documents from plans for performance pieces to photographs to daily reports on the moods of the participants. The archive also contains a wealth of documents on the cancelled 1990 Czechoslovak Spartakiad. The materials are not properly archived and only roughly placed in chronological order. The copies of the documents from the archive cited in this book are in the author's possession.

1938, the three-hundred-meter-long west grandstand was framed on the sides by bricked twenty-eight-meter-high towers for the needs of "cinematographers, photographers and painters."[174] Located on this grandstand, directly above the government box seats, was the platform for the gymnastics directors from where a director used flags and broadcasted commands to conduct the movement of the masses of gymnasts for all Slets and Spartakiads. During the period between the wars, two Workers' Olympiads of the social democratic Workers' Gymnastics Association and one Orel Slet were also held at Strahov Stadium. Sokol contributed to these events by lending its temporary buildings, though in the case of the planned 2nd Communist Spartakiad in 1928 it refused to cooperate – a fact often pointed out in the communist press.

Besides the construction of Strahov Stadium, the state and City of Prague supported Sokol Slets in a number of other ways. The state subsidized the Slets with various discounts, particularly with regards to transportation fares; the City of Prague invested significant funds into enhancing the transportation infrastructure or the landscaping around the stadium. Due to the upcoming 1932 Slet, the company Kolben and Daněk built at the city's expense a completely new, longer and electrified track at the place of the original funicular on Prague's Petřín Hill. The funicular's further development was also closely linked to the mass gymnastics at Strahov: the first major repair was undertaken before the 11th Slet in 1948, and regular revisions or replacement of cables were made before the individual Spartakiads. [175]

174   Balcárek, Ferdinand – Kopp, Karel: "Masarykův státní stadion na Strahově". *Architekt SIA*, 1938, vol. 37, n. 7, p. 112. According to Markéta Svobodová, this was undoubtedly inspired by Amsterdam's Olympic Stadium designed by Jan Wils. Svobodová, Markéta: "Státní stadion v Praze". In: R. Švácha (ed.): *Naprej!*, p. 154.
175   In June 1965, right before the 3rd Spartakiad, a landslide caused the funicular to be shut down, with its operation recommencing in time for the final Spartakiad in 1985. Fojtík, Pavel: *Po kolejích na Petřín*. Dopravní podnik hl. m. Prahy, Prague 2001, p. 31f.

At the time of the Munich crisis of 1938, Strahov Stadium served as a refugee camp for German democrats fearing Nazi persecution in the Sudetenland. Milena Jesenská (famous for her correspondance with Franz Kafka), who led a public campaign on their behalf, praised the spontaneous hospitality of Czechs at the stadium and many other refugee centers in Prague.[176] Hospitality was replaced by cruelty when Strahov Stadium housed German civilians again right after the Second World War. A camp was set up here for Germans and Czech collaborators, and stood out among Prague's camps both in terms of its size and its appalling conditions. According to the information from July 1945, over 1,300 people were imprisoned in the camp, the vast majority being women and children.[177] Germans who were imprisoned here recollect catastrophic hygienic conditions, hunger, as well as frequent beatings, rape, torture and killings right on the athletic field and in the stands of the stadium.[178] These memories have largely been confirmed by Czech sources. For instance, Olga Fierzová, an assistant to the Protestant priest and social worker Přemysl Pitter who had accompanied him on his inspections of the Prague internment camps, described the situation:

176 Jesenská, Milena: Pověz, kam utíkáš – povím ti, kdo jsi. *Přítomnost*. Vol. 15, n. 38 (21 September 1938), pp. 594–595. Jesenská wrote a number of articles in *Přítomnost* on the topic of German refugees. In later texts, she warned against Czech repraisals against German civilians since "revenge never strikes where it should but where it could." See Jesenská, Milena: Nad naše síly. *Přítomnost*. Vol. 15, n. 41 (12 October 1938), pp. 650–651.
177 According to the statistics compiled upon the request of Přemysl Pitter there were 658 German women, 326 men and 195 children imprisoned there. There were also more than one hundred Czech and "other" prisoners. See Pasák, Tomáš: "Přemysl Pitter – zachránce německých a židovských dětí v roce 1945". In: *Přemysl Pitter. Život a dílo*. Pedagogické muzeum Jana Amose Komenského, Prague 1994, pp. 33–34.
178 See for instance Schieder, Theodor (ed.): *Dokumentation der Vertreibung der Deutschen aus Ost-Mitteleuropa. Die Vertreibung der deutschen Bevölkerung aus der Tschechoslowakei*, Vol. 4, Part 2. Deutscher Taschenbuch Verlag, München 1984, pp. 162–164. Among the prisoners at the stadium were also German speaking victims of Nazi persecution, see for instance Scholten, Gerhard. *Zwischen allen Lagern. Leben in einer Zeit des Wahnsinns*. Universitas-Verlag, München 1988.

It was the worst at Sokol Stadium in Strahov where thousands of people had to sleep on the bare ground without any shelter or blanket. The severely ill and children lay in the hot summer sun in unspeakable squalor full of insects. Both the toilets and the paths to them were befouled by those sick with dysentery. They were unable to drag themselves further and remained lying in their own excrement. We found among them an old professor, a friend of the first president T. G. Masaryk, who had once invited him from Germany to teach at the university in Prague. These shameful images desecrated the place that had once been the stage of the great Sokol Slets.[179]

The torture inflicted by members of the revolutionary guard is described in a report of the Prague Police Directorate from early June 1945.[180] Also preserved is a document in which the Prague Funeral Institute exacted from the Police Directorate the payment of bills from July 1945, which included 32 coffins transported to the internment camp at Strahov Stadium.[181] The camp was shut down in September 1945, apparently due to concerns that the dysentery and other contagious diseases would spread to the city.[182]

---

179 Fierzová, Olga: *Dětské osudy z doby poválečné. Záznamy ze záchranné akce přátel Milíčova domu v Praze.* Spolek přátel mládeže a družstva Milíčův dům, Prague 1992, p. 23.
180 The report gives the case of guards tyranizing a woman to such an extent that she remained fully unconscious. The guards […] used cigarettes to burn uncovered parts of her body." Quoted from Staněk, Tomáš: *Tábory v českých zemích 1945–1948.* Tilia, Šenov u Ostravy 1996, p. 80.
181 See also ibid, p. 73. According to the same source, the dead and killed were taken from Strahov and buried in a mass grave at the St. Lazarus cemetery in Břevnov. See Staněk, Tomáš: *Poválečné "excesy" v českých zemích v roce 1945 a jejich vyšetřování.* Ústav pro soudobé dějiny Akademie věd České republiky, Prague 2005, p. 199. Přemysl Pitter's report indicated that the high death rate was also caused by the camp guards stealing food intended for the prisoners. See Archiv bezpečnostních složek (further ABS), E-6 (Ministerstvo vnitra – Správa internačních, sběrných a pracovních středisek Praha), k. 2 (= box), inv. j. 5 (= inventory unit), Zpráva pro ministerstvo vnitra o stavu stravování v internačních táborech, jmenovitě na Strahovském stadionu z 11. 8. 1945. For the extensive use of German prisoners from Strahov stadium as a forced labour, see Fond 119 (Internační tábory Němců), Archiv Hlavního města Prahy.
182 Staněk, T.: *Tábory v českých zemích 1945–1948*, p. 71. The camp was terminated after the "thorough and insistent" urging by Přemysl Pitter, who supposedly showed the appalling

TRANSFORMATIONS IN SLET SYMBOLISM

Along with the "state-ification" of Slets, there occurred in the period between the wars numerous other changes in semantics, choreography and gymnastics instructions. Above all, the understanding of the body and its movements gradually underwent a transformation, much of which was influenced by the innovative trends of figures such as Georges Demény, Emil Jacques-Dacroze and Elizabeth and Isadora Duncan, which were much more readily accepted in the woman's section of Sokol.[183] An important bearer of gymnastics know-how were the American Sokols and their regular appearance at Slets. Augustin Očenášek, one of the main promoters of modern trends (especially rhythmic gymnastics) described in 1926 the change in the understanding of the human body in the age of "fast machines" as such:

> The 1880s and 90s admired a figure with massive rigid arm and shoulder muscles, and excused underdeveloped leg muscles [...] The ideal is now the slim type with long, supple muscles evenly distributed on the torso, arms and legs, and a sharp mind. Sternness, hard jerky movements, petrified positions and rigid endurance that were errantly considered to be expressions of strength have been gradually abandoned. Though the older generation of trainers still adheres to this rigidity in cultivating the athlete's body, utilizing the favored terminology taken from matter (wood, iron, stone) such as a knotty figure, steel muscles and granite-like posture, the younger generation emphasizes that a person is made of flesh, bones and nerves, that his body is alive and not merely matter: less mass in the muscles and bones, but exceptional quality, a beautiful form interwoven with healthy, sensitive nerves![184]

conditions to influential people including the wife of the mayor Vacek. See Fierzová, O.: *Dětské osudy z doby poválečné*, p. 23.

183 See Heczková, L.: "*Tělo v pohybu*", p. 157.

184 Očenášek, A.: "Doslov", p. 107.

An emphasis on the "natural" movement of the body was gradually implemented at Sokol Slets in contrast with Tyrš's idea of the body as an ancient Greek sculpture and exercises as a series of "beautiful postures." "A static beauty does not suffice today," wrote one leading Sokol officials, Viktor Heller, in 1934, adding that "we are introducing exercises of beautiful movement."[185] Symbolic exercises gave way to a movement considered aesthetically worthy due to its usefulness and simplicity. "The exercises should be veracious," noted Sokol gymnastics director Marie Provazníková, "and there should be no feigning anything that is genuinely not happening or that the gymnast genuinely does not feel."[186] Unlike Tyrš's requirement of "segmentation," the idea of an integral movement "running through the entire body, experienced by the entire body as a whole, not by its individual parts, and experienced spiritually" was asserted.[187] The choreography of the performances also underwent a significant transformation. While all Sokols exercised exactly the same movements prior to the First World War, at the first postwar Slet in 1920 half of the female gymnasts performed movements with a phase shift, which enabled the mass of bodies on the stadium field to be divided up and for simple patterns to be made from it. At later Slets this method was even further developed and individual groups of gymnasts (especially the women) performed various exercises, thus creating on the stadium's field a complex composition of shapes. The gymnasts also left their designated marks and moved a few places in different directions with the others in perfect synchronization.[188] This development culminated in the bold choreographed dance of thirty thousand women at the 10th All-Sokol Slet

185 Kozáková, Z.: *Sokolské slety 1882–1948*, p. 32.
186 Provazníková, M.: *Vývoj sletových společných cvičení žen*, p. 45.
187 Ibid, p. 46.
188 Another important choreographic change was the departure from a previous practice in which every exercise was repeated four times, always toward one of the four grandstands. As Marie Provazníková writes, this method, considered at the time to be a matter of fairness to all spectators and even as social justice to the spectators in the standing-room-only places, gave way

of 1938, which completely freed the women gymnasts from their marks and let them freely dance on the stadium's field (only a few hundred select women formed the basic shape of an ellipse).[189]

It was not by accident that all of these changes were first implemented in the performances of female Sokol members, since they were part of the aforementioned feminist strategy of "segregation as emancipation" within Sokol. The leading figures of the women's section in the Czech lands – Klemeňa Hanušová, Milada Malá and Marie Provazníková – willingly accepted modern gymnastic impulses so as to highlight the differences between the male and female exercises and guide the women's gymnastics, in Provazníková's words, "down its own path, physiologically, aesthetically and psychologically distinct from that of the men."[190] Whereas the "segregation as emancipation" strategy in the early years of the 20th century was aimed at overcoming the resistance of the Sokol's male leadership to allowing women's participation in the Slets, it already has a somewhat different objective after the First World War. Emphasizing the difference of the female body and its movements helped ensure the autonomy of both women's gymnastics and its female leadership. In other words, it was a way to exclude men from the world of women's gymnastics. This strategy did not meet with resistance from Sokol's male leadership, but was instead welcomed.

Following the first post-war Sokol Slet of 1920, women were admitted as full members and their presence on the stadium's field became an integral part of the political message of mass gymnastic performances. In the view of aesthetician Otakar Zich regarding the 1920 Slet, "the natural difference between the two sexes" was to comply with two fundamental aesthetic elements – strength and

to a more dynamic choreography in which "the performance does not have to be the same. It's enough that a picture of beauty is provided to all spectators." Ibid, pp. 44.

189 See "Rej pro třicet tisíc cvičenek". In: *Památník XI. sletu všesokolského v Praze 1948.* Sokolský pomocný výbor, New York 1967, pp. 55–56.

190 Provazníková, M.: *Vývoj sletových společných cvičení žen*, p. 43.

grace: "[...] strength without grace would be monstrous, grace without strength effeminate."[191] The national community and its aspirations were expressed using a new gender model that endured until the final Sokol Slet in 1948. While the male participants (along with the military) performed traditional calisthenics, the female gymnasts created a new expressive display of rhythmic gymnastics featuring, in gymnastics director Marie Provazníkova's words, "a continuous stream of soft, fluid and gymnastically worthy movements [...] that touched the spectators' aesthetic sensibilities with unified, disciplined and rhythmic movements, not with rigid endurance."[192] These two gymnastic styles, also apparent in the choreographies, together created the common narrative of the strength and beauty of the Czechoslovak people.

In this semiotic construct, the female body was to symbolize the national community's relationship to its past and to Slavic unity, to embed it even deeper in the natural cycle itself and to embody the nation's spiritual and aesthetical aspirations. This role is well depicted by an article by Eduard Bass, the editor-in-chief of the daily *Lidové noviny*, on the performance by junior women with maypoles at the 1938 Slet. Bass essentialized the junior women in two ways: one as women, the second as members of an ethnic group (Slavic or Czech women): "That's right, the Slav women came with their ancient symbols of budding, blossoming, life and love," wrote Bass, "they came solemnly and seriously, almost as priestesses of an ancient myth [...] They danced with all their beings filled with an amorous melody and a seductive rhythm." Bass also rhetorically asked where else one could find such a "captivating miracle of harmony," providing the answer himself: "only in the Slavic lands does

---

191   Zich, Otakar: "Estetické dojmy sletové". In: J. Hiller (ed.): *Památník VII. sletu všesokolského v Praze 1920*, p. 266.
192   Provazníková, Marie: "Ženský tělocvik sokolský za Tyrše a dnes". In: Rudolf Procházka (ed.): *Památník IX. sletu všesokolského pořádaného na oslavu stých narozenin Dr. Miroslava Tyrše za účasti svazu "Slovanské Sokolstvo"*. Československá obec sokolská, Prague 1933, p. 26.

womanhood, filled with this divine love and reveling in the poetry of song and dance, shine everywhere."[193]

The artist Josef Čapek also saw in this Slet a clear division of symbolic gender roles.[194] The men's calisthenics expressed in his view "male diligence and work" and was an expression of defensive energy, while the "gently supple" exercises of the women "pleasantly and intimately bring to mind home and garden, meadow and forest." The gender differences in the Sokol Slets were considered to be an expression of the "natural" difference between the sexes in terms of their (re)production roles. In response to the question of why the performance by the junior women at the Slet in 1938 received more applause than their male counterparts, Václav Pergl, one of the key Sokol officials, answered:

No matter what becomes of the world, girls will always be more attractive – at least in our country, in Slavic countries. This is already given by the tasks that nature prepares for them and that we at Sokol do not want to artificially suppress. Sokol will never raise our Czechoslovak girls to be amazons. Certainly not. We want them to become healthy women and mothers, while we want our boys to become austere masculine men, whom we are practically raising for work and battle.[195]

Sokol female trainers and officials did not protest such essentialization of their gender and limited view of the potential of the female body. On the contrary, a distinct difference of the women's performance was the best guarantee of their autonomy and equality. Male and female bodies played within the complex ritual of the Sokol Slets an equally important role in representing the national

193 Quoted from Procházka, Rudolf: "29. června". In: Procházka, Rudolf (ed.): *Památník X. všesokolského sletu v Praze 1938*. Československá obec sokolská, Prague 1939, p. 144.
194 Čapek, Josef: [Bez názvu]. *Lidové noviny*, vol. 46, 5 July 1938, p. 3.
195 Pergl, Václav: "Prvý den dorostu 26. VI.". In: R. Procházka (ed.): *Památník X. všesokolského sletu v Praze 1938*, pp. 125–126.

community and their aspirations. Nevertheless, this symbolic equality was fixed to a traditional view of the "natural" division of the male and female role and, instead of weakening the existing patriarchal arrangement, it helped to reinforce it.[196]

196 The tension between the emancipation program and gender segregation is well illustrated by a short essay by gymnastics director Marie Provazníková in which under the telling title "Sokol Women – the Mothers of a Healthy Nation" she argues for the right of women to serve in the military. In: *Lví silou*, p. 20.

THE LEFT AND MASS GYMNASTICS

The Sokol ambition to embody the entire Czech and later Czechoslovak nation was always for the most part wishful thinking. Yet the democratic milieu of the First Republic created favorable conditions for the centrifugal trends that had long existed within the gymnastics movement. In the early 20th century Sokol's sharply anti-clerical stance provided the impetus for the Catholics to create an alternative association, the Orel (Eagle). This organization played an important role in Moravia and in Silesia, and after the creation of Czechoslovakia also in Slovakia, where it adeptly competed with the Sokols under the leadership of Andrej Hlinka.[197] The Sokol ambition to represent the entire national community, however, suffered more from the loss of part of its working-class members. In 1897, Sokol had joined a campaign against Czech social democracy, expelled social-democratic activists from its clubs and called them in its press "riffraff without a nation and homeland."[198]

Social democrats objected to this: "We can no longer watch as our comrades in Sokol clubs are insulted and expelled for their beliefs." They then announced the establishment of the independent Association of the Workers' Gymnastics Clubs, "where we will be able to work to elevate physical and moral instruction in the solid ranks of proletarians fighting for their liberation."[199]

Following the establishment of an independent Czechoslovakia, the relations between the social democratic gymnasts and Sokol were decorous. The two organizations jointly took part in maintaining order after the creation of the republic and especially in suppressing the December Strike of 1920. In doing so, the tension between the moderate and radical wings of the social democratic gymnasts came

---

197 Perútka, Jaromír – Grexa, Ján: *Dejiny telesnej kultúry na Slovensku*. Univerzita Komenského, Bratislava 1995, p. 137.
198 Kössl, J. – Krátký, F. – Marek, J.: *Dějiny tělesné výchovy II.*, p. 77.
199 Ibid.

to a head, which led to the establishment of communist Federation of the Workers' Gymnastic Clubs. This split took place shortly before the planned first Workers' Olympiad, which was originally meant to be held in 1915 but was postponed until 1921 due to the ongoing war. The leaders of the communist gymnasts had originally planned to boycott the Workers' Olympiad and instead conduct their own exercises outside of Prague. Yet literally a few days before the event they changed their minds and hastily began to prepare their own performance in an area of Prague called Maniny.[200] Later communist historiography gave a heroic tint to the haste and confusion in which this counter-move was prepared. The mobilizing announcement of the head of the communist gymnasts issued seven days before the event's commencement is often cited: "The Federal Olympiad will take place in Prague, the preparation of exercises in towns have been halted, all Federation forces are heading for Prague, clubs of Greater Prague and its environs are assigned general work duties, the entire communist proletariat is called to help!"[201] A statement of the main organizer of this first communist Spartakiad, Jiří František Chaloupecký, attesting to the almost miraculous strength of the proletariat masses in building the exercise grounds for over seven thousand gymnasts and temporary wooden stands for one hundred thousand spectators, is similarly cited: "On Wednesday there was still a bare meadow – but by Saturday the communist Coliseum already towered in its place, every nail pierced like a dagger into the heart of anyone who had dishonored the workers in December."[202] The benevolence of state authorities, which issued during the week all necessary official permits and provided transportation discounts, also undoubtedly contributed to the success.

200 The exercise grounds were built where the Vltava's new riverbed would later pass through.
201 Mucha, V.: *Dějiny dělnické tělovýchovy v Československu*, pp. 70–71.
202 Ibid, p. 72.

Thus two leftist mass gymnastic performances were held at the same time in June 1921 in Prague with absolute identical exercises (the participants had originally trained for the same Workers' Olympiad),[203] differing only in the final scene. The events were so similar that a delegation of the Finnish communist athletes mistakenly performed at the social democrats' olympiad.[204] At the leased Sokol stadium on Letná plain, the social democrats' participants showed "moral strength, socialist dedication and all the creative traits hidden in the worker's soul,"[205] as well as loyalty to the new republic. In the final scene of *The Dawn of a New Age*, the two and a half thousand participants put on a mass theater performance in which the symbol of capitalism – a statue of a golden calf – was destroyed and replaced by a giant, four-meter high bust of President T.G. Masaryk. In contrast, the spectators of the communist Spartakiad witnessed a performance of *The Victory of the Revolution* carried out by two thousand participants under the leadership of Dědrasbor, the workers' theatre company. The *Sokol Bulletin* compared the two scenes in a thorough (and ironic) report from both events: "The rightists declared the principle to create, the left to destroy. In their performance, the communists were more successful, despite the scene's disposition; it was at times artfully strong, even mystical in its recitatives on life [...] in its two main figures, revolution and victory, it was demonic. [...] The rightists masterfully employed costumes and colors of the mass, but the content was weak, often distastefully [...] There was no need to build the head [of Masaryk] on a tarnished pedestal of mammon."[206]

---

203 Both performances were essentially copies of Sokol Slets; the only substantial difference was the performance of social-democratic and communist participants with hammers (wooden), which meant to symbolize proletarian work.
204 Kříž, Václav: "Slavnosti Svazu a Federace D.T.J.". *Věstník sokolský* 1921, vol. 23, n. 17, p. 441.
205 *První dělnická olympiáda v Praze 1921*. Česká grafická unie a.s., Prague 1921, unpagin.
206 Kříž, V.: "Slavnosti Svazu a Federace D.T.J.", pp. 440–441. Kříž did not even mention the name "Spartakiad" and spoke about the two events as if they were both named Olympiad.

Later communist gymnastics emphasized its link to this relatively modest event as its main source of inspiration. The main reason was its well (though hastily) chosen name of "Spartakiad," which referred to both the world of physical exercise (Spartacus as a gladiator) and the class struggle.

The example of the Workers' Olympiad and the communist Spartakiad shows that the gymnastics of the left copied the physical *habitus* of Sokol, but also tried to ideologically separate itself from Sokol as much as possible. This is well illustrated in a 1926 article by Klement Gottwald, the later first communist president of Czechoslovakia, entitled "The Sokol Slet and Us."[207] In Gottwald's view, Sokol was created as an instrument of the Czech bourgeoisie in its struggle with the German bourgeoisie, but its class character was largely obscured during the "national oppression" when the interests of the Czech bourgeoisie and those of the Czech proletariat were temporarily similar. After the creation of an independent state, the Czech bourgeoisie achieved its true objective, i.e. "if not a monopoly then at least a leading position in exploiting our own proletariat." Yet Sokol did not lose its importance for the Czech bourgeoisie. The bourgeoisie "endowed" it with a new role: to "obscure the class nature of today's society." The Czech bourgeoisie was apparently at this time oppressing the Czech worker, "skinning him without a knife," but posing as his "brother" in Sokol. The same bourgeoisie will easily find a common language with his German and Hungarian colleagues, but "never fails to incite the Czech proletarian against the German and Hungarian proletarians" at Sokol. They likewise "gleefully pour" millions of public money into the Catholic church

S. K. Neumann rejected their comparison at the time: "Let's not argue over figures – I don't care if its 10,000 more or fewer, only if tens of thousand resolute remain; let's not argue over the precision of the production – it's not about the beauty of the gesture, but about the vigor of the blow that our boys together land on the bourgeoisie and its order; Let's not argue over the size, beauty and gleam – the proletariat was truly on our side." Quoted from Mucha, V.: *Dějiny dělnické tělovýchovy v Československu*, p. 77.

207   Gottwald, Klement: "Sokolský slet a my". *Rudé právo*, vol. 6, 4. 7. 1926, pp. 1–2.

but at Sokol they are clearly a great "free-thinker" and "Hussite." Gottwald's view was then expanded upon by Ladislav Štoll, who in the 1950s became the leading figure of the communist cultural policy, on the occasion of the next Slet in 1932 in the essay *The Political Sense of Sokol*.[208] Štoll also believed that Sokol's historical role consisted of supporting the Czech bourgeoisie in its struggle for the "right to the free exploitation of its own proletariat."[209] The ideological framework of this struggle was created by Tyrš's tract *Our Task, Direction and Goal*, this "sensational pack of high-minded sentences and grandiose words" and the "official fountain of specifically petty-bourgeois moralism."[210] Sokol Slets were then, according to Štoll, the truest expression of Sokol's role in obscuring class differences:

Prague will once again become the stage for great manifestations of patriotism. The assembly of thousands of healthy militarily disciplined gymnasts will impress the crowds. The illusion of a fleeting picture of a mechanically perfect collective performance, the activities of healthy muscles, the thrilling rhythm in the music of marching bodies with colorful papers will mesh in the spectators' heads and will once again conceal for some time the fact of anarchy and the class struggle in society.[211]

The ambivalent relationship of the Czech left to mass gymnastic performances corresponds to the more general phenomenon among Central European leftist movements that imitated nationalistic

208 Štoll, Ladislav: *Politický smysl sokolství*. Karel Borecký, Prague 1932; See also Macura, Vladimír: "Souvislosti Štollovy marxistické analýzy sokolství. O odborné práci Ladislava Štolla Politický smysl sokolství (1932)". *Česká literatura*, 1982, vol. 30, n. 6, pp. 547–550. According to Macura, Štoll here, first verified the possibilities of a Marxist methodology in analyzing the cultural phenomenon and showed "proper sensitivity regarding the mechanisms for creating a bourgeois national myth."
209 Štoll, L.: *Politický smysl sokolství*, p. 11.
210 Ibid, p. 30.
211 Ibid, p. 5. In a 1929 congress resolution the Czechoslovak Communist Party characterized the Sokol as a fascist organization and the DTJ as a social-fascist organization. Kössl, J. – Krátký, F. – Marek, J.: *Dějiny tělesné výchovy II.*, p. 167.

gymnastic movements in their politicizing of the body, aggressive masculinity, opposition to competitive sports and in the creation of a mystical cult and ritual.[212] Mass calisthenics also held a particular charm for the left in that it resonated with the ideological postulate of equality and a distaste for elitist "bourgeois" sports. Supporters of the Proletkult saw in sports and in the principle of fair play "the remnants of a decadent past and the personification of a degenerate bourgeois culture."[213] They called for a new beginning via a "revolutionary transformation of the proletarian physical culture that was to take the form of working gymnastics, of mass gymnastic performances and social excursions."[214] Yevgeny Rjumin, a literary critic close to the Proletkult movement, saw the mass gymnastic performances as an important element for cultivating new Soviet Rituals, particularly May Day parades. The synchronized movement and gymnastic exercises were to provide new content to the May Day parades of Soviet Russia: "The bulky, anxious and chaotic crowd of many thousands is transformed into a harmonious, grandiose, monumental and creative collective of all participants."[215]

Mass gymnastic performances also resonated, like choral singing or recitals, with ideas of the leftist avant-garde. It offered the promise to fulfill the dreams of a mass theater for the masses, removing the barrier between the audience and the actors and transforming

212 Mosse, George L.: *Nationalism and Sexuality. Middle Class Morality and Sexual Norms in Modern Europe*. Howard Fertig, New York 1985, p. 134; also Wheeler, Robert F.: "Organized Sport and Organized Labour. The Workers 'Sports Movement'". *Journal of Contemporary History*, 1978, vol. 13, n. 2, pp. 191–210. However leftist gymnastic movements mainly differed from their nationalist counterparts in their attempt to overcome nationalist boundaries. The joint synchronized exercises of participants from different countries and different ethnicities served this purpose well.
213 Riordan, James: *Sport in Soviet Society*. Cambridge University Press, Cambridge 1977, pp. 101–102. Also see Geldern, James von: *Bolshevik Festivals, 1917–1920*. University of California Press, Berkeley 1993.
214 Riordan, J.: *Sport in Soviet Society*, p. 102.
215 Rjumin, Jevgenij: *Massovye prazdnestva*. GIZ, Moscow – Leningrad 1927, p. 45; See also Zakharov, Alexander V.: "Mass Celebrations in a Totalitarian System". In: Alla Efimova – Lev Manovich (eds.): *Tekstura. Russian Essays on Visual Culture*. University of Chicago Press, Chicago 1993, p. 215.

11. Josef Sudek's photograph of the parade of Sokols during the 1932 Slet, published in the avant-garde journal *Žijeme*.

the crowd into an active artistic collective, a necessary condition of which was the voluntary discipline of the masses.[216] The ambivalent relationship of the art avant-garde to Sokol and its Slets was well illustrated by extensive coverage of the 1932 Slet by leftist life-style magazine *Žijeme*, which combined an admiration for the perfect

216 Perhaps the avant-garde artist most distinctly involved in mass gymnastic performances was Ladislav Sutnar, not only artistically (his famous poster for the 3rd Workers Olympiad in 1934), but also conceptually and choreographically (cf. fig. III).

organization of the Slet and a fascination for the aesthetics of the mass formations (the photographs of Pavel Janák and particularly of Josef Sudek are almost indistinguishable from the pictures taken by Alexander Rodchenko of the Soviet performances) with a harsh indictment of the artistic and political ambitions of Sokol. For instance, theater critic Josef Träger wrote that as long as Sokol's ideology is superficial bourgeois nationalism, "unquestioning loyalty to the state" and "reconciliation with the ruling regime," its aesthetics of "folkloristic stylization" will represent the "blatant discharge of unconcealed dilettantism, in which it will be difficult to decide whether bad taste or helplessness predominates."[217] Träger emphasized the "banality" of the Slet scenes, especially the verbal accompaniment: "Domorázek's verse will long remain an unsurpassed admonitory example of soulless poetry: calendar-like pathos combining within intellectual emptiness and linguistic lameness."

---

217   Träger, Josef: "Sokolstvo a divadlo". *Žijeme*, 1932, vol. 2, n. 3–4, pp. 76–77.

THE COMMUNIST PARTY AND SOKOL AFTER THE SECOND WORLD WAR: THE SEARCH FOR A COMMON DENOMINATOR

After the Second World War the Communist Party's relationship to Sokol radically changed. In the eyes of communists, Sokol was no longer an instrument of big capital and the Sokol Slets were not glitter obscuring class differences, but had been transformed into an important tool of the "national revolution."[218] The Communist Party did not renew its own gymnastics organization after the war and instead recommended that its members join Sokol, which was to become a natural base for the unification of post-war gymnastics. A statement by the party chairman published in the daily *Rudé právo* at the close of 1946 welcomed the preparations of the 11th All-Sokol Slet and called on its members: "Let the Communists be the best and most selfless Sokols fulfilling the great spiritual legacy of Tyrš and Fügner and elevating Sokol to new levels of democracy and progress."[219] The long-time communist sport activist Klement Gottwald now became a member of the Sokol in Prague's Lesser Side, as did a number of other prominent communist leaders.[220]

Sokol's position also changed, even though it viewed with caution the communist courtship and their attempts at unifying gymnastics. With regards to the Communist Party, Sokol President Antonín Hřebík said, "They were previously international, and we

---

218 This change was preceded by a shift in the opinion starting in the late 1930s, especially regarding the 1938 Sokol Slet, which was, according to e.g. Jan Šverma "a massive manifestation of our entire people, documenting its determination to defend democracy, the republic and the country's independence." Šverma, Jan: "Nedáme se!". *Rudé právo*, vol. 18, 3. 7. 1938, p. 1.
219 "Vše pro zdar XI. všesokolského sletu". *Rudé právo*, vol. 26, 22. 12. 1946, p. 1.
220 Klement Gottwald had joined Vienna's Czech social democratic gymnastic club in 1912, took part in the preparations for the Spartakiad in Maniny and later on the development of communist gymnastics in Slovakia where he edited the magazine *Spartakus*. See Kössl, J. – Krátký, F. – Marek, J.: *Dějiny tělesné výchovy II.*, p. 160.

were national. That was incompatible. Today they are a national and state-loyal party."[221] The development of mass gymnastic performance following the Second World War was deeply influenced by the persecution of Sokol during the Nazi occupation. The losses in the ranks of male gymnastic leadership were so significant that we can speak of a discontinuity of personnel. On one night alone, during Operation Sokol on October 7–8, 1941, nine hundred of the highest Sokol officials were arrested, of which only a small minority survived the war.[222] Much greater continuity was maintained in the women's Sokol leadership where considerably fewer losses were suffered. Those Sokol leaders who did survive the persecution and returned from the concentration camps, such as Miroslav Klinger, Josef Truhlář, Viktor Heller and František Bláha, were deeply affected by this life experience. Strong ties to former communist prison mates and an openness to build a "new order" is evident with them.

Sokol was also richer from its experience in unification attempts during the Second Republic (1938–1939) and the Protectorate, which structurally has much in common with the unification attempts during the post-war period. "Simplifying the relations within gymnastics," as unification attempts during the Second Republic were called, offered Sokol a chance to fulfill its longtime dream to monopolize the nation's physical and moral preparation in the spirit "Every Czech a Sokol," though it also threatened the possessively guarded autonomy of the Sokol movement vis-à-vis state authority.[223] Shortly before the occupation, for instance, the *Sokol Bulletin* called for the unification of all gymnastics into Sokol, which was

221 Uhlíř, J. B. – Waic, M.: *Sokol proti totalitě*, p. 110.

222 Provazníková, Marie: *To byl Sokol*. České slovo, Munich 1988, pp. 171–172; See also Uhlíř, J. B. – Waic, M.: *Sokol proti totalitě*, p. 89. Heydrich's decree to dissolve Sokol was part of the campaign.

223 See Waic, Marek: "Sokolská organizace a pokus o sjednocení tělesné výchovy po mnichovském diktátu". In: Václav Hošek – Petr Jansa (eds.): *Psychosociální funkce pohybových aktivit v životním stylu člověka*. Univerzita Karlova, Fakulta tělesné výchovy a sportu, Prague 2000, pp. 116–118.

intended to be a way of overcoming "unfortunate partisanship."[224] Sokol was allegedly predestined for this role since it was derived "from the depths of the national spirit," helped create modern national history, determined its character and represented the nation and its "manly virtue" to other countries. Other gymnastics organizations then "arose from us, borrowing everything down to the last detail from us" and only differed from Sokol in that in serving their parties they "corroded" the unity of the people.[225] Three months later, already under the Nazi Protectorate, Miroslav Kavalír pointed out that in its aim to create a "healthy and morally adept nation," Sokol would play a central role in unifying gymnastics.[226]

Both projects of transforming society – of Sokol and the Communist Party – actually had some similar traits, which became much more distinct now with the communists' struggle for "a national path to communism." This has already been mentioned in the shared distaste for competitive sports and the leftist avant-garde's fascination with mass performance. Yet the affinity between Sokol and the project of "national communism" went even further.[227] In the postwar effort of the Communist Party to show itself as the most loyal heir of national "progressive traditions," the communist leadership had much more in common with Sokol nationalism than with the Proletkult leftist avant-garde. Tyrš's social Darwinism emphasizing

224 Krejčí, Jan: "Za sjednocením". *Sokolský věstník*, vol. 41, 8. 2. 1939, p. 1.
225 Ibid.
226 Kavalír, Miroslav: "Před sjednocením". *Sokolský věstník*, vol. 41, 10. 5. 1939, p. 1; other Sokol authors wrote during the protectorate that Sokol should be responsible for the repoliticizing of our national life," during the First Republic it was to create a new "non-political policy" (Arnošt Bláha) aimed at bonding the "community of language and blood."
(Marie Provazníková). See Bláha, Arnošt: "Na dobré cestě". *Sokolský věstník*, vol. 41, n. 26, 28. 6. 1939, pp. 318–319; Provazníková, Marie: "Láska k vlasti". *Sokolský věstník*, vol. 41, n. 29, 19. 7. 1939, p. 365.
227 For the concept of "national communism", see Kopeček, Michal: *Hledání ztraceného smyslu revoluce. Zrod a počátky marxistického revizionismu ve střední Evropě 1953–1960*. Argo, Prague 2009, pp. 119–142 as well as Sommer, Vítězslav: *Angažované dějepisectví: Stranická historiografie mezi stalinismem a reformním komunismem, 1950–1970*. Nakladatelství Lidové noviny – FF UK, Prague 2011.

the need for progress and constant movement ("stagnation means death") also resonated with the Communist Party's understanding of its own historical role. The communists also modified Tyrš's fight against backwardness into a fight against reactionaries.[228] Similarly, it was relatively easy to reinterpret Sokol Slavic patriotism as socialistic Slavic patriotism and to mention cooperation with the Russian emigrant Sokol as only a marginal and embarrassing episode.[229] Lastly, the Sokol ambition to transform the entire society – the motto "Every Czech a Sokol" did not merely mean formal membership in the gymnastics organization, but the moral and physical renewal of the individual and nation – corresponded to the Communist Party's endeavor to create a new person.

However, this transformative ambition also corresponded to the general radicalization of the post-war discourse that did not care for realism and austerity. Sokol writers, never far from hyperbole and pathos, were now given free reign. Sokol's objective, in the view of e.g., Robert Konečný, was nothing short of "making humanity more humane," which was to be achieved through discipline as the best "school of humanity."[230] The red Sokol shirt did not only express the longing for a social and national revolution; it also meant the desire for an inner revolution, for a person "free in the masses, since he was in agreement with the masses." The Slets were to play a fundamental role in this transformation: "The greatest significance of the Slets in our overly partisan and over-politicized life," wrote Konečný shortly

---

228 For instance, Julius Dolanský stated "Tyrš considered backwardness, i.e. reactionary thinking, to be the worst, murderous crime that could be done to the nation." *Stenoprotokol 34. schůze Národního shromáždění*, 14. 7. 1949 (available online at the Czech and Slovak Digital Parliamentary Library).

229 See for instance Maxa, Prokop: "Slety po stránce slovanské". In: *Deset sletů*, p. 11. Cf. Jan Masaryk's speech given on 17 January 1948 in which he spoke of the Slets as a "blessed work of Slavic unification" and compared them with gymnastic parades in Moscow that he had personally watched from Generalissimo Stalin's box." Masaryk, Jan: *Mezinárodní význam všesokolských sletů*. Nakladatelství Československé obce sokolské, Prague 1948, pp. 8–9.

230 Konečný, Robert: "Slety po stránce jejich psychologického působení". In: *Deset sletů*, pp. 18–24.

before the communists' February 1948 putsch, "was always first and foremost that it clearly showed our people's desire not for what divides us, but for what brings us together. The merit of the 11th Slet will be all the greater with the increase of political partisanship that grow into enormous dimensions. The greater the respect for a party, the less respect for the individual and state." He believed that the Slet should not merely be a spectacle, but should express "the wonderful feeling of a national community" that blurs the boundaries of the words "I, you and we" and should be an expression of a single "will to live freely and to humanly move forward." Writer Václav V. Štech deftly expressed a similar sentiment in describing Sokol Slets as "displaying the anonymous force of a nation in colors and movements, which has the effect of choral singing – a force whose task is to ceaselessly renew the youth of the nation and state."[231] Yet Sokol and its Slets also possessed in the eyes of these writers the ability to resolve all problems of the post-war republic. Štech, for instance, was convinced (in complete contradiction to the post-war mood in Slovakia) that "it is up to Sokol, like no other organization, to resolve our Czechoslovak-ness."[232] The prepared Slet of 1948 was also intended to show the nation's path in questions of morality, which was especially important "in an age of fluctuating values, […] that is not attentive enough to moral questions." Lastly, the Sokol Slet depicted "the purity of the relationship between the Sokol man and Sokol woman, the purity of a man's view of a woman and a woman's of a man."[233]

---

231 Štech, Václav Vilém: "Slety a výtvarné umění". In: *Deset sletů*, p. 33.
232 Ibid, p. 34. Such an idea completely ignored the political reality of post-war Slovakia. Sokol communists did not share any enthusiasm for renewing Sokol; See for instance "Neoživujte mrtvoly". *Nové slovo*, vol. 2, 8. 6. 1945, p. 15.
233 Konečný, R.: "Slety po stránce jejich psychologického působení", p. 22.

THE ALL-SOKOL SLET OF 1948 –
"CAN THE PEOPLE BETRAY?"

The very preparations for the Slet of 1948 created a space in which the common interests of Sokol and the Communist Party, as well as the conflicts between them, became all the more apparent. At the close of 1946, the presidium of the Central Committee of the Czechoslovak Communist Party had supported Sokol in its preparation for the Slet, which was to serve "the matter of the nation's physical fitness, the idea of Slav fraternity" and called on all communists to assist in its preparation.[234] The first and second government of Klement Gottwald, "the honorary chairman of the 11th Slet,"[235] as well as the Prague City Hall under Mayor Václav Vacek, invested hundreds of million Czechoslovak crowns into the Slets, either directly into Strahov Stadium or into urban development work within the broader context of the city. Later Sokol historiography has insisted that the Sokols refused all state aid in order to maintain their political independence.[236] Financial self-sufficiency was, however, always largely illusory, especially in the case of the 11th Slet. At the time of the event the Sokols themselves admitted that the Slet had received "extraordinary support from the state's top officials."[237]

The concrete south and north grandstands were built from state funds (while the makeshift east grandstand was paid for by Sokol), as was the concreted and paved surface of the assembling platform about the size of a small airport (330 × 46 meters) and a number

---

234 "Prohlášení předsednictva ÚV KSČ z 22. 12. 1946 k přípravě XI. všesokolského sletu a vstupu komunistů do Sokola". In: Jaroslav Marek (ed.): *Za socialistický systém tělesné výchovy. Dokumenty od nár. a demokratické revoluce po XV. sjezd KSČ*. Olympia, Prague 1978, p. 29.
235 Uhlíř, J. B. – Waic, M.: *Sokol proti totalitě*, p. 114.
236 See for instance *Jednatel*: "Ze zákulisí posledního sletu". In: *Památník XI. sletu všesokolského v Praze 1948*, p. 142; Waldauf, Jan: *Sokol. Malé dějiny velké myšlenky*, vol. 1. Atelier IM, Luhačovice 2007, p. 241.
237 Köppl, Evžen: "Organizace sletu". In: *Památník XI. sletu všesokolského v Praze 1948*, pp. 24–27.

12. A recruitment poster for exercises at the 1948 Slet. In the background, a shot of the junior women's performance at the 1938 Slet (National Museum).

of buildings in the stadium's vicinity amounting to 90 million Czechoslovak crowns.[238] The City of Prague spent even more (ca. 120 million Czechoslovak crowns) on the Slet grounds. For example, a new water line with a capacity of 300 liters per second was extended to Strahov Stadium with outlets in the locker rooms.

The broader vicinity of Strahov Stadium underwent a dramatic change at the expense of the City of Prague, resulting in the present form of the Břevnov and Smíchov sides of Strahov Hill. Two streetcar circuits and numerous vehicle crossings, underpasses and pedestrian overpasses and underpasses were built on the Břevnov side of the city so that vehicle routes never crossed with pedestrian ways. A special temporary pedestrian crossing was built that even traversed Strahov's medieval walls. On the opposing Smíchov side, two new roads and a new trolley-bus route were built to link downtown Prague with the Slet grounds. The extent of this work is illustrated by the fact that over 1,100 truck loads of granite blocks were needed for cobblestone paving.

Yet the City of Prague also invested outside of Strahov as part of the Slet preparations. Car parks were linked to all arterial roads for non-Prague vehicles with vehicle entry to the center requiring special permission.[239]

A new Florence bus station was opened in downtown Prague right before the Slet. Almost all train stations underwent modifications, particularly Masaryk Station which received a new vestibule with

---

238 Banzet, Jaroslav: "Sletiště". In: *Památník XI. sletu všesokolského v Praze 1948*, pp. 30–32. In addition to this, for instance, the military lent eighty soldier-cooks with field kitchens and fifty thousand porcelain mugs. Sweets for younger students and adolescents were subsidized by the state. The meteorological service built from its funds a broadcasting network of news stations around Prague which, along with the aerial observation network, broadcast to Strahov reports on the formation of storms, their size and direction. See Novotný, František: "Sletové stravování". *Památník XI. sletu všesokolského v Praze 1948*, pp. 210–211. Tvrdík, František: "Povětrnostní služba na sletišti". Ibid, pp. 208–209.
239 Moos, Jindřich: "Do Prahy!". In: *Památník XI. sletu všesokolského v Praze 1948*, pp. 195–197.

ticket windows. Writer Vladimir Thiele[240] described other changes in Prague in connection with the prepared event: One major change was the streetcar crossing at Na Poříčí Street where a corner building in full working order was demolished; it had been "built in the path" and "had long been an obstacle, held up traffic and, as they say, blocked the way."[241] A "beautiful new pedestrian underpass" was built at the corner of Hybernská Street across from Masaryk Station and the street on this "eternally jammed corner" was widened so that both cars and streetcars could pass.

The Astronomical Clock on Old Town Square, damaged during the Prague Uprising of 1945, was also repaired and its chimes, as shown in Jiří Weiss's film on the Slet, symbolically commenced the event.[242]

Following the communist putsch of February 1948, Gottwald's government continued to support the Slet, despite the Sokol leadership's expression that February of "absolute loyalty" to president Beneš and their faith in the "wisdom of his statesmanship."[243]

240 Like its predecessors, the Slet commemorative book was prepared a few months in advance and was gradually modified in accordance with the changing political situation. The preparations began in April 1948 and the first corrections were finished just before the Slet. Supplementary texts (Dolanský, Gottwald, Zápotocký) were added and a number of changes were made upon the censor's orders. In the end, however, publication was forbidden. A Sokol exile managed to smuggle out a rough copy without the pictures and make several photocopies of it (two copies also existed in Czechoslovakia). In 1967 the American Sokol published an abridged version of the commemorative book in which they did not include, in addition to several expert texts, "all forced statements and those individuals that we know either betrayed or disappointed." Instead two later texts on the Slet and communist persecution were included. Pictorial material from the Slet is featured in the publication Ambrosi, Vilém (ed.): *XI. všesokolský slet v Praze*. Svět v obrazech, Prague 1948; See also *XI. všesokolský slet 1948*. Konfrontace, Curych 1976.
241 Thiele, Vladimír: "Praha se připravila". In: *Památník XI. sletu všesokolského v Praze 1948*, pp. 80–82.
242 Heller, Viktor: "Na Staroměstské radnici". In: *Památník XI. sletu všesokolského v Praze 1948*, pp. 156–157. See also Weiss, Jiří: "Natáčíme sletový film". In: Ibid, pp. 182–183. The preparation of Jiří Weiss's two-part Slet film *Song of the Slet* is further proof of generous state support. Weiss was provided with a large crew equipped with walkie-talkies, including roughly twenty professional cameramen with cameras mounted to military jeeps.
243 Quoted from Uhlíř, J. B. – Waic, M.: *Sokol proti totalitě*, pp. 124–125.

In order to ensure that the Slet was successfully carried out, the Communist Party even made far-reaching political concessions and temporarily backed off from its two fundamental and interrelated plans concerning gymnastics. This consisted of, firstly, achieving complete control over Sokol though "action committees", ad-hoc parallel power structures run by the Communist Party set up on all levels of social and political life and, secondly, the rapid unification of all gymnastics and sport into this pacified Sokol so that by early June 1948 "all physical education was only under Sokol."[244] The communist leadership carefully carried out purges in Sokol in light of the Slet preparations and slowed the excessive zeal of some of the local agents of the "action committees". For instance, Marie Provazníková, who clearly opposed the Communist Party, remained a Sokol gymnastics director. Sokol members were aware that the communists wanted a successfully organized Slet that would demonstrate both within and outside the country the stability of the political situation, and they tried to make use of the situation to maintain the highest degree of autonomy. In mid May, Sokol leaders even dissolved the Sokol "action committees" without consulting state or communist authorities, publishing their decision in their own bulletin.[245] The Communist Party ultimately sanctified this decision, thus opposing its own Sokol "action committees". Similarly, it assumed a lax position regarding the unification of gymnastics, which, following its formal announcement in March 1948, it ultimately had to postpone until after the Slet.

However, the willingness of the Communist Party to allow and support the Slet did present practical and moral dilemmas for Sokol

244 Ibid, p. 130. Preparations for the Slet also affected quite remote political realms. For instance, the Ministry of Justice recommended to prosecutors that death sentences to Germans convicted in retribution trials be carried out after the Slet had ended. See Frommer, Benjamin: *National Cleansing: Retribution against Nazi Collaborators in Postwar Czechoslovakia.* Cambridge University Press, New York 2005, p. 338.
245 Kaplan, Karel: *Národní fronta 1948–1960.* Academia, Prague 2012, pp. 107–108.

officials – dilemmas that largely appeared again in organizing the Spartakiad (often by the same people). Many Sokol members refused to take part in the Slet after the communist putsch because they feared the organization would be politically exploited by the communists, and even used leaflets to call for a boycott of the Slet. Sokol President Antonín Hřebík reacted to these calls shortly after the putsch: "There is no reason for the Slet not to be held. Use your Sokol discipline and decisiveness to reject all false news […] disrupting […] the Slet's preparations! Government representatives headed by Klement Gottwald reaffirm that the Slet is in the interest of our entire nation and state."[246]

Yet Hřebík himself, upon being replaced by 77-year-old Josef Truhlář as the head of Sokol, emigrated along with hundreds of other Sokol officials. Many other officials, most notably Marie Provazníková, saw the holding of the Slet as a moral obligation not only to the members who had trained for it, but also to the "brothers and sisters" who had been killed during the occupation, who had dreamed of a Slet in a liberated Czechoslovakia. For them, this event represented the final punctuation to the Sokol past, and they were willing to work with the Communist Party only so that a successful Sokol Slet could be held.[247]

There was also a number of leading figures of the Sokol movement who could envision Sokol under the new regime and for whom cooperation with the communist authority was not merely of a tactical nature. This is especially true of the "old-new" Sokol President Josef Truhlář, who was the only top representative of the First Republic Sokol to remain in its leadership and was therefore of exceptional value for the Communist Party. Truhlář had supported the staged

---

246   Uhlíř, J. B. – Waic, M.: *Sokol proti totalitě*, p. 134.
247   See Provazníková, M.: *To byl Sokol*. Provazníková gives here a harsh assessment of the role of the individual Sokol leaders during February 1948 and the preparations for the Slet, but also comes to terms with her own membership in the action committee of the Czechoslovak Sokol Community. Cf. Waldauf, J.: *Sokol. Malé dějiny velké myšlenky*, Vol. 3, p. 477.

elections in June 1948 as a "worthy introduction to our 11th All-Sokol Slet" and called for the election of a single candidate. "A single candidate will teach us to truly think and act politically and prevent our "beer hall" politics. [...] Only after we learn this, will we be able to have more candidates."[248] It may be that Truhlář was, like many other Sokol officials, excited about the possibilities that the unification of gymnastics (which meant, among other things, the transfer of all property of the dissolved gymnastic organization to Sokol[249]) and the state's open support offered, though only few of them were prepared to fully relinquish the autonomy of Sokol life.[250] Even in carrying out the large-scale purges at Sokol, its presidium, trying to defend its autonomy, announced: "We alone will clean our ranks and will do it the Sokol way."[251] Not even Truhlář was willing to accept the direct assault on Sokol's authority that occurred in connection with Beneš's funeral. In early September 1948 he resigned from his position, stating:

"I'm not running away, but I cannot continue under these conditions! Nor can I for my personal honor, for the Tyrš-instilled manly pride, or for my honor as Sokol president."[252] He was ultimately convinced to remain the leader of the "cleansed" Sokol, and, shortly before his death, was even a guest of honor in the stands reserved for state officials to witness the 1st All-State Spartakiad. The tactical acquiescence of the communist party after February 1948 thus provided an opportunity for a broad range of opposition or adaptation strategies, but also corroded the already quite illusory unity of Sokol leadership. Many of the conflicts that stemmed from the differing strategies vis-à-vis communist authority would come to a head

---

248 Ibid, vol. 1, p. 224.
249 Zákon n. 187 ze dne 14. července 1949 o státní péči o tělesnou výchovu a sport, paragraf 9.
250 Kaplan, K.: *Národní fronta 1948–1960*, p. 106.
251 "Prohlášení předsednictva ČOS ze dne 14. července 1948". *Sokolský věstník*, vol. 46, n. 31–32, p. 451.
252 Uhlíř, J. B. – Waic, M.: *Sokol proti totalitě*, p. 146.

13. Women's entrance at the 1948 All-Sokol Slet at Strahov Stadion in Prague (photo Václav Chochola).

decades later, both within the country and abroad in exile, particularly during attempts to renew Sokol in 1968 and 1989.

The Slet itself, which took place on June 10 – July 6, 1948, was a culmination of the prior First-Republic mass gymnastic performances. In fact, the exercises were very similar to those of the final pre-war Slet, often composed by the same people, and, in the case of the women's round dance (REJ), the performance was repeated (the only time in Slet history). Yet in the number of gymnastic participants and spectators and in the organizational preparations, this Slet eclipsed all previous ones and this would prove a difficult model to surpass for later Spartakiad organizers. The event boasted of a number of firsts: e.g., apparently for the first and last time the figure of a quarter million spectators[253] was reached, and also for the first time in Czechoslovakia did the event receive television coverage, though only for a few receivers within the range of a few kilometers.[254]

The changed political situation was mostly reflected in the inclusion of a separate performance by the trade union juniors and the performance of Soviet gymnasts (as well as the absence of members of the American Sokol) in the Slet program. The young unionists entered to the sound of sirens, a helicopter then dropped on the stadium's field two bouquets of red roses that the gymnasts, singing "Song of Labor" presented to President Gottwald and Prime Minister Zápotocký. The performance itself, to which some of the audience loudly voiced their disapproval,[255] was intended to depict the work process: boys building bridges and towers, girls embodying "more delicate work such as weaving on looms, etc."[256] The performance of Soviet athletes, who seemed for one Sokol writer "so real, alive, beautiful, captivating, so sure and confident and so vividly happy," consisted of well-proven elements of Moscow gymnastic shows: acrobatic motorcycle riding, duo high-trapeze acts and human pyramids on steel structures.[257] The Soviet performance was

---

[253] Libenský, Jan – Martínková, Blažena: "Sletová vystoupení dorostu". In: *Památník XI. sletu všesokolského v Praze 1948*, pp. 99–102.

[254] See Disman, Miloslav: "Praha IV na všech vlnách, ve zvuku i v obraze." *Památník XI. sletu všesokolského v Praze 1948*, pp. 148–149. Another novelty was the introduction of short-wave walkie-talkies for radio reporters who could thus broadcast directly from the stadium's field. According to Disman's testimony, one reporter made use of this opportunity during the military day as well and was hit in by a piece of amunition cartridge which lodged about 3 centimeters deep in his chest. He continued broadcasting despite the injury and was brought to the hospital only after the military performance had ended.

[255] Marek, Jaroslav (ed.): *Za socialistický systém tělesné výchovy. Dokumenty od nár. a demokratické revoluce po XV. sjezd KSČ*, Olympia, Prague 1978, p. 49. See also Dolanský, Julius et al.: *Sto deset let Sokola. 1862–1972*. Olympia, Prague 1973, p. 94.

[256] Libenský, J. – Martínková, B.: "Sletová vystoupení dorostu", pp. 99–102.

[257] Disman, Miloslav: "Sovětští fyskulturníci mezi námi". In: *Památník XI. sletu všesokolského v Praze 1948*, p. 139.

immediately preceded by a composition of a much larger Yugoslav delegation which had arrived in Prague on the same day that the Cominform resolution was released leading to a Soviet-Yugoslav rift. At the end of the performance, seven hundred and fifty Yugoslav sailors formed on the stadium field the enormous word "Tito," which the entire stadium apparently reacted to by chanting "Ti-to, Ti-to."[258]

The ambition of the final Slet, like those before it, was to represent the entire nation. "These aren't just gymnastic clubs of various districts that came together for a joint performance," wrote theater critic Miroslav Rutte of Sokol calisthenics, "that's the nation itself, the people in the purest sense of the word."[259] The spectators and gymnasts coalesced into a single organism, "the people greeted the people," even if, according to newly appointed gymnastics director and pre-war member of the broader Sokol leadership Evžen Penniger, the entire nation did not take part – just "its better, healthy part."[260]

Also appearing was a motif that would later assume a central role in Spartakiads: the transformative role of the mass spectacle on the "unconsecrated, yet sacred grounds of the Sokol stadium at Strahov."[261] The Slet was intended to be a "general test of the all-Sokol, national, state and pan-Slavic future" that, in the view of Sokol President František Bláha, would only be achieved when all youth pass through "our Sokol school of Tyrš."[262]

As in previous Slets, the Sokol-represented nation was portrayed as an organism, but unlike before the radical implications of this

258 See Dedijer, Vladimir: *Tito Speaks. His Self Portrait and Struggle with Stalin*. Weidenfeld & Nicolson, London 1953, pp. 374–375. Also see Bláha, František – Martínková, Blažena: "Sletová premiéra", p. 130; the text however avoided the name Tito.
259 Rutte, Miroslav: "Sokolská prostná". In: *Památník XI. sletu všesokolského v Praze 1948*, pp. 137–138.
260 Penniger, Evžen: "Po sletu". In: *Památník XI. sletu všesokolského v Praze 1948*, pp. 214–215.
261 Disman, Miloslav: "První takt sletové symfonie". In: *Památník XI. sletu všesokolského v Praze 1948*, pp. 66–68.
262 Bláha, František: "O sokolský národ". In: *Památník XI. sletu všesokolského v Praze 1948*, pp. 21–22.

biological metaphor were thought through. A good example is the description of the performance of Sokol juniors by the writer Edmond Konrád. At Strahov he saw "ecstatic consanguinity" in thousands of Czech faces which all represented the "tribe of a single family," their eyes and foreheads created "by the same law."[263] The gymnasts passing through the Strahov gates in a "shapeable flood" embodied the timeless national community: "You once again recognize yourself in this new, more beautiful race, in which you are some way again you and yours, in which we have been we and ours since time immemorial, perhaps since Forefather Czech." The juniors represented for him the "youngest shoots" on the massive national trunk that, though it has lost many a twig, "drives the sap to the farthest ends" (here Konrád is clearly referring to the post-war ethnic cleansing in the borderlands). The exercises of the junior women in particular evoked in Konrád and in many other Sokol writers the idea of an eternal national organism: "And those vibrant beds of spring flowers, that was how your wife was in her spring, and like her, these before your eyes will be good and sweet perhaps quite soon, [...they] will perform the everyday work and cook and give birth and nurse, darn socks and children's underwear and clean and scold."[264] Thus the nation depicted at Sokol Slets was transformed in Konrád's eyes from an elusive historical category into an eternal, i.e. racial, community.[265]

263 Konrád, Edmond: "Duchový Tábor". In: *Památník XI. sletu všesokolského v Praze 1948*, pp. 119–120.

264 Similarly, František Kožík saw in the "slender junior women" future mothers, whose children would already be taking part in the next Slet. Kožík, Fratišek: "Komu patří dík". In: *Památník XI. sletu všesokolského v Praze 1948*, p. 94. Anna Sedlmayerová also considered the exercises as a ritual of sorts in which the mothers relinquish their daughters to the collective. Sedlmayerová, Anna: "Matky". In: Ibid, pp. 102–103.

265 We have also previously come across a similar understanding of the organic metaphor. For example, in the 1920 Slet souvenir program the distinguished Czech anatomist and Sokol official Karel Weigner defended the necessity and benefit of a "program of national eugenics and racial hygiene." Weigner, Karel: "Zdravím k síle národa a ke kráse života". In: J. Hiller (ed.): *Památník VII. sletu všesokolského v Praze 1920*, pp. 30–33.

Yet the organic community created by the malleable mass of Sokol gymnasts was newly interpreted as a new political quality chiming with the new order. "Indeed, the monolithic unity that is best for the nation," wrote František Kožík, whom we will later examine in detail "is in the end the greatest political maturity."[266] Newly elected communist president Klement Gottwald also interpreted the importance of the Sokol Slet in this sense in an open letter to Sokol members from July 3rd, i.e. right after a range of Sokol "provocations" aimed at the new authority. In the letter, in which he addresses Sokol members with "Dear brothers!", Gottwald wrote that the Slet is proof that "our new order [...] is filled with Tyrš's ideas, progress, democracy and Slavic solidarity" and has created unsuspected possibilities for Sokol's development. "Whatever they may say about the 11th All-Sokol Slet," he concluded, "this was the Slet in which the motto 'Every Czech a Sokol" came true."[267] Similarly viewing the transformation of the Sokol collective into a timeless communist collective was Jaroslav Seifert, the later dissident and the only Czechoslovak recipient of the Nobel Prize for Literature, whose verse accompanied the hastily prepared so-called Slet harvest celebrations that were to replace the Slet theatrical scene. At the close, Seifert posed an important question regarding the development of the 1948 Slet: "Indeed, we will all, every single one of us, slice from one bread. It is bittersweet, and a common destiny awaits us all. A few will betray. Can the people betray?"[268]

The course of the Slet and particularly of the Slet parade showed the Communist Party leadership that the response to Seifert's question was positive. New president Gottwald and other members of

---

266 Kožík, František: "Ve jménu vzpomínky". In: *Památník XI. sletu všesokolského v Praze 1948*, pp. 17–19.
267 Gottwald, Klement: "Drazí bratři!". In: *Památník XI. sletu všesokolského v Praze 1948*, pp. 142–143.
268 Seifert, Jaroslav: "My chceme nový, lepší svět. Verše k sletovým dožínkám". In: *Památník XI. sletu všesokolského v Praze 1948*, pp. 162–166. Seifert's verse also accompanied the prior Slet in 1938. See Procházka, R. (ed.): *Památník X. všesokolského sletu v Praze 1938*, pp. 50 and 56.

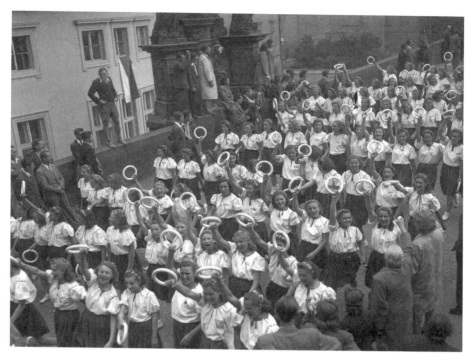

14. Sokol parade in 1948 on the Charles Bridge in Prague (photo Václav Chochola).

the new political garniture had to stand for hours in the tribunes reserved for government officials at Strahov Stadium and on Old Town Square and watch on as thousands of Sokol members systematically insulted them, despite all the precautionary measures taken: they tried to counter the protests by calling for police forces equipped with machine guns and for members of the People's Militia to come to Prague, by organizing their own parallel event management services or by amassing hundreds of volunteers ready to chant slogans prepared in advance. The first incident occurred during the performance of pupils who hailed in front of Gottwald the resigning President Beneš. Protests then continued over the course of the main Slet days and culminated during the Slet parade that over eighty thousand Sokol members including a thousand equestrians took part in. Sokol members hailed Beneš and chanted slogans (also prepared in advance) such as "Strength in Tyrš, faith in Beneš," "They killed Masaryk, we won't give them Beneš," "Let the whole world know, we want Beneš back as president" or "A fist to the face for all comrades." When marching by the government stands at Old Town Square, Sokol members marched in silence and demonstratively turned their heads to face the opposite side.

It was clear to the communist leadership that they had to strongly react to these protests if they wanted to gain control over Czechoslovak gymnastics. At a Communist Party's Central Committee meeting, Václav Kopecký requested that "a pogrom-like spirit be used in confronting the provocateurs at Sokol."[269] In preparing the repression against Sokol members (relatively mild compared to subsequent years[270]) the theory of the aggravation of class struggle, formulated at the Cominform meeting in Bucharest in June 1948, was put to use for the first time.[271] However, the repression, along with the press campaign, provoked a strong public reaction from the leaders of the individual Sokol clubs, resulting in further Sokol protests during Beneš's funeral. In the autumn of 1948, it was clear to the communist leaders that controlling Sokol would not be easy,

---

269 Kaplan, K.: *Národní fronta 1948–1960*, p. 114. Accord to the resolution of the presidium, the "defeatist reactionary elements are trying to place and unleash nests of vipers in Sokol." Quoted from Uhlíř, J. B. – Waic, M.: *Sokol proti totalitě*, p. 141. See also "O čistý štít Sokolstva". *Rudé právo*, vol. 28, 24. 7. 1948, p. 1.

270 Dozens of Sokol members arrested during the Slet were sentenced to fines or several days of punishment. See Kaplan, K.: *Národní fronta 1948–1960*, pp. 111–112. The harshest reactions were caused by the protests of regional leaders and the attendance of Sokol members at the funeral of former president Edvard Beneš. By October 1948, 11,446 Sokol members were barred from the Sokol and more than 1,500 officials were relieved of their positions. Yet this "cleansing" of Sokol came up against passive resistance in the individual clubs. See Šikula, Martin: "Tři poznámky k násilné transformaci Sokola. Regionální sondy do postupné likvidace tradiční spolkové organizace v letech 1948–1952". *Časopis Matice moravské*, 2012, vol. 131, n. 1, pp. 89–116.

271 Uhlíř, J. B. – Waic, M.: *Sokol proti totalitě*, p. 141.

which was not alleviated by the fact that the communists had no clear concept for transforming physical education. In mid 1949, for instance, they were still expecting that the Slets would continue, as attested to by the speech of Julius Dolanský, a literary historian, communist official, and a chief Sokol "educator", at the National Assembly:

"The 12th All-Sokol Slet at the end of our first five-year plan will not only be a jubilant display of Tyrš's Sokol ideas carried out through the absolute unity of physical education as initiated by Klement Gottwald; the 12th All-Sokol Slet will be a victorious celebration of the people's democracy and of all Czechoslovak people."[272] Yet skepticism gradually prevailed in the Communist Party concerning the Sokol's ability to become a tool for the communization of physical education and Gottwald's principle formulated right after the Slet protests was implemented: "Better to have Sokol not work at all, than to have it work against us."[273]

In 1949 to 1953, the attempt to control Sokol gradually turned into its almost complete dissolution. The Communist Party first tried to "dilute" the traditional Sokol community by persuading in particular the proletariat of large factories (often traditionally with anti-Sokol sentiments) to join Sokol. The recruitment of "new Sokol members" was then accompanied by another step – the dissolution of Sokol's traditional organizational structure. First the organization of Sokol by counties was ended in early 1949 by which the obstinate county directorships were done away with, and a new structure aligned with regional administration was put into place. This was followed by a much more radical intervention which consisted of the dissolution of the regional principal of gymnastics organization and its replacement with the production principle. In other words, the participants

272 *Stenoprotokol 34. schůze Národního shromáždění*, 14. 7. 1949 (available online at the Czech and Slovak Digital Parliamentary Library). See also Šikula, M.: *Tři poznámky k násilné transformaci Sokola*, p. 101.
273 Waldauf, J.: *Sokol. Malé dějiny velké myšlenky*, vol. 1, p. 245.

would not exercise where they lived, but where they worked. Lastly the final, most significant change was the "sportification of Sokol," which meant a complete turnaround in the association's physical education policy. The all-round and non-competitive Sokol training that the individual units were meant to follow was to be replaced by competitive sports with members working towards – in imitation of the Soviet model – a performance proficiency badge, still called for some time the Tyrš Proficiency Badge.[274] State authorities were thus taking a clear position in the decades-long dispute between non-competitive gymnastics and competitive sports.

By the end of 1952, the Czechoslovak Sokol Community was dissolved due to its enduring "sectarian club-ism," and a system for the state management of gymnastics was formed. The Voluntary Sports Organization (DSO) Sokol was set up in accordance with the new organizational structure which was to deal with "residual" gymnastics in villages and smaller towns. With the motto "For a rich harvest, for the athletic glory of the village" the DSO Sokol was to become involved in the work of the agricultural cooperatives, organize sports activities for its members and each year organize a harvest celebration. It is not completely clear from these radical changes in the Communist Party's policy towards Sokol to what degree it was an attempt to control the gymnastics movement and to what extent it consisted of a mechanical sovietization of physical education, meaning an imitation of the constantly changed Soviet physical education model that was taking place in other Eastern Bloc countries as well. In any case, the first half of the 1950s saw a severe drop in gymnastic and athletic activities in general, especially in Sokol calisthenics.

Just as it had managed to disintegrate the association's structure and marginalize Sokol calisthenics, another 180 degree turn was prepared beginning in the autumn of 1953. With the decision to

---

[274] Zákon n. 187 ze dne 14. července 1949 o státní péči o tělesnou výchovu a sport, paragraf 8.

begin to prepare the 1st All-State Spartakiad as part of the tenth anniversary of the liberation of Czechoslovakia, we see not only the renewal of traditional mass gymnastic performances, but also a return to traditional Sokol calisthenics. Plans to organize another Slet had never completely disappeared among the formal Sokol officials holding on to various posts of nationalized physical education. Following Gottwald's death, these efforts met with the attempts by political leaders to find a new, post-Stalin legitimacy that also required new rituals. By sacrificing the "Slet" name and replacing it with "Spartakiad," leading representatives of interwar communist physical education could be brought on board for the next Slet. Such individuals, such as Vilém Mucha, shared the belief of former Sokol representatives that an unconditional preference for competitive sports was a threat. The event's name both referred to the first communist Spartakiad in the Maniny area of Prague in 1921 and to Soviet gymnastics. Though the "all-state" adjective was a slavish translation of the Russian word *vschesoyuznaya* (all-union), in its concept the Czechoslovak Spartakiads bore almost no resemblance to the Soviet event of the same name. Indeed, Soviet Spartakiads represented the hierarchical system of athletic competitions in which mass gymnastic performances played only a marginal role during the opening and closing ceremonies. In the parlance of the day, Czechoslovakian Spartakiads possessed Soviet form and Sokol content.

Besides changing the name from Slet to Spartakiad, the state also used a more forceful way to show former Sokol members that a return to mass gymnastic performances did not mean a return to autonomy and to the political position that Sokol held prior to February 1948. Under the name Operation "Sokol" the State Security prepared in 1954–55 an extensive show trial against the "illegal Sokol organization," which it accused of making preparations to renew the Sokol organization in all regions of the country following the expected putsch, of the misusing funds of the former Czechoslovak Sokol Community and of obstructing the Spartakiad preparations.[275] Shortly before the Spartakiad was held, several former high Sokol officials were summarily sentenced to long prison terms; as the "group leader," Viktor Heller received a ten-year prison sentence.[276]

Shortly before the start of this political trial against the former Sokol leaders, another former Sokol top official, Jaroslav Šterc, who had taken part in the preparation of the previous three Slets, drew up the first 20-page confidential draft of the future Spartakiad. In December 1953, he submitted it to his superior, Defense Minister Alexej Čepička, who essentially agreed to it and recommended that the numbers of participants and the organization of the Spartakiad be compared with previous Slets "since the Spartakiad must far exceed it in its magnitude and content."[277] Not long afterwards, the

---

275 ABS, f. Historický fond StB, H 322 (Akce "Sokol"). This investigation included the systematic attempt to analyze the post-war development of Sokol and its leading figures. Most of these reports were written by lieutenant Ludvík Arazím who was promoted in late 1955 for his work in "securing the 1st All-State Spartakiad". (Ludvík Arazím was also one of the Secret Police officers assigned to the writer Pavel Kohout during the normalization period.
He was dismissed in June 1973, however, for "moral and political shortcomings" and rehabilitated in 1990). See Schovánek, Radek (ed.): *Svazek Dialog. Stb versus Pavel Kohout. Dokumenty StB z operativních svazků Dialog a Kopa*. Paseka, Prague – Litomyšl 2006, pp. 362–363. It was relatively difficult for the Secret Police to show Sokol officials as an anti-state group, since many of them were involved in the Spartakiad preparations or had completely withdrawn from public life. Their position is characterized by one of the reports from Action "Sokol": "[…] They are not at all engaged politically, do not speak out at all against the state, though they also never praise it."
276 Though Viktor Heller was among the Sokol leaders willing to cooperate with the Czechoslovak Communist Party after February 1948. See Waldauf, J.: *Sokol. Malé dějiny velké myšlenky*, vol. 1, p. 243. On Heller's later recollection of the trial also see vol. 2, pp. 145–147.
277 Národní archiv (further only NA), f. Státní výbor pro tělesnou výchovu a sport 1949–1956 (further only SVTVS), box 46, unit number 1096, Návrh na provedení I. celostátní spartakiády ze dne 14. prosince 1953. The plenum of the State Committee for Gymnastics and Sports had already approved in October 1953 the idea of holding the 1st All-sports Spartakiad and set up its preparations committee in which a number of former Sokol officials figured. NA, f. SVTVS, k. 66, inv. n. 196, Organisační směrnice pro přípravu I. celostátní spartakiády, Organisační směrnice pro práci výboru I. všesportovní spartakiády při SVTVS ze dne 27. října 1953. Jaroslav Šterc mentions in his book the "historic" weekend meeting on the proposal of the 1st Spartakiad at a cottage in Šerlich in the Orlické Mountains on December 12–13, 1953. Šterc Jaroslav: *Československé spartakiády. Nejmasovější projev naší tělesné výchovy*. Olympia, Prague 1975, p. 44. See also NA, f. SVTVS, k. 63, inv. n. 189, Materiály z porad předsednictva spartakiády 1954 (21. 1. 1954).

preparations for the 1st all-state Spartakiad of 1955, which we will discuss in Chapter 4, were underway. As early as March 1954, an experienced Sokol member, President Antonín Zápotocký, was warning the organizers that there could be no delay: "I must take this opportunity to express my concerns that the Spartakiad preparations are slightly behind schedule. I think that part of the problem here are the incorrect and sectarian views that are still held. The Spartakiad's preparations [...] must be based on all, even old, but good and time-tested national traditions of mass participation, of accessibility and of unity. They must not disregard, but must adopt everything that was good and of the mass nature in our previous Sokol Slets, Olympiads and Spartakiads."[278] With the president's admonition, the post-war gymnastics development came full circle: from the Communist Party's attempt to control and exploit Sokol and its Slets, to the attack on the very essence of Sokol activities as part of the sovietization and "sportification" of gymnastics, to a return to non-competitive calisthenics and mass gymnastic performances.

✕✕✕

The long and complex development of mass gymnastic performances of the second half of the 19th century and first half of the 20th century shows that the human body and its movement are "ideological variables". The same exercises can express completely different political views. Turner exercises depicting the aspiration of the German nation for unification and a "place in the sun" were

On the preparations and organization of the 1955 Spartakiad see also the thorough MA thesis: Lenčéšová, Michaela: *Prvá celoštátna spartakiáda 1955*. FF UKF, Nitra 2015.
278   "Projev prezidenta republiky Antonína Zápotockého na rozšířeném zasedání Státního výboru pro tělesnou výchovu a sport při vládě republiky Československé, konaném ve dnech 27. – 28. března 1954". In: J. Marek (ed.): *Za socialistický systém tělesné výchovy*, pp. 99–102. For the delays, see also AČOS, f. I. celostátní spartakiáda 1955 – Základní dokumenty, Ideový program, plán příprav a návrh rozpočtu I. celostátní spartakiády v roce 1955, p. 5.

adopted by the Sokols, who used the same exercises (though slightly embellished) to show the vitality of the small "Czechoslavic" nation and its own ambition to represent this nation. The Sokol exercises, which expressed a corporeally understood national solidarity that transcended classes, were adopted at the close of the 19th century by the Social Democrats, whose participants used the same exercises to symbolize the strength of an organized working class and social solidarity of the exploited. Added to the palette after the First World War was communist mass gymnastics, which was to demonstrate the inevitability of the class struggle and the ultimate victory of the working masses. Sokol lost its monopoly on interpreting the meaning of mass gymnastic performances during the First Republic, though paradoxically its physical *habitus* expanded into culturally diverse and politically hostile spheres. The over century-long development of the gymnastic movements and their mass rituals represented a rich source of inspiration, meanings, symbols and pitfalls for the organizers of later Spartakiads who – as we shall see in the following chapter – readapted Turner and Sokol exercises to the new political reality.

Symbolism
of the First Spartakiad
in 1955

STALINISM WITHOUT STALIN

The 1st All-State Spartakiad in 1955 began only a few weeks after the unveiling of the Stalin monument. Film footage from the period captures the Spartakiad gymnasts with the statue's almost spotless bright granite in the background on Letná Plain. Nevertheless, the first Spartakiad is characterized by the attempt to dispense with Stalin, to create a post-stalinist ritual in which the central role was not played by the Leader, but by the unsurpassable power of the masses (literary critic and later dissident Sergej Machonin described one of the 1955 Spartakiad performances as "the floating movement of one massive creature, something like the ancient movements of the earth from which the mountains were born and the seas waters first curled in waves"[279]).

The horizontal social geometry of Strahov stadium plain was thus asserted against the vertical Stalin cult of personality on Letná. This

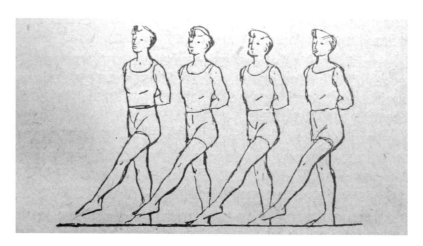

15. Illustration of a synchronized step drill in the book by Jiří Žižka: *Pořadová cvičení.* (Prague 1957).

279 Machonin, Sergej: "Tvář našeho času". *Literární noviny*, 1955, vol. 4, n. 27, p. 2.

is well documented by the opening speech of President Antonín Zápotocký at Strahov Stadium (in which Stalin's name was not once spoken): "Today and on the days to follow the masses will speak here at the Spartakiad at the Strahov Stadium: masses of children, students and apprentices, masses of employees of factories and offices, of shops and fields, masses of youth – of men and women – from cities and villages."[280] The speaker here was not only defining the core of the Spartakiad message, but also its style. Thus in 1955, as well as five years later, socialist realism represented a way of interpreting and aestheticising the concept of *the people*. By comprehensively listing the various groups of people ("masses of adolescents," "masses of employees," "masses of children"), Zápotocký evoked one of the key genres of socialist realism and the fundamental organizational principle of the Spartakiads – the principle of the mosaic. The 1st All-State Spartakiad presented the people as a perfectly symmetric whole composed of clearly designated social and professional groups, the stones in a "mosaic of blinding beauty,"[281] of which each had a clearly defined role.

The individual stones of the socialist mosaic first needed to be clearly defined. Socialist realism was thus characterized more by emphasizing national, class and gender differences than by blurring them. National and regional traits under the motto "socialist content – national form" were flaunted or even newly created (reports of the Spartakiad parade surprisingly emphasized the participation of the German minority).[282] Socialist realism dealt with the category of social classes

280 "Projev prezidenta republiky Antonína Zápotockého". *Rudé právo*, vol. 35, 24. 6. 1955, p. 1.
281 Navrátil, Jiří: "Zpěv o dnešním dnu". *Mladá fronta*, vol. 11, 3. 7. 1950, p. 1; quoted from Macura, Vladimír: *Šťastný věk a jiné studie o socialistické kultuře*. Academia, Prague 2008, p. 161.
282 "The Karlovy Vary Region also contributed to the colorfulness of the parade with the interesting costumes of the dance ensemble of citizens of German nationalility 'Aufbau und Frieden' z Aše." In: "Nejmohutnější přehlídka úspěchů naší tělovýchovy". *Rudé právo*, vol. 35, 4. 7. 1955, p. 2. For general discussion of this trend, see for instance Slezkine, Yuri: "The USSR as a Communal Apartment, or How a Socialist State Promoted Ethnic Particularism". In: Sheila Fitzpatrick (ed.): *Stalinism. New Directions*. Routledge, London and New York 2000, pp. 313–347.

in a similar way. Workers, farmers or the working intelligentsia clearly did not represent social classes in the Marxist sense with their own antagonistic interests, but were instead arbitrarily constructed categories whose roles were to create clearly demarcated pieces of the overall picture of the working people.[283] This social engineering is perhaps most surprising in case of gender since we would expect that the social emancipation of women would be accompanied by a reduction in gender differences in representation. Yet this certainly was not the case in the Spartakiads. Gender differences were clearly defined and emphasized. All aforementioned categories were canonized and unchangeable, but also arbitrary since they did not refer to any "essential" differences and did not create any distinctive autonomy. The principle of the mosaic required that the individual groups differed as much as possible from one another so that there was a distinct border between them and only their otherness allowed them "to speak," to compose the shared image of the people. Socialist realism did not, therefore, strive for uniformity, but for diversity.

In addition to the mosaic, the metaphor of a mechanism could be useful for understanding the specific style of socialist realist Spartakiads. After all, it is no coincidence that the most ideologically charged part of the 1st All-State Spartakiad was the final scene of the performance by the work reserves in which thousands of participants used their bodies to create an image of several enormous turning cogwheels. The metaphor of a mechanism lies in stark contrast with the previous Sokol metaphor of a living organism (to which the Spartakiads during the "normalization" period of the 1970s and 80s would return).[284] The body itself was understood here as

---

[283] See for instance Fitzpatrick, Sheila: "Ascribing Class. The Construction of Social Identity in Soviet Russia". In: Fitzpatrick, Sheila (ed.): *Stalinism. New Directions*, pp. 20–46.

[284] For instance, on the occasion of the 1920 Slet, Otakar Zich announced that Sokol is transforming "innumerable human individuality" into "an organism," into a "perfect social unit." It was for him about "organic connection which occurs from good will and love for common thought" and not "subordination to the mechanical as with a machine." Zich, O.: *Estetické dojmy sletové*, p. 265. This corresponds to Zich's understanding of nation, which in his view is the only natural

a mechanism.[285] Its appearance did not play a major role: the body became a symbol, the bearer of a uniform, weapon, tool, or even other bodies. Its movements were highly stylized as well. In fact, the participants did not perform gymnastics, but symbolic movements representing various activities in society, such as factory or field work, and even the clearly paradoxical performance of gymnastic exercises or sports. Thus the participants did not exercise, but "performed" exercises. In the later discourse among Spartakiad organizers the critical term "formalism" was used for this understanding of the body. Since age was not significant ("Nejedlý is young"[286]), since the genders of the participants could be arbitrarily substituted and since external attributes such as uniforms and headscarves were important, it begs the question of whether other symbols could have substituted the human body. This had, after all, occurred at the 1st All-State Spartakiad – also figuring in the performance along with the human participants at Strahov Stadium were steel structures, tanks, tractors, messenger pigeons and police dogs.[287]

The socialist-realist style of the first two Spartakiads, which was the work of a number of pre-war avant-garde figures (Milča Mayerová, Jožka Šaršeová, Jiří Kroha), clashed with the strong tradition

unit besides the family. All other units based on occupation, social status, religion etc. are artificial and disrupt the natural national organism whose base consists of animal instincts and the "dark subconscious." The role of Sokol, existing outside the realm of both class and parties, is to serve as a national synthesis.

285 The term "mechanization" of the body also appeared in Jeffrey T. Schnapp's well-known work on the Italian theater of masses. Schnapp speaks of "Soviet mechanization and fascist metallization" as "two different ways of conceptualizing the borderline between technologies of mass production and human bodies." While Soviet mechanization strove to demask bourgeois subjectivity and create a rational, classless and sexless society, fascist metallization demonstrated the "iron" will to transform society into a sacred community. Schnapp, Jeffrey T.: *Staging Fascism. 18BL and the Theater of Masses for Masses*. Stanford University Press, Stanford 1996, p. 86. On the history of the mechanism as corporeal metaphors cf. e.g., Morava, Sergio: "From Homme machine to Homme Sensible. Changing Eighteenth-Century Models of Man's Image."*Journal of the History of Ideas*, 1978, 39, 1, pp. 45–60. See also Bröckling, U.: *Disziplin*, p. 121.

286 See p. 139.

287 Nevertheless, the releasing of postal pigeons was a traditional part of Sokol Slets. See for instance Thiele, V.: "Praha se připravila", pp. 80–82.

of the Sokol Slets that had been established by the many gymnastic experts of Sokol origin. Unlike the avant-garde artists, the former Sokol members knew how to prepare the "communist Slet" under time constraints. Along with the various socialist realist elements, strong organizational and symbolic continuity was also apparent at the first Spartakiad. The adult participants were largely former members of Sokol; Sokol instructors were responsible for training them, and those composing the routines were usually the same people who had come up with the Sokol performances. The gymnasts were accompanied by music that had traditionally accompanied Sokol performances, such as Josef Suk's "A New Life" composed for the Sokol Slet.[288] As in the final Slet, the music was conducted by Jan Uhlíř, the gymnasts' costumes were again designed by Karel Svolinský, the photographs were taken by the same photographer, Ladislav Sitenský, and the Spartakiad film was shot by Martin Frič, who had also made a Slet film. To top it all off, sitting in the government box seats at Strahov Stadium next to Politburo members was the nearly 85-year-old Sokol President Josef Truhlář. The resulting shape of the Spartakiad was therefore a compromise, aesthetically often very problematic, between those wishing to restore the Slets in their original form and those who wanted a theater experiment embodying a socialist society.

Whatever the differences between the avant-garde artists, political sponsors and proletariat gymnastic instructors on the one hand, and the Sokol subculture on the other, both sides agreed on the primary aesthetic and symbolic element for the Spartakiads – discipline. In his poem "Choral Singing," for instance, not only did the poet Vítězslav Nezval (quoted in the introduction) effectively link Sokol fraternity to socialist solidarity, he also developed themes of

288 The main composer of Spartakiad music, Jan Seehák, had composed the accompaniment to the exercises at the final two Sokol Slets; Václav Dobiáš also helped create the music for the final Slet and first Spartakiad.

the plasticity of the people that first need to be malleable and controllable for them to be able to "speak" or create figures.

As the literary scholar Vladimír Macura has noted, discipline was not in the eyes of the Spartakiad organizers some kind of external principle that should suppress natural expressions of the individual, but an "inner essence" deformed by everyday life.[289] Marie Majerová, a member of the interwar avant-garde, praised the perfection of disciplined movement compared to "impure" habits: "This extending of arms, squats and push-ups, these are all in fact stylized human movements, cleansed of the ugly involuntary habits of uncontrolled movements, thought through to the beauty of perfection."[290] In the view of the Spartakiad organizers, discipline was to become an inner need, just as Vilém Mucha, an official of workers' gymnastics, wrote: "Finally now, all of the people have to learn how to march well, keep step and in line. What a wonderful spectacle it is to see marching formations at military parades and what a spectacle it would be if we could at least approximate this marching in our May Day parades or on other occasions."[291] Jiří Žižka, another of the key Spartakiad organizers though from the Sokol milieu (an organizer of the 1948 Slet, as well as Slets after 1989), recommended beginning with drill instruction from 3 years of age; a system of sequential exercises at preschools including "simple linear arrangement, changing shapes and assuming certain shapes" was to lead to the transformation of a person into a disciplined individual while still a preschooler.[292]

289 Macura, V.: *Šťastný věk*, pp. 159–160.
290 Majerová, Marie: "Chvála spartakiády". In: Vilém Mucha (ed.): *První celostátní spartakiáda 1955*. Státní tělovýchovné nakladatelství, Prague 1956, p. 8.
291 Mucha, Vilém: *První celostátní spartakiáda 1955: věcí všeho pracujícího lidu Československa*. SVTVS, Prague 1955, p. 17.
292 Žižka, Jiří: *Pořadová cvičení*. Sportovní a turistické nakladatelství, Prague 1957, pp. 6–7. This brochure was first published in 1952 when its author still worked as an instructor for the Central School of the Czech Sokol Community, and after five new editions (always upon the occasion of the Spartakiad) it was published for the last time in 1991.

"SOCIALISM IS A CHILD."
SCHOOL AND JUNIOR DAYS

Like the Sokol Slets (and unlike the later Spartakiads during "normalization") the mass performances of the first three Spartakiads were divided into School and Junior Days and Adult Days. Over 120,000 participants from first-graders to university students performed in the nine pieces and closing scene of the School and Junior Days that took place on June 23–26, 1955.[293]

With the exception of two routines, these were co-ed exercises, even though boys and girls wore different colored uniforms and often performed different exercises to the same rhythm.

The joint entrance of 40,000 participants of the individual gymnastic pieces preceded the performance itself. After filling the entire field of Strahov Stadium, some of the participants (3,000 older schoolgirls in yellow t-shirts and blue shorts) standing in front of the main grandstand where the party elite sat, created "as if with the wave of a wand" a living sign.[294] The girls raised above their heads blue and red pieces of cloth and formed the abbreviations ČSR (Czechoslovak Republic) and SSSR (USSR) and along the sides the years 1945 and 1955, in which the height of a single letter was 18.5 m, the width 15 m and the thickness 3.5 m (i.e. five participants).[295] Other girls knelt and, bowed with their foreheads and hands on the ground, formed the "background" of the message.

The first piece consisted of a performance of 6- and 7-year-old children entitled *The Golden Gate*. The children performed in smaller groups of 28 (14 boys and 14 girls) led by their teachers, who helped them with their positioning on the field and held wound banners

---

293 The Spartakiad program the School and Junior Days was repeated several times with various changes.
294 "Druhý den I. celostátní spartakiády". *Rudé právo*, vol. 35, 25. 6. 1955, p. 1.
295 NA, f. SVTVS, k. 64, inv. n. 190, Podklady pro schůze štábu I. celostátní spartakiády (leden–duben 1955).

16. Performance of students with paper cubes at the 1st Czechoslovak Spartakiad of 1955. The inscription above the gate reads "ready for work and defence of the country" (photo Václav Chochola).

during the routines. The performance, in which the children's movements mimicked e.g. the pistons of a locomotive and wings of an airplane (since, as the daily *Rudé právo* explained, "the future belonged to aviation"[296]), culminated in the final "golden gate."[297] As in the

296 Mládí, radost, mír zní Strahovem". *Rudé právo*, vol. 35, 24. 6. 1955, p. 2.
297 Bašta, Ladislav: *Zlatá brána. Cvičební hodina pro žactvo 1.–2. postup. ročníků všeobecně vzdělávacích škol.* Státní tělovýchovné nakladatelství, Prague 1954, p. 20.

well-known children's game, they passed through the gate formed by the other children, but instead of the threat that one of them would "lose his head," they sang: "Come boys, come girls, through the golden gate to peace, to happiness, to the gold."[298] Another change in the game was that the last child passing through the gate was not "struck with a broom," but instead stood before the others and unwound a blue banner with a white dove while reciting the poem: "Forward, let the white / dove / set out for / the sun, / Fly! Let it pass our greeting to / the entire young / world."[299]

The press of the day praised the performances of these "toddlers,"[300] but gave much more space to the performance that followed by 8 to 11-year-old pupils presenting "education focused on acquiring work habits."[301] Twelve thousand children accompanied by accordion music and in the rhythm of a Russian "Cossack dance" performed the routine with cubes of paper. As the commentary at that time explained, these cubes were not just everyday boxes with red (girls) or yellow (boys) paper glued to it, but "building material" that the children passed around, threw, stacked and built from it "maybe a factory, maybe a dam."[302] It was elsewhere emphasized that even though the routine resembled a game, it was actually the promise of future building efforts. "Yes, today we are still playful small fries, but just wait and see how we will one day build dams and nuclear power plants!" wrote the daily *Večerní Praha*.[303] The piece culminated in the nine-member groups forming rows to show, as

---

298 Ibid, pp. 25–27.
299 Ibid; See Macura, V.: *Šťastný věk*, p. 162.
300 "Skvělé vystoupení mládeže na Strahově". *Zemědělské noviny*, vol. 11, 24. 6. 1955, p. 2.
301 *Program I. celostátní spartakiády 1955*. Státní tělovýchovné nakladatelství, Prague 1955, unpag.
302 "Mládí, radost, mír zní Strahovem". *Rudé právo*, vol. 35, 24. 7. 1955, p. 2; "Vracejí nám milé vzpomínky". *Obrana lidu*, vol. 14, 26. 6. 1955, p. 1.
303 "Třetí den spartakiády: Mládí z továren a polí". *Večerní Praha*, vol. 1, 25. 7. 1955, p. 1. The daily *Zemědělské noviny* reported on it similarly: "They came today to exercise with blocks; tomorrow – several years from now – they themselves will construct the buildings of socialism [...]". In: "Šťastné mládí nadchlo". *Zemědělské noviny*, vol. 11, 26. 6. 1955, p. 1

written in the description, "the unified will of all: taking up work or the struggle for a joyous socialist future."[304]

The children's performance literally embodied one of the main elements of the socialist symbolic universe, i.e. the promise of a happy age in the future. The child's body, movements, voice or smile, played a key role in the Spartakiads since they physically substantiated the future of the communist regime and the feasibility of its ambition to create "a new person." As Macura pointed out, the child's consciousness was at that time believed to have already been formed by the new order and thus unburdened by the "experiences" and "prejudices" that their parents had grown up with.[305] We see this in, for instance, Milan Kundera's poem "Old Woman," or even more explicitly in Stanislav Neumann's verse: "There, where you and I grope forward / while still looking over our shoulders, / there the crowd of pioneer scouts will rush out before us, / lighting the way with red scarves."[306] Macura has also analyzed how the "child's perspective" penetrates to the very cultural code of socialist realism: "[...] the contradictory and complex gave way to simple and clear, tragic to optimistic, passionate to asexual, reflective to enthusiastic".[307] "Socialism is a child," wrote Josef Kainar.[308] The youth thus became a crucial category of socialist classification; only the young could participate in the socialist paradise. Yet linking the idea of paradise and the youth also worked the other way around. Those for whom an adherence to socialism was a given, necessarily became

---

304 *Program I. celostátní spartakiády 1955.* Jana Berdychová later gave this exercise as an example of a quite poorly conceived gymnastics composition that "demonstrably worsened children's posture." Berdychová, Jana: *Funkce tělovýchovných skladeb pro hromadná vystoupení mládeže v systému socialistické tělesné výchovy.* Habilitační práce. Fakulta tělesné výchovy a sportu Univerzity Karlovy, Prague 1960, p. 82.

305 This paragraph is a summary of Macura's analysis of the role of childhood in socialist semiotics. See Macura, V.: *Šťastný věk*, pp. 14–35 and 185–192.

306 Neumann, Stanislav: *Píseň o lásce a nenávisti.* Mladá fronta, Prague 1952, p. 42; Kundera, Milan: *Člověk zahrada širá. Verše.* Československý spisovatel, Prague 1953, pp. 20–21.

307 Macura, V.: *Šťastný věk*, p. 192

308 Kainar, Josef: *Český sen.* Československý spisovatel, Prague 1953, p. 62.

young, regardless of their biological age. In the song "STM" (Competition of Young Creativity), Nezval named all who are "young": "who fight for a happy life with the army of peace," "comrade Stalin," "every communist," the party, Zápotocký and even Nejedlý (the 77-year-old minister of culture).[309]

If "Nejedlý is young," then it is clear that socialist realism was working rather loosely with youth (as well as with other categories of corporeality as we will soon see).

"Youth" was more a value than a biological category. This is evident in Spartakiad routines in which children performed as "young adults" and imitated the world of adults – even in those parts of the performances in which, according to descriptions of the pieces, they were intended to play. This approach to the cult of the youth is one of the attributes in which fascist and socialist symbolisms differ.

In fascist rituals, as J. A. Mangan points out, the display of the active body of young men and women play an utterly irreplaceable role, though one that is completely different from that which we see here.[310] Its objective was to embody the "myth of renewal." This myth is considered a defining mark of "generic fascism," i.e. a particular type of a political movement characterized by a vision of "a national community rising like the Phoenix from a period of stifling decadence that almost destroyed it."[311] The marching and exercising young bodies of men and women of fascist rituals embodied the fascist regime's ambition to renew the national community through unbridled violence and racially hygienic sex. While young men demonstrated their desire to kill and be killed for the sake of

---

309 Nezval, Vítězslav: *Křídla. Básně z let 1949–1952*. Československý spisovatel, Prague 1952, p. 15.

310 Mangan, J. A.: "The Potent Image and the Permanent Prometheus". In: Mangan, J. A. (ed.): *Shaping the Superman. Fascist Body as Political Icon – Aryan Fascism*. Frank Cass, London 1999. For a general overview of the fascist aestheticizing of politics see Gentile, Emilio: *The Sacralization of Politics in Fascist Italy*. Harvard University Press, Cambridge, MA 1996; Berezin, Mabel: *Making the fascist self. The political culture of interwar Italy*. Cornell University Press, Ithaca 1997.

311 Griffin, Roger: *The Nature of Fascism*. Pinter Publishers, London 1991, p. 38.

racial purity, young women displayed their healthy bodies prepared to give birth to the next generation of even more determined and even purer fighters (and of more mothers). The fascist sexualization of young bodies was completely absent in early Spartakiads and therefore in the socialist context the border could be blurred between children and older youth, as well as between boys and girls, which was not possible in the fascist context. In socialist realism, youth is presented as non-biological, asexual and "eternal," while in fascist art youth is regenerating and thus mortal.

A NEW SHIFT BEGINS

The routine that best captured the organizers' ambitions to differ as much as possible from the Sokol Slets and come up with a completely new type of composition was that of the apprentices of the "State Work Reserves."[312] Entitled "A New Shift Begins," it entailed over nine thousand "up-and-coming innovators and Shakhanovites."[313] and was a choreographically demanding performance

17. A performance by the apprentices of the work reserves entitled "A New Shift Begins" for the 1955 Spartakiad at Strahov Stadium.

312 The State work reserves was a short-lived pedagogical experiment of secondary apprentice education based on the Stalinist model. See the entry "Státní pracovní zálohy" in Franc, Martin – Knapík, Jiří (eds.): *Průvodce kulturním děním a životním stylem v českých zemích 1948–1967.* Academia, Prague 2011, pp. 869–871.
313 AČOS, f. I. celostátní spartakiáda 1955 – Základní dokumenty, Ideový program, plán příprav a návrh rozpočtu I. celostátní spartakiády v roce 1955, p. 3.

that surpassed all previous Sokol compositions in the way it moved large mass formations on the exercising field. The piece culminated with an image in which the boys in dark blue costumes created a picture of eleven cogwheels that turned as they slowly jogged. The girls in short white skirts and yellow blouses ("Oh, you white angels of the work reserves!" praised Marie Majerová[314]) arranged themselves into rows linking the individual cogwheels. As the girls performed successive squats, their rows produced a wave-like effect which, according to the accompanying commentary of Martin Fryč's Spartakiad film, represented fields of grain (though the daily *Rudé právo* interpreted the rows of women as symbolizing chains as the pulleys between the cogwheels[315]). The cogwheels were momentarily transformed into flowers and then back to their original form, since, as the daily *Zemědelské noviny* wrote, "a country of advanced industry controlled by the people has to bloom, after all."[316] At the very end, the girls formed with their bodies a five-pointed star inside the largest cogwheel.

The press praised the performance of the work reserves as "unquestionably the best" piece at the Youth Days[317] and foreign guests confirmed its success. Nikolai N. Romanov, the chairman of the All-Union Committee for Physical Education and Sports in the Soviet Union, considered the performance to be a milestone in the international history of physical education.[318] Following the fiasco of the closing image[319] the Communist Party hastily ordered three repeat

---

314 Majerová, M.: "Chvála spartakiády", p. 7.
315 "Slavná přehlídka mládí a krásy pokračuje". *Rudé právo*, vol. 35, 25. 6. 1955, p. 2.
316 Dumasová, Jiřina: "Vlajky vylétly opět na stožár". *Zemědělské noviny*, vol. 11, 3. 7. 1955, p. 2.; quoted from Macura, V.: *Šťastný věk*, p. 160. See also Machonin, Sergej: "Čas růží". *Rudé právo,* vol. 35, 4. 7. 1955, p. 3.
317 [Caption under a photo of the work reserves performance]. *Rudé právo*, vol. 35, 30. 6. 1955, p. 1.
318 "Odnášejí si nejkrásnější dojmy". *Zemědělské noviny*, vol. 11, 28. 6. 1955, p. 2.
319 It is difficult to reconstruct what the closing scene looked like. According to the preserved technical description, it was meant to take the following form: "After the flags were shot up when the spectators were gazing upward, the performance of the acrobats would begin on the structure

18. Conclusion of the "A New Shift Begins" performance by the apprentices of the work reserves during the 1955 Spartakiad (National Museum).

work-reserve performances, even on the Adult Days and always at the end of the day's program.

The enthusiasm of the day for this performance is best depicted by Pavel Kohout's article "Praise for the Creative Reserves" on the front

under the balloon. Acrobatic exercises are used for this performance. After the exercise the participants will unroll a 120 m2 picture with the portraits of comrades Stalin and Gottwald and will descend down the prepared ropes to the main platform. Forty meters before the main platform the descending direction will change into an ascent and they will pass at a height of 50 meters over the main grandstand. At this final moment the platform above the central structure is raised to a height of 15 meters, the four rotating arms of the central structure begin to turn and the ribbons unwind. The arms of the rotating structures also start turning and the participants release the colourful streamers." NA, f. SVTVS, k. 64, inv. n. 190, Podklady pro schůze štábu I. celostátní spartakiády (leden – duben 1955), nám. ZTV, I. CS 1955, 64, Technický popis závěrečného obrazu I. celostátní spartakiády. See crushing criticism of the performance in: Janoušek, Vladimír: "Scény při tělovýchovných slavnostech". In: *Vědecká konference o teoretických a metodických základech masových tělovýchovných vystoupení (19. – 20. 2. 1956)*. Institut tělesné výchovy a sportu, Prague 1956, pp. 159–162.

page of *Rudé právo*.[320] After initially admitting that he disliked gymnastic performances, Kohout articulated the problems that he as a television journalist faced in verbally describing the monumental movement of the gymnasts:[321] "This is where we stop with thinking up, with playing with lofty and feathery words that come and go like a mayfly. Instead, something else of unalterable worth ignites in the heart. Peace is this kind of word, and the working class is this kind of concept [...] and that which you see on Strahov's greenish field is the youth of the working class, the reserves of the working class, the country's creative reserve." As Macura pointed out, Kohout also attacked intellectualism and verbose "literatism" for the inability to conceive and designate a new collective work of the new person.[322] In fact, Kohout's description of "Strahov's greenish field" is not poetic hyperbole – prior to the 1955 Spartakiad 1,800 tons of Strahov sand were dyed in mixers with twelve tons of green dye that, nevertheless, lost its color and instead colored the participants green when it rained.[323] The performance of the work reserves evoked in Kohout a long history of class struggles from "the smoke of the barricades" in 1848, to the shot from the Aurora, to the "song of our glorious February." In his view, the work reserves were also the "true face of our country's youth," and not those who, "in an attempt 'to elevate themselves above their ordinariness' fluffed up their boyish hair and dressed like dandy-freeloaders." Kohout saw in the performance a confidence "full of pride" in the new working class, whom he addressed in the article's conclusion: "Here's hoping that you turn the gear of a real machine in the same way, that we will always find that you are the same as we have come to know you at Strahov Stadium."

---

320 Kohout, Pavel: "Chvála tvořivých záloh". *Rudé právo*, vol. 35, 30. 6. 1955, p. 1.
321 Pavel Kohout also took part in the concept of the military's performance at the first Spartakiad in 1955.
322 Macura, V.: *Šťastný věk*, p. 155.
323 Kouřimský, Gustav: *Spartakiádní areál Strahov*. Olympia, Prague 1982, p. 21. See also NA, f. SVTVS, k. 68, inv. n. 201, Zprávy o stavu příprav I. celostátní spartakiády a její hodnocení.

In its explicit symbolism and overall choreography, the composition completely defied the tradition of Sokol performances. The piece's choreographers, Marie Rejhanová and Jožka Šaršeová, were not associated with Sokol, but were part of the leftist avant-garde, for which work-aestheticizing choreographies were nothing new.[324] Šaršeová was a prominent dancer and choreographer, having studied dance in Hellerau where she met artists such as V. Meyerhold and M. Chagall, and worked with a number of Czech avant-garde directors, such as Jiří Frejka, Jindřich Honzl and E. F. Burian.[325] Her transition from small avant-garde stages to mass gymnastic performances of the 1950s may have been influenced by her trips to the Soviet Union. In 1937, she had taken part in a May Day parade on Red Square as a member of a delegation of unionists. There she was most captivated by (besides her kiss with comrade Kalinin) the running of thousands of unsaddled horses from Soviet stud farms and the performance of tankers: "A tank flew out from the lower end of the square manned by a sturdy lad [...] It flew across the entire Red Square at an incredible speed and only after it had disappeared from sight did many other tanks set out with beautiful, strapping young men, the hope, strength and youth of this great land."[326]

Šaršeová certainly was not the only one to cross smoothly over from the inter-war avant-garde to socialist realism. Other creators of Spartakiad pieces included dancer and choreographer Milča Mayerová, who, for instance, had choreographed Jean Cocteau's Dadaist *The Wedding Party on the Eiffel Tower* and posed for Teige's design

---

324   Cf. from the Soviet avant-garde e.g. the performance of the Blue Blouse theater collective entitled *Ford and Us* that included gymnastic performances with stylized work movements in the background of a large cogwheel, or the performance *Machine Dance* by the Moscow Ballet School captured in a Margaret Bourke-White photograph from 1931 in which young dancers form the image of assembly-line production. See Deák, František: "‚Blue Blouse' (1923 to 1928)".
The Drama Review, 1973, vol. 17, n. 1, pp. 35–46; Wilk, Christopher (ed.): *Modernism. Designing a New World, 1914–1939*. Victoria & Albert Museum, London 2006, p. 18.
325   Šaršeová, Jožka: *Tak to jsem já…*, Mladá fronta, Prague 1981, p. 62.
326   Ibid, pp. 140–141. See also Šaršeová paper in the *Vědecká konference o teoretických a metodických základech masových tělovýchovných vystoupení*, p. 165.

of Nezval's poem *Abeceda*. Mayerová's piece for women *The Sower: A Song from the Fields and Orchards* served for the 1960 Spartakiad.[327] Moreover, as we will see in more detail in chapter four, the socialist-realism architecture of Strahov stadium was designed by another member of the interwar avant-garde, Jiří Kroha. The involvement of a number of avant-garde artists in the first Spartakiads confirms the well-known thesis of Boris Groys who asserts that Stalinist persecution of avant-garde artists conceals a deep kinship between the modernist avant-garde and socialist realism.[328]

In Groys's view, Stalinism realized the avant-garde's radical dream that art should cease to merely depict life and begin to transform it based on a full-scale and bold artistic vision, though this calls for the artist to become at a certain point a political leader. Ultimately, this all-encompassing aesthetic project – the total art – could only be carried out by the only, supreme artist – Stalin.[329]

Šaršeová herself linked the avant-garde era with mass gymnastic performances. In 1955, she wrote in the daily *Lidové noviny*:

"I've long wanted to work with a large collective in a large space, to use all my experiences and to see if I was able to work with expressive means of physical movement and mass gymnastic performances."[330] The Spartakiad composition represented for her a large theater project in which the laws of theatricality needed to be thoroughly applied and not only "flirted" with. When viewed as theater, a specific trait of mass gymnastic performances is that the mass, not the individual, is the actor. Yet this by no means weakens the overall effect of this "great artwork," but enhances it: "The expressive

327 Mayerová, Milča: *Rozsévačka. Píseň z polí a sadů. Skladba pro ženy.* STN, Prague 1958.

328 Groys, Boris: *The Total Art of Stalinism, Avant-Garde, Aesthetic Dictatorship, and Beyond.* Princeton University Press, Princeton 1992.

329 In general, organizers of the first Spartakiad strove for the broadest involvement of artists – whether they were linked to the avant-garde past or not. Cf. e.g., entry "Beseda spisovatelů s tělovýchovnými pracovníky" in Franc, M. – Knapík, J. (eds.): *Průvodce kulturním děním a životním stylem*, pp. 149–150.

330 Šaršeová, Jožka: "Nová kapitola". *Literární noviny*, 1955, vol. 4, n. 28, p. 3.

possibilities of the collective are not the sum of the individuals, but the exponential increase of their possibilities." Šaršeová fully carried out her concept at the next Spartakiad in 1960 for which she created the piece for women entitled *Life: Victory over Death*. In it, the gymnastic element almost completely disappeared and the massive choreography of the monolithic ensemble of women prevailed. Nearly 30,000 women "exercising" in long white dresses formed the shape of a globe with meridians and parallels and with a diameter of nearly 200 meters. The image changed colors according to how the women – as instructed by short-wave radio[331] – covered their heads alternately with red (symbolizing the "horrors of war") and blue (symbolizing "international solidarity") scarves.[332] At the end of the performance the women formed the image of a blossoming landscape in which "communist women throughout the world shake hands following the victory over the averted threats of war."[333] Rejhonová, the co-author of the aforementioned piece with the work reserves, then at the same Spartakiad reused the motif of cogwheels and created in the piece *To New Tomorrows* the closing image of "the massive gear of an atomic machine," which surpassed the performance of the work reserves in its sophistication and dynamics, but share with them the same symbolism and approach to the human body (cf. fig. XI).[334]

331 Serbus, Ladislav – Kos, Bohumil – Mihule, Jaroslav: *Historický vývoj a základy tělovýchovných vystoupení v ČSSR*. STNP, Prague 1962, p. 88.
332 Commentary to the film by Krejčík, Rudolf: *Symfonie psané pohybem. Tradice hromadných tělovýchovných vystoupení*. Krátký film, Prague 1987, 88 minut. See also Šotola, Jiří – Šiktanc, Karel: *II. celostátní spartakiáda*. STN, Prague 1961.
333 Riedlová, Ludmila: "Život vítězí nad smrtí". *Teorie a praxe tělesné výchovy*, 1961, vol. 9, special issue: Výsledky výzkumu II. celostátní spartakiády 1960, pp. 31–33. Riedlová points out here a number of problems that accompanied the performance of this piece. The spectators did not understand its complex symbolism, the women participants, quickly rounded up from large factories and offices, did not have enough training, and the women instructors preferred practicing other pieces for women and gave up practicing this piece.
334 See Papoušek, Jaroslav: *II. celostátní spartakiáda. II. část: Mládí a krása*. Krátký film, Prague 1960, 44 minut.

In addition to involving the interwar avant-garde, the work-reserves piece also illustrated a new interpretation of gender symbolism. It may seem at first glance that the Spartakiad barely altered the gender symbolism of the Sokol Slets and the pre-war gender order in general. Men and women performed exercises separately, were dressed in gender specific colors (dark blue symbolizing manual work, white symbolizing purity and innocence), the choreographers seemingly attributed traditional roles to the two sexes: women expressed through symbolized work in fields their connection to the world of nature and the household, while men flaunted strength and an innovative spirit by embodying industrial work. Moreover, the accounts of the performances often brought to mind the Sokol discourse between the wars. Marie Majerová,[335] for instance, spoke of the women's performances in these terms: "That which rose from the depths of the Czech and Slovak land of Mánes's influence, image after image transformed into Rusalka's waving, into the tenderness of cradles, into the dance of nymphs. Your routine had the lightness of lake waves and the loving grace of friendly embraces. It convinced us that gymnastics makes the body beautiful. [...] nothing binds men together more than joint work, joint efforts, a joint struggle. The success and satisfaction of joint work, of joint efforts, of a joint struggle was evident in your performance. You are builders, men, and you will be fighters for many years to come [...] Your strength will become power, if you don't grow weary."[336]

However, the Sokol gender model clearly did not correspond to the social reality or to the ideological ambitions of the communist regime of the mid 1950s. The country was going through a radical industrialization that successfully undermined traditional gender

---

335 Marie Majerová herself had performed as an instructor of the workers' gymnastics at the Spartakiad held at Maniny in 1921.
336 Majerová, M.: "Chvála spartakiády", p. 1 a 6.

roles.[337] Despite the Stalinist rediscovery of family values,[338] there was little room on an ideological level for bucolic images of women's traditional village and domestic life. After all, the students of the State Work Reserves that had performed *A New Shift Begins* were part of the large-scale mobilization of work forces for industrial projects, in which a new working class was to be created regardless of sex. In fact, we do not encounter here the traditional gender model, but a different overall narrative and a different understanding of the human body led to the creation of a completely new model that we can perhaps call the "engineered gender." This was not anchored in the world of unchanging family values as it was with Sokol, but in the social engineering of a new ruling elite that planned and redrew a new society using arbitrarily formed categories. In the view of this elite, gender was merely a convenient way to create a certain image of society in a style that best corresponded to socialist realism – to the mosaic in which the individual components did not mean anything by themselves and could only convey meanings as a whole. The choreographers of Spartakiad performances utilized a fact well known to anthropologists, namely that the sexual differences between the male and female body create a stable binary opposition that enables society to be represented as a whole composed of two equally sized but radically different components.[339] Thus gender served here simply as a way to indicate differences and

---

337   See Kalinová, Lenka: *Společenské proměny v čase socialistického experimentu. K sociálním dějinám v letech 1945–1969.* Academia, Prague 2007.

338   Dissolution of the Zhenotdel, the women's department of the Central Committee of the Communist Party of the Soviet Union in 1930 or laws making divorces more difficult and banning abortions (both in 1936) can be seen as manifestations of a Stalinist return to family values. See Fitzpatrick, Sheila: *Everyday Stalinism. Ordinary Life in Extraordinary Times. Soviet Russia in the 1930s.* Oxford University Press, Oxford – New York 1999, pp. 152–156; Goldman, Wendy: *Women at the Gates. Gender and Industry in Stalin's Russia.* Cambridge University Press, Cambridge 2001.

339   Douglas, Mary: *Purity and Danger.* Routledge & Kegan Paul, London 1978, p. 115; Synnott, Anthony: *The Body Social. Symbolism, Self and Society.* Routledge, London – New York 1993, pp. 228–235.

to allow for symbolic play with binary opposites, not to refer to a hierarchical world of "natural" sexual differences. The gender roles were for the most part divided arbitrarily here.[340] Theoretically the roles could have been swapped in the Work Reserve's piece (i.e. the boys would depict the grain and the girls the industrial cogwheel) without disrupting the overall narrative of the Spartakiads. The chosen arrangement of shapes for the piece also suggests this: while the "female" fields of grain formed a straight line, the "masculine" industry was represented by circles, i.e. the exact opposite of the traditional gender morphology of the Sokol Slets.[341] The only real task of these symbolic elements consisted of how they differed from each other. In fact, it was often impossible to tell in the Spartakiad compositions of this period whether the participants were male or female, and sometimes even the choreographers themselves did not maintain the gender separation. At the 1960 performance of the Association for Cooperation with the Military (Svazarm), for instance, both the male and female participants used their bodies, regardless of gender, to create the shape of parachutes.[342]

In contrast, we often find in socialist realism the use of traditional gender models even though they did not relate to sexual differences. The fact that gender binary opposition is not necessarily bound to the physical opposition between the male and female body is illustrated in e.g. Karel Pokorný's famous statue *Brotherhood*. This superb example of socialist realism created in 1947 depicts the male figure of a Czechoslovak partisan, who plays the female role in the binary opposite to the male figure of the Soviet soldier, whom he

340 For a general overview of the changing understanding of physicality in communist gymnastics see Oates-Indruchová, Libora: "The Ideology of the Genderless Sporting Body: Reflections on the Czech State-Socialist Concept of Physical Culture". In: Naomi Segal, Roger Cook, Carl Stychin and Lib Taylor (eds.): *In/determinate Bodies* Macmillan, London 2002, pp. 48–66.
341 For instance, the piece *Youth from the Villages* (DSO Sokol) featured a swapping of tradicional gender colors: the boys performed in yellow outfits, and the girls in blue. See Mucha, V. (ed.): *První celostátní spartakiáda 1955*, p. 91.
342 Šotola, J. – Šiktanc, K.: *II. celostátní spartakiáda.*

tenderly and submissively embraces.[343]Countless paintings showing Stalin and his "younger brothers" – leaders of Soviet Bloc communist parties such as Klement Gottwald, Mátyás Rákosi or Bolesław Bierut – possessed the same logic. While Stalin standing in the foreground and gazing upwards to the shining future is older, larger and stronger, his "weaker halves" look upon him with admiration.

The arbitrary and engineering use of gender symbols during the 1st All-State Spartakiad was part of a grand, but short-lived experiment in which society was perceived as a set of mechanical parts and the human body as a means for depicting non-human symbols. This experiment clashed with the entrenched tradition of representing the nation and understanding the human body, with a tradition that soon began to vigorously assert itself.

---

343 The eroticizing of the Czechoslovak-Soviet relationship was not uncommon. See e.g., Jiří Kolář's poem "My People": "And then I saw my people accept the most horrific death with a smile / And then I saw my people and the Red Army. / Two lovers." Kolář, Jiří: *Sedm kantát*. Družstvo Dílo, Prague 1945, pp. 8–9. See also Janáček, Pavel: "Listopad ve znamení Théty". *Tvar*, 2001, vol. 12, n. 1, p. 1 a 4.

THE UNBEARABLE HEAVINESS OF FOLKLORE:
FOLK DANCE AND SPARTAKIADS

The Adults Day program, held on July 2–3, 1955, opened with the Jamboree of Costumed Groups which consisted of a folklore performance of four hundred groups with three thousand pairs. Represented along with the Bohemian regions were Moravian Slovakia, Hanakia, Wallachia and Lachia, as well as all three regions of Slovakia. The jamboree culminated in a "joint dance of joy and victory"[344] under colorful maypoles that were to express the idea of "the unity of nations in Czechoslovakia in building a peaceful socialist future."[345]

The diversity of costumes and their origin from all over Czechoslovakia ("a thousand village boys and girls from Moravian Slovakia"[346]) became suitable material for many variations on the theme of melting differences together into a whole, and one of the few opportunities to speak openly about an "even closer, even friendlier bond" between Czechs and Slovaks.[347]

Besides the unity of a "healthy and pure" people[348] the folklore presentation was also intended to depict its history. It was typical for the Spartakiad's mosaic-like testimony that this key part of the overall narrative in the symbolic division of labor was allocated and assigned to the dancing folklore groups. The other pieces, with a few exceptions, had their symbolic focal point in the present, in its celebration, in its expectation of an even better future. This was, after all, the basis of the symbolism of the youth performances – the embodied promise of a great future. Yet the performances of the folklore groups turned to the past, showing where the current happiness

---

344 Mucha, V. (ed.): *První celostátní spartakiáda 1955*, p. 125.
345 Ibid.
346 "Téměř čtvrt milionu diváků tleská druhému dni dospělých". *Rudé právo,* vol. 35, 4. 7. 1955, p. 2.
347 "Ej, vy ztepilí šuhaji v čižmách, ej, děvčata v suknici rudé ". *Práce*, vol. 11, 3. 7. 1955, p. 2.
348 "pozdravili nás písní a tancem ". *Stadion*, 1955, vol. 3, n. 28, p. 14.

came from and the obstacles that needed to be overcome. Instead of a non-problematic glorification of the grandeur of the national past, this was an aestheticization of the history of the class struggle. "The history of our country accompanies them," the daily *Zemědělské noviny* wrote, "their costumes bear the ancient elements of the people's creativity, as do the embroidery stitches made by the pricked fingers of little girls who grew up and grew old during serfdom. [...] The Beskydy Mountains region is no longer impoverished, the young Wallachian and Lachian men proudly carry themselves and if they bow their heads in dance, it is only to their beautiful women."[349]

Though some observers such as the writer František Kožík were touched by strong emotions in viewing this performance ("Why hide behind dark glasses? Tears are not a sign of weakness, but the ability to deeply feel."[350]), this was one of the most absurd and aesthetically most problematic performances. The intimate aesthetics of folklore based on the uniqueness and non-transferability of local traditions clashed with the massive Strahov Stadium and its aesthetics of uniformity and geometrization. As in many other aspects of Spartakiads, this was not a communist innovation, but the adaptation and modification of previous Sokol practices.

Joining folk dance with gymnastic performances had first occurred in the 19th century, even though there was at that time a completely different (we could even say "opposite") understanding of physicality and political position. In the 19th century, folklore performances became part of the rituals of "official nationalism"[351] (e.g., seven hundred villagers from eighteen Moravian domains performed "national dances" to celebrate the opening of the Olomouc – Prague

349 "Zářiš v kráse, země má". *Zemědělské noviny*, vol. 11, 3. 7. 1955, p. 1.
350 Kožík, František: "Živé pohlednice ze Strahova". *Večerní Praha*, vol. 1, 4. 7. 1955, p. 3. Kožík bemoaned all Slets and Spartakiads (and then the Slets again). See for instance Kožík, František: "Slet ve vzpomínce". *Lidové noviny*, vol. 46, 11. 7. 1938, p. 6; Kožík, František: "Sokolátka se sjíždějí". In: R. Procházka (ed.): *Památník X. všesokolského sletu v Praze 1938*, p. 83.
351 R. W. Seton-Watson came up with this term to describe the aristocracy's reaction to the protesting national movement. Viz Anderson, B.: *Imagined Communities*, p. 86.

railway line in 1845[352]), while Sokol Slets were presented as part of the Czech national "counter-culture." The Slets were originally quite modest affairs that could not compete with folklore festivities. The third Sokol Slet was then held as part of the Czech-Slavic Ethnographic Exhibition of 1895. The exhibition's success provided the Sokols with a framework for their future performances and also influenced its content; Sokol gymnasts presented, among other things, exercises based on Janáček's music inspired by folk dance.[353] After the First World War, the relationship between gymnastic performances and folklore festivals was reversed and "folk" dance groups were invited to take part in Sokol or Orel Slets.[354] Elements of folk dances thus increasingly became part of gymnastic performances. At the 1938 Slet, for instance, the junior women's performance around several hundred maypoles with yellow chaplets on their heads in reference to folk song motifs was a success.[355]

The performances by folklore groups at Spartakiads are thus one of the examples, even if extreme, of a more general "folklorism" phenomenon, i.e. the politicization of folk traditions. As Josef Jančář has pointed out, as far back as the age of Romantic nationalism this politicization was aimed at unifying folk culture and blurring local and regional differences to create a national folklore and national popular culture. Folklore was thus transformed into a modern symbolic product that could be successfully employed in

352 Jančář, Josef: "Dokonalost prostého života. Lidová kultura, folklor a folklorismus". *Dějiny a současnost*, 2004, vol. 26, n. 6, p. 29.

353 Nolte, C. E.: *The Sokol in the Czech Lands to 1914*, p. 130.

354 At the 11th All-Sokol Slet of 1948, folk dances were part of the so-called Sokol harvest celebrations that replaced the traditional Slet scene. Their ethnographic part was compiled by Karel Plicka with a team of ethnographers. Karel Svolinský worked on their artistic components and Jaroslav Seifert wrote a series of verses for them. Forty ethnographic groups danced, accompanied by their own bands, not therefore to a uniform "folk" rhythm. Buddeusová, Nora: "Sletové dožínky". In: *Památník XI. sletu všesokolského v Praze 1948*, p. 161; Seifert, Jaroslav: "My chceme nový, lepší svět. Verše k sletovým dožínkám". Ibid, pp. 162–166.

355 See for instance Procházka, R. (ed.): *Památník X. všesokolského sletu v Praze 1938*, pp. 121–122.

seemingly completely unrelated and alienating environments, such as the platform of a train station during an inauguration ceremony or the geometrical space of Strahov Stadium. Communist ideologists seized upon this tradition of politicizing folk culture and further developed it. Some composers of Spartakiad pieces such as Bohumil Kos referred to the famous Soviet dancer and choreographer Igor Alexandrovich Moiseyev,[356] who described how evolution cleanses and "crystallizes" folk dance.[357] In the process of the constant appearance and disappearance of new elements, Moiseyev believed that "foreign elements" introduced in dance only briefly survive and quickly die as unnecessary, while everything that gives "national and distinctive traits" to dance is preserved and passed down from generation to generation. Like any other discipline of Soviet art, choreography has the same "folk form" and "socialist content": If folk form divides the dance of one Soviet nation from another, the content brings them back together, showing them their shared origin and destination. [...] The themes of patriotism, the friendship of nations, the heroics of work are common to all folk dances. This "socialist content" of folk dances allows the differences in "folk form" to be overcome and for a joint folklore performance to be created at the stadium that obviously did not correspond to any local dance tradition, but instead represented the "joyful creative art of the people".[358]

Yet ethnographers disliked the joint performance of folklore groups. Some Slovak experts (at considerable personal risk) opposed the participation of local dance groups in fearing the loss of the final remnants of authenticity of their folk dance forms.[359] Slovaks also

---

356 For more information see e.g. Moiseyev's obituary in the *New York Times*. Anderson, Jack: "Igor Moiseyev, 101, Choreographer, Dies". *The New York Times*, vol. 157, 3. 11. 2007.

357 Mojsejev, Igor A.: "Úvod". In: Milan Horák – Bohumil Kos – Miroslav Kremlík (eds.): *Sborové písně a tance Sovětské armády*. Naše vojsko, Prague 1952, pp. 112–114.

358 "Manifest jednoty, síly a lásky k vlasti". *Svobodné slovo*, vol. 11, 3. 7. 1955, p. 1.

359 Personal letter to author by Ivan Murín, May 10, 2006.

voiced their opposition to the representation of Slovakia through folklore. In his 1958 article, Vladimir Mináč sounded the battle cry against "the unbearably pleasant heaviness of folklore" and against "folklore rentiers" profiting from the representation of Slovaks to others (especially in Prague) as a "nation of shepherds with bare bellies" making clogs and singing songs.[360] He also rejected the Prague "shoulder patting" which he considered humiliating, even if well intentioned.

Folklore performances were last part of the mass gymnastic performances at the 1960 Spartakiad. Performing here under the title of *Song of the Homeland* were dozens of costumed ensembles presenting "images of our village life": an exaltation of Morana, the Slavic goddess of winter and death, and the welcoming of Spring, the sowing and harvest of grain and the final harvest dance.[361] In the new organic model of Czechoslovak Spartakiads during the "normalization" period, the preparations for which had already begun in the mid 1960s, a representation of the history of the people could no longer be separated from the overall narrative and be left to the folk dance ensembles. Spartakiads held during the "normalization" period employed more sophisticated instruments, particularly the gymnastic performances of women accompanied by the "national" music of Bedřich Smetana, Antonín Dvořák and Leoš Janáček to connect with the nation's past. The female body (as much as possible exposed) became more a symbol of the people's regenerative power than dusty folk costumes.

---

360 Mináč, Vladimír: "Tíha folklóru". *Literární noviny*, 1958, vol. 7, n. 12, p. 1. It is difficult to imagine that Kundera was not aware of Mináč's term "unbearable heaviness" that features prominently at the beginning of the article. Mináč was a major Slovak literary figure and his text on the first page of *Literární noviny,* the most important literary journal of the time, especially on the sensitive Czech-Slovak topic must have been widely discussed in Prague literary circles. Moreover, the topic of folk dance and music occupied Kundera for quite some time; it features heavily in his first novel *The Joke.*
361 Šotola, J. – Šiktanc, K.: *II. celostátní spartakiáda.*

Another change in the relationship between folklore and mass gymnastic performances occurred during the "normalization" period. The Spartakiad performances themselves were gradually becoming part of the folklore, i.e. regularly repeated events that neither the gymnasts nor the spectators considered to be an expression of a specific ideology. Instead, they were already taking part in the Spartakiads due to their apparent intrinsic value of a deeply embedded tradition with a distinctive national element. Like the folk dances, the mass gymnastic performances were simply something that "we" and only "we" did and still do. This trend was even more pronounced in the post-1989 Slets, which once again incorporated the performances of costumed ensembles.[362]

362 See for instance Fišerová, Eva (ed.): *XIII. všesokolský slet, Praha 2000*. Česká obec sokolská, Prague 2001, p. 137.

SOKOL MEMBERS FROM THE FACTORIES AND OFFICES

The jamboree of costumed ensembles was followed by the rest of the Adult Days program. This consisted of two performances of the "unionist gymnastics" simply entitled *Men from the Factories and Offices* and *Women from the Factories and Offices* and one joint performance of men and women of the Voluntary Sports Organization Sokol (DSO Sokol). Despite the slapdash titles and organizations stemming from recent experiments in bringing physical education under state control, this part of the 1st All-State Spartakiad actually most resembled the Sokol Slets. The similarity was so great that even the exile weekly *Čechoslovák* declared this Spartakiad to be a Sokol undertaking: "The image of the 1948 Slet and even of Slets from before the war is repeating at Strahov Stadium! We never wrote that the Spartakiad is collapsing. Those living with their nation, even in exile, are taking away one correct message from this image: Sokol is surviving in the people's blood even despite the cruelty of the seven-year foreign onslaught!"[363] Participating in the DSO Sokol's piece was even a large Sokol delegation from abroad (mainly of the Vienna Sokol), which literally embodied the harmony of the national community despite the Iron Curtain across the border.

Most reminiscent of the Slets were the performances of the trade union men, choreographed by Jaroslav Šterc. The daily *Rudé právo* printed a photograph of their performances across the entire front page in which only Jiří Kroha's socialist-realistic pylons over the Gate of Athletes tell us that this is not a photograph from the Sokol Slet.[364] Šterc's calisthenics completely copied a Sokol performance at the final Slet, and the costume of black exercise pants and white

---

363 Quoted from Zídek, Petr: "Soudružky a soudruzi, tužme se". *Lidové noviny*, příloha Orientace, vol. 18, 25. 6. 2005, pp. I–II.

364 *Rudé právo*, vol. 35, 3. 7. 1955.

t-shirts also contributed to the visual similarity. This likeness was certainly important for the activation of the severely disoriented Sokols, but represented a problem for communist propaganda. It was still too early in 1955 to openly and wholeheartedly acknowledge and exploit it. Moreover, the working class needed to be somehow embodied in the mechanical model of the Spartakiads. Therefore, some new elements were incorporated into the beginning and end of the performance to signalize that what had been witnessed at Strahov in 1955 was fundamentally different from the Sokol Slets.

19. A performance by 16,200 Revolutionary Trade Union men for the 1955 Spartakiad at Strahov Stadium (photo Václav Chochola).

Flag-bearers holding red banners of the Revolutionary Trade Union Movement were positioned at the start before the entrance of 16,000 men. At the performance's conclusion the men created some fifteen hundred arrow-like formations by joining two lines of four men with their hands on each other's shoulders (see fig. 15 and 26b). Another gymnast then stood at the forefront with an extended right arm holding a small red flag. Writer and dissident Ludvík Vaculík, who, along with the journalist Jiří Lederer, had been one of the "trade union men" in this formation at Strahov Stadium, nostalgically recalled this moment ("I strongly felt how much I needed to have my strong personality and my will smothered by the common will.")[365] Although such "formalism" did not correspond to Sokol's new gymnastic practices, it strongly evoked Tyrš's aesthetic principles and those of the early Slets that indulged in such tense poses, the held positions that expressed aspirations to higher ideals.

While the performance itself differed only minimally from those of the Sokol Slets, the radio commentary at the stadium and later observations in the press made radically different claims. This thoroughly Sokol performance was interpreted as an expression of the working class's commitment to stand up to the "tyranny of capitalists." It was to express "the long and arduous path that the working class had to take to achieve these objectives."[366] *Rudé právo* offered its interpretation of the massive entry in fifty-four columns of three which had already been used at previous Slets: "How much force is in the working people, in their solid unity. Nobody could ever stop these armies rolling forth; they would be crushed just like those who had dared to oppose the united people in February 1948."[367]

---

365 Vaculík, Ludvík: "Paže tuž, vlasti služ!". *Lidové noviny*, vol. 19, 11. 7. 2006, p. 12. See also Vaculíks article on the 1965 Spartakiad: Vaculík, Ludvík: "Hudbou, tancem a písní…". *Rudé právo*, vol. 45, 1. 7. 1965, p. 3.
366 "Síla jednotného lidu". *Rudé právo*, vol. 35, 3. 7. 1955, p. 1.
367 Ibid.

20. A performance by the Revolutionary Trade Union women for the 1955 Spartakiad at Strahov Stadium (photo Václav Chochola).

Similarly, the performance of the *Women from the Factories and Offices*, composed by former Sokol official and Slet choreographer Stáza Levá, completely resembled women Sokol performances from the previous two Slets. It differed only in its bolder, "sportier" costumes[368] and a newly conceived "grand entry" that, in the words

---

368 At the Slet in 1948, women performed in skirts low enough to cover their knees. The shorts in which they performed in 1955 were only used at the final Slet in athletic competitions.

21. A performance by the Revolutionary Trade Union women for the 1955 Spartakiad at Strahov Stadium (photo Václav Chochola).

of Sergej Machonin, revitalized the field "with the gentle rhythm of marching in place."[369] Yet there was a need to reinterpret for the new political reality the traditional Sokol exercise with a single indian club on the motifs of national songs. Their performance was intended to show how "thanks to the Red Army's liberation, women are entering equally alongside men into a joyous life in the people's democracy."[370] In addition to women's emancipation, *Rudé právo*

369 Machonin, Sergej: "Čas růží". *Rudé právo*, vol. 35, 4. 7. 1955, p. 3.
370 AČOS, f. I. celostátní spartakiáda 1955 – Základní dokumenty, Ideový program, plán příprav a návrh rozpočtu I. celostátní spartakiády v roce 1955, p. 2.

also saw in the piece an expression of women's share in building socialism: "After all, you won't find a place anywhere in our vast socialist workshop where a woman's hand is not helping; you won't find a corner not warmed by the presence of a woman, by her determination to take a stand anywhere a man is fighting for a better life."[371]

The biggest clash between Sokol practices and the socialist interpretation appeared in the "performances of representatives of our new vilage,"[372] meaning in the joint performance of the men and women of DSO Sokol. This was also a piece choreographed by former Sokol women officials and largely made up of traditional Sokol calisthenics. Yet the piece was intended to depict the "new vilage" life, and was thus intended to obscure the Sokol practices. The joint performance of men and women was in itself innovative, since a strict division of gender had always been typical of Sokol Slets. Although men and women now performed together, the gender difference was not obscured for most of the performance, but instead served as a compositional element (e.g., men kneeled, women stood or vice-versa). For the most part, however, the choreography and the performance itself drew from the Sokol repertoire and the "socialist content" needed to be incorporated from external elements. Forced interpretations of Sokol calisthenics did not come across as overly convincing. *Rudé právo*, for instance, first compared the women in the performance to grain and the men to combines "harvesting" these women: "In their rhythmic movements, the women express the continuous growth and the waves of endless fields of grain, while the men, in columns of eight, depict the successful work of reapers, harvesting the rich crop."[373]

---

371   "Květiny bílé po cestě…". *Rudé právo*, vol. 35, 3. 7. 1955, p. 2.
372   [Caption for the photo of the performance]. *Rudé právo*, vol. 35, 3. 7. 1955, p. 2.
373   "Nejmohutnější přehlídka úspěchů naší tělovýchovy". *Rudé právo,* vol. 35, 4. 7. 1955, p. 3.
Only at the very end of the performance did the piece employ an explicit narrative style typical for the 1950s and which we would hardly see in the last Slets. At the end of the piece, small groups of eight participants (men and women separately) joined hands over their heads, thus created "two thousand mandels" to symbolize the harvesting of grain. The joy from the harvest was then

Sokol associations were also apparently meant to tamper down the verses that accompanied the performances at the stadium. The author of these short poems, El Car (real name: Karel Jiráček), was a correspondent for the communist press between the wars and the founder of an amateur group performing choral recitation combined with rhythmic movements – the Red Commando Brigade. As Jiráček recalled in the early years of "normalization," his relationship to Sokol had been strained since he was a young child in the Libeň quarter of Prague:

"Our political convictions were expressed through skirmishes with the boys who attended Sokol and called us "social-dem turkeys," which we couldn't let pass unpunished."[374] The Sokol exercises were thus accompanied by chants from a completely different cultural code: "The air smells of bread and happiness / like a breeze from the fields and meadows brings to the face / the sound of the combines is music to the ear. / Joyful harvests, the time has come, / when the youth rises from the barn while singing / until the last stacks the heavy cob."[375]

The experiment in combining the Sokol tradition of mass gymnastics and amateur proletarian poetry, whose charm lay in provoking bourgeois society, did not work and El Car did not accompany any other Spartakiad pieces with his poetry.

---

expressed by dancing in pairs in a total of two hundred and fifty circles, at the end of which "the men lift their dancing partners up high like in furiant dance." (Ibid.) According to the ideological program presented to the Political Secretariat of the Central Committee of the Czechoslovak Communist Party, this was to be "an expression of joy over the rich harvest expressed by the dance, and a tribute to the supreme bailiff – the president of the republic." AČOS, f. I. celostátní spartakiáda 1955 – Základní dokumenty, Ideový program, plán příprav a návrh rozpočtu I. celostátní spartakiády v roce 1955 .

374 Jiráček, Karel: *El Car vzpomíná. Z historie dělnického Agitpropu.* Orbis, Prague 1971, p. 11.
375 Quoted from Mucha, V. (ed.): *První celostátní spartakiáda 1955*, p. 159.

PERFORMANCES OF THE ARMED FORCES

If the adult performances at the 1st All-State Spartakiad strongly resembled the Sokol performances at the final two Slets, then the daylong gymnastic performance of the paramilitary organization Svazarm departed from that tradition entirely. The obstinate attempt to surpass at all cost the Sokol Slets in the number of pieces and participants was most apparent in this part of the Spartakiad. The individual Svazarm sections and their "non-human" attributes paraded through the stadium designed to celebrate the strength and beauty of the human body. Over 650 "Svazarm motorists" performed stunts on motorcycles and tractors (the commentary in the press of that period did not explain the participation of tractor drivers in the performance). Aviation model builders wanted to show off their models, but even before they could get from the assembly area to the parade, fierce wind and rain smashed their models.[376] The Svazarm pigeon fanciers followed them with a bit more success, releasing fifteen thousand pigeons with messages of greetings to various locations around the country and beyond the borders. Svazarm cynologists presented "the importance of training dogs to guard state property and to defend the state borders of our state [sic!] from the enemy."[377]

Parachutists then demonstrated their basic skills – "landings, falls, rolls and jumps" – and created with their bodies at the end the image of a red star suspended by the seven strings from a white parachute.[378] Ten parachutists even landed on the stadium field. A group of thirty airplanes formed the word "MÍR" (PEACE) above the stadium, turned around beyond the stadium and rearranged themselves into the letters "I. CS" (abbreviation for the 1st All-State Spartakiad).[379] This, like other Svazarm performances completely denied

---

376 Ibid, p. 192.
377 *Program I. celostátní spartakiády 1955.*
378 "Připraveni k budování a obraně vlasti". *Rudé právo*, vol. 35, 5. 7. 1955, p. 2.
379 Ibid.

the aesthetics of the Sokol Slets based on an implicit symbolism of the human body and its movements. Yet a place was found for them in the mechanical model of Spartakiads since the event ultimately demonstrated the richness and diversity of the people.

The final day of the 1st All-State Spartakiad belonged to the army corps. Though military performances had been part of the Sokol Slets since 1920, it played here a much more prominent and independent role (though Sokol choreographers had a hand in the military's Spartakiad performances). The first piece consisted of a performance by DSO Red Star and the troops of the Ministry of the Interior that was choreographed by Jaroslav Šterc. The participants were accompanied by brassy music and dramatic verse: "A hero with his clean shield goes before us / the Soviet security force; / we want to beat the enemy like Felix Dzerzhinsky / and his Cheka will remain our model! [...] And if someday the murderer's hand wants to disturb our children's peaceful sleep / New Prague will be like Tábor of old / we will fight in the spirit of Gottwald."[380] The explicit symbolism of the 1950s is best captured by the piece's conclusion in which the participants formed fifteen concentric circles in the national colors. They were surrounded by two lines of border guards with guns (the first line lying, the second kneeling) forming an enormous five-pointed star across the 200-meter breadth of Strahov Stadium. The very center of the circle was then entered by a platoon of carriers in white exercise outfits, who lifted the male and female participants on a metal structure. A red banner bearing a portrait of "comrade Stalin" fluttered in their hands. The five thousand participants then sang: "A statue of Stalin will stand for hundreds of years over Hussite Prague."[381]

380   Archiv tělesné výchovy a sportu Národního muzea (dále ATVS NM), f. Spartakiády (1953–1990), k. 2, Scénář mluveného slova rozhlasem při Dnu ozbrojených sil I. celostátní spartakiády dne 5. července 1955 v Praze na Strahově, p. 2.
381   Ibid, p. 1.

Though the ideological content of this message was absolutely clear even without the verbal accompaniment, its effect on the viewer is questionable. The layering of the distinct symbols, like the use of the human body as mere visual material, did not allow the spectators to form their own interpretations and prevented their active involvement. The piece also suffered from some technical shortcomings. Stalin's portrait, for instance, was inadvertently concealed: owing to the stadium's massive dimensions the people in the stands could hardly see the red banner, let alone what was portrayed on it. The fact that the border guards aimed their weapons at the stands also probably did not produce the desired associations. Lastly, the overall effect was not enhanced by the color of some soldiers' exercise outfits, which though intended to represent the red on the national flag, was instead pinkish.

The military began its performance by portraying the historical narrative of the Nazi occupation and Soviet liberation entitled Liberation into a New Life. The central motif of all legitimization efforts, i.e. gratitude to the Soviet Union and to "its wonderful people" was fully played out here.[382] The soldiers formed with their bodies a map of Czechoslovakia that stretched the entire length of the stadium with two formations on it indicating the "focal points of the Czechoslovak resistance": Banská Bystrica and Prague.[383] Dramatic music and the kneeling of the participants symbolized the "oppression of Hitler's occupation."[384] Then the red curtain at the Gate of Athletes parted and two Soviet tanks bearing Soviet soldiers and Czechoslovak

382 Mucha, V.: *První celostátní spartakiáda 1955: věcí všeho pracujícího lidu Československa*, p. 20.
383 Ibid, p. 2. The closing scene of the Military Day at the 11th All-Sokol Slet in 1948 had a very similar script. Miloslav Disman describes how there appeared at Strahov "the image of a republic whose borders were created by our military, police and border guards and whose red, blue and white surface was formed by the ranks of Sokols in the Garibaldi like red shirts, the women's white exercise outfits and the blue eyes and outfits of our junior women." Disman, Miloslav: "Duha z Prahy do Košic". In: *Památník XI. sletu všesokolského v Praze 1948*, p. 160.
384 "Vzpomínka na léta vzdálená i blízká…". *Rudé právo*, vol. 35, 6. 7. 1955, p. 1.

and Soviet flags drove out onto the Strahov Stadium field. Both formations of soldiers representing the uprising then came together and created a five-pointed star in the middle of the Czechoslovak map and then walked to greet the arriving tanks and their crews. After embracing one another and brief joint maneuvers, the soldiers and tanks left the stadium together.[385]

The Strahov performances were to show "a new type of military,"[386] i.e. a military that is both fully prepared to defend its country, but also a "peaceful military" not separated from the people, a military that knows how to rejoice ("life in the people's democratic military is joyous"[387]). We frequently encounter such paradoxical connections within the context of Spartakiads and they refer to deeper contradictions within the semiotic "world of socialism," which weakens the appeal of its rituals, particularly when compared to fascist celebrations (Susan Sontag wrote that "certainly Nazism is 'sexier' than communism"[388]). Spartakiads could not merely show the strength of the working class, they had to express the participation of farmers and, of course, the working intelligentsia in the same breath. Likewise, they had to refrain from glorifying the uniqueness of their own country and instead create a symbolic space for other communist countries, and, above all, express Czechoslovakia's complex oneness/separateness. With historical references to the Hussites, it roused itself to stand up to the eternal enemy in the West, but also could not forget about the friendship with the people's democracy of East Germany even with the proletariat of capitalist countries. It celebrated folk simplicity, but also emphasized the high cultural level and sophistication of the national community.

385 ATVS NM, f. Spartakiády (1953–1990), k. 2, Scénář mluveného slova rozhlasem při Dnu ozbrojených sil I. celostátní spartakiády dne 5. července 1955 v Praze na Strahově, p. 3. See also "Vzpomínka na léta vzdálená i blízká…". *Rudé právo*, vol. 35, 6. 7. 1955, p. 1.

386 AČOS, f. I. celostátní spartakiáda 1955 – Základní dokumenty, Ideový program, plán příprav a návrh rozpočtu I. celostátní spartakiády v roce 1955, p. 4.

387 "Skvělá ukázka připravenosti naší lidové armády". *Rudé právo*, vol. 35, 6. 7. 1955, p. 2.

388 Sontag, S.: *Under the Sign of Saturn*, p. 102.

Stalin was obviously exceptional, but he too also had to be presented as a regular person connected to the people.[389] These contradictions, which I have by no means exhausted, made it impossible to create an aesthetically impressive ritual as the Nazi Nuremberg Rallies had been. In its performance the military could not only demonstrate its own strength (which is the most popular and easiest theme of mass spectacles), but also had to show its "human face." This could also account for why women also took part in most of armed forces performances in the 1st All-State Spartakiad. Part of each military performance was devoted to dance. For instance, in the military piece entitled *Physical Preparation – An Integral Part of The Combat and Political Preparation* consisted of troops in uniforms, with helmets and rifles ("the rifle barrels shining with a dark gloss") – elements of combat preparation, namely hand-to-hand combat, were presented.[390] In the end, however, they laid down their weapons in stacks, put their arms around each others waists and danced Slovak dances for men.[391] Game-like elements were incorporated into other pieces and commands such as " Ready for the competitive game of carrying a comrade!"[392] resounded all over the stadium. An Otto Ježek poem also captured the contrast between the soldiers in combat and in peace: "Windswept men, / brawny and rigid / listen to supple music, / how it bends and straightens them, / perhaps they themselves are a beautiful song, / perhaps they will begin to dance together."[393]

The *Soldiers Exercising with Children* demonstration, in which nearly 1,000 soldiers and 4,500 boys and girls aged 10–14, went even

---

389 See Macura, V.: *Šťastný věk*, pp. 101–120. Yet Macura constructed here a dialectic unity of these two positions.
390 "Skvělá ukázka připravenosti naší lidové armády". *Rudé právo*, vol. 35, 6. 7. 1955 p. 2.
391 *Program I. celostátní spartakiády 1955*.
392 ATVS NM, f. Spartakiády (1953–1990), k. 2, Scénář mluveného slova rozhlasem při Dnu ozbrojených sil I. celostátní spartakiády dne 5. července 1955 v Praze na Strahově, p. 4.
393 Ježek, Otto: "Jsme připraveni". *Obrana lidu*, vol. 9, 5. 7. 1955, p. 1. The poem has other remarkable verses as well!: "[…] bronze-tanned / They're already here! They're already here! […] / Go ahead, spectator, find the words / for how they formed lines! or "Comrade, you're not so hardened / your heart is ringing right now / Admit that you're moved."

further in representing a "new type of military". *Rudé právo* described the performance:

> The marching troops stopped in the middle of the field for a short rest. An officer commands that they take leave, the soldier's "hurrah!" resounds through the stadium, and suddenly children from all sides of the stadium run to the soldiers. They call, waving to the soldiers, romping around with them and literally hanging on them, creating the impression throughout the stadium of loud, vibrant grapes. The stadium erupts. Suddenly all these smaller groups open into circles studding the field. [...] The soldiers form from the circles a snake that twists around the entire field.
> The children imitate a clumsy bear, a jumping frog, a spry horse [...] girls dance, weave and turn around their soldiers. The people in the stands applaud the entire time.

The absurdity of this performance led the Spartakiad organizers themselves to harshly condemn it much later. In a 1987 three-part documentary on the history of the Spartakiads, footage of the soldiers performing with children is accompanied by commentary:

"Some of the pieces were marred by inappropriate aesthetics of the 1950s. The inappropriate basic concept and strained adaptation of folklore led to a formalism of forced merriment that was accentuated by the hollow pathos of accompanying poetic verses."[394] Even while it was being prepared, this performance met with resistance, especially from the parents of the adolescent girls who were supposed to perform with "their soldiers."[395]

---

394 Krejčík, Rudolf: *Symfonie psané pohybem. Tradice hromadných tělovýchovných vystoupení. Část II: Strahovská vystoupení 1947–1965*. Krátký film, Prague 1987.
395 NA, f. SVTVS, k. 68, inv. n. 201, Zprávy o stavu příprav I. celostátní spartakiády a její hodnocení.

✕✕✕

The aesthetics and symbolism of the first and second Spartakiads reflected the ambitions of the early communist regime to radically change society and the individuals themselves. They also reflected the vacuum of legitimization that appeared with the departure of the "cult of personality." This was to be filled through a traditional Sokol portrayal of the national community. It is this dependence, both ideological and practical, on the Sokol tradition that gives the first two Spartakiads a unique hybrid form. Nevertheless, the inconsistency of the Spartakiad narrative is partially concealed by the overall style of these Spartakiads, i.e. the mosaic-like depiction of the whole using isolated "stones." This mechanical understanding of the Spartakiad narrative is reflected in a distinct interpretation of the human body that served as a mere bearer of other symbols. The next chapter will examine how radically the Spartakiad style changed in the second half of the 1960s and ultimately resulted in the complete rejection of the mechanical model of society during the "normalization" Spartakiads. In its place, the organism and family became the central metaphor for later Spartakiads.

Spartakiad Symbolism During the "Normalization" Era

SPARTAKIADS WITH A HUMAN FACE

The first truly post-Stalinist Spartakiad, the 1965 Spartakiad, reflected the political and social thawing of the mid 1960s, as well as that period's trends in culture and fashion. In many ways this Spartakiad, which bore the motto "In the name of health, power and beauty, for a happy, peaceful life, for the victory of communism!", heralded the radical changes in symbolism in gymnastic practices of later Spartakiads held during the "normalization" period. The preparations for the 1965 Spartakiad saw several important changes in the ranks of key organizers. The Spartakiad organization staff was headed by one of the few former Slovak Sokol officials, gymnastics trainer Julius Chvalný. He was joined by the younger generation of Sokol officials, namely Jiří Žižka and Eva Bémová. The new leadership was responsible for the preparations of the 1965 and later Spartakiads. The 1965 Spartakiad was characterized by a completely new stage direction. Unlike previous Spartakiads, particularly the 1st All-State Spartakiad, which lasted for several weeks with dozens of performances and was separated into school children, juniors, adults and military days,

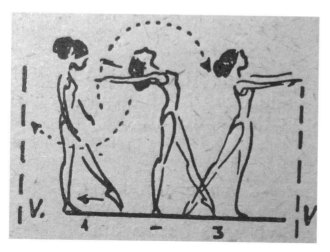

22. An illustration from an instruction manual of the women's performances for the cancelled 1970 Spartakiad.

the 1965 Spartakiad was to have a single four-day cycle consisting of two afternoons of events: *A Song of Peace* and *Victory Is Ours*, which twice repeated (*A Song of Peace* on July 1st and 3rd, *Victory Is Ours* on July 2nd and 4th). The number of participants on Strahov field was also dramatically reduced compared to the 1960 Spartakiad (from 722,000 to 356,000), as was the number of performances (from 19 to 12). The shortened Spartakiad program provided the Spartakiad staff's program commission, which had reviewed the coordination of the choreographed performances and musical accompaniment, the space to create an integrally compact artistic whole, even though this was not fully achieved until later Spartakiads held during the "normalization" period. Another change that required a drastic reduction in the number of participants, especially in district Spartakiads, was the shift away from the forceful way of recruiting participants. Regional Spartakiads were dropped and a greater emphasis was placed on district and county Spartakiads. It was in these district Spartakiads that for the first time that exercises of parents with preschool children became part of the program under the leadership of Jana Berdychová.

The changed atmosphere is also attested to by the organization of the state-wide Spartakiad for the deaf, blind and physically disabled athletes that for the first and last time took place concurrently with the Spartakiad at Strahov Stadium. Although the synchronized exercise to musical accompaniment probably was not the best sports activity for disabled athletes, their participation at the socially prestigious Spartakiad, where the symbolic body of the nation was formed, had considerable emancipatory significance. In an international context, this was a very early expression of respect for disabled athletes since it was not until 1988 that the Paralympics first took place in the same city as the Olympic Games.[396] One of the most remarkable

---

[396] It was also an unusual phenomenon within the context of Eastern European sports. The response of a certain Soviet sports official to a Western reporter's question of whether

pieces of the 1965 Spartakiad was the military's performance of *Victory Is Ours* in which several dozen wheeled armored transporters entered the Strahov Stadium field as the performing military personnel jumped off of them one by one.[397] A weaker aspect of this powerful entrance, as the choreographer of the performance Ivo Fibiger later admitted in an interview, was that the stadium's architecture prevented the vehicles' exhaust emission from dispersing; instead it lingered among the participants and only slowly rose among the spectators in the stands.[398] This piece directly embodied the tension between the two ways of understanding the human body: the body as a mechanical machine as opposed to the body as a living organism. Leaps from human pyramids were witnessed here for the first time in this military composition. Another remarkable piece was the co-ed performance of junior apprentices entitled *We Are Transforming the World with Our Work* in which thirteen thousand participants danced in a cha-cha rhythm on the "largest dance floor in the world."[399] Modern concepts of gymnastics and choreography were then evident in the performance of the advanced female gymnasts with banners entitled *Moving toward Beauty*. Among the interesting children performances was that of the eight to eleven-year-old boys with boxes that they used to show the development of panel-housing construction.

Soviet athletes will take part in the 1980 Paralympic Games is well known: "There are no invalids in the Soviet Union!" See for instance Phillips, Sarah D.: "'There Are No Invalids in the USSR!' A Missing Soviet Chapter in the New Disability History". *Disabilities Studies Quarterly*, 2009, vol. 29, n. 3, p. 1. For more on the representation of physical otherness and disability see Kolářová, Kateřina (ed.): *Jinakost – postižení – kritika. Společenské konstrukty nezpůsobilosti a hendikepu.* SLON, Prague 2012.

397 The cost of using armored transport came to 4,876,728 crowns. See Vojenský historický archiv (VHA), f. MNO – 1965, k. 153, inv. n. 446, Zpráva o prověrce finančně ekonomické činnosti štábu a podřízených útvarů vytvořených pro zabezpečení III. celostátní spartakiády.

398 Interview with Ivo Fibiger, 20. ledna 2006, Prague. Author's archive. See also for instance Vorel, Miroslav: "Hygienicko-technický průzkum III. CS". *Teorie a praxe tělesné výchovy*, 1966, vol. 14, n. 8, p. 485.

399 Krejčík, Rudolf: *Symfonie psané pohybem. Tradice hromadných tělovýchovných vystoupení. Část II: Strahovská vystoupení 1947–1965.* Krátký film, Prague 1987.

The change in concept of the 1965 Spartakiad was also reflected in the commemorative publication, traditionally published right after the Slets or Spartakiads had ended. Respected writers Arnošt Lustig and Ota Pavel penned the book's introduction, which, instead of leading the reader into a commemorative book, resembles more a philosophical essay on the nature of human memory.[400] The writers completely avoided references to the political framework of the Spartakiad, and there is no mention here of the Soviet Union, the Communist Party, or even socialism for that matter. There are also no references to Sokol. Instead, a historical link is constructed between the Spartakiads and the ancient cult of the healthy body and to the proletarian gymnastics of the First Republic. The Spartakiads cultivated in both writers a pride for "the human content of the concept of a person" and to an affection for the expression of "strength and health of the people of one country." The Spartakiad's "beauty of healthy human bodies, of boys from factories, of girls with white skipping ropes" is contrasted in the text with the image of the "horrible beauty" of Dresden burning. In its levity and playfulness, the photographic section of the book completely eludes the genre of Slet or Spartakiad publications. Apart from a few traditional shots of the geometrical patterns of the exercises at Strahov Stadium (though even here a Jiří Jírů photograph showing an endless sea of the soldiers' bent backs is completely at odds with the previous presentation of Spartakiad performances), the photographs encourage the reader to view the Spartakiad as a true social event. They show the confusion of the large disordered crowd, the spontaneous use of idle time such as flirting, or the sunbathing of junior women in the stands. The journalistic (as opposed to propagandistic) feel of the book is further supported by e.g., a series of Karel Novák's photographs in which a pair of attractive female greengrocers overturn a wheelbarrow with oranges and apples, or

---

400 Lustig, A. – Pavel, O.: "Úvod, k němuž jsme nechtěli hledat název".

23. A performance by older female pupils entitled "My Country Is a Blossoming Meadow" at Strahov Stadium during the 1965 Spartakiad (National Museum).

by the humorous celebration of otherness in a photograph by Adolf Vrhel, which shows the single blond head of a girl among a hundred marching girls with black hair.

Although in some aspects the 1965 Spartakiad heralded the later Spartakiads of the "normalization" period, it distinctly differed from them in two directions. One of these was that the 1965 Spartakiad was characterized by an experimental and even playful search for new methods and genres that would create a more welcoming, less rigid and disciplinary face. The "normalization" Spartakiads were instead distinguished by the use of tried-and-true methods and a fear of innovation and changes. The second difference was that the 1965 Spartakiad was, at least judging by the extent of press coverage, probably the least important Spartakiad in the eyes of its

Communist Party patrons. The party's main concern was that the Spartakiad not become too expensive. During the preparations, the party leadership slashed the event's budget and reduced the number of performances to twelve. The concept itself of mass gymnastic exercises was openly criticized. The Ministry of Education had drafted shortly before the 1965 Spartakiad a thorough critique of the previous Spartakiad training, which in its view led to a "gross violation of systematic physical education work and the disruption of a school's smooth operation." The Ministry also pointed out that "mass gymnastic performances are in direct conflict with the development of young people's interest in physical education and sports" and that this conflict between the requirement for joint exercises and the students' interest in competitive sports increases with the participants' age, which apparently leads to a "general aversion toward physical fitness activities." Also criticized were the forceful methods of recruiting participants ("the strict requirement of mass participation") resulting in "a serious disruption in the development of character," since the students would "feign interest without inner conviction." In the next Spartakiad, warned the Ministry, "voluntary participation cannot be made obligatory" in this way.[401]

The cancelled 1970 Spartakiad represented another step on the path from the socialist-realist tinged first two Spartakiads to the "normalization" Spartakiads based on a return to traditional Sokol family and patriotic values. Even more than the previous Spartakiad, the integration of the individual performances into two coherent

---

[401] AČOS, f. IV. celostátní spartakiáda 1970 – Základní dokumenty IV. CS 1970, Náměty pro IV. CS, Náměty na koncepci dalších celostátních tělovýchovných slavností (3. 4. 1965). Criticism of the planned event was even stronger before the prepared 1970 Spartakiad. According to the minutes of a Spartakiad staff meeting concerning the proposals for the performance pieces, Vojtěch Trapl appealed to the military representatives present; "Dr. Trapl: Asks for help in one thing. There is a large discussion over the Spartakiad. Voices for the Spartakiad are undemocratically being suppressed. He asks officials for help." See AČOS, f. Výběr skladeb 1960–1975, Záznam diskuse k předvedení ukázky skladby armády (28. 4. 1968?). See also Kössl, J. – Krátký, F. – Marek, J.: *Dějiny tělesné výchovy II.*, pp. 240–241.

program parts was sought in its preparation. The first of these, entitled *Spring*, in which the pieces of pupils and juniors were presented, was to express through modern music and rhythm "the upcoming joyful life of the young generation."[402] The second part, *A Song of Hope*, was to develop the theme of the cooperation among generations and the friendship of Czechs and Slovaks. Taking into account the "country's new federalist arrangement" the organizers replaced "all-state" in the event's title (a reference to the Soviet model) with "Czechoslovak" (the ordinal number also disappeared from the title of the "normalization" Spartakiads so as not to evoke the cancelled 1970 Spartakiad).[403] The decoration of Strahov Stadium was also to be more austerely conceived than previously. In charge of the decorative concept, architect Josef Hrubý (one of the designers of the succesfull Czechoslovak Pavilion at the 1958 Expo in Brussels) wrote, "In coming up with the decorative plan, the designers chose elements that would have more of a subconscious effect instead of trying to create forced allusions in form and content."[404] This shift is most apparent from a gender perspective, in which the Sokol concept of "segregation as emancipation" was dusted off on an organizational and content level. In documents concerning the preparation of the Spartakiad, the autonomy of "female organisers" was emphasized in the creation and training of Spartakiad performances for women, and this autonomy was to continue to be a principle in the organization of sport-for-all in the period between the Spartakiads.[405] This shift in content is documented e.g. by a description of a Spartakiad piece for women written by Eva Bémová and Hana

402 Král, Antonín: "IV. ČSS – Světová gymnastická slavnost". *Teorie a praxe tělesné výchovy*, 1969, vol. 17, n. 9, p. 514.

403 NA, f. KSČ – Ústřední výbor 1945–1989, Praha – předsednictvo 1966–1971, svazek 99, a.j. 164/4, Zpráva ÚV ČSTV Stav příprav IV. československé spartakiády.

404 AČOS, f. IV. celostátní spartakiáda 1970, Libreto pro výzdobu strahovského areálu k IV. československé spartakiádě (první polovina srpna 1969).

405 See for instance "Z diskuzních příspěvků na plénu". *Československý sport*, vol. 17, 23. 5. 1969, p. 2.

Stárková, which was intended as an "expression of a woman of physical and spiritual beauty [...], a declaration of woman-mother, of the bearer of new lives, of new branches on the nation's tree." The magazine *Tělovýchovný pracovník* (Gymnastic Worker), designed for former Sokol trainers, even published in 1968 an article written by the physician Alena Martinovská entitled "The Second Sex in Gymnastics," which hardly could have been published during the previous period – a fact that the author herself emphasized in the text.[406] Martinovská first welcomed that the era had ended in which the policy of employing women in jobs (often health-hazardous) for men was reflected in physical education. She then explained in detail why women are not and cannot be equal to men in sports. She defined the female body almost exclusively in terms of its deficiencies in comparison with the male counterpart, which it surpasses in a single indicator – the relative amount of body fat. The best athletic activities for women are, in her view, those that "help develop a natural sense for rhythm and contribute to physical grace and expressions of femininity." This is one example of the conservative backlash that we encounter in many other spheres of the cultural and political discourse that took place during the Prague Spring.[407]

Spartakiads did not become a central topic of the Prague Spring, which occurred during a period of little Spartakiad activity. The conceptual work for the fourth Spartakiad was essentially ready and there was still plenty of time before the training itself, planned for September 1969, started. In the spring of 1968, Czechoslovak gymnastics was dealing with the much more pressing issue of renewing the Czechoslovak Sokol Community, which soon turned into

406 Martinovská, Alena: "Druhé pohlaví v tělocvičně". *Tělovýchovný pracovník*, 1968, vol. 14, n. 12, pp. 164–165.
407 See in particular the chapters of Barbora Havelková, Hana Havelková and Jan Matonoha in Havelková, Hana – Oates-Indruchová, Libora: *The Politics of Gender Culture under State Socialism. An Expropriated Voice*. Routledge, New York 2014. Yet Martinovská's view to a certain extent counters the principle of "segregation as emancipation" advocated by female Sokol activists since it introduces a hierarchical relationship into the distinction between men and women.

a public dispute over which of the former Sokol members had the right to act on behalf of Sokol. One side consisted of the preparations committee of the Czechoslovak Sokol Community associating former persecuted or deposed Sokol officials such as one-time deputy Sokol President Blažena Martínková or gymnastic director Miroslav Kavalír (even Sokol's first ever female gymnastic director Milada Malá was involved here), who demanded the restoration of Sokol's organizational autonomy, the rehabilitation of individual members and the return of Sokol property.[408] A number of public intellectuals who were not part of the Sokol community came to their support. For instance, in March 1968, Milan Machovec called for persecuted Sokol members to join, without recrimination, in the fight against "the poison of Stalinist centralism" and the "overly organized" gymnastics apparatus.[409] Machovec also highlighted the contrast between the Spartakiads, which people attended "to gain credit" or to make it easier for them to go abroad, and Slets, which expressed the free decision of Sokol members and were a "display of the nation's moral strength."

Spartakiad organizers, mostly coming from Sport-for-All Association (*Svaz základní tělesné výchovy*) of the official Czechoslovak Physical Education Association (*Československý svaz tělesné výchovy a sportu*), were unwilling to cede the Sokol legacy to the preparations committee of the Czechoslovak Sokol Community. It was decided at the extraordinary congress in June 1968 to rename the Sport-for-All Association as the Sokol Gymnastics Association, to introduce the Dr. Miroslav Tyrš Medal as a coveted gymnastic award and, on the occasion of the next Spartakiad, to rename Strahov Stadium as Dr. Miroslav Tyrš Stadium.[410] In an emotional statement they point-

---

408 K pokusu o obnovu Sokola v roce 1968 see Waldauf, J.: *Sokol. Malé dějiny velké myšlenky*, Vol. 2, pp. 463–485.

409 Machovec, Milan: "Patří ‚Sokol' jen minulosti?". *Svobodné slovo*, vol. 24, 28. 3. 1968, p. 3.

410 Prokešová, Hana: "Jsme pro název Sokol". *Základní tělesná výchova*, 1968, vol. 13, n. 7, pp. 1–2. See also "Tyršův odkaz náhle na roztrhání". *Mladá fronta*, vol. 24, 20. 6. 1968, p. 6.

ed out that they represented tens of thousands of members and thousands of trainers of the former Sokol, who "did not fold their hands in their lap and did not stand aside, but actively accompanied the country's people through the good and bad."[411] Yet after the Soviet intervention in August 1968, an agreement was reached between the two Sokol camps on the formation of a joint Sokol movement as part of the Czechoslovak Physical Education Association, which at the beginning of "normalization" was immediately called a "grave political mistake."[412] Apparently, as part of this compromise, Jiří Žižka proposed in January 1969 in a ten-page plan for "Sokol Physical Education" that the term "Slet" once again be used in place of "Spartakiad" (though he also recommended that the Spartakiad five-year cycle be maintained instead of the Sokol tradition of a Slet every six years).[413]

The new party leadership had long wavered over canceling the 1970 Spartakiad.[414] In early October 1969, the Central Committee of the Czechoslovak Physical Education Association had called for party officials to finally decide whether the Spartakiad would take

411 AČOS, f. IV. celostátní spartakiáda 1970 – Zápisy ze schůzí ÚŠ IV. CS, Prohlášení Všem členům odborů ZTV ČSTV! (undated – June 1968).

412 Marek, Jaroslav – Málinka, Ján: *Zpráva o činnosti Československého svazu tělesné výchovy za období 1967–1972*. Olympia, Prague 1973, p. 94.

413 AČOS, f. IV. celostátní spartakiáda 1970 – Zápisy ze schůzí ÚŠ IV. CS, Poslání, hlavní úkoly a obsah sokolské tělesné výchovy.

414 On 10 July 1969, the presidium of the Central Committee of the Czechoslovak Communist Party expressed "the full support of the party" for the Spartakiad, but also requested the views of others party and state bodies for a definitive decision. The Bureau of the Central Committee of the Czechoslovak Communist Party for The Management of Party Work in the Czech Lands recommended in mid October 1969 that the Spartakiad be postponed until 1971, especially with regard to the position of Prague's communist officials, "according to whom the consolidation of public order in Prague is at such a point that there is the risk that the mass performances could be misused." The year 1971, when the fiftieth year of the first Spartakiad, the founding of the Czechoslovak Communist Party and the Federation of Worker Gymnastic Clubs were commemorated, also apparently enabled the laying of a foundation for an ideological concept completely different from that of the All-Sokol Slets, which up until now have been interwoven with contemporary Spartakiads." See NA, f. KSČ – Byro ÚV KSČ pro řízení stranické práce v českých zemích, Praha, sv. 54, a. j. 92, Zpráva o stavu příprav a politických předpokladech konání IV. čs. spartakiády.

place, and if so in what way.[415] It acknowledged that the "persistent influence of members and officials of the former Czechoslovak Sokol Community" represented a serious political risk, but also warned that a cancellation of the Spartakiad could be interpreted as a "political weakness or the inability of the physical education organization" and lead to "moral demobilization." On the other hand, a successfully held Spartakiad, perhaps devoid of the Spartakiad parade, could "contribute to the consolidation of relations not only in the gymnastics movement, but also to a certain extent in society, especially among the younger generation." Based on external (i.e. party) pressure, the Czechoslovak Physical Education Association Central Committee ultimately cancelled the 1970 Czechoslovak Spartakiad in late October 1969 and instead organized Gymnastic Festivals on a local level.[416] As a replacement event, a Spartakiad of the militaries of Warsaw-Pact countries took place in 1973 at Strahov stadium that was viewed by, along with President Gustáv Husák, the leaders of the occupying troops.

The cancellation of the 1970 Spartakiad is interesting proof of the pessimism of party leaders regarding their ability to rapidly stabilize the situation in Czechoslovakia and its concerns about the extent and force of the Sokol subculture. The worries of political leaders stemming from the planned 1970 Spartakiad and its ensuing cancellation tellingly suggest that the Spartakiads represented to a certain extent an autonomous political ritual that was more than a mere tool in the party's hands. If we accept the premise that the meaning of political rituals is to conceal the contradiction between ideological claim and social reality, we see that the Spartakiad only had a limited capability to mask these contradictions.

---

415 AČOS, f. IV. celostátní spartakiáda 1970 – Základní dokumenty IV. CS 1970, Stav příprav a některé problémové otázky IV. československé spartakiády (3. 10. 1969).
416 See for instance "Proč se nebude konat spartakiáda?" *Zpravodaj tělovýchovných slavností 1970*, 1969, vol. 1, n. 1, pp. 1–2.

"NORMALIZATION" SPARTAKIADS AS AN IMAGE OF SOCIAL COHESION

The cancellation of the 1970 Spartakiad had one important benefit in the organizers' eyes: It provided sufficient time to complete a new model of gymnastic performances that was maintained until the end of state socialism. The basis for the new Spartakiad narrative moved away from the image of a perfectly functioning mechanism that the first Spartakiads had presented and returned to the Sokol depiction of the nation as an organism. Individual symbolic components were no longer mechanically arranged one after another, but created a firm and enclosed organic whole. The symbolism of the performed pieces – happy childhood, the beauty of the female body, masculine courage – formed the image of a single and unchanging national organism, the national body. In addition to the organism, the metaphor of the family and its unchanging and uncompetitive world was increasingly asserted.

Instead of the professional groups that had formed the core of the first Spartakiads, compositions based on age and gender differences became the basic structural components for all three Spartakiads in the 1970 and 80s. Instead of workers and farmers, present and future, spectators saw men, women and children. The military performance fully complied with this plan and was to a certain extent its culmination. Dressed only in "snow-white shorts," the conscripts did not so much represent the military as they did the masculinity of the Czechoslovak people. The strict gender structure of "normalization" Spartakiads somewhat disturbed the two co-ed pieces, namely the performance of young apprentices and that of the "upcoming socialist intelligentsia" of universities.[417] Yet in both cases gender was the main organizational principle. In the performance of university

---

[417] "Za život plný krásy". *Rudé právo*, vol. 65, 28. 6. 1985, p. 3. It was also admitted that the men make "a kind of 'grid' against the backdrop of female grace".

students at the 1975 Spartakiad, for instance, the male students were meant to "show a bit of courage, improve their dexterity and acquire more strength," while the female students were to "refine the expression of their movements."[418] The only piece that remained largely stuck in the aesthetics of the 1950s was that of the Svazarm (though even here only the men performed, in contrast to the 1950s and 60s). The paramilitary performance on massive steel structures came across as highly inorganic, and the fact that it remained in the Spartakiad program was probably the result of political and organizational compromises. In later interviews, Spartakiad organizers spoke about these performances with a certain degree of scorn.[419]

The structure of the "normalization" Spartakiads provided a distinct interpretation or narrative of the Czechoslovak people. It thus continued in the trend that had been begun during the preparations for the 1965 Spartakiad and which had moved from the fragmented "mosaic-like" structure of the first two Spartakiads to a coherent and cohesive concept. Practicality prevented all performances, even during the "normalization" period, from being included in a single program, as there were too many compositions, and too many gymnasts and spectators who wanted to take part. All three "normalization" Spartakiads were therefore composed of two afternoon programs consisting of seven or eight pieces. Although Spartakiad organizers claimed that each afternoon program had its own concept,

---

418 Staněk, Jaroslav: "Premiéra na Strahově. Rozhovor se spoluautorkou skladby vysokých škol Helenou Livorovou". *Rudé právo*, vol. 55, 18. 6. 1975, p. 8. Yet the classification of university students as a separate category harked back to the "mechanical" logic of the first Spartakiad. The expert report on this piece writes: "The performance of a separate piece by university students for the first time in the history of mass gymnastic performances provided this social group with the chance to show its engaged attitude toward socialist gymnastics and toward the needs of the entire society." Seliger, Václav a spol.: "Výzkum fyziologické a pedagogické náročnosti skladeb hromadných vystoupení na Československé spartakiádě 1975". *Teorie a praxe tělesné výchovy*, 1976, vol. 24, n. 11, p. 673.

419 According to e.g., Vratislav Svatoň, the only positive aspect of the steel para-structures was that after the Spartakiads they could be made into green houses in private gardens. Interview with Vratislav Svatoň, April 10, 2000, Prague. Author's archive.

it was in fact a rather even distribution of the compositions into two units so that the contrasts between the individual pieces would be preserved and the program would evenly progress. A contrast was particularly achieved by alternating pieces for men and then for women, as well as those of various age categories.[420] The second afternoon program of the 1975 Czechoslovak Spartakiad had, for instance, the following structure: Women/ Parents with children/ Men / Older school-girls / University students / Younger school-boys / Junior women / Military. The organizers gradated the Spartakiad program by ending each afternoon block with a performance by the military which, in its discipline, strenuousness and dynamics far outstripped the other pieces. The military's performance was almost always juxtaposed with that of junior women or women which had immediately preceded it. In all three Spartakiads the performances of women and soldiers were also repeated in both program blocks, though different women were used for the women's repeat performance. The only innovation to the program in 1980 and in the final Spartakiad that followed was the inclusion of a separate common composition for junior women and women, which satisfied the overwhelming interest among women to participate. Concealed behind the changes in the program lay an even more fundamental change: the transformation of the very understanding of the human body's symbolism. It was no longer a bearer of other symbols such as flags, uniforms or weapons, but itself became a symbol. Having played a minimum role in the 1950s, the body's external appearance now became the focal point. The muscular bodies of the tanned soldiers symbolized society's ability to defend itself against the enemy. The Spartakiad organizers contrasted it with the "natural aesthetic

---

420   It was explicitly requested in the concept of the 1975 Spartakiad that "male and female components be sensibly alternated, also regarding co-ed pieces." AČOS, f. Československá spartakiáda 1975 – Odbor hromadných vystoupení, Koncepce hromadných vystoupení na V. ČSS v Praze na Strahově ze dne 30. 6. 1973, p. 2.

qualities of the female body,"[421] which referred to a world of unchanging natural reproduction cycles and also served to aestheticize the national community. The Sokol gender morphology also returned to Spartakiad compositions. As Pavel Belšan wrote: "The choreography's ground plan must remain true to its ideological and creative concept, respect the participants' age-specifics, their gender and the degree to which they can master gymnastic techniques."[422]

As we will see, the change in how the human body was viewed led to a strong emphasis on sexual differences through e.g., strikingly different outfits for male and female compositions. This was not merely the objectification of the female body; the Spartakiads offered a dynamic link between the image of the woman and man that together testified to the beauty of life under late socialism, anchored in unchanging, "natural" values. The division of labor by gender is well captured by Jan Pilař's poem "To the Women at Strahov": "I once saw / a vast field with tulips / Today they bloomed / on Strahov Plain / on slim stems / palms of petals / caressed tenderness / saved for children / and one woman / joined to another / until it was full of the colors / of our country. // You men/ will hardly hold your tears back / when you see flowers / sunflowers and roses / and poppies dancing / in the middle of the stadium / drenched with the beauty / of motion and tones / with your eyes you will sow a promise in the flowerbeds / that you will protect the hearts of their linden trees." /[423]

The movement of the participants was not intended to directly symbolize a certain idea or activity, but itself was to be a symbol. It was austere and resilient in its compositions for men, and supple and dancing in those for women. Yet it also utilized an authentic

421   Pinkava, Jindřich: "Estetika a sport". *Teorie a praxe tělesné výchovy*, 1967, vol. 15, n. 11, p. 670.

422   Belšan, P.: "Choreografie a funkce náčiní, nářadí a režijních prostředků", p. 51.

423   Pilař, Jan: "Ženám na Strahově". In: Otakar Mohyla – Karel Procházka (eds.): *Verše ze Strahova*. Olympia, Prague 1985, unpagin.

child-like movement, whose spontaneity and clumsiness testified to the happiness of childhood much better and much more convincingly than the pathetic poems about youth that were part of the previous Spartakiads. The stadium's architecture was also transformed with all the socialist realist decorations removed, such as the classical columns from the Gate of Athletes and the pylons with sculptures and emblems of friendly countries. A stark grey cement structure remained that was austerely decorated with the flags of communist countries whose only function was to allow the interaction of the masses of spectators with the masses of participants.

The style chosen for the Spartakiads, which predominately worked with the implicit symbolism of the human body without external signs and symbols, was not conducive to the portrayal of the enemy. Spartakiad symbolism only implied that the enemy was anyone who separated himself from the nation's body without being able to directly embody that enemy. The image of the enemy therefore needed to be completed by accompanying texts and commentary. While the enemy of the 1950s and 60s was, above all, an external enemy, namely in the form of the American nuclear threat and "agitators" living in exile, the "normalization" construct of the enemy focused on depicting the inner enemy. This fits with the general metaphor of an organism defending itself against infection, filth and contamination. If the West was depicted negatively, then it was usually within the context of supporting the inner enemy: anti-communist forces in the West supporting various "schemers," "political charlatans," or "shamans" spreading "fictions and inanities" and, as in 1968, trying to pull off a counter-revolution.[424] In the Spartakiad discourse of

---

[424] See "Strahovské finále". *Rudé právo*, vol. 55, 28. 6. 1975, p. 1; Stano, Jiří: "Čtyři součásti čtvrté spartakiády. Harmonie, kázeň, síla, důvěra". *Rudé právo*, vol. 55, 5. 7. 1975, příloha "Haló sobota", pp. 1–2; Marek, Jaroslav a kol.: *Politickovýchovné působení funkcionářů, cvičitelů, trenérů a učitelů tělesné výchovy při přípravě Československé spartakiády 1985*. Olympia, Prague 1985, p. 5; Marek, Jaroslav – Svatoň, Vratislav: *Politickovýchovné působení funkcionářů, cvičitelů, trenérů a učitelů tělesné výchovy při přípravě Československé spartakiády 1990*. Olympia, Prague 1989, p. 3.

"normalization", the enemy lost its planetary dimension and took the form of spiteful, inflexible and embarrassing notes in the margins. The theme of the enemy was emphatically articulated in 1980 in connection with the Olympic Games in Moscow and the campaign against Charter 77. The author of the guidelines for the political education of Spartakiad participants, Jaroslav Marek, warned in 1980 that "we are witnessing an increased anti-Czechoslovak campaign" and should intensify the political-educational work so that the Spartakiad can "document the collapse of anti-Czechoslovak anti-communist imperialistic propaganda and the bankruptcy of the dissident groups, i.e. the remnants of the anti-socialist forces in our country."[425] In *Rudé právo*, Davis Cup team coach Pavel Korda added: "As a former participant, I admire not only the performances themselves, but also the grandeur surrounding them – the organization, transportation and supplying, as well as the enthusiasm of the spectators. I truly believe that even those who go out of their way to criticize everything see it in a similarly positive light. They certainly leave here with nothing to say."[426]

Yet the semiotic construct of Spartakiads based on the metaphor of an organism had one significant disadvantage compared to the previous Spartakiads. It was difficult to articulate one of the main themes behind the event that, with the onset of "normalization", had intensified rather than weakened, i.e. gratitude for the Soviet Union and its military. The logic of "normalization" Spartakiads, which focused on representing the national body, did not allow for a direct portrayal of the Soviet Union in the form of a performance by Soviet gymnasts, as was the case at the 1948 Sokol Slet and at Spartakiads up until the Prague Spring. No guests performed at "normalization" Spartakiads with one exception: Czechoslovak compatriots from the

425 Marek, Jaroslav: *Politickovýchovné působení funkcionářů, cvičitelů, učitelů tělesné výchovy a trenérů při přípravě Československé spartakiády 1980.* Olympia, Prague 1980, p. 3.
426 "Hluboké dojmy ze Strahova". *Rudé právo,* vol. 60, 28. 6. 1980, p. 8.

West.[427] A traditional part of all three pre-1968 Spartakiads was the raising of the Czechoslovak and Soviet flags accompanied by the singing of both anthems. At the 1975 Spartakiad, the Soviet flag was replaced by a symbolic red banner and, since a red banner has no anthem of its own, this also resolved the problem of how the people in the stands would behave or misbehave during the singing (broadcast live) of the Soviet anthem.[428] Gratitude to the Soviet Union therefore had to be expressed in the commentary that followed. The daily *Sport*, for instance, explicitly linked the opening ceremonies of the 1975 Czechoslovak Spartakiad with the liberation and the occupation: "[The participants] are coming to thank those who have led them all the way to this day, to pay homage to a great friend who thirty years ago helped us in our worst hour and has continued to do so whenever the need arises."[429]

The Spartakiads held during the "normalization" era closely resembled each other. Not only did they share an identical structure, the individual compositions for the various individual age categories were almost indiscernible and told the same story. The organizers themselves admitted within closed circles that some of the pieces, such as that of the soldiers, of the Svazarm and of the apprentices, were "actually already a fourth variation of a certain type of performance."[430] Another aspect that now remained almost unchanged was Strahov Stadium, which had previously been dramatically transformed with each Slet or Spartakiad. The stadium's decoration for the individual "normalization" Spartakiads differed only in the changed

---

427 The abundant community of Czechoslovak compatriots from Eastern Blok countries was not at all represented.

428 This minor semiotic change played a certain role in the post-1989 discussion within Sokol on the degree of collaboration with the communist regime. See Waldauf, J.: *Sokol. Malé dějiny velké myšlenky*, vol. 3, p. 599.

429 "Společná cesta". *Československý sport*, vol. 23, 1. 7. 1975, Spartakiádní příloha Československého sportu, p. 1.

430 Kos, Bohumil: "Vývojové tendence v tvorbě a režii pohybových skladeb". In: *Sborník ze semináře FTVS UK Praha*, p. 46.

numerals above the side entrances commemorating the anniversary of the liberation by the Soviet army and in the slight modification of the main slogan of Spartakiads displayed over the main Gate of Athletes. This "development" is well attested to by the disinterest of the sponsors of the Spartakiad ritual in ideological innovation: the 1975 Spartakiad was held under the slogan "For Peace, For Socialism," the 1980 Spartakiad went with "For peace – For Socialism" and the 1985 Spartakiad opted for "For Socialism – For Peace."

That the "normalization" Spartakiads remained more or less unchanged was in itself one of the primary messages of these rituals: after the turmoil and turbulences of the 1950s and 60s, and especially 1968, a time of peace and "successful social consolidation" had now arrived.[431] "Only people satisfied and happy, people surrounded by security," wrote *Rudé právo* in 1975 "could create what the participants and viewers created at Strahov Stadium – a giant and spontaneous demonstration of sincere gratitude for freedom and for a life in peace, and a display of profound trust in our communist party."[432] Similarly, the metaphor of an organism, to which all semiotic components of the "normalization" Spartakiads were bound, also refers to a world of unchanging natural phenomena. "normalization" peace was even juxtaposed with capitalist neurosis. *Rudé právo* compared the view of the exercising youth with the West: "On the other side of the world, their generation is succumbing to mental illness, fear and horror. They are frightened by the unemployment of their parents, scarred with pessimism and skepticism, and driven to despair. Our young people are happy. They are confident of the future, believe in the force of our shared breath and step."[433]

---

431 Marek, J. a kol .: *Politickovýchovné působení funkcionářů, cvičitelů, trenérů a učitelů tělesné výchovy při přípravě Československé spartakiády 1985*, p. 19. According to Marek, the 1975 Spartakiad demonstrated "the complete isolation of anti-socialist forces."

432 Houfová, Jarmila: "Skvělá přehlídka mládí a krásy socialistického Československa". *Rudé právo*, vol. 55, 30. 6. 1975, p. 1.

433 Stano, Jiří: "Čtyři součásti čtvrté spartakiády. Harmonie, kázeň, síla, důvěra". *Rudé právo*, vol. 55, 5. 7. 1975, příloha "Haló sobota", pp. 1–2.

The motif of stability and security was closely linked, again through the organism metaphor, with the other main message of Spartakiads, e.g., social cohesion. The Spartakiad was to express, "that which is characteristic of our socialist society," which is "cohesiveness," "collectiveness" and "moral and political unity."[434] The circle became the basic choreographic component and rhetorical figure of the "normalization" Spartakiads. This "symbol of unity and cooperation and an ancient Slavic representation of the sun"[435] was formed by three thousand secondary school students in the opening ceremony of the 1980 Spartakiad accompanied by Václav Hons's verses: "All of us in the great circle of happiness / we all came together / as gratitude for good work / for the moment of wisdom / smelling of bread / smelling of forest [...]".[436] Spartakiads created the image of the people as a unified "national collective,"[437] of a single national body joined "through the shared beating of our hearts."[438] The sensed existence of a national community was embodied at Strahov Stadium and the awareness of belonging to a single national community was depicted there: "The rings, groups of people that did not know each other, that had never before seen each other, but who believed and knew that hundred of thousands of others were working on the same thing, merged into oceans of beauty."[439] The opening and closing rituals were especially suited to developing the theme of social cohesion. In the closing scene of the 1975 Spartakiad, for instance, soldiers formed an enormous five-pointed star whose arms

---

434 "Skvělé vítězství". *Rudé právo*, vol. 55, 1. 7. 1975, p. 1.

435 Chvalný, Július et al.: *Československá spartakiáda 1980*. Olympia – Šport, Prague – Bratislava 1981, p. 167.

436 See for instance AČOS, f. Československá spartakiáda 1980, Spartakiáda se otvírá (Václav Hons). Václav Hons was later one of the few poets who composed a ceremonial poem for November 17th 1989. ("I will quietly lay / snow flowers / to this drop of blood / of the glorious 17th of November.") See Hons, Václav:"17. listopad". *Rozhlas*, 1989, vol. 16, n. 53, p. 2. See Janáček, P.: "Listopad ve znamení Théty".

437 Stano, Jiří: "Československá spartakiáda". *Rudé právo*, vol. 60, 1. 7. 1980, p. 3.

438 Bonhardová, Nina: "Odkaz ČS spartakiády 75". *Rudé právo*, vol. 55, 4. 7. 1975, p. 8.

439 Stano, J.: "Československá spartakiáda"

stretched all the way to the far ends of the stadium. Representatives of the other fourteen pieces surrounded the star around the stadium's perimeter in square formations. In the middle of the star the military performers formed a four-level human pyramid while "The Internationale" was sung, with a single soldier on top raising his arms to the sky.[440]

The new model of "normalization" Spartakiads also much better illustrated the intermingling of age categories, thus testifying to the "strong link between generations and their social unity."[441] A feature particular to the "normalization" Spartakiads was the ability to present not only the motif of youth as in all preceding Spartakiads, but also the theme of old-age.[442] Film cameras regularly focused on the grey hair of both men and women performing as proof of the wholeness of the "Spartakiad oeuvre." Division of the Spartakiad program by age and gender enabled contemporary society to be presented as a happy family in which women were in charge of the "comfort of the home," men worked and protected the country, children played, adolescents prepared for future roles according to gender, older participants passed on their experience and augmented the family image with a grandparent figure. The metaphor of the family also penetrated into spheres where it did not semantically

---

440 Five years later the soldiers came up with a different motif. To the sound of the "Victory Will Be Ours" march they formed with their bodies an enormous symbol of the Olympic Games in Moscow crowned with a five-pointed star. At the same time on the opposing side of the stadium women participants in white outfits and scarves of different colors formed five Olympic circles in the five different colors. After the image was created, verses of "A Tribute to the Olympics" were broadcast: "Long live the friendship between nations of the entire world; long live Olympic ideals [...] Let's hope the fomenters of misunderstanding remain ignored." The participants then left the stadium to the sound of the march "Across the Scorched Earth, Across the Bloody River." "Mládí, radost, krása, síla". *Rudé právo*, vol. 60, 27. 6. 1980, p. 3. The formation of participants into the shape of Olympic rings was also part of the Olympic ceremony for the 1936 "Nazi" Olympic Games, as is evident in Riefenstahl's film *Olympia*.
441 "Spartakiádní proud". *Rudé právo*, vol. 55, 16. 6. 1975, p. 1.
442 Ladislav Serbus suggested that as part of the "Respect for old age program," special pieces specifically for older participants be prepared. Serbus, L.: "Diskusní příspěvek". In: *Sborník ze semináře FTVS UK Praha*, pp. 36–37.

belong. For instance, the performance of the youngest pupils, which traditionally evoked themes of socialization and education, reminded a *Rudé právo* reporter at the 1980 Spartakiad of a "larger family of sorts" in which the accompanying teachers and trainers represented the performing children's mothers.[443]

---

443 "Strhující premiéra na Strahově". *Rudé právo*, vol. 60, 27. 6. 1980, p. 1.

PARENTS AND CHILDREN PERFORMING EXERCISES

Perhaps the shift in Spartakiad semiotics to family values is best illustrated by a "normalization"-era novelty, the Parents and Children composition, which was presented in more or less identical form at all three Spartakiads. This piece featured mothers (sometimes even fathers and grandparents) performing with their children three to five years of age (though the youngest "gymnast" was only twenty months[444]) simple exercises and games played to children rhymes.[445] This performance contradicted a whole array of socialist-realist Spartakiad principles, instead demonstrating the new symbolic priorities of the "normalization" Spartakiads. It showed the unchanging, indisputable and apparently apolitical values such as a mother's love for children, children's joy and spontaneity, life optimism and "pleasant comfort of our families."[446]

It can even be said that this piece became a kind of ideological climax of the "normalization" Spartakiads. Former opponent of the Parents and Children exercise performance Jiří Žižka also confirmed this when he admitted that "the Parents and Children piece will become the symbol of the 1975 Czechoslovak Spartakiad."[447]

---

444 Krejčík, Rudolf: *Československá spartakiáda 1980*. Krátký film, Prague 1980, 63 minutes, cinematography Vladimír Skalský.

445 A nearly eighty-page sociological study based on 115 interviews with families exercising at the Spartakiad was published. It shows, for instance, the percentile ratio of adult participants: only father 8 percent, only mother 52 percent, alternating parents 17 percent, parents alternating with grandparents 15 percent, only grandparents 7 percent, other person 1 percent. The intelligentsia prevailed among parents (42 percent); home-keeping women were also numerous (8 percent). Only 10 percent of them were members of of the Czechoslovak Communist Party, while nearly 60 percent were ČSTV members. Only 10 percent of the parents had never before participated in a Spartakiad. The average age of the children was 3.75 years. The study also shows that, besides Spartakiad propaganda, the popularity of the parents and children exercises was mainly disseminated through word of mouth: two thirds of the parents recruited other parents to exercise. Hudeček, Jaroslav: *Cvičení rodičů a dětí na Československé spartakiádě 1975*. Vědecká rada Ústředního výboru Československého svazu tělesné výchovy, Prague 1977.

446 "Cvičenci opět nadchli Strahov". *Rudé právo*, vol. 60, 28. 6. 1980, p. 1.

447 Žižka, Jiří: "Dramaturgie hromadných tělovýchovných vystoupení ČSS 75". *Teorie a praxe tělesné výchovy*, 1975, vol. 23, n. 6, p. 325.

197

24. Parents and children exiting Strahov Stadium after performing at the 1975 Spartakiad (National Museum).

The evaluation committee that selected the pieces for the 1975 Spartakiad also expected that the "effects that this piece will have on the public and on the Spartakiad's overall atmosphere will be like no other."[448] *Rudé právo* also expressed its approval when it deemed the Parents and Children exercise the "most graceful Spartakiad piece."[449] Just as the work reserves' performance in 1955 became the central motif of the first Spartakiad, the Parents and Children's performance depicted in condensed form the essence of the ideological message of "normalization" Spartakiads. A scene in the Parents and Children piece, in which the children, after a brief separation from their parents when they performed by themselves, ran to their mothers who took them in their arms and spun around with them,

---

448 AČOS, f. Výběr skladeb 1960–1975, Hodnocení skladeb pro Československou spartakiádu 1975, p. 2/3.
449 Caption for the photo of performance of parents and children. *Rudé právo*, vol. 60, 30. 6. 1980, p. 8.

can be juxtaposed with the collective image of the work reserves' cogwheels and fields of grain. ("The boys and girls run to seek refuge in the loving arms of their parents," *Rudé právo* wrote, "Come, my little one, you're my whole world.")[450] It was such a touching scene that according to a Western journalist the Secretary General of the Communist Party burst into tears.[451]

The shift in the symbolism of the Spartakiads is also well illustrated by the fact that it was by no means easy to push this piece through. Jana Berdychová (born in 1909), who had worked with mass gymnastics (especially with the youngest children) since her youth, came up with the idea for the piece. Her co-ed piece for the youngest pupils entitled *Our Toys*, in which ten thousand six to eight-year-old children of Prague and its vicinity performed, had opened the All-Sokol Slet of 1948. In her commentary to this performance, she outlined the main principles of her work: "To surprise the viewer with the children's considerable freedom in their physical expression; from a psychological and physiological standpoint, the unrestricted movement of children this age is a necessary requirement. It does not have to be done in unison, but a common rhythm carries the children through free play, marching and other games involving imitation.[452] Berdychová avoided anti-Sokol recourse and became personally involved in the Sovietization of Czechoslovak gymnastics and the creation of new physical education curricula at schools.[453] Her professional life was devoted to matters of gymnastics for the

450 "Manifestace zdatnosti a krásy". *Rudé právo*, vol. 60, 28. 6. 1980, p. 3. See also "O nejmladší cvičence". *Rudé právo*, vol. 55, 27. 6. 1975, p. 8.

451 Werther, Betty: "The Show of the Shows – Or Something Close". *International Herald Tribune*, vol. 9, 12. – 13. 7. 1975, p. 14. *Rudé právo* published a photograph in which ČSTV chairman Antonín Himl gives Husák a symbolic gift – "a sculpture of a mother and child exercising". In: "Pozdrav účastníkům spartakiády". *Rudé právo,* vol. 55, 24. 6. 1975, p. 1.

452 Berdychová, Jana: "Naše hračky". In: *Památník XI. sletu všesokolského v Praze 1948*, pp. 37–38.

453 See for instance Berdychová, Jana – Georgieva-Chaloupková, Marie: *Tance sovětských národů. Popis s obrázky a hudebním doprovodem*. Nakladatelství Československé obce sokolské, Prague 1951.

youngest children and to the creation of mass gymnastic performances. After the first Spartakiad, she argued that the general principles applied for adult performances cannot merely "somehow be applied" to children and youth, but that pieces specifically for these age categories had to be created. The idea of parents and children performing exercises together was first mentioned in her 1960 doctorate work for Charles University's School of Physical Education and Sports.[454] When three years later she submitted a proposal for her own choreographed piece involving parents and children for the 1965 Spartakiad, she was met with criticism from the Spartakiad staff.[455] The following objections appear in the preserved record of the evaluations committee whose task it was to choose the best Spartakiad pieces:

Comrade Žižka: There are comrades who do not feel that it is the proper expression, nor is it logical. We want children to be in school, in the collective, but here they are with their parents, playing with them. There the role of the parents is theatrical, circus-like.

Comrade Nováková: It bothers me that too much individual care is given to the children. This could make things complicated when the child returns to the collective.

Comrade Volek: We must avoid there being any cuddling. The disparity must not be such that it causes undesirable associations with family values.[456]

In a later interview, the 97-year-old Berdychová recalled the conflict with the main organizer of the first Spartakiads Jaroslav Šterc: "And Šterc declared all over the country that Berdychová was spoiling the

454 Berdychová, J.: *Funkce tělovýchovných skladeb pro hromadná vystoupení mládeže*, p. 150.
455 The piece was eventually performed only at local-level Spartakiads.
456 AČOS, f. Výběr skladeb 1960–1975, Hodnocení skladeb 29. 4. 1963 (Děti naše květy). See also AČOS, f. Výběr skladeb 1960–1975. Závěry komise předsednictva ÚV ČSTV ke spartakiádním skladbám předváděným ve dnech 29. a 30. 4. 1963.

children, that she was dragging them and their mothers into the gyms even though she knows that we have a lack of exercise space. He spread this around. I really had to fight him."[457] For the organizers of Spartakiads in the 1950s and 60s, the exercising of parents and children represented a foreign element that disturbed the overall testimony of a ritual about society as a mechanically perfect machine. Yet in the 1970s and 80s "undesirable associations with aspects of the family" were no longer a problem and the Parents and Children performances were fully incorporated into the new model of the happy family. For the author of the idea of parents exercising with their children, the 1975 Spartakiad was an opportunity to present this idea to the public and to build a network of groups involved in this exercise throughout the country.[458]

Berdychová believed that the compositions for the parents and children performance should be based on the specificity of this intergenerational performance and should further strengthen its uniqueness. Qualities particular to the young children's exercise performance were "spontaneity, beauty and purity, children's movement, family love, caring for children, playfulness, and the dynamics and authenticity of children's expressions".[459] The exercise was not intended to transform the children's movement, "to purify it" of "unpleasant unconscious habits" as Marie Majerová had requested during the first Spartakiad in 1955, but was to "enhance and emphasize" children's expression. The choreography of these pieces was based on simple round shapes, semicircles and circles that allowed for a different number of pairs to perform exercises in them. For instance, groups of children and parents exercised around several

---

457 Interview with Jana Berdychová, 23. ledna 2006, Prague. Author's archive.
458 See Urban, Ivo: "Dobře si je vychováme. Rozhovor s Janou Berdychovou". *Rudé právo*, vol. 55, 5. 6. 1975, p. 8.
459 Berdychová, Jana: "Vývojové tendence skladeb pro rodiče a děti na čsl. spartakiádách". In: *Sborník ze semináře FTVS UK Praha*, pp. 83–87. See also Berdychová, Jana: "Problematika dětských tělovýchovných skladeb pro hromadná vystoupení". *Teorie a praxe tělesné výchovy*, 1978, vol. 26, n. 11, pp. 678–684.

dozen flowers made of colored pads that were randomly placed on the stadium's field. This solved the problem of the frequent turnover of participants during training hours. The children did not exercise on the place markers since this "rids them of their natural playfulness and is an unnatural interference with a child's mentality." If the children lost interest in an exercise, it was not their fault. Instead, flaws were to be sought in the "concept of the piece on the whole." The pieces were also intended to sufficiently "maintain an awareness of the emotional expressions between a child and its partner." The aim of the exercise was not to transform, to socialize a child, but to alter society to the child's image.[460] The uniqueness of the Parents and Children performance was further emphasized by the media. All three primary documentary films from "normalization" Spartakiads as well as television reports contained the same long shot of a specific child who was completely ignoring the exercise and playing his own game. The documentary film of the 1980 Spartakiad shows e.g. a roughly three-year-old boy playing with the sand on the field instead of exercising. This is accompanied by ironic commentary: "Not everyone understands the responsibility of a public exercise performance; some are more interested in the sand piles at Strahov Stadium."[461] *Rudé právo* also reported on the "soloists," children who were wandering away from their parents, building sand castles from the Strahov sand or pouring sand on the feet of adult participants. The media at that time did not view this play as a disruption of discipline and order, but praised them for the "spontaneity of children's

---

460 The political innocence of this performance did not so fully apply in the case of the parents. According to the author, the piece was to provide the parents with a) inspiration for their own exercising with children, b) a comparison with the development of other children, c) "a feeling of belonging to the whole," d) "an opportunity to demonstrate a good relationship toward the thirty-year construction of the republic." Berdychová, Jana: *Skladba pro rodiče a děti.* Olympia, Prague 1974, p. 4.
461 Krejčík, Rudolf: *Československá spartakiáda 1980.* Krátký film, Prague 1980.

expression,"[462] which was one of the fundamental messages of the Spartakiads held during the "normalization" period. Yet the weaker the discipline motif, the stronger the theme of peace. The performance was therefore intended to express the joy of a childhood "unthreatened by bombs falling on the roofs of their homes."[463]

462 Houfová, Jarmila: "Spartakiáda – velkolepé dílo statisíců". *Rudé právo*, vol. 65, 1. 7. 1985, p. 2. Ten years prior to this *Rudé právo* has reported that during a rehearsal at Strahov the children had become so immersed in building sand castles that steam rollers had to be used to level the exercising field for the next performance. See "O nejmladší cvičence". *Rudé právo*, vol. 55, 27. 6. 1975, p. 8.

463 "Za život plný krásy". *Rudé právo*, vol. 65, 28. 6. 1985, p. 3; See also "Manifestace zdatnosti a krásy". *Rudé právo*, vol. 60, 28. 6. 1980, p. 3.

AN AMIABLE BACKGROUND: FEMALE PERFORMANCES AT SPARKIADS DURING THE "NORMALIZATION" ERA

Another ideological highlight of "normalization" Spartakiads consisted of the performances of women that further developed the central theme of family happiness and peace in a socialist country. Two of the three "normalization" performances of women were accompanied by classical music. In 1975, women performing with indian clubs were accompanied by Bedřich Smetana's pieces *From Bohemia's Woods and Fields* and *The Vltava*, and in 1985 they performed holding ribbons to Antonín Dvořák's *Slavonic Dances*[464] (in 1980, the introductory piece "Prologue," performed by students from the secondary schools of Prague and Central Bohemia, was accompanied by Leoš Janáček's "Slet" *Sinfonietta*, originally composed for the 1926 Slet[465]). It was in classical music that the composers of the "normalization" Spartakiad pieces were able to find the perfect means to effectively link the traditional ideas of the 19th century on national unity with even more traditional ideas of the role of a woman as the "provider of life." The female body and the classical national music together created the image of unchanging, timeless collective happiness. As we have previously explained, in their ability to

---

464 The idea to use *Slavic Dances* was not completely new. Music scholar Jiří Dostál speculated in the 1948 souvenir program, "how exercises would look to Dvořák's Slavonic Dances if they had been composed for calisthenics." Dostál, Jiří: "Živel organizující množství". In: *Památník XI. sletu všesokolského v Praze 1948*, p. 154–156. In the same period, Otakar Šourek mentioned among the compositions led by a "Sokol spirit" Dvořák's *Slavonic Dances* and Janáček's *Sinfonietta*. Šourek, O.: *Slety a umění hudební*, p. 41.

465 Janáček's relationship to Sokol, of which he was a member, was completely ignored in articles on the 1980 Czechoslovak Spartakiad, despite the fact that the relationship was previously publicaly discussed e.g. in a 1956 conference. See Procházka, Zdeněk Horymír: "Hudba jako nedílná součást hromadného vystoupení". In: *Vědecká konference o teoretických a metodických základech masových tělovýchovných vystoupení*, p. 99. On Janáček's *Sinfonietta* see Šourek, O.: *Slety a umění hudební*, p. 36.

25. A performance by 12,000 women at Strahov Stadium the inscription reads: "For peace, for socialism" during the 1975 Czechoslovak Spartakiad (photo Marie Hlušičková).

express the depth of the national past, these performances replaced the inorganically appearing performances of costumed groups at previous Spartakiads.

In approving the women's pieces for the 1975 Czechoslovak Spartakiad in December 1973, staff members expressed considerable concerns regarding this "experiment." It was the first time that classical music was to be used as the musical accompaniment and the organizers were troubled by, among other things, their "responsibility to Smetana."[466] The creative process was also unorthodox: the performances were usually made by first coming up with the content (the exercises) and then composing the music to it. Now, however, the musical part was given and the movements had to be created to

---

[466] AČOS, f. Výběr skladeb 1960–1975, Hodnocení skladeb pro Československou spartakiádu 1975, 14. 12. 1973.

fit it. A discussion on the participants' outfits was also held. Some of the staff members did not like that the women were to perform to classical music in long pants and smocks. For instance, one of the few Slovak members of the evaluation committee said: "Women can wear pants in the parade, but Indian clubs together with trousers? No way." Jarmila Kostková, who had belonged to the younger Sokol generation and had composed a number of Spartakiad pieces, argued that not even the "more feminine" alternatives fully satisfied: "Smetana did not see women in t-shirts either." *Rudé právo* even informed of dissenting letters arguing that Smetana's music would be degraded by the accompaniment of an exercise performance."[467] At the same time, however, both the communist press and organizers placed high hopes in the performance. Professor Serbus expected the piece to have the effect of patriotic education. "I don't want to exaggerate," he said, "but the performance might evoke an ecstatic patriotic sentiment of sorts. If it is done properly." Antonín Král emphasized the emotional force of the piece: "it will give people goose bumps, there will be a sea of tears – and rightfully so." *Rudé právo* assured that ultimately the performance at Strahov won over all its doubters with its beauty: "The masses of spectators understood, they feel how our tradition is beautiful, democratic and truly of the people, how the national classics form a vivid and vibrant part of our current happy, peaceful days, part of the life of nations advancing on the path of the Great October Revolution. Thanks to you, women, providers of life and joy."[468]

The women's performance at the 1975 Spartakiad had two parts as well as two groups of female participants; nearly two thousand "advanced gymnasts" in orange t-shirts with two indian clubs and ten thousand women with a single indian club in blue mini-dresses (though the cut of this outfit more resembled a kind of shortened

---

467 "Pod avantgardním rudým lidstva znamením". *Rudé právo*, vol. 55, 30. 6. 1975, p. 3.
468 Ibid, p. 3.

work coat).[469] The first part utilized livelier parts of Smetana's work *From Bohemia's Woods and Fields* for the dance-like exercise, while the second part, based on *Vltava* was mainly composed of bold choreographic changes and transitions in which the women moved to up to forty place marks away – using their bodies to render Smetana's idea of "a torrential current gradually emerging from tiny springs."[470] The river's powerful current was to be depicted by dozens of massive arrows formed by the women at the performance's conclusion.[471] As *Rudé právo* pointed out, the performance did not merely portray the river's current, "but the image of a nation's life, flowing peacefully and then wildly in the torrid rapids, leading out into a wide breadth."[472]

The same creative team[473] returned to national classical music for the 1985 Spartakiad. Unlike Smetana, the *Slavonic Dances* by "cosmopolitan" Dvořák much better met the needs of dance gymnastics. Yet even here the massive choreography of the entire stadium was applied, especially at the beginning of the piece. In white smocks and green knee skirts while holding small hoops and ribbons, the women formed in each corner of the field the shape of linden leaves, and then these shapes, in probably the boldest choreography in Spartakiad history, moved in a dancing step toward the middle where their four points touched and created the shape of a four-leaf clover. At the conclusion of the performance, roughly thirty concentric circles of women split off from their exactly even rows and formed the image of an "enormous sun."[474] In an obvious "reference" to the famous round-dance of the women from the 1938 Slet an impressive

469 Chvalný, Július: *Československá spartakiáda 1975.* Olympia, Prague 1976, unpaginated.
470 "Společná cesta". *Československý sport*, vol. 23, 1. 7. 1975, Spartakiádní příloha Československého sportu, p. 1.
471 AČOS, f. Výběr skladeb 1960–1975, Hodnocení skladeb pro Československou spartakiádu 1975, 14. 12. 1973.
472 Pešek, Jaromír: "Strahovský koncert". *Rudé právo*, vol. 55, 5. 7. 1975, p. 5.
473 Eva Bémová, Květa Černá a Draha Horáková.
474 "Za život plný krásy". *Rudé právo*, vol. 65, 28. 6. 1985, p. 3.

contrast between the geometrical perfection of the grid of place markers and the spontaneous and dynamic central form was thus formed. As it had done ten years earlier, the 1985 performance thematized the link between Czech classical music, the landscape and history on the one hand, and the female body on the other, though this time in a much more aesthetically impressive form.

The women's performance at the 1980 Czechoslovak Spartakiad was not accompanied by classical music, but by a modern rhythm and the singing of Waldemar Matuška, whose later emigration to the USA shocked the party.[475] Although the music was contemporary, the understanding of the women's role in society, which the piece was intended to express, was wholly traditional. This is also attested to by the song's lyrics, which developed themes of a harmonious home: "Let the flute of birds play on / and the doomsayer owl fall mute / let our home continue to blossom in joy / an amiable backround." This piece and its interpretation in the press clearly represents an apex of the return to traditional family values during the "normalization" period. A brief published description of the piece tells us that the author based it on the principle that "the health, fitness and grace of a woman form the basis for an orderly, harmonious and stable family and thus a healthy society."[476] Unlike the other pieces that avoided direct narrativization, the women's performance was to depict the story of "a woman's mission in a socialist society,"[477] just as *Rudé právo* reported on it:

"Mother and child. The authors of this ode to women devoted a great deal of space to the time-honored bond of motherhood. A spring of the innermost feelings of the provider of life gushed forth from it. The equal

---

475 After Matuška's emigration, František Janeček, who penned the hit *Poupata* (Buds) for the following Spartakiad received his confiscated attic apartment on Wenceslas Square. After 1989, Matuška sued in vain for it to be returned.
476 Chvalný, J. et al.: *Československá spartakiáda 1980*, p. 166.
477 "Domov náš, vlídné zázemí...". *Rudé právo*, vol. 60, 27. 6. 1980, p. 3.

voice of a man's spouse, caring for home comfort after the everyday bustle, sounded like a bell. Child's crying, disheartening her with worries of the fate of the family hearth. The dramatic tension in the piece was reflected in the alternation of dynamic exercises, in the enclosing of the islands of shapes portraying the unraveling of everyday worries. The glowing coals of sleepless nights have dimmed. A calm has settled in. [...] A child once again peacefully plays or falls into a sweet sleep. He wakes with a smile to the dewy morning, and his mother wakes from a dream to today's joyful reality, expressed by the mirth and dancing encouraging her to love, work and live to the fullest."[478]

How should these patriarchal references be interpreted? This was largely a return to the gender model of the Sokol Slets. Still, it cannot be said that patriarchal values won out in "normalization" Spartakiads, since there is no dominant counter-image of a creative, working and fighting man to the subordinate image of the woman taking care of the "amiable backround." The values that women embody in their performance – peace, stability, family comfort – were central (not secondary) values of the "normalization" society. As in other areas of "normalization" culture, women's symbolic significance dramatically increased with the regime's shift in values.[479] Thus the women's performances at the Spartakiad represented better than any other the remarkable gender order of the "normalization" culture in which submission was dominance.

---

478   Ibid.
479   Cf. Havelková, Hana – Oates-Indruchová, Libora: *The Politics of Gender Culture under State Socialism. An Expropriated Voice.* Routledge, New York 2014.

JUNIOR WOMEN AND "BUDS"

The performances of the junior women (15 to 18-years-old students or members of gymnastic clubs) at Spartakiads during the "normalization" period were an important part of society's image as an organism. The performance possessed distinctly dance-like attributes whose choreography was full of round shapes, emphasizing a "specifically female collective expression of movement."[480]

The movements, choreography, but above all interpretations in the press and film commentary suggested themes of growth, maturation and blossoming, with this well-worn metaphor obviously possessing strong sexual connotations. Other references that were not of a gender-specific "female" type and which had been present in previous Spartakiads (work, play, education and competitiveness, as well as courage, persistence and defense of country) were completely absent. A key word that appeared in describing the junior women's performance was "tender." Under their headlines of "The Breath of the Tender Youth" or "A Poem of the Tenderness of Girls," *Rudé právo* described how "thin-legged girls" in "white mini-skirts" presented "a lyrical poem on the tenderness and desire of girls that will soon intensify into a maternal feeling."[481]

Even infrequent references to the world of work and education quickly veered toward the family. The junior women thus showed in their performance that "their future is bright," that "they would not live without uncertainty [sic], that they would work for the happiness of their families, of their children, for society."[482] If in the 1950s youth was an expression of an attitude towards life ("Nejedlý

---

480 *Československá spartakiáda 75. Program hromadných tělovýchovných vystoupení Praha--Strahov.* Olympia, Prague 1975, unpaginated.

481 "Pod avantgardním rudým lidstva znamením". *Rudé právo*, vol. 55, 30. 6. 1975, p. 3; "Manifestace zdatnosti a krásy". *Rudé právo*, vol. 60, 28. 6. 1980, p. 3; "Báseň o dívčí něze". *Rudé právo*, vol. 65, 29. 6. 1985, p. 3.

482 "Manifestace zdatnosti a krásy".

26. Performance of the older female pupils at Strahov Stadium during the last Spartakiad in 1985 (National Museum).

is young"), "normalization" Spartakiads sexualized youth. That which was emphasized in youth was, as in the Sokol Slets or fascist rituals, its reproductive potential.[483]

The male view of the junior women, both controlling and consuming, was also developed as a theme. Rudolf Krejčík's 1980 documentary film assures the viewer that during the junior women's exercises "everyone gets his money's worth," and footage of the junior women exercising are mixed with the gazing, hungry eyes of a male spectator.[484] The junior women provided a "delight for the viewer's eyes"[485] and the press reported on the sexual tension, the

---

[483] An emphasis on the physical appearance of the female participants is attested to by the instruction guidelines for the junior women's piece at the 1975 Spartakiad. "Having the height of the girls in the basic groups more or less the same contributes to an aesthetic appearance. This should be taken into consideration when choosing the girls." Fialová, Milka – Rejhonová, Marie: *Skladba pre dorastenky.* Šport, Bratislava 1974, p. 7.

[484] Krejčík, Rudolf: *Československá spartakiáda 1980.* Krátký film, Prague 1980.

[485] Houfová, J.: "Skvělá přehlídka mládí a krásy socialistického Československa". *Rudé právo,* vol. 55, 30. 6. 1975, p. 2.

"teasing" between the soldiers and junior women (*Rudé právo*, for instance, noted the chanting of conscripts during the Spartakiad parade: "No matter if they're fat or thin, the junior women our vote win!"[486] or "With our tan bodies and white shorts we greet the junior women."[487])

The eroticizing of the junior women's performances was also carried over to the performances of the category one age group lower, i.e. that of the 11 to 14-year-old school girls. In communism's collective memory, the performance of these girls ("Buds") at the 1985 Spartakiad symbolizes the phenomenon of Spartakiads (or of "normalization" as the case may be) as such. The exercises themselves were not anything out of the ordinary, and we find the same motifs in previous Spartakiad pieces of the same age category. As in earlier years, the popularity among the school girls was based more on an "adult" than a "children's" interpretation of the piece. In 1980, for instance, this composition of "future ladies" contributed to "improving the aesthetics of expression through movements," since, as *Rudé právo* pointed out, "they will soon be attending ballroom dancing classes."[488]

"Buds" differed in that the authors first succeeded in involving the "normalization" pop-culture so that the music accompaniment to the Spartakiad piece became a real hit. "Normalization" radio played it as part of its daily repertoire and television quickly produced a video clip in which the popular group Kroky is accompanied by a group of twelve junior women participants while it plays its "disco-polka" right in the gym.[489] In February 1985 the song *Buds* was also released as a single. This was not the first attempt to turn the music accompaniment of a Spartakiad piece into a hit. In 1975 the organizers had attempted to popularize Elena Lukášová's

---

486   "Báseň o dívčí něze". *Rudé právo*, vol. 65, 29. 6. 1985, p. 3.
487   "Řeka mírového života". *Rudé právo*, vol. 65, 1. 7. 1985, p. 2.
488   "Cvičenci opět nadchli Strahov". *Rudé právo*, vol. 60, 28. 6. 1980, p. 1.
489   See Štichová, H. (ed.): *Retro spartakiáda 1955–1985*, p. 42.

version of "Singing to the Sun," which had accompanied the junior women's performance. Although the song had a catchy melody and the organizers had systematically promoted it during all Spartakiad events as the main theme song, it did not become a popular hit. The fact that the lyrics contained direct ideological references such as the "flag of peace" or "red roses," or that it was still too early in 1975 for the public to sing the same hit as the communist sponsors of Spartakiads, may have had something to do with this.

In a joint interview for *Rudé právo* from 1985, František Janeček, who wrote the song *Buds*, and pop singer Michal David recall that it was Jarmila Kostková who had involved them in the Spartakiad. Kostková, a former Sokol official, had noticed that much of the audience for Kroky performances consisted of girls of the "older school girl" category.[490] Michal David praised the female Spartakiad participants for singing the song along with him, thereby creating an "absolutely unique" fourteen-thousand voice choir, and at the end of the interview expressed his hope that the "Buds turn into the most beautiful flowers that enrich our peaceful country."[491] Although the "Buds" piece did not deviate in any way from the other Spartakiad productions during the "normalization" period, it well illustrates the nature of the moral economy at that time. A trade was made in which the school girls received as accompaniment a song sung by a pop-star with a catchy melody and innocuous or at least ambivalent lyrics (they only had to "walk toward tomorrow") and Spartakiad organizers in return received the very useful image of enthusiasm, loyalty and "female maturation."[492]

---

490 "Nechť rostou do krásy. S Michalem Davidem a Františkem Janečkem o ‚poupatech'". *Rudé právo,* vol. 65, 28. 6. 1985, p. 8.
491 Ibid.
492 According to *Rudé právo* the girls transformed in the piece "from girls into lovely young women, very nearly approaching the female beauty of their mothers." "Koukněme se na poupata…". *Rudé právo,* vol. 65, 1. 7. 1985, p. 5.

SOLDIERS AND THE CRISIS OF MASCULINITY

The men's performance at "normalization" Spartakiads did not form a symbolic counterbalance to the women's. There were far fewer male participants training in the men's pieces than there were women and the men usually only occupied half of the place markers at Strahov, i.e. seven thousand places instead of the usual nearly fourteen thousand.

Even *Rudé právo* admitted that there "were the most concerns" with them and that they preferred sports to traditional calisthenics.[493] There were so few men that for the 1975 Spartakiad the organizers opted to prepare a joint piece with the junior men, who could be more easily "motivated." This was not only about the number of participants, but also the nature of the performance itself. Of all the Spartakiad pieces, the men's performance most resembled the traditional Sokol calisthenics. For most of the "normalization" period the Sokol associations were more a hindrance than anything else, and it was only in the 1985 Spartakiad that organizers openly embraced this tradition in using Suk's *Into a New Life* marching song. The men's performance lacked the size and pathos of the women's or the dynamism of the military pieces. This was largely caused by the very age of the men, most of whom belonged to the same generation that had taken part in the final Slet. Thus the men's pieces aged five more years with each passing Spartakiad. The creators had to therefore ensure that the "exercises for the older participants were not ridiculous."[494]

---

493   See Staněk, Jaroslav – Marek, Rudolf: "Tleskali cvičencům do kroku". *Rudé právo*, vol. 55, 28. 6. 1975, p. 8; "Spartakiádní impuls všedním dnům". *Rudé právo*, vol. 60, 3. 7. 1980, p. 8. This is evidenced by e.g. a *Rudé právo* interview with the head of the men's Tesla Žižkov gymnastics club training: "I couldn't imagine my life without the gymnastics club and collective. I therefore don't understand why the interest of men in gymnastics is, to their detriment, so low. […] I do feel, however, that men's gymnastics has not been promoted enough. Why, for instance, don't the posters promoting the Spartakiad have exercising men on them?" – "Pět vyznání z milionu". *Rudé právo*, vol. 55, 1. 5. 1975, p. 8.

494   AČOS, f. Výběr skladeb 1960–1975, Závěry ze schvalování skladeb dne 19. 4. 1974 v TJ Bohemians.

The weakness in numbers and symbolism was reflected in e.g. Jiří Střecha's impressive 12-minute documentary film *The 1985 Czechoslovak Spartakiad* consisting of a collage of Spartakiad pieces.[495] The director only gave three seconds to the men's exercise, and even that was probably for the sake of meeting the obligation to present the Spartakiad program in its entirety. The participants of the men's piece were not referred to in the press as fighters or builders, but almost exclusively as fathers (especially popular was the pleonasm "family fathers"), and though there was no direct mention of the elderly, terms such as "maturity" and "experience" predominated. Although the symbolic "weakness" of the men's pieces during the "normalization" period consisted mainly of the internal development of the gymnastics movement, meaning the feminization of gymnastics, it also corresponded to a more general phenomenon of the crisis of masculinity during the "normalization" period.[496]

The role of the symbolic counterbalance to the women's pieces that had been held by the men's pieces at Sokol Slets had to be taken over by the military during "normalization". The military was very successful in accomplishing this task, and their pieces were always considered the highlight of the performances at Strahov. Yet their performances at district Spartakiads, where their mechanical precision formed a strong contrast with the lack of coordination and general confusion in other pieces, were even more impressive. If it is said that most of the "normalization" Spartakiad pieces were variations on the same genre, this applies even more so to the military's pieces. Spartakiad organizers were aware of this and had warned following the 1975 Spartakiad: "It will be difficult to find a new direction for the compositions of the Czechoslovak army since

---

495 Střecha, Jiří: *Československá spartakiáda 1985*. Krátký film, Prague 1985, 12 minut.
496 Ivo Možný summed it up as such: "A man lives in the family of a woman. A woman lives in a family that she isn't content with. A man lives in the family of a woman not content with the family." Možný, Ivo: *Moderní rodina. Mýty a skutečnosti*. Blok, Brno 1990, p. 111.

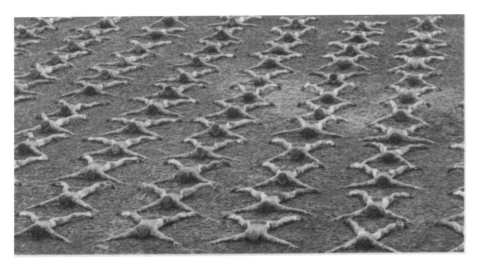

27. Zdeněk Lhoták photograph from the *Spartakiad* series documenting the military's performance at a district Spartakiad in Prague in 1985.

this genre probably cannot be further advanced in terms of gymnastics."[497] The individual pieces performed by the military barely varied at all, and thus symbolically affirmed at each Spartakiad the regime's stability and permanence. All were composed of a dynamic and even breath-taking entrance, in which nearly fourteen thousand soldiers – accompanied only by their hollering "hurrah" – sprinted from Strahov Stadium's three entrance gates toward the grandstand reserved for government officials. It took less than forty seconds for them to occupy all of the stadium's place markers to perform "in front of their commander."[498] The dramatic effect of the entrance ("A bull is coming through the east gate, / a rose ring in his nostril,"

497   Seliger, V. a spol.: "Výzkum fyziologické a pedagogické náročnosti skladeb hromadných vystoupení", p. 674. The authors of the article also question the appropriateness of "exercises on the bodies of participants lying down which to a certain extent contradicts the principles of health and aesthetics." Ibid.
498   "Neplánované krycí zabarvení". *Československý sport*, vol. 23, 30. 6. 1975, p. 6.

28. Zdeněk Lhoták photograph from the *Spartakiad* series documenting the military's performance at a district Spartakiad in Prague in 1985.

wrote Jaroslav Čejka in the poem "A Dream of the Stadium"[499]) was further increased by a flyover by fighter planes, which "exceeded a thousand kilometers per hour just fifty meters above the stadium."[500] Thanks to months of training several hours a day and weeks of rehearsals at Strahov Stadium, the performance itself could be composed of difficult exercises and a complex choreography that no other piece could compare to.[501] The soldiers formed abstract,

499 Čejka, Jaroslav: "Sen o stadiónu". In: O. Mohyla – K. Procházka (eds.): *Verše ze Strahova,* unpagin.

500 "Strahov plný ruchu". *Rudé právo*, vol. 55, 21. 6. 1975, p. 8.

501 The military piece required four hundred hours of practice. See Veselý, Josef (ed.): *Směr Strahov. Sborník nejdůležitějších informací, metodických návodů, námětů, básní a písní k rozvíjení kulturně výchovné a sportovní činnosti v průběhu přípravy a konání Čs. spartakiády 1990.* Naše vojsko, Prague 1989, p. 11. See for instance the interview with one of the co-authors of the military piece Jiří Kašpar – Matoušek, Jaroslav: "Cvičení, jaké svět neviděl". *Rudé právo*, vol. 55,

rectangular compositions (*Rudé právo* thought they resembled "Žižka's Hussite wagon fort"[502]) and avoided any round shapes that were exclusively for the women's pieces. A highlight of the military compositions consisted of the "live fireworks," i.e. acrobatic leaps of select military gymnasts from a five-meter-high human pyramid into the arms of other waiting soldiers.[503]

Part of the symbolism here was also the soldiers' courage in facing the risks of this performance in which the spectators would "hold their breath." Injuries occurred quite often during rehearsals; this is attested to by a secret military report from October 1965 in which the individual injuries are listed, including serious injuries requiring several months of treatment, such as concussions (in most cases – 57 percent – caused by two heads colliding), vertebrae fractures and spinal cord injuries.[504] Yet the report concludes that the total "losses" of less than four percent did not exceed the planned quota for normal combat exercises.[505]

The body of men in these military's pieces was more exposed than was the case in other pieces. The color of the tanned skin throughout Strahov Stadium was one of the most impressive Spartakiad symbols. *Rudé právo* accurately wrote that soldiers dressed only in "snow-white shorts" and white sneakers performed "in the simplest,

21. 5. 1975, p. 8. Yet the perfection of the military performances lay in opposition to one of the basic traditional elements of Sokol and Spartakiad performances, i.e. that the performances were not intended to be of the elite and that the exercises were aimed at the public at large, at the masses, in the sense that everyone was supposed to be able, with a little effort and practice to perform the exercises.

502 Jelínek, Jan – Kropáč, Zdeněk – Stano, Jiří: "Obdiv obráncům vlasti". *Rudé právo*, vol. 65, 1. 7. 1985, p. 5.

503 "Pod avantgardním rudým lidstva znamením". *Rudé právo*, vol. 55, 30. 6. 1975, p. 3. The pyramids of soldier bodies first appeared at the 1960 Spartakiad.

504 VHA, f. MNO – 1965, k. 241, inv. n. 767, Zpráva velitele západního vojenského okruhu o úrazovosti příslušníků armády při III. celostátní spartakiádě.

505 The many injuries are also attested to by the fact that the military's expenditure of over 140,000 crowns in compensation since it was considered to be work-related. VHA, f. MNO – 1965, k. 153, inv. n. 446, Zpráva o prověrce finančně ekonomické činnosti štábu a podřízených útvarů vytvořených pro zabezpečení III. celostátní spartakiády.

yet most effective outfit." The military's performance was the only one (except for perhaps the junior women) in which an emphasis was placed on a body's perfect appearance. In the photographs of other performances we see, along with bodies satisfying the day's ideals of beauty, also less perfect bodies as proof of Spartakiad's mass appeal and that it was for all of the people. Yet the military's pieces did not allow for any imperfections. The soldier's muscular tanned bodies, often photographed from below so that they stood out against the sky, testified to both the "strength" and "beauty" of the Czechoslovak people. The eroticizing of the military performances evokes the cult of the body of the late 19th century in both Turner and Sokol exercises.

Photography and film footage documenting the muddy bodies of soldiers in their struggle against the elements was a specific genre for representing the military pieces. This was also a frequent motif with other Spartakiads and Sokol pieces and was extensively developed by both Jiří Weiss in his documentary film *A Song of the Slet*, and by cinematographer Jan Špáta in Rudolf Krejčík's documentary film *The 1975 Czechoslovak Spartakiad* (moreover, the filmmakers ironically played with the lyrics to the Spartakiad song "Singing to the Sun"). Yet it was only in the near nakedness of the military participants that this genre came to the fore. Perhaps Zdeněk Lhoták best utilized it in his photographic series *Spartakiad* taken at a single Prague district Spartakiad in 1985. In an interview, Lhoták described how the bad weather, which transformed the stadium into a stinking muddy lake, turned a boring work assignment to document a district Spartakiad into an extraordinary aesthetic experience and an artistic challenge.[506]

---

506 Interview with Zdeněk Lhoták, 10. dubna 2001, Prague Author's archive. According to Lhoták, the stench was caused by the fact that the grass had been fertilized a few days prior to the performance. See also Lhoták, Zdeněk: "Model Society". *Aperture*, 1998, vol. 47, n. 152, p. 53.

Lhoták had been able to make the most of the ten-minute performance to take a series of photographs combining details with views from the upper reaches of the stadium. This series eventually won international awards (second place in the World Press Photo sports category in 1986), but did not correspond to the usual representation of the Czechoslovak military, and Lhoták claims to have encountered resistance in publishing the photographs. This seems to have been more a case of caution on the side of certain editors, since the genre of the muddy soldiers was an enduring part of the Spartakiad's visual representation. The soldiers' struggle with the stadium's muddy field and the climbing of slippery bodies by other recruits evoked a number of useful ideological motifs. In addition to the obvious motif of overcoming adversity, it was mainly a message of a shared fate with one's country and the merging of the army with the people. *Rudé právo* described the military's piece at the 1975 Czechoslovak Spartakiad as such: "The soldiers boldly assailed the muddy ground. There they were no longer tan and white, but merged with the color of the stadium's field. They seemed to be blending with, to be growing into the earth – an earth whose peace and calm was entrusted to their hands – the Czechoslovak People's Army."[507]

507 Houfová, J.: "Skvělá přehlídka mládí a krásy socialistického Československa". *Rudé právo*, vol. 55, 30. 6. 1975, p. 2.

A RETURN TO SOKOL

One of the telling shifts that occurred during the three Spartakiads held during the "normalization" period consisted of a change in how the Sokol tradition was viewed. For most of the "normalization" period the organizers avoided direct references to Sokol and its Slets – a contrast with the preceding Spartakiads where the Sokol tradition was directly followed up on or even competed with. *Rudé právo* went the farthest in this, declaring only the "revolutionary legacy of the workers' Spartakiads" and the three state-wide Spartakiads as representative of the traditional gymnastic performances.[508] Journalists at *Rudé právo* sought out elderly participants (most of whom had previously belonged to Sokol) who would boast of taking part in the 1921 communist Spartakiad at Maniny in Prague.[509] In fact, it was not the Sokol tradition itself that was feared, nor a comparison of the Slets and the Spartakiads. In their size, organizational preparations, choreography and the level of difficulty of their performances, the Spartakiads had long surpassed the Sokol Slets. This was actually a "normalization" reaction to the revival of Sokol in 1968. *Rudé právo* in particular adhered literally to the text "Lessons from an Assessment of the Past Development of the Physical Education Organization," in which Sokol was named

---

[508] See for instance "Strahovské finále". *Rudé právo*, vol. 55, 28. 6. 1975, p. 1; "Hold tradici i dnešku". Ibid, p. 1; "Slavná tradice". Ibid, p. 3. *Rudé právo* did not avoid the continuity of the mass gymnastic performances, but did avoid using the words "Slet" and "Sokol." In 1985, it e.g. referred to an eighty-year-old participant who had been "an active participant of all mass gymnastic performances at Strahov since 1920." In: "Sjednoceni touhou uspět". *Rudé právo*, vol. 65, 27. 6. 1985, p. 8.

[509] See for instance Felt, Karel: "Vrátit se ještě jednou". *Rudé právo*, vol. 60, 28. 6. 1980, p. 8. *Rudé právo* even dusted off the ancient rivalry between the communist and social democratic gymnastic movement. It reprinted a reader's letter reminiscing how in 1921 they had marched around the Letná stadium, where the "rightist olympiad" were being held, on their way to Maniny: "Musicians 'blew' *Down with All Tyrants and Betrayers* and we saw there how many members of the DTJ tore the emblems from their caps and joined us. Křivánek, Josef : "…a to nám napsali". *Rudé právo*, vol. 55, 28. 6. 1975, p. 8.

as the main factor causing the rift and "rightist deviations" during the Prague Spring.[510] Other media designated for a different audience was somewhat more relaxed regarding Sokol traditions. For instance, Krejčík's documentary on the 1980 Spartakiad referred in the introduction to the tradition of Sokol Slets, particularly the 1938 Slet, and quoted from the writings of Miroslav Tyrš.

Nevertheless, the final Spartakiad in 1985 saw a reversal in the relationship to the Sokol tradition. For the first time during the "normalization" period a direct historical line was drawn between the Slets and Spartakiads. In addition to the traditional laying of wreaths at the tombs of revolutionary leaders at Vítkov Hill, the Spartakiad ritual was broadened to include a tribute to Miroslav Tyrš at his tomb in the Olšany Cemetery.[511]

References to Sokol appeared in the performances themselves at the 1985 Spartakiad – both in the women's performance, in which the famous swarm of women from 1938 and 1948 was evoked, and the men's entrance to Suk's Sokol march "Into a New Life." The three-part historical documentary film on gymnastic performances entitled *A Symphony Written by Movement* and completed in 1988 shows a clear developmental line from the Sokol Slets to the last Spartakiad. The 1948 putsch does not represent a significant turning point within the film's structure: the first part of the film describes the development from Tyrš to the 1938 Slet, the second part the post-war performances at Strahov in 1947–1965, and the third the Spartakiads during the "normalization" era.[512] This shift was part of a more general search for the lowest common denominator among the events' spectators, participants and directors. The Sokol

---

510   "Poučení z hodnocení vývoje tělovýchovné organizace v uplynulém období schválené XII. plenárním zasedáním ÚV ČSTV dne 25. září 1971". In: J. Marek (ed.): *Za socialistický systém tělesné výchovy*, pp. 200–215.

511   "Generálka se vydařila". *Rudé právo*, vol. 65, 27. 6. 1985, p. 1.

512   Krejčík, Rudolf: *Symfonie psané pohybem. Tradice hromadných tělovýchovných vystoupení. Část II: Strahovská vystoupení 1947–1965*. Krátký film, Prague 1987.

tradition, which was always an important part of the participants' motivation and of their family histories, was once again acknowledged as possessing officially recognized value.

František Kožík's biography of Miroslav Tyrš was published in 1987 and in many ways characterized the important change in how the Sokol past was viewed. Kožík is of such importance in examining the continuity and discontinuity of Czechoslovak mass gymnastics that a more detailed look is warranted.

František Kožík came from a traditional Sokol family. His father, a judge, left the Catholic Church with the rest of his family and became a gymnastic director at the Sokol in Uherské Hradiště. Upon his death he was, in accordance with his wishes, buried in his ceremonial Sokol costume.[513]

František Kožík was also a lawyer by trade, but made a name for himself as a writer in the early days of the Nazi occupation with the publication of his first biographical novel *The Greatest of the Pierrots*, which, according to the criticism of Václav Černý at that time was "an unabashed example of opportunist play with a national audience."[514] In 1942, Kožík became a dramaturge for the protectorate radio ("It certainly was not a good time," he wrote in his memoirs, "but I knew that it was now up to me to keep broadcasting Czech plays, otherwise German broadcasting would take over their time."[515]). A year later he even took part in a Nazi-organized expedition of European writers to mass graves in Katyn, from where he left with the "belief that a beautiful opportunity for those who heed the call of the age is offered by a united Europe, protected by

513 Kožík, František: *Vzpomínky.* Orbis, Prague 1995, p. 266.
514 Černý, Václav: *Paměti II. Křik Koruny české: 1938–1945. Náš kulturní odboj za války.* Atlantis, Brno 1992, pp. 193–197.
515 Kožík, F.: *Vzpomínky,* p. 208. Kožík received from Emanuel Moravec a national award as one of the writers who "served the Nazi idea and would continue to serve it." See Černý, V.: *Paměti II. Křik Koruny české,* p. 300.

German troops."[516] After the war, Kožík had to answer for his activities before a committee of writers chaired by Václav Černý who in his memoirs mocked him for appearing before the committee "in the impeccably decorated and ironed uniform of a Czechoslovak lieutenant in reserves, even with patent-leather shoes as if he had just arrived from the barricades – that is, if there are even any patent-leather lieutenant barricades.[517] Nevertheless, during the preparations for the 11th All-Sokol Slet, Sokol appealed to him as a long-time member to edit the prestigious Slet commemorative book.[518]

In 1952, Kožík once again appeared in the role of an eyewitness of the Katyn massacre, but this time called it "groundless slander, deserving of condemnation."[519] Three years later, now as director of the official state entertainment industry, he became involved in promoting Spartakiad, and his prose and verse then accompanied all Spartakiads from 1955 to 1985, when he spoke of the event as a "magnificent gift to the party."[520]

516   "Básník F. Kožík o Katynu". *České slovo*, vol. 35, 8. 5. 1943, p. 5. Kožík's testimony and its various transformations are clearly documented in a study by Borák, Mečislav: "Zločin v Katyni a jeho české a slovenské souvislosti". In: Miroslav Šesták – Emil Voráček (eds.): *Evropa mezi Německem a Ruskem. Sborník prací k sedmdesátinám Jaroslava Valenty*. Historický ústav Akademie věd České republiky, Prague 2000, pp. 505–522. See also ABS, f. Agenturní svazky, a. n. 785 938 (Medard).

517   Černý, Václav: *Paměti III (1945–1972)*. Atlantis, Brno 1992, p. 59. See also Kožík, F.: *Vzpomínky*, p. 238.

518   Kožík, F.: *Vzpomínky*, p. 256. See also for instance Kožík, František: "Všechno bylo nečekaně krásné a nové". In: R. Procházka (ed.): *Památník IX. sletu všesokolského*, p. 146.

519   Kožík, František: "Katyň očima pravdy". *Práce*, vol. 8, 13. 3. 1952, p. 6. Reprinted as "Svědectví o ,katynském případu'". *Rudé právo*, vol. 32, 14. 3. 1952, p. 3. Here Kožík wrote that he had read through several of the victims' diaries and that it was clear that they were referring to German captivity.

520   See for instance Kožík, František: "Jeden a půl miliónu". In: Ctibor Rybár – Jan Novotný (eds.): *V rytmu krásy a radosti. 15 let československé tělovýchovy*. Státní tělovýchovné nakladatelství, Prague 1960; Kožík, František: "Než mávl červený praporek". *Literární noviny*, 1960, vol. 9, n. 26, p. 1; Introductory text to Mohyla, O. – Procházka, K. (eds.): *Verše ze Strahova*, unpag. In 1956 he was an involuntary witness to the Hungarian uprising in Budapest. For Kožík's somewhat inaccurate testimony of the Budapest events (Ernö Gerö was apparently hanged from a lamppost) see Kožík, F.: *Vzpomínky*, pp. 291–298. In the late 1950s, Kožík became an informant for the Secret Police, was given the code name Medard and less than successfully spied

Kožík already presented at the 1960 Spartakiad a wholly non-marxist, though strongly nationalistic story of the arduous path of Czechoslovak gymnastics through history all the way to its culmination in the form of Spartakiads based on the notion, which he understood quite literally, that a nation consists of a single collective organism.[521] In Kožík's view the phrase "a healthy soul in a healthy body" does not apply only to individuals, but also to entire nations. The freedom of Slavic nations went hand in hand with physical ability, which is attested to by the painting of mid-19th century Romantic Josef Mánes, "who convincingly portrayed that noble and robust race." Likewise, a healthy national spirit was evident in the valor of Czech knights and the rigor of Hussite men and women. Yet Kožík believed that the nation's physical ability also declined during the "dark" ages when the national spirit was suppressed. "The unhealthy national soul listlessly endured a general weakness," wrote Kožík, "the entire nation had drooped shoulders and a sunken chest, if we do not count the rising class of the bourgeoisie that suffered from obesity." Tyrš and Sokol then ensured that the awakening national spirit was accompanied by a revival of the national community's physical powers. Hovering over Czechoslovak physical culture between the wars was "an unhealthy fog of all the diseases of professionalism." The Czechoslovak people had to wait until their "true liberation" in May 1945 for a real boom in physical education. After the communist putsch of 1948, the national body was "newly oxidized and got fresh air" and gymnastics and sport was finally unified and freed of all "influences of the selfish and ambitious interests of individuals and parties."

on Jaroslav Seifert. ABS, f. Agenturní svazky, a. n. 785 938 (Medard). See also Stehlík, Michal: "Spisovatel František Kožík a Státní bezpečnost. Cesta ke konci spolupráce 1968–1982". In: Pavel Andrš – Jana Čechurová – Luboš Velek et al.: *Posláním historik. Pocta prof. Robertu Kvačkovi k 80. narozeninám.* Nakladatelství Lidové noviny, Prague 2012, pp. 611–622.

521 Kožík, František: "Jeden a půl miliónu", unpagin.

Kožík's 1987 biographical novel on Miroslav Tyrš entitled *Věnec vavřínový* (The Laurel Wreath) presents a wholly unproblematic picture of the national past.[522] There is no trace of the leftist criticism of Sokol – the national pathos, the corporatism, feigned non-partisanship, the bourgeois moralizing. Tyrš is portrayed as a man of a socially conscious, aesthetically sentient spirit, but also of a perfectly wrought body. It was through Sokol that Tyrš attempted to convey his physical perfection to the broader Czech national community that up until then had suffered from idleness ("Weakened muscles, drooped shoulders, bent spine. They therefore weren't even able to think about resisting oppression"[523]). A physically and mentally competent nation trained in Sokol discipline was then able to rise up like a "bastion against western Germanism."[524] Here Kožík was successfully dusting off the traditional Sokol historical narrative for the needs of the newly discovered interests of communist leadership in previously taboo national traditions and festivities. In 1988, he received the title of National Artist and the approval of regime-favored and anti-Semitic writer Alexej Pludek.[525]

After the Velvet Revolution of 1989 (just as in 1968), Kožík became involved in renewing Sokol ("we brought our ardor into its impoverished ranks"[526]) and celebrated in his writings the new political power embodied by the Civic Forum political movement.[527] His verse also appears as the introduction of the commemorative book for the first post-communist Slet in 1994 ("We are watching over your legacy / on guard – / against the enemy, envy and treachery. / We know our mission and objective: / a clean shield – and always

---

522   Kožík, František: *Věnec vavřínový.* Československý spisovatel, Prague 1987.
523   Kožík, F.: *Věnec vavřínový*, p. 75.
524   Ibid, p. 154.
525   See for instance Pludek, Alexej: "K neuvěřitelným narozeninám. Národní umělec František Kožík osmdesátiletý". *Rudé právo*, vol. 69, 16. 5. 1989, p. 5.
526   Kožík, F.: *Vzpomínky*, p. 362.
527   Kožík, František: "Nezapomenutelné vánoce". *Lidová demokracie*, vol. 45, 30. 12. 1989, p. 4.

at the front!"[528]) It is clear from Kožík's memoirs published a year later that he did not consider the changed views accompanying his work to be conjuncturalism. Instead he viewed the arc linking his post-war recollection of the "beautiful face of president Masaryk" to the post-1989 celebration of Václav Havel as the constant in which he consistently contributed to and sacrificed himself for the "national destiny" despite all the political upheavals.

✕✕✕

In several ways, the story of the final three Spartakiads disrupts the set view of the Czechoslovak "normalization". First of all, it is clear that Ladislav Holý's theory on the ardently guarded border between the private and public sphere, which was supposed to represent one of the cornerstones of "normalization" stability, did not apply here.[529]

The Spartakiad example shows that, in addition to the weekend-house culture and other escape strategies, there were also many "more engaged" forms of the "normalization" *modus vivendi*. The Spartakiads also are not an example of an invasion of privacy, "a politicization of the private," as Paulina Bren characterized it in her study on "normalization" television series.[530] Instead, the opposite process was taking place that we could call the privatization of the

---

528   Kožík, František: "Myšlenka Tyršova". In: *XII. všesokolský slet. Praha 1994*. Česká obec sokolská, Prague – Litomyšl 1995, p. 7.
529   Holý, Ladislav: *The Little Czech and the Great Czech Nation. National Identity and the Post-Communist Transformation of Society*. Cambridge University Press, Cambridge 1996.
530   Bren, Paulina: *The Greengrocer and His TV*: the Culture of Communism after the 1968 Prague Spring. Cornell University Press, Ithaca 2010. The term was originally used by Lauren Berlant to describe the reduction and "privatization" of the public sphere and citizenship during the Reagan years. Berlant, Lauren: *The Queen of America Goes to Washington City. Essays on Sex and Citizenship*. Duke University Press, Durham 1997.

political, i.e. a symbolic application of the private world's values to the public sphere of political and social matters. By visualizing the public sphere as the private sphere, as family, the alienation of political power and of the "normalization" society was concealed.

Secondly, the rigidity of "normalization" Spartakiads seemingly corresponds with the general historical view of "normalization". Stemming mainly from dissidents' reflection of the age, namely Václav Havel's characterization of "normalization" as "timeless," the prevailing view of "normalization" is that of a period distinguished by a waning vitality of the ruling elite, ideological fading, and the dawdling away of days under a tedious regime that was on its last legs. This was not, however, the case for the Spartakiads. That Spartakiads were unchanging was the intentional choice of their organizers, and this in itself contributed to the creation of an image of peace and stability. It seems that the unchanging facet of "normalization" Spartakiads was not a reflection of social reality, but instead an attempt to symbolically "mask" the deep social changes that were disrupting the stability of the power relations existing at that time. Yet the desire for "peace and order" was not only limited to the party's ruling elite for the sake of maintaining power. It was also shared by a significant part of society terrified of hasty social changes. Not only was "normalization" society not "timeless," it was exposed to severe modernization and demographic changes, innovations in technology, the waning of experiences from World War II, the globalization of culture and an increase in free time, among other things. As far as physical education is concerned, there was a dramatic increase in individual and competitive sports to the detriment of traditional calisthenics, especially among men, which led to the almost total feminization of gymnastics, which had originally been exclusively a male, paramilitary "sport."

Finally, neither do "normalization" Spartakiads support the theory of a gradual dissolution of the ruling power and the regime's ideological burnout. Spartakiads therefore did not share the fate of other communist rituals as Christel Lane describes for the Soviet Union, or Roman Krakovský recounts for the Czechoslovak May Day festivities.[531] On the contrary, as a social ritual the "normalization" Spartakiads enjoyed great success and utilized consensual symbols to create the image of a stable and cohesive solidarity. The fact that prominent avant-garde artists no longer took part in them and that similarly prominent foreign guests such as Tristan Tzara and Fernand Léger no longer applauded them[532] does not change anything (the only exception was Juan Antonio Samaranch, President of the International Olympic Committee, a regular guest at the Spartakiads and at East German Turnfests, who as the former Spanish sports administrator and minister of sports under the Franco regime knew a thing or two about mass choreography). After all, "normalization" Spartakiads were not designed to dazzle metropolitan artists and intellectuals, but to have an effect on "normalization" society at large.

531 Lane, Christel: *The Rites of Rulers. Ritual in Industrial Society – the Soviet Case.* Cambridge University Press, Cambridge 1981; Krakovský, Roman: *Rituel du 1er mai en Tchécoslovaquie: 1948–1989.* L'Harmattan, Paris – Budapest – Torino 2004.
532 Raúl Castro also witnessed the 1960 Spartakiad, proclaiming it one of the wonders of the world. See *Československá spartakiáda 1980. 100 otázek a 100 odpovědí.* Mladá fronta, Prague 1980, p. 4.

The Organization
of Spartakiads

In mobilizing hundreds of thousands of gymnasts, tens of thousands trainers and thousands of organizers, the Spartakiads were one of the greatest operations in logistics, a "test" of state socialism. The enormous organizational task that they represented became in itself a political symbol, a promise that the state would manage other organizational challenges just as efficiently. In this sense, the Spartakiads were to be a kind of substitute for inept state planning. In this *ersatz* state planning, each individual ultimately was to end up on his place marker and perform in perfect lucidity the tasks assigned to him by an expert team. Similarly, the organization of Spartakiads and the participants' performances were a promise of the creation of a "new person" and a "new society." A key ideological aspect of the communist regime – the transformation of a sprawling crowd into a sovereign, but also highly malleable people – took center stage every five years. A single social being, a single national body was, through strict discipline, to rise from the mass of individualism. The Spartakiad organizers themselves were aware of this almost mystical transformation, as attested to by the words of Vilém Mucha regarding the time needed to practice: "There are only nine months from September 1954 to June 1955. The same amount of time needed for a fetus to be born."[533]

This chapter examines several key aspects of the organization of Spartakiads, though it certainly does not completely cover all the issues and problems that the preparation of this social ritual represented. We will first explore the creation and implementation of a specific professional discourse among the top Spartakiad organizers, who were largely former Sokol officials. The core of this discourse was formed by adapting their professional experiences and specific gymnastic practices to the milieu of state-socialist gymnastics; its starting point was the harsh criticism of practices of the

533 Mucha, V.: *První celostátní spartakiáda 1955: věcí všeho pracujícího lidu Československa,* p. 11.

first half of the 1950s, including the first Spartakiad of 1955. The crucial influence of former Sokol members is evidenced by a more general phenomenon typical for the stabilization phase of a communist regime: the expertization of decision-making not only in highly specialized matters, but also in fundamental conceptual questions. In the example of Spartakiads, it is evident in how the political leadership, having learned their lesson from the confusion and ineffectiveness of the "revolutionary" phase of communism, increasingly left decision-making up to non-party experts. The organization and management of the first 1955 Spartakiad, discussed separately here, illustrated the failure of "revolutionary" work methods that necessitated the direct involvement of the highest party bodies. Beginning with the 2nd Spartakiad of 1960, a stable management system based on a professional staff of several hundred experts was set up that worked on the endless five-year cycles of Spartakiads. The greatest organizational challenge consisted of the work with the gymnasts themselves, their training and accommodation in Prague. This will be examined in another part of the chapter, focusing on the creation of a "useful," analytical crowd and the difficulties that – as the organizers themselves admitted – were presented by the unpredictable behavior of the participants. While these issues are explored here from the organizers' perspective, the next chapter will take a look at these matters from the participants' views. Following up on the first chapter of this book, the architectural framework, within which the transformation of the participants into an analytical crowd took place, will be examined – both the tangible architecture of the Strahov complex and the intangible architecture of the marked field. The final part will focus on the expenses related to Spartakiads within the specific milieu of state socialism's moral economy.

PROFESSIONAL DISCOURSE

The professional discourse on the Spartakiads, which gradually developed in specialized workplaces such as Charles University's Faculty of Physical Education and Sports and the Scientific Council of the Czechoslovak Physical Education Association, formulated the guidelines by which the Spartakiad compositions were to be created, trained and organized. This discourse consisted of articles in specialized journals and, above all, the internal discussions among Spartakiad experts as "ritual specialists." This discussion was quite practical at its core: it was a *de facto* generalization of deep personal experiences with the exercising, creation and organization of gymnastic

29. Shooting Martin Fryč's film on the 1955 Spartakiad (photo Václav Chochola).

performances.[534] Former Sokol members took part in most of the expert discussions, and thus the ensuing professional discourse was strongly influenced by fundamental theoretical works of Sokol figures, including Tyrš and, above all, Augustin Očenášek (whose working class and mining background was emphasized[535]). Inspired by European trends of the day, Očenášek had attempted to modernize Sokol exercises. The Spartakiad discourse also adopted from the Sokol milieu a critical spirit and tendency to constantly seek new possibilities for creating and training Spartakiad compositions.

The first significant confrontation of Spartakiad specialists was the scientific conference "Theoretical and Methodical Foundations for Mass Gymnastic Performances" in February 1956, which reacted to problems concerning the preparation and run of the first Spartakiad. All basic principles of the later Spartakiad professional discourse already appeared in this discussion. Many of the talks addressed critically the policy of "sportification" of Sokol, i.e. replacing traditional calisthenics with competitive sports. They also criticized the explicit political symbolism, or the "formalism" of the 1st All-State Spartakiad. A leading figure of the discussion and of the professional critical reflection in general was Ladislav Serbus, originally a Sokol instructor and secondary school gym teacher, who, following the February 1948 communist putsch, became a member of the Central Committee of the Czechoslovak Sokol Association, the founder and rector of the Physical Education and Sports Institute (1953–58) and later the dean of Charles University's Faculty of Physical Education and Sports.[536]

534 Ladislav Serbus e.g. stated that he had drawn his conclusions from, in addition to research, "his own experience as a participant, instructor, teacher and author of gymnastic performance pieces." Serbus, Ladislav: "Historický vývoj masových tělovýchovných vystoupení u nás". In: *Vědecká konference o teoretických a metodických základech masových tělovýchovných vystoupení*, p. 1.
535 Penniger, Evžen: "Poznámky k referátům". In: *Vědecká konference o teoretických a metodických základech masových tělovýchovných vystoupení*, p. 171.
536 Serbus returned the the previous discussion thirty years later, See Serbus, L.: "Diskusní příspěvek", pp. 36–37. See also Kössl, Jiří: "Za univ. prof. PhDr. Ladislavem Serbusem".

The basic strategy of the Spartakiad experts, which then actually legitimized all other aspects of the Spartakiad discourse, was their defense of the Sokol practice as part of the progressive national tradition. This consisted of several basic arguments. First, Ladislav Serbus believed there was a need to separate the Sokol practice from Sokol ideology and distinguish between the physical exercises and the physical culture. For this purpose, Serbus drew from Stalin's text *Marxism and Problems of Linguistics* in comparing physical exercises to language and the physical culture to literature.[537] While language (or physical exercises) can serve both a capitalist and socialist order, literature (or the physical culture) serves either a bourgeois or socialist order. To support this argument he stated that social-democratic and later communist gymnastics had taken over the practice of Sokol exercises, and gave the specific example of parallel or (from the perspective of gymnastics) identical gymnastics performances from 1921: of the first communist Spartakiad and of the first social-democratic Olympiad. Serbus deduced from this that it would be incorrect to assume that by establishing a new socialist order there would be created new physical exercises typical for a socialist physical culture. He also emphasized "for the information of those comrades fond of violent changes," that a socialist physical culture "would not fall from the sky." The change would come – here he quoted Stalin – by "gradually amassing elements of a new quality, i.e. by the gradual dying off of elements of the former quality."

Another argument used by Serbus in his text was the assertion that even though the Sokol ideology and Sokol leadership served the bourgeoisie, the Sokol membership was working-class and its

---

Teorie a praxe tělesné výchovy, 1987, vol. 35, n. 11, p. 704; Serbus, Ladislav: *Tělesná kultura v podmínkách socialistické alternativy vědeckotechnické revoluce. Plán věd. práce Univ. Karlovy v Praze "Socialistické Československo dnes a v roce 2000"*. Fakulta tělesné výchovy a sportu Univerzity Karlovy, Prague 1973. Also see the extensive personal collection of Ladislav Serbus kept in the National Archive (f. 1369).
537 Serbus, L.: "Historický vývoj masových tělovýchovných vystoupení u nás", pp. 4–5.

exercises contributed to strengthening the physical and moral power of the working class. Proof of this was the fact that active Sokol members included the second communist president Antonín Zápotocký and his father, the prominent trade union leader Ladislav Zápotocký, who had participated in a number of Slets and had even been the founder of several local chapters (even though he was later expelled from Sokol).[538] Serbus and other writers could also fall back on the then statements of the communist party which tried to win Sokol membership over to its side, e.g., Klement Gottwald's aforementioned 1926 article "The Slet and Us."

A third argument that somewhat contradicts the previous two was the assertion that Tyrš's ideas and Sokol's role in the "struggle for national liberation" were in fact always progressive and in accordance with Marxist doctrine. It was not difficult to support this argument with plenty of fitting quotes from Klement Gottwald during the preparation for the 11th All-Sokol Slet of 1948 and when the communist party openly embraced the Sokol tradition.[539]

Not only was the rehabilitation of calisthenics and their mass performances based on the acceptance of the axiom on Sokol's progressiveness, a return to Sokol's understanding of "natural" movement was also derived from it. In criticizing hitherto practices, the work of Augustin Očenášek is often cited with its emphasis on every movement being physiologically justifiable, efficient and purposeful and its eclipsing of the symbolic aspect.[540] Yet at the 1st All-State Spartakiad, movement often did not come from "the biological need of

---

538 Cf. "The Speech of President Antonín Zápotocký at the Assembly of the State Committee for Gymnastics and Sports." Zápotocký's ambivalent relationship to Sokol is also apparent in his novel *Rudá záře nad Kladnem* (A Red Glare over Kladno) in which he describes, among other things, Lenin's interest in Sokol and his recommendation to control it rather than creating a parallel workers' gymnastics movement. Zápotocký, Antonín: *Rudá záře nad Kladnem*. Práce, Prague 1951, p. 313.

539 Serbus, L.: "Historický vývoj masových tělovýchovných vystoupení u nás", pp. 14–15.

540 The exercises of the first Spartakiad represented for former Sokol creators a return to obsolete "theatrical" forms of Sokol exercises performed before and immediately following the First World War.

the exerciser's organism"[541] (a frequent complaint of former Sokol members), but instead was intended to imitate various work tasks or symbolize the work of industrial and agricultural machines. "It is unnatural for a grown person," protested Serbus, "to consciously assume the role of a factory machine, a mandrel, mowing machine, etc. [...] Is it then our goal for those exercising to move as mechanically as a machine works?" Especially problematic was the imitation of sport disciplines. As Evžen Penniger writes, Sokol had adverse experiences with it in the past.[542] Included in the exercises of the 1912 Slet, for instance, was a highly stylized way of disc-throwing, which allegedly resulted in the participants never properly learning how to throw the disc. Penniger worried that such exercises at the 1st All-State Spartakiad, in which the trade union juniors demonstrated the disc throw with both their right and left hands, would have similar consequences. In his theoretical work of mass gymnastic performances, Serbus therefore recommended that the "laws of biomechanics" be respected at the next Spartakiad and that the exercises be composed of the "utmost economic" and graceful movements: "A biomechanically proper movement is also graceful, and thus aesthetically pleasing. It is a movement performed with the amount of energy that corresponds to the purpose that it strives for, or to the content that it should express."[543]

541 Holomek, Antonín: "Diskusní příspěvek". In: *Vědecká konference o teoretických a metodických základech masových tělovýchovných vystoupení*, p. 137.
542 Penniger, Evžen: "Poznámky k referátům", p. 170.
543 Serbus, L. – Kos, B. – Mihule, J.: *Historický vývoj a základy tělovýchovných vystoupení v ČSSR*, p. 124. However, the expert criticism was for the most part ignored in preparing the Spartakiads, and the stylized movements and games also appeared in the following 1960 Spartakiad: The expert assessment of the piece for the younger pupils entitled A Joyous Spring explains: "The games used, however, lost their character and were performed in a stylized manner, therefore losing their joyousness. The participants' interest in practicing other parts dropped; the children listlessly practiced them, especially the boys. The number of participants in the clubs dropped. The practices were then transferred to the schools where they were obligatory." See Blablová, Jarmila: "Radostná jar. Skladba mladšího žactva 9–11letého". *Teorie a praxe tělesné výchovy*, 1961, vol. 9, zvláštní číslo: Výsledky výzkumu II. celostátní spartakiády 1960, pp. 11–12.

Another requirement stemmed from the demand for a "natural" movement of the participants: the composition's adequate symbolism. According to Serbus and other former Sokol creators, the compositions were to express those ideas that could be expressed through collective exercises and were to avoid "formalism," i.e. the external display of non-gymnastic significations. This was once again a reaction to former Slet practices in which theatrical elements often overshadowed the exercises themselves. The Sokol organizers had only recently held tempestuous discussions on the modernization of Sokol exercises in accordance with international trends at that time. With its explicit symbolism, the formation of participants into letters and shapes, the 1st All-State Spartakiad had completely contradicted this trend. Serbus writes that a Spartakiad composition "cannot strive to fill the role of a political editorial,"[544] but must indirectly affect spectators with the beauty of the participants' synchronous movements and their joy from the exercises. ("The ideological effect [of the piece] will certainly be greater on the spectators – even if a political tendency is not explicitly expressed in it – if it is performed masterfully than if a piece with ideological attributes is performed poorly.[545]) Authors of Spartakiad pieces, such as Jarmila Kostková, criticized ideologically tinged compositions that exceeded the "expressive possibilities of a calisthenics performance."[546]

For instance, the piece for the trade union men and women at the first Spartakiad was intended to express the following ideological message: "The pieces should express the glorification of work and its

On criticism of surviving "formalism"in Spartakiad pieces See Holub, Miroslav: "O příštích spartakiádách". *Plamen*, 1960, vol. 2, n. 8, pp. 150–151.

544 Serbus, Ladislav: "Závěr diskuse o teoretických a metodických základech masových tělovýchovných vystoupení". In: *Vědecká konference o teoretických a metodických základech masových tělovýchovných vystoupení*, p. 185.

545 Serbus, L. – Kos, B. – Mihule, J.: *Historický vývoj a základy tělovýchovných vystoupení v ČSSR*, p. 128.

546 Kostková, Jarmila: "Některé poznatky ke zlepšení postupu při hodnocení a výběru skladeb pro větší tělovýchovné slavnosti". *Vědecká konference o teoretických a metodických základech masových tělovýchovných vystoupení*, p. 112.

victory. They should show the share of versatile physical education in preparing the new socialist person to perform his great tasks in building up socialism. An exercise should depict work in various production sectors from strenuous manual labor to the ease and facilitated tempo in using mechanization, which should be expressed by the exercise's appropriate tempo. It should also be a tribute to work, peace and friendship with the USSR." As Kostková pointed out, it was this kind of unfeasible assignment that discouraged many from submitting projects to the competition. Those who did submit them opted for one of three strategies:

"1) they resorted to symbolism and verbal expression of the theme, 2) they did not take the theme into consideration, 3) they partially observed the requirements, which was evident in the unbalanced nature of their concept."[547] This discourse also included an attempt to suppress "non-gymnastic means." The material for a Spartakiad piece was to be the human body itself and its movements,[548] not, as was the case in the 1st All-State Spartakiad, portraits of statesmen, flags of socialist countries, pathetic verse, machines, animals or weapons.

Another part of the Spartakiad discourse was the general idea of aesthetics of mass performances as a "new art" and its principles.[549] Examining Spartakiads were expert aestheticians such as Jaroslav Volek and Antonín Sychra, the latter whose assessment of Spartakiads followed up on the artistic criticism of Slets by his

547 Ibid. The discussion of whether the Spartakiad was primarily a political or gymnastics activity continued later as well. For instance, the professional assessment of the 2nd All-State Spartakiad in 1960 believed the gymnastics aspect of Spartakiads to be less important. "We propose accepting the ideologically political and propagandistic view as the first and foremost. This enables us to assess the share of the 2nd Czechoslovak Spartakiad in the cultural revolution in our country in terms of the participants and spectators." See "Hlediska pro hodnocení II. celostátní spartakiády". *Teorie a praxe tělesné výchovy*, 1961, vol. 9, special issue: Výsledky výzkumu II. celostátní spartakiády 1960, pp. 2–5;
548 Serbus, L. – Kos, B. – Mihule, J.: *Historický vývoj a základy tělovýchovných vystoupení v ČSSR*, p. 114.
549 Berdychová, J.: *Funkce tělovýchovných skladeb pro hromadná vystoupení mládeže*, p. 5.

father-in-law, Jan Mukařovský, a member of the Prague Linguistic Circle.[550] Yet more important for the Spartakiad itself was the thinking of experienced authors of Sokol and Spartakiad performances who had developed Tyrš's original theories that favored the aesthetic perspective over that of the gymnastic.[551] Ladislav Serbus formulated some of the fundamental principles on which the "beauty of gymnastics" would be based. It is, above all, the technical mastery of the composition that enables movements to be made simultaneously. Overly difficult exercises hindering the synchronization of the participants should therefore be avoided. The exercise should use the effect of contrasts (e.g., alternating low and high positions, slow and fast rhythms), gradation, i.e. placement of the most difficult and most impressive exercises at the piece's conclusion, harmony achieved by repeating individual motifs or the symmetric division of the field. He went on to point out the importance of an element of surprise that would comply with Tyrš's principle of "harmony following disharmony."[552]

In reference to Tyrš, he recommended interspersing the dynamic chain of movements with a moment of stillness in which the gymnast's movement would stop (though not for the three seconds recommended by Tyrš) so that a certain component of the choreography would stand out.[553] He also devoted considerable attention to the colors of the outfits that played a key role in terms of the color

550 Serbus, L. – Kos, B. – Mihule, J.: *Historický vývoj a základy tělovýchovných vystoupení v ČSSR*, p. 99; See also Serbus, Ladislav: "Ideové pojetí a estetická funkce tělovýchovných skladeb". In: *Sborník ze semináře FTVS UK Praha*, pp. 60–65. See also the work of Vilém Hohler who studied the aesthetics of Spartakiads systematically, for instance in: Hohler, Vilém: "Základní estetické aspekty skladeb III. CS". *Teorie a praxe tělesné výchovy*, 1966, vol. 14, n. 4, pp. 251–254.

551 Serbus, L. – Kos, B. – Mihule, J.: *Historický vývoj a základy tělovýchovných vystoupení v ČSSR*, p. 54.

552 Tyrš, Miroslav: *Cvičení veřejná a závodnická*. Československá obec sokolská, Prague 1932, p. 275.

553 For choreography of Spartakiad pieces, see Belšan, P.: "Choreografie a funkce náčiní, nářadí a režijních prostředků", pp. 48–57.

effects during the synchronous movements. In a veiled criticism of the Soviet influence, Serbus deemed some of the outfits of the first Spartakiad as "unacceptable and foreign," not suiting "our national sentiment."[554]

One of the basic ways of gauging the Spartakiad's "gymnastics beauty" was by examining the spectators' reaction. The frequency and length of the applause were professionally studied and processed, and spectator surveys were evaluated.[555] The professional discussion pointed out that the pieces were not supposed to pander to the audience, but to aesthetically instruct them.[556] For instance, in a 1975 article entitled "How to View the Individual Pieces," Pavel Belšan instructs the *Rudé právo* reader how to perceive the Spartakiad pieces, which components should be noticed and how to evaluate them.[557]

Another principle for a Spartakiad piece, again in reaction to mistakes of the 1st All-State Spartakiad, was the suitability of the

---

554 Serbus, L.:"Historický vývoj masových tělovýchovných vystoupení u nás", pp. 23–24. The colors of the participants' outfits for the closing scene was, in the author's view, a "deterring example." Later open criticism of Soviet gymnastics also appeared. Vilém Hohler e.g. wrote about the Soviets' performance at the Friendship Evenings of the 1965 Spartakiad: "It is apparent, for instance, that in our cultural context the Soviets' piece seems conservative, even kitsch." HOHLER, V.: "Základní estetické aspekty skladeb III. CS", pp. 251–254.

555 "Certain colleagues noted in reports the amount of applause, its force and where it was coming from during the piece," states a report on the research work of the Scientific Council of the Central Committee of the Czechoslovak Gymnastics Association during the 1975 Spartakiad. NA, f. ÚV ČSTV, k. 390 (1975).

556 Třešňáková, Vlasta: "Úloha cvičebních úborů při hromadném vystoupení". In: *Vědecká konference o teoretických a metodických základech masových tělovýchovných vystoupení*, p. 150. According to the author, the spectators most strongly reacted to the changes in formations and play of colors caused by unexpected movements and gave the most applause to such effects in all pieces, which should attest to the "general public's low level of professional knowledge." Since mass gymnastic performances have been neglected since the last Slet, "the education of the general public in this direction has petrified." See also Břicháček, Josef – Petrák, Bořivoj – Syručková, Drahomíra: "Ideově výchovné působení II. CS na diváky Strahovského stadiónu". *Teorie a praxe tělesné výchovy*, 1961, vol. 9, special issue: Výsledky výzkumu II. celostátní spartakiády 1960, pp. 38–40.

557 Belšan, Pavel: "Jak se dívat na jednotlivé skladby: nejen překvapivá geometrie". *Rudé právo*, vol. 55, 28. 6. 1975, p. 6.

exercise to the participants' age and gender.[558] Jana Berdychová criticized the excessive demands placed on the youngest, often pre-school children, who at the district Spartakiads in 1955 had been subjected to several hours of lining up and waiting. In the afore-mentioned review from 1956, Berdychová wrote, "they are usually present at the flag-raising ceremony [...] they are meant to stand at attention before the spectators on the sun-scorched field; they are meant to be attentive despite not understanding the speeches."[559] According to Berdychová, the weak physical condition of a five to seven-year-old child (though due to a lack of older children, even four-year-olds) "prevents the child from coping with the consider-able demands related to the lining-up, rehearsals, waiting and stand-ing, during which you can see the child gradually drooping, to the point of collapse." Berdychová also pointed out that the children often sat for over an hour on the field as "a decoration or border" for another performance, in cold weather dressed only in their ex-ercise outfits, in hot weather with no hat under the scorching sun. The press, Berdychová claimed, unreasonably praised such exercises as "heroism." Other experts criticized that the ideological content of Spartakiad compositions was beyond the intellectual abilities of young children. An analysis of the composition for the youngest pu-pils (six to eight years of age) entitled *Fairytale* drew the following conclusion:

The theme of *Fairytale* that well-being comes from work and that happiness should be sought in work is certainly very valuable. We observed to what extent the children understood this idea. It was to our great surprise that, even though the idea is served as fairytale,

558 Serbus, L. – Kos, B. – Mihule, J.: *Historický vývoj a základy tělovýchovných vystoupení v ČSSR*, pp. 122.
559 Berdychová, Jana: "Příspěvek k problematice tělovýchovných vystoupení dětí s hlediska pedagogického". In: *Vědecká konference o teoretických a metodických základech masových tělovýchovných vystoupení*, pp. 63–64.

preschool children were not aware of the ideological content of the exercise and did not understand the idea properly. Preschool children find gratification in the immediate experience from the verse, music and movement; they do not ponder the content of the accompanying words or the symbolism of the movements. They will soon forget the interpretation of their teacher and instructor. [560]

Ideas on "natural movement" also involved a return to the Sokol gender discourse based on the intellectual climate of organic nationalism and the belief in essential, natural differences between the sexes. In her doctorate thesis, Jana Berdychová tried to base this re-established gender discourse on the natural developmental differences between boys and girls. In her view, children's exercises should be strictly divided by sex, since boys and girls have different abilities and interests in physical education due to their distinct biological nature. While boys should undertake simple but physically demanding and dynamic exercises and devote their energy to competitive sports, girls should focus on dance exercises with a difficult choreography, since, especially during puberty, "they long to publicly perform."[561] Berdychová also writes: "This very age of adolescence provides quite specific prerequisites for subtle expressions of feeling in movement, and both the choreographers and the music composers should utilize this magic of adolescent girls. No other age of youth provides an opportunity for such sensitive expression."[562]

That her views were more the rule than the exception is supported by the minutes of a Spartakiad evaluation commission meeting. This commission was tasked with choosing the best submissions for Spartakiads compositions, discussed shortcomings with the authors,

560   Hintnaus, Ladislav: "Pohádka. Cvičení nejmladšího žactva 6–8letého". *Teorie a praxe tělesné výchovy*, 1961, vol. 9, special issue: Výsledky výzkumu II. celostátní spartakiády 1960, pp. 9–10.
561   Berdychová, J.: *Funkce tělovýchovných skladeb pro hromadná vystoupení mládeže*, p. 87.
562   Ibid.

and thus established a canon for creating them. The evaluation committee, predominantly made up of Slet organizers and the authors of Slet pieces such as Jaroslav Šterc and Eva Bémová, insisted on the precise defining of gender roles and their strict separation. The largest discussion in the commission was caused by a submission for the 1965 Spartakiad entitled *My Country Is a Blossoming Meadow* for which the author, Jarmila Žerovnická, proposed that sticks be used as tools, but the entire commission disapproved. Božena Drdácká offered her opinion: "If we got rid of the sticks and made changes that would make the piece more artistic, then it isn't all that bad; the creators could improve it by May by using ribbons or flowers."[563] The piece did in fact appear at the 1965 Spartakiad; they got rid of the sticks and the girls performed with two flowers attached to a ribbon (see fig. 17). The commission also carefully examined the other submissions, ensuring that their masculine or feminine nature be preserved and ordering them to be "feminized" or "masculinized" as necessary.[564]

The professional Spartakiad discourse based on the Sokol tradition obviously had its opponents, especially among the leftist art avant-garde. Jožka Šaršeová, for instance, harshly criticized Serbus's speech at the 1956 conference. In her view, a return to Sokol exercises would be inadmissible since its "form stopped at the level required by the bourgeoisie, i.e. a form that created a strong healthy worker, that increased the self-confidence of the Czech bourgeoisie, of a 'Czech person' against the oppression of the German bourgeoisie." Instead, there was the need to try new forms, since "artistic experiments, bold and necessary as they are, must correspond to the constant experiments of the revolutionary party that rebuilt and recreated our country." The Spartakiad pieces were to be "combative"

563 AČOS, f. III. celostátní spartakiáda 1965, Hodnocení skladeb 29. 4. 1963. For more on Božena Drdácká, see Strnad, Miloš: "Životní jubileum doc. dr. Boženy Drdácké, CSc.". *Teorie a praxe tělesné výchovy*, 1987, vol. 35, n. 3, p. 192.
564 AČOS, f. III. celostátní spartakiáda 1965, Hodnocení skladeb 29. 4. 1963.

and as such needed "all weapons, better, ever newer weapons." Šaršeová opposed "necessary rules and unwritten laws for gymnastic pieces," that she felt hindered creative potential and discouraged spectators. Yet shortly after the 1st All-State Spartakiad it was clear, at least in professional circles, that the Spartakiads would not become an experimental space of theater for the masses, but would remain in tow of the Sokol Slet tradition.

In addition to this professional discourse aimed at improving the Spartakiad pieces, there was also a purely "scientific" examination of Spartakiads. This was apparently intended to give mass exercises the scientific status that other areas of physical education enjoyed. Along with features of unity, mass character and ideology, one of the cornerstones of socialist gymnastics was supposed to be its scientific quality.[565] Socialist sports science had already acquired in the 1950s its institutional background and own scientific journals, including the magazine *Teorie a praxe tělesné výchovy* (Physical Education: Theory and Practice) which imitated the Soviet model *Teoriia I Praktika Fizicheskoi Kultury*.[566] Unlike analyses of top-level sports which entail a certain amount of verifiable data and the possibility of international scientific cooperation, it was extremely difficult to maintain the illusion of scientific work in "Spartakiadology."[567]

---

565 See for instance "Statut vědecké rady ÚV ČSTV". *Teorie a praxe tělesné výchovy*, 1962, vol. 8, p. 488.

566 The Soviet model was faithfully copied by other Eastern Bloc countries as well; East German sport had e.g. its own professional magazine *Theorie und Praxis der Koerperkultur*.

567 Yet even outside of Spartakiad research the attempt to apply methods of the exact sciences to the social sphere, where these laws did not apply and where there was very little quantitatively comprehensible data, led to unconvincing results and mere "scientific" posturing. In fact, often no verifiable data could be found behind the curtain of the professional terminology. A typical result of such quasi-research was an article by Miloš Zeman, later the prime minister and president of the Czech Republic, from 1973 entitled "A Complex Prognostic Model of Czechoslovak Physical Education" printed in *Theory and Practice of Gymnastics*. Zeman presented here a brief report on the ongoing prognostic project that was to represent up until 1990 "a constant instrument for managing Czechoslovak physical education in terms of both their closer and more remote perspectives." This result was to be achieved using then normal prognostic methods of "brainstorming" and the computer simulation of a complex model of 140 variables, 600 basic

For instance, the magazine *Teorie a praxe tělesné výchovy* published in 1966 the article "Expended Energy In Mass Performances at the 3rd All-State Spartakiad," whose authors included Serbus and Berdychová.[568] The article was accompanied by photographs of two ten-year-old children holding hands (probably a boy and girl) and wearing masks with tubes attached to bags on their backs. Transmitters are mounted on their masks. The photograph was intended to show the "indirect calorimetry" method in which exhaled air captured in the Douglas bags was analyzed. The transmitters were for the "wireless transmission of heartbeat capacities."[569] The article, full of charts, graphs and data for the various performances of the 1965 Spartakiad, ultimately reached the conclusion that their "physiological efficiency" was "relatively good."[570] Besides the methodological difficulties that the authors themselves admit (e.g., the bags hindering the participants during exercises), such research completely neglected the essence of mass performances in which generally it was not the movements themselves that were difficult, but the spatial orientation, the synchronization with the other participants and, above all, the hours of waiting and arrangement, often in cold weather, rain or extreme heat.[571] The gymnastics officials were also

equations and 60 "loops of feedback." The model worked with variables such as "Marxist-Leninist ideology," "socialist lifestyle" or "ideological education in physical education." Zeman, Miloš: "Komplexní prognostický model Československé tělovýchovy". *Teorie a praxe tělesné výchovy*, 1973, vol. 21, n. 5, pp. 263–271.

568   Seliger, Václav a spol.: "Energetický výdej u skladeb hromadného vystoupení na III. CS". *Teorie a praxe tělesné výchovy*, 1966, vol. 14, n. 3, pp. 137–153. The same research with the same methodology was conducted during the preparations for the Spartakiads during the normalization period, see Seliger, V. a spol.: "Výzkum fyziologické a pedagogické náročnosti skladeb hromadných vystoupení", pp. 644–685. Hrčka, Jozef: "Celoštátna spartakiáda 1980 a výskum". *Teorie a praxe tělesné výchovy*, 1979, vol. 27, n. 11, pp. 699–701.

569   Seliger, V. a spol.: "Energetický výdej u skladeb hromadného vystoupení na III. CS", p. 137.

570   Ibid, p. 153.

571   In 1965, there was undertaken extensive "bioclimatic" research of the temperature to which the participants had been exposed at Strahov. The air temperature reached up to 40.5 °C, the temperature of the concrete surface of the assembly area rose to 34 °C, the temperature in the dressing rooms, where it was usually forbidden to open windows, was 28 °C. As the results warned, the situation became worse with the crowd of participants: "[…] there is a kind of mutual

aware that the Spartakiads would not contribute to improving the physical condition of the Czechoslovak society. As one of the Slovak experts noted, "As time goes by, the more we see spider-like physiques: thin arms and legs and big bellies."[572]

Sociological and pedagogical studies, aimed at e.g. "ascertaining that (sic!) parallel to the preparations of the 1960 Spartakiad it would be possible to perform basic tasks at schools and to derive from them basic recommendations for the youth performances at the 1965 Spartakiad".[573] Unfortunately for the Spartakiad organizers, this normative research objective was rarely met. The magazine *Teorie a praxe tělesné kultury* e.g. published in 1966 the article "The Influence of practicing the Spartakiad Piece 'One for All' on the Moral, Motor and Functional Development of 11–13 Year-Old Boys."[574]

As part of the "pedagogical experiment" the school boys were divided into three groups: one group practiced only for the Spartakiad, the second group combined practice with physical education curricula and the control group underwent normal physical education. The researchers found that while the boys in the control group improved in all monitored categories, the group practicing for the Spartakiad and the combined group showed a significant and moderate drop in performance, respectively. The boys focusing on only the Spartakiad exercises worsened in their running speed, stomach muscles, number of pull-ups and push-ups and were also much less satisfied with physical education than those boys from

emanation of heat that occurs in the flow of participants which gives off even more heat." Vorel, M.: "Hygienicko-technický průzkum III. CS", pp. 483–487.

572 Hrčka, Jozef: "O niektorých problémoch športovo-rekreačnej aktivity občanov a voľného času". In: Jozef Hrčka et al.: *Voľný čas a športovo rekreačná aktivita občanov. Príspevky zo seminára Vedeckej rady SÚV ČSZTV.* Šport, Bratislava 1974, p. 6.

573 Kozlík, Jaroslav: "Jak v podmínkách příprav na II. CS se plnily zákl. úkoly tělesné výchovy ve školách". *Teorie a praxe tělesné výchovy,* 1961, vol. 9, special issue: Výsledky výzkumu II. celostátní spartakiády 1960, pp. 24–25.

574 Adamus, Milan a spol.: "Vliv nácviku spartakiádní skladby 'Jeden za všech- ny' na morální, pohybový a funkční rozvoj chlapců ve věku 11 až 13 let". *Teorie a praxe tělesné výchovy,* 1966, vol. 14, n. 4, pp. 226–232.

the control group (an almost 40% difference). This result was confirmed by previous research that had revealed a "significant drop in discipline" among pupils practicing for the Spartakiad, especially in seventh-grade boys. Yet the same research also showed that the situation was better for eighth-graders: "Less of a drop [in discipline] is evident in eighth-graders, who also do not like practicing for the Spartakiad, but who are more aware of the consequences if they do not take part in gymnastic performances."[575]

Every Spartakiad was also accompanied by extensive anthropometric research. In the 1950s and 1960s, scientists led by anthropologist Vojtěch Fetter measured at district and state-wide Spartakiads the basic physical dimensions (body height, weight, chest circumference) of several thousand participants (e.g., more than 5,000 people in 1965). The results were machine processed by the State Planning Commission.[576] In the 1980s, the number of examined participants increased (to 10,000) as did the number of monitored indicators that included dozens of physical dimensions and the measurement of fourteen skin folds.[577]

The research results were then published in large multi-volume monographs.[578] It was important for anthropologists to show that the exercise participants did not represent from an anthropological

575   Kozlík, J.: "Jak v podmínkách příprav na II. CS se plnily zákl. úkoly tělesné výchovy ve školách", pp. 24–25. Other research showed the ineffectiveness of Spartakiad exercises. According to its findings, the women's exercises (also at the 1965 Spartakiad) were only "slightly more demanding than ordinary walking." Seliger, V. a spol.: "Energetický výdej u skladeb hromadného vystoupení na III. CS", p. 148.

576   See for instance Fetter, Vojtěch – Suchý, Jaroslav: "Základní tělesné rozměry cvičenců III. CS ve srovnání s rozměry cvičenců I. a II. CS". *Teorie a praxe tělesné výchovy*, 1966, vol. 14, n. 6, pp. 348–360; See Vorel, M.: "Hygienicko-technický průzkum III. CS", p. 486.

577   Bláha, Pavel: "Antropologický výzkum konaný v souvislosti s ČSS 1985".*Teorie a praxe tělesné výchovy*, 1986, vol. 34, pp. 502–504. See also: AČOS, f. Antropologický výzkum Československé spartakiády 1985.

578   Bláha, Pavel a spol.: *Antropometrie československé populace od 6 do 35 let. Československá spartakiáda 1980*, část 1 a 2. ÚNZ hl. m. – ÚV ČSTV, Prague 1982, 1984; Bláha, Pavel a spol.: *Antropometrie československé populace od 6 do 55 let. Československá spartakiáda 1985*, 4 vols. Ústřední štáb Československé spartakiády, Prague 1985–1987.

perspective a specific, select category, which would allow for the measurements to be applied to the entire Czechoslovak population. At the same time, however, this cast doubt on the claims made by the Spartakiad organizers that practicing the gymnastic pieces contributed to physical fitness. The anthropologists drew from research on the physiological difficulty of the performances of the 1980 Czechoslovak Spartakiad, which showed that even the military's choreography, which had exceeded many times over the difficulty of most other pieces in terms of energy expended, corresponded to plain walking at a speed of 5.6 km/h or bike riding at 15 km/h. They then deduced from this that "the physique of the participants could not in any way be influenced by the strain during practice for and the Spartakiad itself. The physique can only be influenced by long-term and highly intensive physical activity."[579]

The way in which the participants were subjected to the techniques of discipline and also scientifically examined in detail brings to mind Foucault's view of biopower, in which authority grasps the power over the human body (and thus also over the individual) through scientific analysis. Yet as in many other aspects of Spartakiad, this Foucauldian association is merely on the surface. Knowledge of the physical dimensions of the participants (or measuring the carbon dioxide in plastic bags) did not lead to any greater control over their bodies and did not even serve the Spartakiad organizers, despite the scientists' assurance that their research would contribute to better composed Spartakiad pieces. This was more another case of how individual social groups and communities (in this case scientific) appropriated a political ritual profusely sponsored by the state.

---

579 Bláha, P. a spol.: *Antropometrie československé populace od 6 do 35 let. Československá spartakiáda 1980*, část 1, p. 23; Bartůňková, Staša et al.: "Funkční a energetická náročnost skladeb ČSS 1980". *Teorie a praxe tělesné výchovy*, 1981, vol. 29, pp. 145–152. This research also showed that the pulse rate for many of the performance pieces reached only 122 per minute, while that of children aged five to fifteen did not drop during spontaneous physical activity under 150 per minute.

THE "CALL TO ARMS" FOR THE 1ST ALL-STATE SPARTAKIAD IN 1955

The organization and especially the management structure of the 1st All-State Spartakiad fundamentally differed from later Spartakiads. The first event took place within the organizational framework of Stalinist physical education, which, though it strove to unite gymnastics, instead resulted in the splintering of a previously quite efficient Sokol system copied by several smaller competing movements. In addition to the State Committee for Physical Education and Sports, the trade unions, DSO Sokol and ministries of education, of labor, of national defence and of national security were also involved in the management of the 1st Spartakiad. Yet the direct involvement of the highest communist bodies, which intervened in the most minute detail of the preparations, was most typical for it. In later years the communist party was limited to merely an overseeing role. The first Spartakiad faced considerable problems from the very start, mainly because the preparations began late – roughly a year and a half before the event was to be held. Sokol Slets, relying on the volunteer enthusiasm of its nearly million strong members and whose preparations were made by a staff of experienced experts, had usually started planning work on the event three years in advance. As we will see, due to the rigidity of the physical education system and difficulties in securing supplies, the preparations for the event essentially had to be commenced immediately following the end of the previous Spartakiad. In attempting to top the Sokol Slets, the inexperienced organizational apparatus took on a much more difficult task than it was able to manage in the short timeframe. This led to the later constantly criticized "call to arms," i.e. the attempt to overcome the accumulated delays through the extraordinary use of human and material resources right before the Spartakiad was to start. (As we will later see, the "call to arms" was an integral and necessary part of state-socialist rule and not specific to late Stalinism).

The biggest problem for the organizers was coming up with enough gymnasts. Here it became clear that putting something like a Sokol Slet on, but without Sokol taking part, would be extremely difficult. As late as November 1954, i.e. when practices for the performances should have already been intensively underway throughout Czechoslovakia for two months, the number of participants was negligible.[580] Both in factories, where the trade unions were supposed to organize the practices, and in villages, where this task fell to the DSO Sokol, there was a lack of adult male participants in particular. Only 14,000 men at all Czechoslovak factories were practicing, much fewer than at the final Slets. The situation was especially bad in Slovakia. At the J. V. Stalin Factory in Martin, where, among other things, Czechoslovak tanks were produced, only ten men and twenty women were practicing for the Spartakiad. In the entire Žilina region there were just over a thousand adults of all categories practicing. The situation in the Bohemian and Moravian regions was not much better. In Třebíč, for instance, it was reported that there was "not a single person practicing for the Spartakiad, not a single poster in the town, and no mention of it at association meetings" and from the total of seventeen thousand Czechoslovak crowns allotted for the Třebíč gymnastics there was only two hundred left for the Spartakiad.[581] The situation in the villages was slightly better, though only a little over a third of the associations, decimated by the Stalinist "sportification of Sokol," joined in the practices there.

580 The following description is based on a hundred page long document: AČOS, f. I. celostátní spartakiáda 1955, Stenografický záznam zasedání rozšířeného výkonného výboru I. CS 1955, 7. 11. 1954. Architect Jiří Kroha's talk defied the discussion's generally pessimistic tone: "Indeed, all of our socialist work is born of obstacles and difficulties, but we have shown again and again that these are not insurmountable for us, that we can overcome them guided by the teachings of our glorious work class [...] and that the heroism of our worker lies in overcoming these obstacles."
581 Yet during the period between the wars Sokol life was relatively strong here. For example, the six hundredth anniversary of the city's establishment was celebrate by a march of 1,500 uniformed Sokol members accompanied by the music of a twenty-four member Sokol band. Historie jednoty. Sokol Třebíč (Cf. www.sokol-trebic.cz/historie-jednoty Accessed 12. 12. 2014).

Moreover, those practicing in the villages ran into problems such as seasonal work (the chairmen of the collective farms allegedly announced that "if the potatoes aren't harvested there will be no Spartakiad") or a lack of gymnasiums. The Agricultural Cooperatives often used the former Sokol halls to store grain, arguing that "feeding the nation takes precedence." Despite the constant protests of sports organizers, it continued this storage practice in the spring of 1955 and many of those practicing for the Spartakiad had to do so in local pubs which, as workers of the State Committee for Physical Education and Sports bitterly noted, had not been used for storage.[582]

The organizers also encountered the resistance of a number of sports associations that "see their one and only task in taking care of the soccer team." The numbers of those practicing for the Spartakiad among sports clubs was even reduced as the weather improved in the spring of 1955 and their members were able to play sports, especially soccer.[583] Spartakiad organizers had to battle here with the consequences of the Stalinist policy of "Sokol's sportification." Sports clubs were not willing to abandon their newly acquired position and questioned the authority of the constantly changing state supervision. The secretary of the Central Council of Trade Unions and the second-in-command in the organizational hierarchy of Spartakiad preparations, Jaroslav Kolář, gave as an example the attendance by officials of the State Committee for Physical Education and Sports at a meeting of a sports club in Tachov. The officials had to hear from the club chairman that here "they don't like being inspected, they couldn't care less and that every inspector is shown the exit door." The chairman also declared that the club's female

---

582 Neither did the passivity of the National Front partners contribute to a more successful recruitment. For example, the Czechoslovak Socialist Party, whose membership had traditionally meshed with Sokol (the party's post-February 1948 chairman Miroslav Klinger was a former Sokol gymnastics director), had recruited by mid April 1955 in all regions a total of 89 participants. See NA, f. Ústřední akční výbor Národní fronty 1948–1955 (dále ÚAV NF), k. 56, inv. n. 26, Příprava na konání I. celostátní spartakiády.

583 Ibid.

members were not going to perform at Strahov, or at a district Spartakiad, "since they exercise in shorts and the women would like to exercise in skirts." He also refused to start practicing for the Spartakiad until the club received money to insure the participants and to repair the former Sokol hall. District sports officials responsible for meeting the Spartakiad quotas responded to such displays of obstinacy by ceasing to fund clubs or by banning its activities. They then took away the members performance classifications and their athletic badges.[584]

Nevertheless, the numbers for potential participants remained low. The dogged and often forceful attempt to enlist Spartakiad participants seemed "strange" to top sports representatives such as Vilém Mucha, a key figure of interwar and post-war communist gymnastics. He complained that there was a lack of "that past enthusiasm [...] we never had to send anyone to Prague [...] they used to go there voluntarily. Back then, nobody requested that the organizers buy them the exercise outfit. They all paid for it themselves, since they wanted to take part in the amazing festivities in Prague." The organizers encountered here a fundamental problem of the communist regime: you can't take away a society's autonomy and mobilize it at the same time. If the Communist Party's leadership wanted to have a Spartakiad, they also had to provide autonomous space for "that enthusiasm." The Spartakiad organizers soon realized that the success of the Spartakiad hinged on the involvement of the individual clubs and that "sitting around and creating red tape in central, regional and district committees would not save or help anything." They tried to find different ways, often quite desperately,

---

584 See also Appelt, Karel: "Poznámky k dotazníkové akci". In: *Vědecká konference o teoretických a metodických základech masových tělovýchovných vystoupení*, pp. 120, 122. In a poll taken during the first Spartakiad, athletes often gave the financing of their club as their main reason for participating. Prague golfers, for instance, practiced for the second Spartakiad in order to keep their sole golf course in Lišnice from being destroyed. See Sedlák, Prokop: *Historie golfu v českých zemích a na Slovensku*. Svojtka & Co., Prague 2004, pp. 107–108.

to get around the absence of an autonomous gymnastics movement. They futilely appealed to the "great revolutionary experience" of trade unionists, or attempted various organizational experiments. For instance, they formed Spartakiad committees in every district which were to coordinate the preparations. Yet this only led to the passivity of the sports organizations that, as officials complained, "feel that the Spartakiad is not their responsibility, but that of the Spartakiad committees." The committees were then quickly dissolved and the individual sport units received the target figures for participants that they had to meet. This did not solve the problem since those units that reached their target figures had no incentive to acquire more recruits. Jaroslav Kolář then dramatically announced the need to "do away with all target figures, reject them as reactionary and defeatist, and mobilize on a broad front." It was also proposed that paid sport officials, especially those in Slovakia, take part in Spartakiad practices, but even this minimum requirement was "not received with great enthusiasm." The fact that ultimately enough participants were actually found to fill the Strahov Stadium field for nineteen performances, and so that the district and regional Spartakiads could be held, was the result of two pragmatic concessions. First, the organizers abandoned their original idea that the Spartakiad would be a "new socialist gymnastics" affair, and actively attempted to involve "former virtuous, lower-ranking Sokol workers," who, according to Alexej Čepička needed to be distinguished from the "conscious lackeys of the bourgeoisie."[585] The second was to fill the void of volunteers with students, on whom it was much easier to apply the necessary pressure. This was the case e.g. with the Svazarm pieces, in which, upon the intervention of the Ministry of Education, Svazarm members were replaced by secondary school students. This also made use of the fact that the gymnastics

---

585 AČOS, f. I. celostátní spartakiáda 1955, Stenografický záznam zasedání rozšířeného výkonného výboru I. CS 1955, 7. listopadu 1954.

instructors at schools could much better maintain the continuity of callisthenic exercises than those at gymnastics clubs.

Not only were the organizers of the 1st All-State Spartakiad missing the enthusiasm and dedication of the Sokol clubs, they were also lacking the experience of the top Sokol officials. "We have so many problems that our hair is turning gray," said the head of the trade unionists Jaroslav Kolář, "it's no excuse that we've never organized a Spartakiad or even a Slet,"[586] The increasing delays led to the direct involvement of the highest bodies of the Communist Party. The incompetent general František Janda was dismissed from the head of the Spartakiad preparations and replaced by the young and energetic Václav Pleskot.[587] In a defensively tinged New Year's speech, President Zápotocký declared Spartakiads to be among the state's top priorities when he said: "We won't allow ourselves to be rattled or intimidated. [...] We will meet our plans, move forward with our events, and especially prepare the 1st All-State Spartakiad as an expression of the unstoppable development of the physical and psychological forces of our youth, guaranteeing our victory."[588] From January to July 1955 the politburo and the secretariat of the Communist Party's Central Committee met twelve times to discuss the Spartakiad.[589] A Central Committee commission to oversee the preparations and implementation of the 1st All-State Spartakiad was set up and consisted of officials of four departments of the Communist Party's Central Committee. Three days before the start of the first Spartakiad, on 20 June 1955, the politburo then established another commission of the Communist Party's Central Committee and empowered it in its daily meetings "to take all necessary

586   Ibid.
587   For more on Pleskot, see Zídek, P.: "Soudružky a soudruzi, tužme se".
588   Quoted from Mucha, V. (ed.): *První celostátní spartakiáda 1955*, p. 11.
589   NA, f. SVTVS, k. 65, inv. n. 191, Usnesení porad štábu spartakiády 1954 až 1955, Zpráva o přípravách a výsledcích I. celostátní spartakiády 1955. The Politburo approved details such as the design for the main Spartakiad poster. See NA, f. SVTVS, k. 46, Tajné spisy 1955, n. j. 184, Pleskot Novotnému 28. února 1955.

operative and organizational measures to ensure the successful run of the 1st All-State Spartakiad."[590]

The party's direct involvement in organizational matters greatly accelerated the preparations, though it did not prevent the considerable confusion that arose right before the Spartakiad and during it. On 21 June 1955, i.e. during the general rehearsals and just two days before the opening ceremonies, the party's special operative commission was still dealing with the fact that the extension to the east grandstands designed by architect Jiří Kroha was still not finished and ordered that it be completed and cleaned up within two days at 6 am (the scaffolding removed by 10 am).[591] On the terraces of this grandstand they also remade at the last minute a round target several meters large that bore the sports insignia of Czechoslovakia and other communist countries.[592] This delay was caused by the party officials themselves when they decided less than a month before that these targets bearing the portraits of politburo members of the Czechoslovak Communist Party and USSR were inappropriate. A day later, on the eve before the event began, the party commission, concerned by reports of ticket sales, ordered the Spartakiad staff "to designate in shifts on 24 June a total of 20,000 to 25,000 gymnastic participants to be used to fill certain areas of the stands if necessary."[593] It also realized at the last minute that members of the People's Militia in civilian dress would have to be added to the

---

590 The draft for the final report on the 1st All-State Spartakiad characterized the party's involvement as such: "Just a half year ago it seemed that not enough had been done for the Spartakiad's preparations [...] Once again the party showed in the crucial moments how important its help is in being able to stir up enthusiasm in the masses, in being able to overcome all obstacles and difficulties." NA, f. SVTVS, k. 68, inv. n. 201, Zprávy o stavu příprav I. celostátní spartakiády a její hodnocení.

591 AČOS, f. I. celostátní spartakiáda 1955 – Politické materiály, Zápis z porady komise ÚV KSČ pro zajištění I. celostátní spartakiády, konané 21. června 1955 u soudruha Šalgy.

592 NA, f. SVTVS, k. 65, inv. n. 192, Zápisy operačních schůzí štábu spartakiády 1955.

593 AČOS, f. I. celostátní spartakiáda 1955 – Politické materiály, Zápis z 2. porady komise ÚV KSČ pro zajištění I. celostátní spartakiády, konané 22. června 1955 v kanceláři n. 30 na stadionĕ.

Socialist Youth event security in the parade, since "the young can not cope."[594] This confirmed a previous characterization of Socialist Youth officials: "[...] although most of them don't mess anything up, they also don't do anything."[595] The improvised nature of the management is attested to by orders of the party's commission, such as "verify whether the report is true that yesterday 16,000 children did not receive lunch,"[596] or the command to the police to monitor whether at the lodging houses the wake-up call, times for breakfast and departure to the assembly places were being followed, and, in the case of delays, "to properly warn the supervisors."[597] Following the first performance, the politburo, upon the urging of the Sparta-kiad directorship, decided to cancel the closing performance[598] and replace it with several repeat performances by the work reserves.

The improvisation of the entire first Spartakiad is also evidenced by the fact that only after it had ended did party and sports bodies begin to deal with establishing the Spartakiad tradition. As part of the overall assessment of the Spartakiad, the politburo decided to organize these state-wide events in regular four-year cycles, taking into account the international sports calendar so that it would not collide with the Olympic Games and international youth festivals.[599]

594 AČOS, f. l. celostátní spartakiáda 1955 – Politické materiály, Zápis z porady komise ÚV KSČ pro zajištění l. celostátní spartakiády, konané 21. června 1955 u soudruha Šalgy.
595 AČOS, f. l. celostátní spartakiáda 1955 – Politické materiály, Stenografický záznam zasedání rozšířeného výkonného výboru l. CS 1955, 7. listopadu 1954.
596 AČOS, f. l. celostátní spartakiáda 1955 – Politické materiály, Zápis z 6. porady komise ÚV KSČ pro zajištění l. celostátní spartakiády, konané 25. června 1955 v 9.00 hod. na strahovském stadionu. The organisational chaos was also noted by a prominent medical doctor Josef Charvát in his memoires Charvát, Josef: *Můj labyrint světa. Vzpomínky, zápisky z deníku.* Galén, Prague 2005, pp. 397–398.
597 AČOS, f. l. celostátní spartakiáda 1955 – Politické materiály, Zápis ze 7. porady komise ÚV KSČ pro zajištění l. celostátní spartakiády, konané dne 25. června 1955 v 19.45 hod. na strahovském stadionu.
598 AČOS, f. l. celostátní spartakiáda 1955 – Politické materiály, Zápis z 8. porady komise ÚV KSČ pro zajištění l. celostátní spartakiády, konané dne 27. června 1955 v 17.00 hod. na strahovském stadionu.
599 NA, f. SVTVS, k. 65, inv. n. 191, Usnesení porad štábu spartakiády 1954 až 1955, Zpráva o přípravách a výsledcích l. celostátní spartakiády 1955.

It was therefore proposed to make an exception and organize the second Spartakiad after just three years for 1958 to commemorate the tenth anniversary of the Victorious February (the communist putsch in February 1948) and then to hold all ensuing Spartakiads at four-year intervals. According to this plan, the third Spartakiad was to take place in 1962 as the celebration of the one hundredth anniversary of Sokol's founding. The proposal also stipulated that the term "Spartakiad" be reserved exclusively for mass performances of the entire gymnastics movement on a district, regional and state-wide scale.

A RETURN TO A TRIED-AND-TRUE PRACTICE

After the first Spartakiad had ended, the event was assessed on several levels[600] and it was agreed that a change was needed in the management of non-competitive gymnastics to avoid unnecessary haste and confusion. The first cautious step to return to the Sokol tradition and autonomy was the formation in early 1956 of the gymnastics directors' council of the State Committee for Physical Education and Sports headed by gymnastic directors Jaroslav Šterc and Josefa Racková. Following the establishment of the Czechoslovak Physical Education Association in late 1956, the Sport-for-All Association was set up as one of its three basic components.[601] Its leadership mainly consisted of former Sokol officials: among those joining Šterc and Racková were Jiří Žižka, Antonín Král, Eva Bémová and Draha Horáková, whose main task was to revive the Sokol tradition of calisthenics in preparing for the quickly approaching second Spartakiad. They did not, however, completely succeed in this task. Less than a half year before the district Spartakiads of the second Spartakiad (which as a failed experiment had been organized a year before the regional Spartakiads and final Strahov Spartakiad) the discontent National Front declared that the participant numbers were "utterly insufficient." For instance, fewer than fifteen hundred men were practicing in the City of Prague, fewer than three hundred in Karlovy Vary and "so far not one man" in the Příbram district. What's more, the organisers apparently still had no idea of the recruitment situation.[602] The party secretariat once again set up

---

600   A conference of gymnastics experts had previously been held in September 1955. Kostková, Jarmila: "Podmínky vzniku Svazu ZTV – ZRTV". In: J. Kostková (ed.): *Svaz základní a rekreační tělesné výchovy*, p. 11. The aforementioned conference of gymnastics experts held in February 1956 produced a more thorough assessment.

601   Later renamed the Association of Basic and Recreational Gymnastics; during the Prague Spring and shortly after it bore a number of other names.

602   NA, f. ÚAV NF, ved. odb. 23. 1. 1959, Informativní zpráva o stavu nácviku na II. celostátní spartakiádu, pp. 1–3, příloha n. 15.

a commission of the Communist Party's Central Committee to assist in the Spartakiad, though, as it emphasized, this "does not mean that the Central Committee of the Czechoslovak Physical Education Association is not responsible for the preparations and run of the 2nd All-State Spartakiad."[603]

The commission's main role was to "monitor and inspect," or "assist in resolving important political matters," but not to deal with organizational details, as was the case in 1955 when the same commission dealt with how many dumplings a Spartakiad meal should have, banned the sale of ice cream in the Strahov dressing room premises or oversaw the process of stuffing straw mattresses. The party's role of monitoring instead of managing was attested to in a later interview with then Association chairman František Vodsloň:

"Tonda Novotný [President Antonín Novotný] called and told me that the Spartakiad would be held under the slogan 'Socialism Won in Our Country'. That was 1960, and it was written on the gate where the athletes entered the stadium. Šterc and Racková came to me with the entire plan for the Spartakiad. They were enthusiastic for the mass gymnastic performances which they had already organized under the Sokol. As the chairman, I only monitored things and watched the rehearsals. He [President Novotný] would always call to find out how things looked, how much there would be and so on. I would have to tell him how everything was going, how many people would be in the parade on Wenceslas Square, he had to know who was joining us from abroad [...] I would also have to give a report on that and he'd present it to the politburo."[604]

603 NA, f. KSČ – Ústřední výbor 1945–1989, Ideologické oddělení (05/3), sv. 11, a.j. 66, Usnesení sekretariátu ÚV KSČ z 16. 3. 1960.
604 Interview with František Vodsloň, 8. January 2000, Prague. Author's archive. František Vodsloň described here how he became chairman of the Czechoslovak Physical Education Association: "It was more or less as a punishment. There was a meeting of writers and I defended them. I was against Hendrych [...] and as a result they immediately transferred me to physical education. Novotný called me and said that the politburo had decided that I would move to physical

Despite the organizational difficulties of the second Spartakiad, an organizational model was established during its preparations that continued until the end of state socialism. The Communist Party abandoned its attempts to directly intervene in the preparations and management of Spartakiads. The responsibility for carrying out these events fell almost exclusively to former Sokol officials who were members in the aforementioned Sport-for-All Association.[605] This association prepared almost all the Spartakiad performances for the second and third Spartakiads (1960, 1965). During the period of "normalization", its share gradually diminished as the role of the Ministry of Education increased in the Spartakiad preparation.[606] The association returned to the tried-and-true practices used in organizing Sokol Slets and Sokol exercises in general. Unlike the 1950s, the gymnastic clubs, and therefore also the Spartakiad practices, were organized on a residential and not a production basis. This means that most of the participants practiced where they lived, not where they worked. Therefore, the trade unions, which had or were supposed to have played an important role in preparing the first Spartakiad, fell completely out of the Spartakiad organization picture. The association's establishment led to a revival of the

education. I told them, listen, I'm going to be fifty soon, I'm not about to twirl on the high bar. And he said that he knows that I'd graduated from a gymnastics school and has the brochure that I'd written on the terminology [...] so that he doesn't want to hear any excuses. Gymnastics will finally have someone that understands it; before it had always been someone who didn't understand it (laughs), before me some General Janda did it. He said, what can some General Janda possibly know about gymnastics compared to you who went through it all."

605 However, party leadership was not satisfied with this state as attested to by a resolution of the secretariat from 1962: "The Czechoslovak Physical Education Association has not yet led a sufficient fight against individualism, prima-donna-ism, selfishness, self-complacency, [... that are] the residue of a bourgeois upbringing and self-serving view of sports [...] We still see the remnants of bourgeois Sokol and scouting ideology. Our gymnastics movement is only very gradually creating a new tradition corresponding to our present-day socialism." NA, f. KSČ – Ústřední výbor 1945–1989, Ideologické oddělení (05/3), sv. 11, a.j. 66, Usnesení 152. schůze sekretariátu ÚV KSČ ze dne 24. ledna 1962, p. 5.

606 For a survey of organizational bodies, see Drdácká, Božena: "Podíl svazu ZRTV na čs. spartakiádě v r. 1990 (východiska)". In: *Sborník ze semináře FTVS UK Praha*, p. 32; See also Přerovský, Jan: "Podíl školství na přípravě Československé spartakiády 1985". In: Ibid, pp. 18–21.

activities of many defunct or dying former Sokol clubs that could then, often under the same leadership, continue in their former activities. As in Sokol, the leadership of the association was intensively involved in dealing with the trainers, especially through their personal discussions at regular trainer meetings and through its magazine *Basic Physical Education* whose publication was mainly intended for trainers. The association's activities largely coincided with the preparations for Spartakiads, and its organization and agenda were fully subordinate to the Spartakiad cycle.

The Sokol principle of "segregation as emancipation," which we described in the first chapter, was once again thoroughly implemented in the Sport-for-All Association and in the organization of Spartakiads. The association's heads were always the men's and women's gymnastics directors ("náčelník" and "náčelnice"), whose main responsibility was the rehearsal of "their" Spartakiad pieces. The men's gymnastics director was responsible for the male and coed pieces (e.g. of universities), the women's gymnastics director for the women's and children's pieces.[607] As during the preparations of the Sokol Slets, the female Spartakiad organizers possessively guarded their autonomy by making the women's pieces distinctly different from those of the men. It was under Eva Bémová and Draha Horáková that *pohybovky*, exercises intended to teach the women more economical, harmonious and aesthetically pleasing movements, came into being. The success of this program was reflected, especially during "normalization", in the association's distinct feminization, in which the female members – pupils, juniors and women – made up seventy percent of the members.[608]

---

607 See for instance Žižka, Jiří: "Tělovýchovná vystoupení ve svazu ZRTV". In: J. Kostková (ed.): *Svaz základní a rekreační tělesné výchovy*, p. 103.
608 According to research from the period of late socialism, adolescent girls preferred sports (first choice – 53 percent) to basic gymnastics (second choice – 21 percent) as their physical education class activities. Hlaváč, František: "Zájmy pubescentních dívek a jejich postoje k tělesné kultuře". *Teorie a praxe tělesné výchovy*, 1988, vol. 36, n. 7, pp. 423–427.

While the Communist Party was forced to allot to the Spartakiad organizers a great deal of independence in preparing this political ritual, this did not mean that it also gave them political autonomy. Although most of the creators of the Spartakiad concept, the authors of the performances and the participants themselves belonged to the Sport-for-All Association, this association was not the organizer of Spartakiads. The central Spartakiad staff, which was dissolved immediately following the end of the event, was formed *ad hoc* roughly three years in advance for the management of each Spartakiad. Its makeup barely changed from one Spartakiad to the next since it included the same group of experts who were the only ones capable of preparing a Spartakiad. Yet its organizational discontinuity was important so that the Spartakiad did not become an affair of the Sport-for-All Association as a kind of pseudo-Sokol movement, but remained "a gift of the Party." Although there were numerous proposals for it to become a permanent institution that would specialize in the preparation of Spartakiads, this never came to pass.[609]

The central Spartakiad staff was an organization apparatus consisting of several hundred members and a complex inner structure with a quasi-military mode of operation (strict hierarchical organization, controlled information flow, backup plans, codes for telephone communication, etc.). Beneath them were the regional (or municipal) and district Spartakiad staff that oversaw the district Spartakiads. Following the federalization of Czechoslovakia, republic staffs were also added to it. Yet the central staff in Prague retained key competencies since, as gymnastics director Jarmila Kostková said, "despite the republic bodies, everything is controlled by the federal organ."[610]

---

609   See for instance Žáček, Rudolf: "Závěry z orientačního průzkumu organizačního provozu východní části strahovského areálu v době III. ČS". *Teorie a praxe tělesné výchovy*, 1966, vol. 14, n. 4, pp. 247–249; "Spartakiádní proud". *Rudé právo*, vol. 55, 16. 6. 1975, p. 1.
610   AČOS, f. Československá spartakiáda 1975, Připomínky k řízení nácviku skladeb na ČSS 1975.

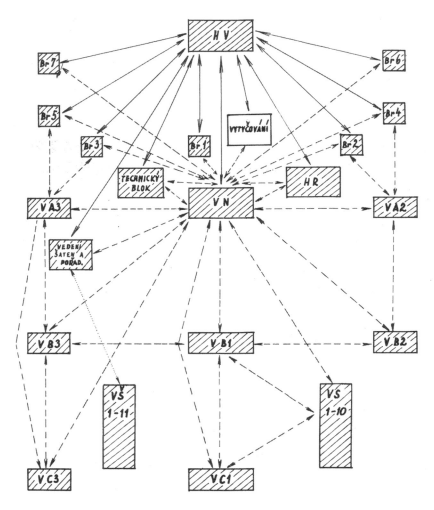

30. Communication diagram of position heads at Strahov Stadium during the 1975 Spartakiad. Abbreviations key: VN – Assembly Head, VA, VB, VC – heads of individual assemblies, HS – Gymnastic director, VS – Head stand of the assembly field, VŠ – Head stand of dressing rooms, Br 1–7 – Heads of individual stadium gates, HR – Head directors. The leadership system is governed by the simple rule that one can only give commands to a space that can be viewed from the leader's stand. So, for instance, the space beyond the eastern stands can't be commanded from the leader's bridge located in the western stands.

It was also the central staff's responsibility to coordinate the various organizations taking part in Spartakiads, which, in addition to the Czechoslovak Physical Education Association, included above all the Ministry of Education, Svazarm, the military and the Prague Regional National Committee. These organizations also set up their own Spartakiad staffs.

The core of the central Spartakiad staff consisted of the Mass Performance Department which – as with the Slet preparations – was further split into a number of commissions and sub-commissions. The most important of these was the Steering Committee, usually led by the men's and women's gymnastics directors of the Sport-for-All Association, which was in charge of processing the Spartakiad program proposal as well as directing the mass performances. This commission consisted of several sub-commissions: dressing room, parade and place-marker sub-commissions. Perhaps the place-marker sub-commission best serves to illustrate the complexity of the Spartakiad organizational web: at its head were the set-up leader and his representatives, under whom were the heads of the "eighths" and their representatives in charge of positioning the place markers in the various sections of the Strahov Stadium field (the technical preparations and storage of place markers also had its heads and their representatives); these heads then oversaw the work of the various place-marker setters, technicians and storage personnel; over ten intermediaries ensured smooth communication. In all, there were nearly 120 workers. Along with the Mass Performance Department, there were a number of other smaller departments such as the Financial Department, the Food Department and Foreign Department overseeing foreign guests (compatriots in particular). For the three weeks when the Spartakiad preparations were at their peak, all of these departments were on constant call, night and day.[611]

---

[611] NA, f. ÚV ČSTV, k. 267, Řízení Československé spartakiády ČSS 1980 v hl. městě Praze.

A return to Sokol's organizational forms and to the dominant role of the former Slet organizers obviously did not mean that all the confusion that marked the first Spartakiad simply disappeared. Each Spartakiad was accompanied by the much criticized "call to arms" and serious problems arose concerning the scheduling of construction work at Strahov. Late and poor construction even led to a tragic accident in 1965. During the line-up for rehearsal of a piece for older pupils entitled All for One in front of dressing-room building no. 5 a pillar for the local radio equipment collapsed.[612] The pillar's cast iron structure hit four fourteen-year-old boys from northeast Slovakia. One of them, Josef Maskalík of the town of Svidník suffered a fractured skull and brain contusion and died from his injuries in the hospital. The other boys apparently survived their injuries.[613]

612 "Neštěstí na Strahově". *Československý sport*, vol. 13, 30. 6. 1965, p. 2.

613 AČOS, f. III. celostátní spartakiáda 1965, Závěrečné hodnocení III. celostátní spartakiády 1965.

SPARTAKIAD FIVE-YEAR PLANS

Though the Spartakiad staffs were assembled more than three years before the event was held, the staff's core personnel were constantly at work on the Spartakiads, usually as part of various Sport-for-All Association committees or of Charles University's Faculty of Physical Education and Sports. The Spartakiad preparations were essentially carried out in constant cycles, as a kind of Spartakiad five-year plan.

The first year of the Spartakiad five-year plan, i.e. the year following the previous Spartakiad (e.g. 1981), was crucial in terms of creating a general concept for the event. Immediately at the start of the first year a commission was set up to prepare the next Spartakiad that was to operate until the Spartakiad staff was chosen the following year. Operating as part of the Czechoslovak Physical Education Association, this commission drafted basic "ideological-political concepts" and had them sanctified by the party's bodies.[614] As Spartakiad preparations gradually turned into a routine, the drafting of these documents and their approval became a mere formality. The basic ideological concept of the Spartakiads almost never changed – the Spartakiads were intended to demonstrate the mass appeal and advancement of Czechoslovak physical education, the care of the party for the people's well-being and, above all, gratitude to the Soviet Union for its liberation of the country in 1945 – only different motifs were accentuated. During the 1980 Spartakiad, for instance, support for the XXII Summer Olympic Games in Moscow was emphasized. The first year of the Spartakiad five-year plan was also the brainstorming period when there was the chance to critically contemplate the further development of the mass gymnastic exercises without the pressure of specific organizational and practical tasks. The comments and suggestions of the various Spartakiad

---

[614] See for instance Demetrovič, Ernest: "Diskusní příspěvek". In: *Sborník ze semináře FTVS UK Praha*, pp. 33–35.

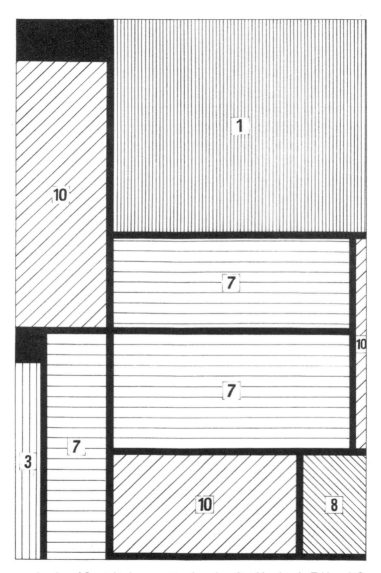

31. Choreography plan of Spartakiad composition based on Piet Mondrian's *Tableau I: Composition with Black, Red, Grey, Yellow and Blue* from 1921 that Spartakiad organizer Pavel Belšan submitted at a 1986 seminar.

departments and regional representatives of the gymnastics movement were processed, and work seminars and conferences of Spartakiad experts were organized. In January 1986 a comprehensive seminar was held at Charles University's Faculty of Physical Education and Sport, where key figures of the Spartakiad organization presented radical plans to transform the entire enterprise. They discussed the possibility of involving computers not only in the Spartakiad preparations, but also in creating the Spartakiad choreography.[615] Vratislav Svatoň proposed here remuneration for the tens of thousands of voluntary trainers; Pavel Belšan presented the plan to use Mondrian paintings as the basis for spatial choreography of Spartakiad compositions, supplementing his proposal with elaborate sketches. Many of the ideas were not aimed at the next Spartakiad, but the one after that, in this case the Czechoslovak Spartakiad planned for 1995.[616]

The second year of Spartakiad preparations (e.g. 1982) saw the basic organizational framework of the Spartakiads established and the choreographies created. At the beginning of the year, the federal government prepared a resolution on the Spartakiad that listed the obligations of the individual partners and released funds for modifications and repairs of Strahov Stadium. In the same period the commission for the Spartakiad preparation chose who would choreograph the Spartakiad performances. This was usually done in the form of a two-round competition, in which first the composition's basic concept and a rough sketch of the movements involved were submitted. In the second round, after the central staff had already been established, those chosen were then invited to exercise their piece in reduced numbers and present it to the steering committee. The winners would then incorporate the commission's suggestions and present a final version of the piece for approval. The basic

615   Interview with Pavel Belšan, 10. February 2006, Prague. Author's archive.
616   Král, A.: "Funkce OHV z hlediska příprav skladeb a koordinace činnosti složek tělovýchovného hnutí", p. 17.

32. Manufacturing indian clubs for women's performances at the 1975 Czechoslovak Spartakiad.

creative work on the Spartakiads had to be completed in the early phase of the Spartakiad preparations since this determined which tools and equipment, outfits and shoes needed to be produced – and the inefficient Czechoslovak consumer industry only managed with great difficulty to fill this order. This was the case even though the Spartakiad requirements were, upon resolution of the federal government, prioritized and additional hard-currency means were released to meet their needs. There was also the need to negotiate with partner organizations, such as the Ministry of Education, Svazarm and the military, and to sign the relevant agreements with them. A system for practicing the pieces already had to be in place at this point. By the end of the year, practice performances of the choreographed pieces were underway, followed by their performance for the heads of the Czechoslovak Gymnastics Association, Spartakiad staff and communist party "guests."

The third year of the Spartakiad five-year plan (e.g. 1983) prepared ground for the start of gymnastic training the following year. The choreographers created their detailed descriptions that included a breakdown of the participants' individual movements. The Spartakiad staff also acquired recordings of the music for the individual pieces and placed orders for the production of gramophone records (later cassette tapes) with the musical accompaniment. In cooperation with the film production company Krátký film and Czech Television, instructional films were prepared for practices. These were even distributed on video cassettes for the final Spartakiad. The steering committee completed its work on the program of the Spartakiad performances at Strahov, meaning that it determined the order of the pieces and prepared the opening and closing ceremonies, as well as the program for the interludes between the individual parts.

The Spartakiad's "peripheral" events were also arranged in this year so that they were not a burden to the organizational apparatus during the crucial fourth and fifth year. This mainly consisted of preparations of the Spartakiad parade, but also the sports and touristic parts of the Spartakiads and of the international Friendship Evenings.

At the start of the fourth year of the Spartakiad five-year plan (e.g. 1984) the descriptions of the individual pieces were issued to help the trainers in the practices. Trainer sessions, in which the authors of the pieces presented and explained the methodology of their exercises to the trainers, took place in several rounds. Spartakiad preparations began to gather momentum at the start of the school year in September when practices began in earnest at schools and gymnastics clubs. Following the Sokol model, the so-called "fire message" launched this phase of preparations in which relay runners with lit torches headed for the local stadiums and particularly

Strahov Stadium where the Spartakiad fires were lit. By then, the various schools and clubs were to have acquired the relevant tools and equipment, and Spartakiad outfits and shoes were to have been purchased at subsidized prices, though this timeframe was clearly never adhered to. During the autumn, inspections were made in the various districts to check on the number of participants and the

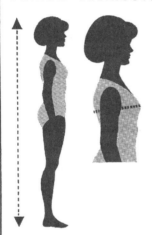

PRINCIP VELIKOSTNÍHO SYSTÉMU

Rozměry výrobků jednotlivých velikostí vycházejí ze základních tělesných rozměrů postav, pro které jsou určeny, t. j. z výšky postavy a obvodu hrudníku.

Pro dětské výrobky stačí k určení velikosti znalost tělesné výšky. U výrobků pro dospělé je nutno znát obvod hrudníku a výšku, případně obvod pasu (u některých výrobků stačí znát jen některé uváděné rozměry, např. pro výběr nátělníků, slipů a gymnastických úborů jen obvod hrudníku).

Výška postavy
se měří od temene hlavy k zemi.

Obvod hrudníku
se měří v podpaží tak, aby krejčovská míra byla vedena přes prsní hroty.
Naměřené hodnoty se udávají v centimetrech.

TABULKY

Na základě popsaného změření postavy je možno stanovit a označit potřebnou velikost cvičebního úboru dle tabulek pro jednotlivé skladby.

V tabulkách jsou hodnoty obvodu hrudníku, výšky (případně obvodu pasu) vytištěny slaběji. Odpovídající velikost je vytištěna silně.

SKLADBA Č. 1 „RODIČE A DĚTI"

Děti — Hrací kalhoty Dulinka, pulover kr. ruk. Ida

Výška postavy	86 — 95	96 — 105	106 — 115	116 — 125
Velikost	90	100	110	120

Ženy — Pulover a dlouhé kalhoty — souprava Pompa

Výška postavy	82 — 87	88 — 93	94 — 99	100 — 105	105 — 111
do 162 cm	2 — 42	2 — 45	2 — 48	2 — 51	2 — 54
nad 162 cm	3 — 42	3 — 45	3 — 48	3 — 51	3 — 54

33. "Principles of Size System" from the brochure *Information on the Sizes of Gymnastics Attire*, published by several textile companies for the needs of 1975 Spartakiad participants.

quality of the practices. The basic constructions at Strahov and at the stadiums in towns holding the district and regional Spartakiads were to have been completed by early winter. An agreement had to be signed with the military on the assistance provided by several hundred soldiers in carrying out the event. Detailed plans of Spartakiad logistics also needed to be completed by the year's end: plans for the participants' transportation to Prague, their accommodations in school, food, health care and for their free time; transporting the participants and spectators to Strahov, ticket sales, etc.

The first half of the fifth year of the Spartakiad five-year plan, i.e. the year that the Spartakiads were held (e.g. 1985) was obviously the most hectic. By the start of the year the participants were to already know all the individual parts of their piece and, to commemorate Victorious February, select groups of participants were to present for the first time an entire piece in public. The state of the Spartakiad practices were constantly checked throughout the spring, and serving this purpose was a system of regular reports from the bottom to the top of the Spartakiad organizational pyramid, as well as systematic inspections from the center in each district. These district Spartakiads, which took place in April and May with a member of the central Spartakiad staff present, served as a true test of the participants and organizational apparatus. The district Spartakiads played an important role in integrating and coordinating the "basic units," of which every Spartakiad piece was composed, and they determined which of these would take part in the Spartakiad finale at Strahov. These units, made up of a relatively low number of participants (e.g. nine or sixteen), were the basic choreographic component and the smallest organizational unit.

Recruits living in the military tent town in the Vypich area of Prague trained for the entire month before the start of the Strahov event. Prague had to be prepared for the onslaught of the participants. The area around Strahov, the path the parade would take, and the primary train stations to which the participants would arrive in Prague were all festively decorated in accordance with a pre-approved plan. As we will later see, the Spartakiad was also an occasion for numerous repairs to the city. All modifications at the Strahov complex had to be completed by the beginning of June, with the Strahov university dormitory turned over to the Spartakiad staff so that it could be used as a dressing room facility. An operative leadership of the staff was also formed at that time which was almost constantly holding meetings and dealing with the unforeseen situations that arose. In the weeks preceding the Spartakiad, the security bodies carried out extensive measures that also involved the military. For instance, during the first Spartakiad of 1955 the air force command gave the order to "maintain from dawn to dusk two S-102 planes on first-level alert, six S-102 planes on second-level alert."[617] The stadium itself was divided into zones with various security levels that could be accessed only with special permission. In 1975, for example, the Spartakiad staff issued thirteen different official passes authorizing entry to various parts of the stadium. The highest authorization, i.e. the right to enter all parts of Strahov Stadium, was held by the owners of the universal red pass with a yellow stripe that, if it also had a red star, allowed entry to the stands for government officials, to the roof of the west and east grandstands and to the Spartakiad control rooms.[618] After the Spartakiad had ended there was still several months of clearance work. This mainly consisted of moving materials, e.g. ten thousand "Spartakiad" cots or changing the dressing facilities back into a dormitory, but mainly of the administrative and final bookkeeping for the event. A preliminary assessment of the Spartakiad was also made and the conclusions were presented as a report to the head of the Czechoslovak Physical Education Association and to the party. A more detailed assessment then followed in

---

617 VHA, MNO – 1955, k. 314, inv. n. 1531, Návrh nařízení pro zabezpečení státních hranic v průběhu trvání I. celostátní spartakiády 1955.
618 *Průkazky a pásky pro činovníky, ostatní pracovníky a pořadatelský sbor ČSS 1975.* Sportpropag, Prague 1975.

which suggestions of the partner organizations were incorporated and which served as a basis for the preparations of the next Spartakiad. Autumn of the final year of the Spartakiad five-year plan also saw the awarding of Spartakiad organizers with athletic and sometimes even state honors. This phase was not always faultless, as we can read in the report of the Ministry of National Defense. A chief administrator complained that the work on the first Spartakiad was not deserving of so many honors and recommended that the number awarded be reduced by half. In his view the criteria for selecting them was not sufficiently strict and demanding: "How could the highest honor go to First Lieutenant Pláteník, who was demoted to the reserves, since his activities in the Spartakiad staff involved his getting to know a certain female official of the same staff which ended up breaking up his marriage [...]."[619]

The wrap-up work also included archiving documentation material produced during the Spartakiad's preparations. A special documentation commission was in charge of this and its task was to ensure that a "correct and objective" view was prepared for the "development of traditions in the Czechoslovak gymnastics movement." Following the completion of the final Spartakiad in 1985 the establishment of a "Hall of the Czechoslovak Spartakiad Traditions" at Strahov Stadium with "complete documentation and modern audio-visual technology" was seriously considered.[620]

---

619 VHA, f. MNO – 1955, k. 708, inv. n. 4197, Hodnocení I. celostátní spartakiády, Zpráva náčelníka hlavní kádrové správy F. Říhy.

620 Košák, Stanislav: "Diskusní příspěvek". In: *Sborník ze semináře FTVS UK Praha*, pp. 89–91. Košák justified his proposal with the spontaneous tourist interest in Strahov Stadium. Numerous tourist excursions allegedly headed there, including those of foreign tourists, to whom the guides would give a dubious explanation while showing the stadium's empty field through the closed entrance gates.

PHYSICAL AND IDEOLOGICAL TRAINING FOR THE SPARTAKIAD

In addition to the constant cycle of "Spartakiad five-year plans" the Spartakiad organizers also used the term "Spartakiad year."[621] This was the nine months from the start of practicing the Spartakiad pieces in September at the beginning of the school year until the actual performance at Strahov Stadium in early July. The complete transformation of hundreds of thousands of individuals into perfectly synchronized and conscious gymnastic participants was to take place during this period. The Spartakiad practice not only disciplined the participant's body, it was also intended as an opportunity to "create the features of a socialist personality in an unforced and systematic way" and to contribute to "the creation of a socialist way of life for workers and of a uniform ideological upbringing of youth."[622]

However, the organizers' greatest efforts were aimed at controlling the participants' bodies. Here they could build on the Sokol tradition and their own experience from Sokol or other institutions of discipline such as the military. According to many organizers, the process of the "sportification of Sokol" in the first half of the 1950s led to the weakening of Sokol techniques of disciplinization. Vilém Mucha complained in 1955 that in many Spartakiad performances "keeping in step, alignments and arrangements were quite often pitiful."[623] Much attention was focused on drill exercises that, as Vratislav Svatoň emphasized much later at the very end of state socialism, "allow the instructors and officials to easily manipulate the exercise participants, save time and are a test of conscious discipline

---

621 E.g., Marek, J.: *Politickovýchovné působení funkcionářů, cvičitelů, učitelů tělesné výchovy a trenérů při přípravě Československé spartakiády 1980*, p. 32.

622 Marek, J. Et al.: *Politickovýchovné působení funkcionářů, cvičitelů, trenérů a učitelů tělesné výchovy při přípravě Československé spartakiády 1985*, p. 21.

623 Mucha, V.: *První celostátní spartakiáda 1955: věcí všeho pracujícího lidu Československa*, p. 17. See *Československá spartakiáda 1980 a ďalší rozvoj masovej telesnej výchovy*. Oddelenie propagandy a agitácie ÚV KSČ, Bratislava 1980 (edition: Fakty a argumenty, n. 6).

34. Rehearsal for the 1955 Spartakiad in the gym of a Prague elementary school (photo Václav Chochola).

35. Rehearsal for the 1955 Spartakiad. Performance of Revolutionary Trade Union members at the Municipal Library in Prague (photo Václav Chochola).

and order."[624] The exercises themselves did not only require that the movements be remembered and executed properly, but also that one's body be under complete control. To create the impression of collective movement it was important to eliminate all elements of the individuality of movement. The brochure *Instructions for Pupils and Youth Exercising at the 1st All-State Spartakiad* stated: "Don't rely on on there being a lot of you and think that something will not be noticed in the large numbers. The slightest jutting out from a row, any imprecise movement of arms, improper bowed or raised head, the slightest movement in which you adjust your clothing or hair – everything is visible and disrupts the overall impression."[625] The synchronized movement of the participants made every movement that diverged from the prescribed plan apparent and created a paradoxical effect in which, despite the vast number of participants, each of them stood quite visibly and "legibly" alone. The distribution of the participants' bodies on the stadium field according to a pre-designed geometrical grid represented a visual strategy transforming the social field into a kind of analytical crowd. An individual's only relationship to the other participants was the geometrical composition of the piece; all other relations were considered unwanted as attested to by the following commands: "If someone next to you feels sick or faints, do not pay any attention and continue with the exercise! This is not being unfriendly: you can't do anything about it anyway and the health services will take care of him."[626]

624 Marek, Jaroslav – Svatoň, Vratislav: *Politickovýchovné působení funkcionářů, cvičitelů, trenérů a učitelů tělesné výchovy při přípravě Československé spartakiády 1990*, p. 19.
625 *Pokyny pro žactvo a dorost cvičící na I. celostátní spartakiádě*. Štáb 1. celost. spartakiády, Prague 1955, p. 24.
626 *Pokyny pro žactvo a dorost cvičící na I. celostátní spartakiádě*, p. 26. The uniformity of the participants' appearance was to be similarly consistent. Spartakiad organizers repeatedly warned female participants not to let their bra straps show and griped over the "tasteless and contemptible habit" of exercising with watches, earrings, ring or necklaces. See for instance Třešňáková, V.: "Úloha cvičebních úborů při hromadném vystoupení", p. 150.

The disciplining of the body was to occur in "dialectical unity" with ideological indoctrination.[627] The ideological instruction of Spartakiad participants was not the responsibility of the former Sokol members, but of the sporting officials from the communist milieu. In the 1950s and 60s this was mainly Vilém Mucha, while in the 1970s and 80s this role fell to the "conscious, advanced party member" Jaroslav Marek.[628] The duration of the nine-month Spartakiad practices was accompanied by an elaborate "ideological-educational plan" divided into individual quarters. At the 1980 Spartakiad, for instance, the following topics were to be discussed:

In the 3rd quarter of 1979: the significance of the 1980 Czechoslovak Spartakiad, the significance of the Slovak National Uprising; in the 4th quarter of 1979: the 1980 Czechoslovak Spartakiad as the successor and implementer of progressive and revolutionary traditions of the gymnastic performances of the Czech and Slovak nation, Successes of our society as emphasized in the conclusions of the 15th Congress of the Communist Party; in the 1st quarter of 1980: the history of the Olympic Games and their importance in Moscow, Soviet physical culture; in the 2nd quarter of 1980: the 35th anniversary of the culmination of our national resistance and of the liberation of Czechoslovakia by the Soviet army, 35 years of success for Czechoslovak gymnastics and sports, Preparations for staying in Prague (an explanation of the instructions and ensuring that all participants of the 1980 Czechoslovak Spartakiad understand them).[629]

627 Marek, J. – Svatoň, V.: *Politickovýchovné působení funkcionářů, cvičitelů, trenérů a učitelů tělesné výchovy při přípravě Československé spartakiády 1990*, p. 22.
628 See Budský, František (ed.): *Vilém Mucha*. Olympia, Prague 1976; Kössl, Jiří: "Profesor Jaroslav Marek šedesátiletý". *Teorie a praxe tělesné výchovy*, 1989, vol. 37, n. 12, p. 767. Along with these main figures, hundreds of other workers were active in the political-educational divisions of the various Spartakiad staffs. Their regular reports are an important source for monitoring moods among participants (see the following chapter).
629 Marek, J.: *Politickovýchovné působení funkcionářů, cvičitelů, učitelů tělesné výchovy a trenérů při přípravě Československé spartakiády 1980*, p. 32.

The main emphasises during these instructional sessions was placed on the "creation of a class Marxist-Leninist historical consciousness" based on the history of mass gymnastic performances.[630] Most of the instructional publications explaining to the trainers what they should convey to the participants focused on an appreciation of the tradition of mass gymnastic performances. The participants were to learn to distinguish between progressive and reactionary elements of Sokol gymnastics, to learn the secrets of the sectarian struggles of leftist gymnastics which led to the organization of the first Spartakiad in 1921, and also to appreciate the "nation-wide" nature of the 1938 Slet and the reactionary nature of the Slet that followed in 1948. The reasons why Spartakiads were better than Sokol Slets and how they gradually became a unique expression of the Czechoslovak people, unparalleled in the world, were also stressed to the participants. They were taught of the effect of "counter-revolutionary forces" in physical education during the Prague Spring and about how they had attempted to cast a doubt on the social role of mass gymnastic performances.

The basic form of these sessions consisted of "discussions on exercise mats." The instructors themselves, guest political-educational workers, or even witnesses of past events were to hold discussions with the participants in an accessible form. For the younger participants, ideological issues were to be simplified as needed. The methodological writings for instructors of the 1985 Spartakiad entitled *The Relay Race of Czechoslovak Spartakiads* discuss ideological matters in the form of simple questions and answers. The instructor was supposed to ask the children questions such as: "Tell me children, who among you can explain what it is to be a slave?" The children's responses were to include fascist subjugation, as well as Spartacus and his uprising. Another question: "Who among you

---

630 Marek, J. et al.: *Politickovýchovné působení funkcionářů, cvičitelů, trenérů a učitelů tělesné výchovy při přípravě Československé spartakiády 1985*, p. 11.

can tell me in your own words what a relay race is?" The correct response was to involve the Spartakiad exercises from the first Spartakiad in 1921, to the 1955 Spartakiad, all the way to the Spartakiad being prepared at that time: "Today it is we who are running a leg of the famous gymnastic performances. Even you, little Honza, even you little Eva, Ivona, Jana, Petra [...] Before us, even our daddies, mommies, grannies and uncles ran a leg of this race." In response to the purpose of Spartakiad exercises, they were to say that they do it so that they don't become obese and so that they are healthy."And he who is healthy is also a good student [...]will turn into a good worker and a brave guardian of the socialist society." The trainers were instructed to take an interest in the actual views of the participants, not to act from a position of power and to be aware that "errant" and "unsocialist" views might appear among them since, as Jaroslav Marek wrote, "opinions are not inherited."[631] Marek elsewhere wrote: "[...] we have to take an interest in our gymnasts' opinions, how they approach certain issues and why, and we have to try to help them so that they rid themselves of errant views that lead to errant behavior."[632]

The successful effect of these political-educational endeavors is doubtful. A 1960 report, for instance, includes the following: "Despite some good results we must admit that the 'Discussions on Exercise Mats' were in many cases only held as a formality or not at all. Shortcomings in political-educational work were apparent in matters of discipline, especially among adolescents, e.g. in Brno."[633] As we will see in the next chapter, the Spartakiad largely failed as a didactic project, yet at the same time the attempts at ideological

631   Marek, J.: *Politickovýchovné působení funkcionářů, cvičitelů, učitelů tělesné výchovy a trenérů při přípravě Československé spartakiády 1980*, p. 30.

632   Marek, J. et al.: *Politickovýchovné působení funkcionářů, cvičitelů, trenérů a učitelů tělesné výchovy při přípravě Československé spartakiády 1985*, p. 26.

633   NA, f. KSČ – Ústřední výbor 1945–1989, Ideologické oddělení (05/3), sv. 40, a.j. 324, Zpráva o zajištění politicko-výchovné práce mezi cvičenci při II. CS z 11. 6. 1960.

control document the far-reaching totalitarian ambitions of the state-socialist project.

A condition for accepting the ideological message – as ideological workers were constantly repeating – was for the participants to take part in the Spartakiad practices voluntarily. This requirement was never fully met over the course of the Spartakiads' existence, except for possibly the cancelled one in 1970. The greatest coercion of the participants, as we have already shown, took place during the first Spartakiad. In later years, most of the adult participants voluntarily took part in the Spartakiad practices as part of their involvement in the Sport-for-All Association. However, the situation at schools, where practicing for the Spartakiad was never based exclusively on the pupils volunteering, was another matter. From one Spartakiad to the next (and especially in preparing for the 1965 Spartakiad) the requirement that the next Spartakiad be organized fully on a voluntary basis was always repeated, though never fully came to be.[634]

As with all preceding Spartakiads, the need to recruit "volunteer participants, if possible" was also emphasized in planning for the final Spartakiad in 1990.[635] The very definition of "volunteering" also came into play. It seems as if the organizers meant by this that the participants had the right to refuse to practice without having to face any consequences for this decision. But this did not mean that only those who felt like it would practice. This is attested to by complaints from the Spartakiad organizers of the "wrong understanding of what it means to volunteer" from 1969: "The principle of volunteering is applied in recruiting, but this is often understood

634 See for instance "Pojetí III. CS, její program a časové uspořádání". *Teorie a praxe tělesné výchovy*, 1961, vol. 9, zvláštní číslo: Výsledky výzkumu II. celostátní spartakiády 1960, pp. 61–63.
635 Kos, B.: "Vývojové tendence v tvorbě a režii pohybových skladeb", p. 48. As late as 1989 Vratislav Svatoň was emphasizing the importance of the participant's free choice: "What mistake are we making when schools and classes that will practice the Spartakiad exercises are designated by directive for the sake of organizational simplicity [...]?". Marek, J. – Svatoň, V.: *Politickovýchovné působení funkcionářů, cvičitelů, trenérů a učitelů tělesné výchovy při přípravě Česko- slovenské spartakiády 1990*, p. 16.

and explained as literally "whoever wants to can practice." There is almost no talk of the positive aspects of the Spartakiads and of their benefit, which plays into the hands of those who did and do not have a positive view of the events."[636] The participants themselves held varying views of the exercises in the different practice phases. A survey taken during the 1965 Spartakiad in 1965 showed, for instance, that among junior women (i.e. the category that was traditionally the least difficult to recruit) only a little over half of the participants practiced completely voluntarily; the others described their participation as "partially voluntarily," "partially forced" or "completely forced."[637]

However, the vast majority of those same junior women expressed satisfaction with the exercises and the desire to take part in the next Spartakiad. The first phase of the practices in which the participants had to endlessly repeat the same sequence of movements was obviously not popular, but after mastering the entire piece and performing it repeatedly in public, the participants' relationship to the choreographed performance often changed.[638] Great motivation, particularly for those participants not from Prague, was the actual Spartakiad event at Strahov Stadium, which they viewed as a "reward" for practicing the whole year. Participation in the Spartakiad was thus the result of a mix of coercion, an established routine and incentives, as well as the participants' own interest and even their enthusiasm.

636 AČOS, f. IV. celostátní spartakiáda 1970 – Základní dokumenty IV. ČS 1970, Informace o přípravách na IV. ČSS v OV a MV ČTO. The report further states: "Along with a lower interest in practicing, it means that the number of participants at district Spartakiads will be significantly lower than before, probably by about 50 percent. This generally shows that there is a greater interest in practicing among women than among men."

637 Škrobánková, Zora – Kroupa, Jaroslav: "Vliv nácviku skladby 'Jaro země mé' na rozvoj pohybové paměti a kultury pohybu cvičenek". *Teorie a praxe tělesné výchovy,* 1966, vol. 14, n. 4, pp. 245–247.

638 See for instance Marek, J. – Svatoň, V.: *Politickovýchovné působení funkcionářů, cvičitelů, trenérů a učitelů tělesné výchovy při přípravě Československé spartakiády 1990*, p. 15.

SPARTAKIAD PARTICIPANTS IN PRAGUE: TRANSPORTATION, ACCOMMODATIONS AND FOOD

The biggest challenge for organizers understandably occurred upon the participants' arrival to Prague. Despite careful planning and constant verifying, they were unable to control the mass of people and transfer the image of perfect organization from the exercising field to the participants' conduct in Prague. Constantly repeated orders and prohibitions regarding their stay in Prague show that the goal of transforming the participants into an obedient mass was not achieved. The main problem did not consist of a lack of organizational work or of the resources that were consumed at Spartakiads in a seemingly unlimited amount, but in the many unforeseeable aspects of this ritual. Obviously, a great unknown was the weather which both the spectators and participants (the latter of whom also had to spend several hours at an open-air meeting place) were exposed to in the unroofed stadium. A much greater problem was posed by the unpredictable behavior of the participants. The organizers complained that "though they think through and plan for all possibilities, one factor cannot be foreseen even though it is one of the most important: the behavior of the participants themselves."[639]

Spartakiad participants were lodged almost exclusively in Prague schools, which among other things meant that Prague schools had to end their academic year at least a week early (with the university dormitories at Strahov ending a month early). Even so, all Spartakiads faced a shortage in lodging capacity. Though the standard of 2.5 m² of floor space per participant was usually complied with, a limiting factor was the schools' washroom facilities.[640] Despite the extremely cramped standards (1 water faucet or sink per 10 to 12 people,

---

639 Wolf, Augustin: "Hygiena stravování na spartakiádě". *Výživa lidu*, 1955, vol. 10, n. 6, p. 1.
640 NA, f. ÚV ČSTV, k. 268, Zásady pro další řešení ubytování aktivních účastníků Československé spartakiády 1985.

1 toilet per 20 women, 1 toilet + 1 urinal per 40 men) it was difficult to accommodate all the participants in schools. Special washrooms were therefore set up in the courtyards of schools, which, however, further complicated matters since women could not then be housed in such facilities. According to the organizers' reports, the conditions at accommodations for the first Spartakiads did not even meet basic hygienic standards. For example, an extensive health report on the 1965 Spartakiad, which praised distinct improvements made in comparison with the previous Spartakiad, noted several basic shortcomings: most lodgings lacked a sufficient number of washbasins and a general lack of showers, especially when the demand was high following the exercises. Forty percent of the accommodations had no showers, only fifteen percent had a constant supply of hot water, twenty percent had intermittent hot water and the rest had only cold water. Half of the accommodation facilities were completely lacking toilet paper.[641] At first, the participants slept on straw mattresses that were filled for the Spartakiad needs and then emptied after the event had ended. During the "normalization" Spartakiads, the participants slept on special Spartakiad cots that were notoriously unstable. The participants usually brought their own sleeping bags or blankets and pillows with them to Prague.

The participants' behavior at their lodgings was probably less than exemplary. This is evident in e.g. the Housing Rules for participants of the 1975 Czechoslovak Spartakiad, whose individual instructions and restrictions were obviously based on past adverse experiences.[642] In the very first sentence the Spartakiad organizers felt the need to emphasize that the "lodgings [are] socialist property and as such are protected by law." In addition to the usual ban on alcohol

641 Matějcová, Anna: "Orientační průzkum podmínek cvičenců na III. CS v Praze z hlediska zdravotního". *Teorie a praxe tělesné výchovy*, 1966, vol. 14, n. 4, pp. 249–250.
642 AČOS, f. Československá spartakiáda 1975 – Ústřední štáb Československé spartakiády 1975, Pořadatelský odbor, ubytovací komise, Ubytovací řád pro cvičence Československé spartakiády 1975.

(and card playing) it was also forbidden to "damage the walls of the lodgings by gluing posters to them," "hammering nails into the walls," "interfering with the electrical wiring," "remaining in the lodgings after the participants have departed" or "having an open flame." The Housing Rules also pointed out that "there is no charge for opening the lodging after closing hours."

36. A special Slet and Spartakiad tram circuit at Břevnov during the 1960 Spartakiad in Prague (photo Václav Chochola).

In terms of logistics, the transport of participants and spectators to Strahov Stadium or to the Spartakiad parade was the most difficult aspect. Although Spartakiad organizers could follow up on the infrastructure work conducted during the previous Slets, the inundation of participants and spectators often exceeded Prague Public Transportation's capacity and also had a negative impact on other transportation in Prague. For instance, special buses had to be used in the Prague 6 district since many of the streetcar lines ended in two specially designed and still preserved loops in the Dlabačov area of Prague 6 near Strahov. Three color-coded routes of twenty special streetcar and four special bus lines marked "Stadium" were designated for spectators and participants. Serving the first three Spartakiads as well as the final Slet were trolley-buses that ran e.g., in intervals of 17 seconds in 1960.[643] As in other areas, here too it was most difficult to control the unpredictable behavior of Spartakiad passengers. Prague Public Transportation futilely announced: "If the vehicle is full, do not overload it by cramming yourself in. Doing so delays both this vehicle and those that follow."[644] As apparent in the amateur documentary film *Zelená pro Strahov* (Green Light for Strahov) on transportation during the 1980 Spartakiad, many buses lost a window due to overcrowding, which also caused some subway stations to temporarily close – especially in transporting participants to the Spartakiad parade. Many of the participants then had no other choice but to heed Prague Public Transportation's advice and walk up Strahov Hill to the event.

The logistical problems in transporting, lodging and feeding the participants during the rehearsals for the final performances often resulted in the need to have the participants wake up very early in the morning or to rehearse the pieces late at night. The rehearsal

643 Papoušek, Jaroslav: *II. celostátní spartakiáda. II. část: Mládí a krása.* Krátký film, Prague 1960, 44 minutes.
644 AČOS, f. Československá spartakiáda 1975, Informace pro cvičence a návštěvníky Čs. spartakiády 1975 (vydaly Dopravní podniky hl. m. Prahy).

schedule for adult women for e.g., the 1975 Spartakiad at Strahov went as follows: Wake-up call and breakfast 2:25 a.m.; transportation to Strahov 3:40 a.m.; line-up 5:00 a.m.; rehearsal including entry and departure 7:00 a.m.; use of dressing rooms after the performance 10:00 a.m.; transportation from Strahov 11:00 a.m.; lunch 12:20 p.m.[645] Rehearsals for military and university participants took place even earlier.

37. Pictogram from the brochure *Health Tips for Participants of the 1980 Czechoslovak Spartakiad*. Accompanying text "Do not consume large quantities of ice cream or smoked meats. We do not recommend that athletes consume alcoholic drinks, including beer."

The provision of meals for the Spartakiad participants was extremely difficult from an organizational standpoint. Data from the second Spartakiad in 1960, in which over five million meals were served (1,834,000 breakfasts, 110,000 snacks, 1,425,000 lunches, 1,660,000 dinners) gives a rough idea of the organizational work involved. The Meals Committee or the Ministry of the Internal Trade officials encountered a number of organizational obstacles. Along

---

645 AČOS, f. Československá spartakiáda 1975, Režim cvičenců Československé spartakiády 1975.

with feeding the gymnastic participants, they also needed to have food available for the Spartakiad's other non-gymnastic participants and visitors.[646]

Not only were Prague's alimentation supply capacities exhausted, the feeding of participants also strained the supply limits of the country itself. During e.g. the first Spartakiad, potatoes had to be scratched from the menu since the autumn harvest had not been a good one and the spring ones soon ran out, but also because "there was no guarantee that the required number of peelers would be available."[647] The goal of a well-balanced menu also had to be abandoned since it would have been "very difficult for us to serve vegetable meals often."[648]

The feeding of the participants is also an interesting example of how the "new person" project failed.[649] This massive catering action was for Spartakiad organizers and dieticians a unique opportunity to change "old" eating habits and to promote a "proper" and "rational"

646 Hock, Jaromír: "Problematika stravování při II. CS". *Výživa lidu*, 1960, vol. 15, n. 6, pp. 88–89. See also NA, f. SVTVS, k. 46, Tajné spisy 1955, n. j. 184, Zpráva o zajištění zásobování při I. celostátní spartakiádě ze dne 28. února 1955.

647 Krupička, Jiří: "Organisace stravovací služby při I. celostátní spartakiádě". *Výživa lidu*, 1955, vol. 10, n. 4, pp. 53–54.

648 "Péče o hygienu výživy o spartakiádě. Rozhovor s MUDr. Neradilovou z pražské KHES". *Výživa lidu*, 1955, vol. 10, n. 7–8, pp. 104–105. "[...] we couldn't take into account the various regional customs – some children from Slovakia rejected the favorite Czech food of baked pasta with ham." Ibid. Health officials at the 1960 Spartakiad complained of the "deterioration of food quality" due to the "considerable dustiness of the assembly areas and field." See Král, J. – Mathé, E.: "Zdravotnický průzkum II. CS.", pp. 52–53.

649 Despite significant efforts (e.g. for the 1960 Spartakiad there were printed ten million educational labels on matches), the attempt to use Spartakiads for health education ended up with similar results. Miroslava Klímová-Fügnerová, the author of the famous instructional book *Naše dítě* (Our Child) complained that "educational work among Spartakiad participants apparently is not easy," adult participants "underestimate the threat of illness and surprisingly fear being vaccinated!" Moreover, health education during the first Spartakiad failed due to organizational chaos: "The health workers did not know the exercise times and addresses for the clubs, not to speak of their lack of interest in arranging discussions." The weak results of the health education attempts were summarized in a brief conclusion: "We still have not improved the hygienic culture of our people." Klímová-Fügnerová, Miroslava: "Zdravotnickou osvětou k úspěchu spartakiády". *Výživa lidu,* 1960, vol. 15, n. 4, pp. 49–50.

diet.[650] Yet this experiment did not succeed. For instance, at the 1960 Spartakiad the easily digestible and high calorie meal of butter cakes with curd cheese and cocoa was served as a main dish. According to Jiří Krupička, one of the catering organizers, this "meal was certainly nutritious, tasty and packed with more calories than any of the other meals," though he himself admitted that it was inconsistent with the "customary tastes of our consumers," and therefore was "the subject of most of the complaints about the food during the first days."[651] Krupička further stated that the "dissatisfaction of those eating was so great that the meal had to be scratched from the menu and replaced with normal kinds of food such as beef goulash and potatoes or a pork and vegetable mix." The attempt to add the Malcao cocoa drink and an "excellent" cheese spread to the breakfast menu met with a similar fate. "We kept hearing that white coffee would be better than cocoa, and that cold-cuts would be better than cheese spread," writes Krupička. The lack of success with similar experiments led to the conclusion that the participants "derailed from their customary way of life" in an unusual environment, "under physical and mental strain [...] need food that is as close as possible to that which they are accustomed."[652] The preserved menus from "normalization" Spartakiads reveal that cold-cuts were now always offered for breakfast.

The matter was made worse by the fact that dietology itself had undergone a rapid transformation since the 1950s.[653] This is well evident in the drinking regimen. According to complaints by nutritionists, the menu for the participants of the first Spartakiad,

---

650 See for instance Hock, J.: "Problematika stravování při II. CS", pp. 88–89.
651 Krupička, Jiří: "Prvé poznatky z II. celostátní spartakiády". *Výživa lidu*, 1960, vol. 15, n. 9, pp. 136–137.
652 Hock, J.: "Problematika stravování při II. CS", pp. 88–89.
653 This was also obviously a personnel failure. The medical report from the 3rd Spartakiad stated that children in the dormitories were served foul-smelling and undercooked potatoes and that instances of theft by the dormitory staff occurred. Matějcová, A.: "Orientační průzkum podmínek cvičenců na III. CS v Praze z hlediska zdravotního", pp. 249–250.

which was proposed by medical doctors of the Institute for Physical Education, professionally assessed by the Institute for the Study of the People's Alimentation and ultimately approved by the Ministry of Health, "neglected fluids," forcing "children to find their own sources however possible."[654] This was rectified by an emergency supply of drinking water at Strahov provided by a special Spartakiad commission of the Czechoslovak Communist Party's Central Committee.[655] Yet this was not merely a case of neglect: the participants were often warned not to drink too much. This was partly a practical measure as evident in the *Instructions for Pupils and Adolescents Exercising at the 1st All-State Spartakiad*, which advised the participants: "not to drink more than is necessary so that you do not have to go to the bathroom frequently,"[656] but also a belief among experts of the harmfulness of drinking. A leading expert in nutrition and the author of a number of professional publications, Dr. Zdeňka Luhanová was still warning participants in 1960 that "when the summer heat forces us to drink more fluids, we should try to limit our intake to avoid digestive problems from an excessive amount of fluids and to prevent too much sweating."[657] In diet, as in many other regards, the Spartakiads were not an example of a successful social experiment, and instead demonstrated the power of ingrained social patterns.

654 "Péče o hygienu výživy o spartakiádě. Rozhovor s MUDr. Neradilovou z pražské KHES", pp. 104–105.
655 AČOS, f. l. celostátní spartakiáda 1955 – Politické materiály, Zápis z porady komise ÚV KSČ pro zajištění I. celostátní spartakiády konané 21. června 1955 u soudruha Šalgy.
656 *Pokyny pro žactvo a dorost cvičící na I. celostátní spartakiádě*, p. 25.
657 Luhanová, Zdeňka: "Jedeme na spartakiádu". *Výživa lidu*, 1960, vol. 15, n. 4, p. 52.

THE DISCIPLINARY SPACE OF STRAHOV STADIUM

Strahov Stadium and the entire logistics background represented a disciplinary space *par excellence* aimed at transforming a disorganized crowd into an analytical mass. The stadium's architecture, whether its tangible features in the form of the dressing facilities, assembly areas, field, stands or control centers, or its intangible aspects especially the network of place marks, was intended to ensure the absolute visibility and "legibility" of the participants and also allow for the people's unmediated view of themselves. A wholly unique interaction between the human body, architecture and political power was occurring here.

38. Departing the stadium during the 1960 Spartakiad (photo Václav Chochola). The prompt departure and entrance of the participants to the stadium was one of the main logistical problems of Spartakiad organization.

Mass gymnastics performances as the regular arrangement of bodies based on abstract geometrical rules can be carried out in any space. This was historically one of the main reasons why it spread so quickly. Yet Strahov Stadium provided the Slets and later the Spartakiads with a specific frame, largely shaping their choreographies and dictating their maximum size (as well as their minimum size as the Sokols learned to their detriment in 1994). It also became part of the Spartakiad mythology: the march through the Gate of Athletes was considered in particular a life-changing liminal experience.

Strahov Stadium, whose development, dictated by the rhythm of Sokol Slets, we examined in the first chapter, underwent periodical transformations even after Sokol was abolished – only now it was based on the Spartakiad five-year rhythm. The construction of a completely new stadium was considered during the preparations of the first Spartakiad.

Ultimately, time constraints and organizational turmoil forced the plans for a new stadium to be abandoned and the modifications to Strahov stadium to be merely cosmetic, though with all the more decorative socialist-realistic embellishments designed by Jiří Kroha's studio.[658] In a short essay in *Architektura ČSR* (Czechoslovak Architecture) magazine, Kroha, in an apparent rebuke of his functionalist predecessors, explained that he was striving for "a new design that was comprehensible and close to our people" and that subdued the "hard and monotonous effect of reinforced concrete."[659] In addition to modifications to the stadium's surroundings in which the Spartacus sculpture in particular stood out and functionally replaced the former dominant sculpture of a falcon with outspread

---

658 AČOS, f. I. celostátní spartakiáda 1955 – Základní dokumenty, Ideový program, plán příprav a návrh rozpočtu I. celostátní spartakiády v roce 1955, p. 10. See also Svobodová, Markéta: "Věčný ruch a věčná nespokojenost nad Strahovským stadionem". *Stavba*, 2004, vol. 11, n. 2, pp. 14–19.

659 Kroha, Jiří: "Státní stadion na Strahově – úprava pro I. celostátní spartakiádu". *Architektura ČSR*, 1956, vol. 15, n. 1–2, pp. 136–138.

wings, Kroha mainly focused on modifying the east grandstands. The main motif became the festive decoration of the Gate of Athletes that was framed by high pylons with monumental sculptures and topped off by a "dynamic" parapet of medallions and numerous banners. Kroha's task was not limited only to Strahov; the architect also took it upon himself to plan the Spartakiad parade and the decorations for the city.[660] Kroha's work on the Spartakiad was his final project and most likely the final socialist-realist architectural project anywhere in Czechoslovakia. As described in detail by Kimberly E. Zarecor, his MANU (Master Studio of a National Artist) studio was dissolved following the Spartakiad.[661] In the same issue of *Architektura ČSR*, the architect of prior modifications to the stadium, Ferdinand Balcárek,[662] cautiously criticized Kroha's changes as inorganic and "overly ornate." Balcárek felt that the modifications to the Gate of Athletes required "larger and more basic forms," that its design suffered by the fact that the "architect probably overlooked the stadium's 2.5 meter eastward slope." Kroha's decorations were completely removed for the next Spartakiad in 1960 and the east grandstands were rebuilt in the international style by Josef Hrubý and František Cubr, designers of the Czechoslovak Pavilion at EXPO 58 in Brussels.[663]

660   Zarecor Elman, Kimberly. *Manufacturing a Socialist Modernity: Housing in Czechoslovakia, 1945–1960.* University of Pittsburgh Press, Pittsburgh 2011.

661   Kroha's fall went hand in hand with the decline in Soviet-styled architecture. See Day, Adrew: "The Rise and Fall of Stalinist Architecture". In: James Cracraft – Daniel B. Rowland (eds.): *Architectures of Russian identity. 1500 to the present.* Cornell University Press, Ithaca 2003. Day points to the example of the post-war reconstruction of Stalingrad to exemplify the lowered faith of the party elite in architects and how they were gradually replaced by building planners.

662   Balcárek, Ferdinand: [Bez názvu]. *Architektura ČSR*, 1956, vol. 15, n. 1–2, p. 138.

663   Cubr, František – Hrubý, Josef: "Architektonické úpravy a výzdoba strahovského areálu pro II. celostátní spartakiádu 1960". *Architektura ČSSR*, 1960, vol. 19, n. 10, pp. 703–706. See also Kramerová, Daniela (ed.): *Bruselský sen. Československá účast na světové výstavě EXPO 58 v Bruselu a životní styl 1. poloviny 60. let.* Arbor vitae, Prague 2008, p. 237. In collaboration with the Czechoslovak Film Enterprises Barrandov a recording studio was also created that replaced the live orchestra used up until then. See Kouřimský, G.: *Spartakiádní areál Strahov*, p. 14.

39. The photo of Military performance at Strahov Stadium during the 1960 Spartakiad shows the eastern stands of the Strahov Stadium remodelled in the international style by architects Josef Hrubý and František Cubra.

The final significant modification of Strahov Stadium, a definitive construction of the three-storey east grandstands with the Gate of Athletes, which was the only component that was still partially wooden, was planned for the fourth Spartakiad in 1970. In January 1967 the incomplete old east grandstand was demolished by detonation, but the construction of a new grandstand stagnated.[664]

The delay in construction was also one of the reasons that led to the cancellation of the 1970 Spartakiad, though the main reason undoubtedly lay in the fear of insufficiently "normalized" participants.

664 Honke-Houfek, Olivier – Kuna, Zdeněk – Stupka, Zdeněk: "Spartakiádní stadion na Strahově – východní tribuna". *Architektura ČSR*, 1975, vol. 34, n. 7, pp. 301–306.

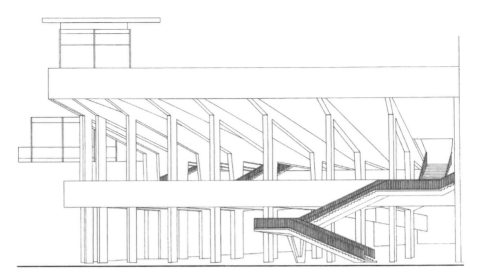

40. Linear perspective of Strahov Stadium's eastern grandstands from a northern view created in March 1968 by the architect Olivier Honke-Houfek as part of the 1970 Spartakiad preparations. In the left part we see one of the balconies that served to direct entrances of the gymnasts; the stairway in the right part provided spectators with access to the bridge over Spartakiad Avenue and entrance to the grandstands.

The east grandstands, over four hundred meters long, were completed by the Armabeton state company in September 1973 on the occasion of the 3rd Summer Spartakiad of Warsaw-Pact Armies. This new grandstand represented the largest investment project of the Czechoslovak Physical Education Association in its history with the grandstand covering a twenty-five meter swimming pool with spectator stands, a sauna, an 18 x 12 meter fencing arena and the central control room for the mass gymnastic performances.[665] A ten-meter-wide gallery that led along the entire length of the east

[665] Also located here were two gyms approximately 600 m² in size and a number of other operations and office rooms. Originally, the Spartakiad staff's archive, the primary source of this work, was also to be located here. In the early 1990s the Czech Sokol Community allegedly saved it from being destroyed, storing it on their own premises.

grandstand on the first floor bridged the Spartakiad Avenue, which was closed to the public due to the line-up of the participants. This resolved one of the logistical nightmares of previous performances at Strahov in which the movement of spectators intersected with the entering participants. The construction of the east grandstand and the reconstruction of the west grandstand significantly changed the ratio of standing places to seating. While in 1960 nearly three quarter of the places were standing room only (100,000), in 1975 over two thirds of the spectators were seated (88,000). In practice, however, the grandstands remained overcrowded, e.g., at the 1975 Spartakiad the 192,000 spectators was an attendance record.[666] With the construction of the east grandstand, Strahov Stadium acquired its definitive form that essentially remained unchanged throughout the "normalization" period. The construction of a special "presidential" footbridge prior to the final Spartakiad that linked Evžen Rošický Stadium with Strahov Stadium and that was built to "eliminate one of the most serious operating problems that entailed entering spectators and honored guests crossing in the areas in front of the west grandstand of the Spartakiad Stadium," was the only other distinct modification.[667]

In terms of Spartakiad logistics and the production of an organizable analytical mass, the Strahov dressing room "town" played an essentiel role. These facilities not only served as locker rooms and showers for the participants, they were also used to transform the unformed mass of participants that arrived at Strahov from various directions and mixed and mingled, into an organized mass prepared to assume their positions at place markers on the Strahov field. The capacity of the dressing rooms handcuffed the Spartakiad

666 Chvalný, J.: *Československá spartakiáda 1975*, unpagin.
667 AČOS, f. Československá spartakiáda 1985, Usnesení vlády ČSSR ze dne 17. 11. 1983 n. 287, Zpráva k návrhu usnesení vlády ČSSR o opatřeních pro zajištění příprav Československé spartakiády 1985.

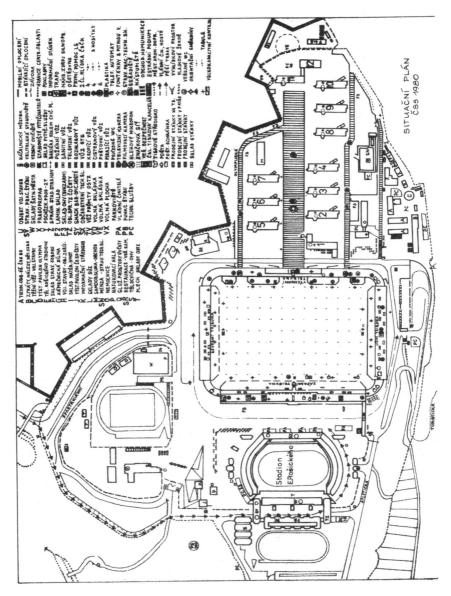

41. Layout of Strahov Stadium and dressing-room town prepared for the 1980 Spartakiad.

organization in that it limited the total number of participants.[668] Up until 1960, the dressing rooms were always wooden; the first lower dressing room, referred to as "the dormitory" (later block 1) of the Strahov dressing room town, was built as a trial for the 1960 Spartakiad. The remaining eleven dressing rooms were added before the next Spartakiad in 1965. The organizers praised the new dressing rooms since the removal of the gapped planks eliminated not only the unpleasant draft, but also "did away with the undisciplined behavior of the male participants caused by dressing room walls they could see through."[669] Between Spartakiads the dressing rooms served as student dorms for roughly five thousand students of the technical universities built during this period in the nearby Dejvice district of Prague. The dormitories had to be transformed into dressing rooms before each Spartakiad, which meant that the furniture had to be moved from the students' rooms to specially designated places in each dormitory block, the door handles disassembled so that the doors could not be locked, the tilt windows secured, the specially made Spartakiad showers prepared and notices mounted on the walls informing that "For safety reasons marching in step is forbidden."[670]

The technical layout of the dormitories was built to conform to the needs of the Spartakiads with wide hallways and stairways (both 3.6 meters), wide doors (1.25 meters) and oversized common showers, but was also marked by a lack of interest in technical aspects not directly related to the Spartakiad. For instance, the Strahov dormitories had a perfect public broadcasting system used to line up the participants, but also a totally inadequate heavy-current electrical

---

[668] See for instance Šterc, Jaroslav: "Řízení tělovýchovných podniků". In: *Vědecká konference o teoretických a metodických základech masových tělovýchovných vystoupení*, p. 109.
[669] Žáček, R.: "Závěry z orientačního průzkumu organizačního provozu východní části strahovského areálu".
[670] Kouřimský, G.: *Spartakiádní areál Strahov*, p. 47. See also "Čísla kolem Strahova". *Lidová demokracie*, vol. 36, 25. 6. 1980, p. 3.

42. Arrangement of gymnasts for a performance at the 1st Czechoslovak Spartakiad in 1955. The still wooden dressing rooms can be seen in the upper left part (photo Václav Chochola).

system and heating. The poor technical condition of the buildings, especially the constant power outages, led to the "Strahov incident" two years following the completion of the dormitories in which the students, chanting "We want light!", set out from the dormitories to Prague Castle and to the city's center. The brutal police intervention resulted in a wave of solidarity actions and gravely threatened the legitimacy of President Novotný's leadership.[671] Student clubs

671 See contemporary film document by Jan Němec *Strahovské události* (1968). See also Pažout, Jaroslav: "'Chceme světlo! Chceme studovat!'. Demonstrace studentů z vysokoškolských kolejí v Praze na Strahově 31. října 1967". *Paměť a dějiny*, 2008, vol. 2, n. 1, pp. 4–13.

in these dormitories (especially block 7) were later one of the first and longest enduring venues for the independent music scene.

The arrangement of participants in the dressing rooms was already begun by their "intentional" assignment to one of the 2,032 rooms, always twenty-four participants per room. Under the supervision of the floor leader, the line-up continued in the corridors of the individual floors that were designed sufficiently wide and stable to bear the weight of the participants. From here the groups descended the oversized stairways to the various assembly places located between the dormitories. Only then did the formations of participants move to the assembly area consisting of an extensive space lined on both sides by dormitories and ending with the Gate of Athletes at the east grandstand. Here the participants assembled in three phases into the definitive shape for entering the stadium, and were divided according to which entrance they were to use. The assembly area was supervised by the entrance commander from a special, still currently visible balcony in the middle of the east grandstand. In a 1984 interview, entrance commander Antonín Trpišovský boasted that at a given moment he was conducting the movement of up to 200,000 participants: "There would be, for instance, one performance piece on the field, two to four more prepared on platforms A, B and C, a fifth at the assembly area, a sixth in the dressing rooms, a seventh leaving Strahov and an eighth arriving. I have to be aware of them all. If you don't know what's going in the background, you don't understand the Spartakiad."[672]

The entry of the participants into the stadium was limited by the capacities of the individual entrances that posed yet another problem in organizing mass gymnastic performances. During the Slets, only the east grandstand was used for the participants' entry and

---

[672] Hanzlíková, Míla: "Spartakiáda není jen akce". *Náš domov*, vol. 35, 31. 8. 1984, pp. 1–3. By assembly areas A, B and C, Trpišovský meant the individual sections of the mass of participants waiting in various prepared stages in the areas between the blocks of dressing-rooms.

departure from the field. They entered through the Gate of Athletes and departed through the two adjacent gates. The four gates in the corners were used exclusively for spectators to enter the seating tribune and standing-room areas. The entrances and departures therefore often took longer than the performances themselves, creating a distinct genre of the Slet performances with complex visual effects. During the 1st All-State Spartakiad, the arches in the west tribune were already being used for departure, but the organizers continued to complain about the duration of the entrances. The original plan for the Days of Pupils and Adolescents to commence with the joint entrance of 90,000 participants thus had to be abandoned.[673] Although Strahov's six-hectare field was large enough to accommodate that number, it was impossible to get the participants on and off the field within a reasonable time. Starting with the next Spartakiad, the participants had access to the remaining gates, i.e. a total of seven gates: the sixty-meter Gate of Athletes could accommodate 72 participants entering at once, while up to 36 participants could enter at once through each of the other six roughly 20-meter gates. Entrances and departures were thus markedly facilitated to the point that "normalization" Spartakiads were essentially seamless in this regard. The entry of the military for their piece was even accomplished in a mere forty seconds. Yet the entrances and departures of the participants through multiple gates required much more preparation and organizational work than that originally done for the Sokol Slets.

More important than Strahov's physical architecture for the exercises themselves was the intangible and largely invisible architecture of the network of place marks. Over the course of the Slets and Spartakiads there was gradually formed on the wooden barriers around the field and especially on the stadium's field an increasingly

---

673 AČOS, f. l. celostátní spartakiáda 1955 – Základní dokumenty, Ideový program, plán příprav a návrh rozpočtu I. celostátní spartakiády v roce 1955, p. 7.

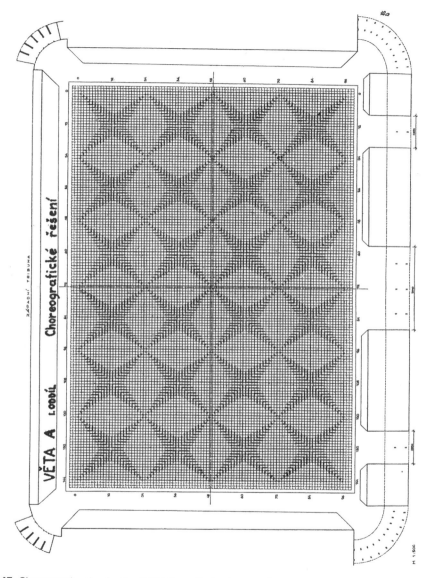

43. Choreography plan for the 1975 Spartakiad military performance documenting the "social geometry" that every Spartakiad piece was based on.

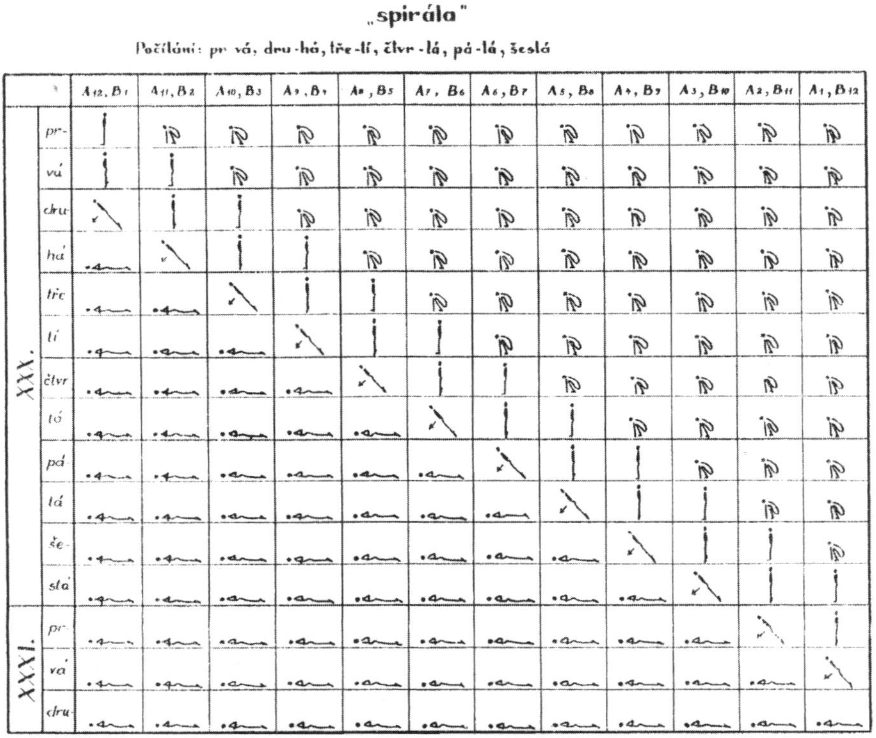
„spirála"
Počítání: pr vá, dru-há, tře-tí, čtvr-tá, pá-tá, šestá
A12, B1
A11, B2
A10, B3
A9, B4
A8, B5
A7, B6
A6, B7
A5, B8
A4, B9
A3, B10
A2, B11
A1, B12
XXX.
pr-
vá
dru-
há
tře
tí
čtvr
tá
pá
tá
še-
stá
XXXI.
pr-
vá
dru-

44. Chart of choreographic changes in the military piece for the 1975 Spartakiad. This table shows the movement of twelve soldiers forming the smallest organizational unit of a piece in the individual beats.

complex system or network of signs intended to ensure smooth entrances and departures and seamless spatial transitions during exercises.[674] The network of place marks created an analytical mass in which each participant had a precisely designated place defined by the intersection of x and y axes. Contrary to the spirit of Sokol and later Spartakiad rhetoric, his body was not part of a uniform mass,

674 Kouřimský, G.: *Spartakiádní areál Strahov*, p. 22.

but instead completely individualized and "legible" to the spectators and other supervisors. In this, the Spartakiads and Sokol Slets fundamentally differ from other mass rituals, such as the Nazi's Nuremberg rallies or communist May Day parades where the position of the individual participants was determined in relationship to others (e.g., at arm's length).

A simple network of place marks had previously been used at the Sokol field on Letná Plain. First stone then wooden blocks were used as markers; from 1932 metal markers were used. The Strahov Stadium field was originally covered with a network of 16,000 markers, but later anthropometric research showed that, due to the physical growth of the population, the gap between the participants needed to be slightly increased. The gaps between the place markers thus gradually increased to 185 centimeters at the final Slet in 1948, another five centimeters at the 1955 Spartakiad and were ultimately set at 195 centimeters for the "normalization" Spartakiads, at which the spacing allowed for 13,824 participants. This arrangement sufficed for the Sokol Slets since in the simple and sparse spatial changes of those compositions the participants only had to move forward or backward or to the sides on the axis of place markers.[675] The complex entrances of the Sokol Slets had been directed using signal flags with spikes that could be driven into the field's surface, or actual people were used as markers. Every entrance had to be arranged separately and the constant running around of these designated markers disrupted the overall effect of the performance.

Almost all performances at the 1st All-State Spartakiad employed a marker system taken from Sokol Slets and for some of the pieces the entrances were longer than the performances themselves (the

---

675 The markers were first used in 1891. Until then, the mass of Sokol gymnasts had to be arranged and tediously straightened out during the course of the exercises. The gymnasts first left their places and moved to other place markers ten years later. See Belšan, P.: "Choreografie a funkce náčiní, nářadí a režijních prostředků", p. 50. See also Zedník, F.: "Orientace cvičenců na cvičišti při II. CS".

longest consisted of a 21-minute entrance for the trade union women with the performance itself only taking 14 minutes).[676] Some pieces with more complex choreography, such as those by the work reserves, utilized, in addition to the network of place marks, additional signs on the stadium's field.[677] "Mushroom markers" were introduced at the next Spartakiad. These had a round protruding head attached to a stem-like peg that could be inserted into the drainage system.[678] Each piece had its own color-coded sign and also differed in shape depending on whether it was designed for entrances, departures or the performance itself. While each piece was marked separately during the first Spartakiad, beginning with the second Spartakiad the marking was always done for the entire afternoon program, so that people acting as markers did not have to run around during the performances and between them. During the "normalization" period, a total of forty thousand markers of fifty different types were used for each Spartakiad.[679] The use of light signals instead of physical markers[680] was considered starting with the second Spartakiad, though this was never implemented and the system that had gradually developed from the Sokol model was used until the end of communism.[681]

676 Žáček, Rudolf: "Několik metodických závěrů pro tělovýchovnou praxi ze zkušeností z I. celostátní spartakiády". In: *Vědecká konference o teoretických a metodických základech masových tělovýchovných vystoupení*, p. 118. Brdíčková, Miroslava: "Nástupy a odchody při tělovýchovných vystoupeních". In: Ibid, p. 153.

677 The positioning of the signs of the individual pieces was governed by a basic network of signs (positioned right next to it).

678 Kouřimský, G.: *Spartakiádní areál Strahov*, p. 27.

679 "Strahov plný ruchu". *Rudé právo*, vol. 55, 21. 6. 1975, p. 8.

680 Zedník, F.: "Orientace cvičenců na cvičišti při II. CS", p. 156; Hanzlíková, M.: "Spartakiáda není jen akce", pp. 1–3.

681 Zedník, F.: "Orientace cvičenců na cvičišti při II. CS", p. 156.

THE BUDGET OF SPARTAKIADS IN THE MORAL ECONOMY OF STATE SOCIALISM

The allegedly astronomical costs played an essential role in the post-1989 discussion on the further fate of Spartakiads. These were contrasted with the Slets that were supposedly financed wholly from Sokol funds and were instead meant to generate a profit for Sokol. Yet this is only true if we do not count the massive indirect subsidy that the state and city of Prague provided throughout the course of the Slets. For instance, the Czechoslovak Sokol Community planned the 10th all-Sokol Slet in 1938 with a balanced budget of 23 million crowns,[682] in which the costs for stadium modifications and other Slet needs were to be paid for by the revenues from the sale of two and a half million tickets and from the concession sales of e.g., "Slet cigars and cigarettes."[683]

The city of Prague alone invested more than twice that amount, i.e. 52 million crowns, into Slet preparations.[684] Yet if we compare Spartakiads with Slets, it is clear that the communist events represented a much greater burden on public budgets. Sokol-member volunteer work and member fees obviously greatly contributed to the success of Slets.

There is no simple answer to the question of how much Czechoslovak Spartakiads cost. Quantifying costs is not easy, nor is determining what these costs meant in the moral economy of state socialism. Although the archives are full of partial Spartakiad budgets, surprisingly there is no overall Spartakiad budget whose compliance would have been overseen by some corresponding institution. For unlike the Slets, no organization was established during the Spartakiads to assume responsibility for proper budgeting and for the

---

682 Pluhař, Jan: "O činnosti dozorčího sboru". In: R. Procházka (ed.): *Památník X. všesokolského sletu v Praze 1938*, pp. 288–290.
683 Mayer, Stanislav: "Zpráva sletového finančního odboru". Ibid, pp. 299–300.
684 Stavěl, Jiří: "Co dala sletu Praha". Ibid, pp. 306–308.

consequences arising from overspending. The main organizer of Spartakiads, the Spartakiad staff, was an *ad hoc* group set up as part of the Czechoslovak Physical Education Association without clear competencies vis-à-vis other state bodies. Despite protests from the State Planning Commission, the Spartakiads did not become part of the five-year plan and a government resolution was passed separately for each of them that roughly quantified costs for the Spartakiad preparations. In explanatory memoranda to these resolutions, it was admitted that Spartakiad expenses could not be accurately quantified. "By government resolution," one such memorandum from 1980 states, "it is impossible to express all specific measures and all forms of support of state bodies, especially of national committees at all levels, in the preparations for Czechoslovak Spartakiads. We therefore suggest assigning the general task to all departments and national committees to provide multilateral support and assistance to Spartakiad organizers; it is expected that the specific means and scope of this support will be mutually agreed to."[685]

The overall budgets, whether part of the government resolution or internal documents of the Czechoslovak Physical Education Association, never included all institutions that shared the Spartakiad costs.[686] When in 1986 preparations for the final Spartakiad began, the Czechoslovak Physical Education Association based its budget in internal documents on the total costs of 673 million crowns for the 1980 Spartakiad and 524 millions for the 1985 Spartakiad.[687] Yet the actual costs were apparently much higher since the Association

---

[685] NA, f. Úřad vlády ČSR/ČR, Praha – usnesení vlády n. 78, podklady (unfiled), Opatření pro zajištění příprav Československé spartakiády 1980 v České socialistické republice.

[686] NA, f. ÚV ČSTV, k. 288, Materiál pro schůzi předsednictva ÚV ČSTV dne 21. 1. 1986, Návrh ekonomického a materiálního zabezpečení ČSS 1990.

[687] For instance the government's budget proposal for the planned 1990 Spartakiad brought protests from the Ministry of Education as well as the Ministry of Defense. The former protested that the budget neglected some essential items amounting to tens of millions of crowns, while the latter pointed out that the planned expenses were considerably underestimated (the Ministry of Defense had planned to spend 20 million not 10 million crowns). AČOS, f. Československá spartakiáda 1990, Náčelník správy bojové přípravy, generálpluk. Miloslav Zíka Úřadu

was unable to accurately quantify the costs for the previous Spartakiads. This is attested to by e.g. an interview with Zdeněk Šimůnek, head of the economic department of the Association's Central Committee, for the Slovak daily *Sport* from late October 1989. In this interview, Šimůnek estimates the total cost of the planned 1990 Spartakiad at 830 million crowns.[688]

Spartakiads were mainly financed by the Czechoslovak Physical Education Association, though a number of ministries and other organizations also financially contributed. For instance, along with providing for its military choreography, the Ministry of Defence also provided the Spartakiad staff with thirty trucks, drivers, fuel and 250 soldiers that helped with the Spartakiad preparations for four months (modifying the dressing rooms and preparing the stadium's field).[689] During the performances, the military field kitchen and three hundred soldiers then assisted in feeding the participants.[690]

In time, state-owned companies became increasingly involved in financing Spartakiads – either through direct contributions to district Spartakiads or through the trade unions, which supported the participants and instructors in various ways. The Eastern Slovak Ironworks provided employees taking part in the Spartakiad with financial contributions for exercise outfits and for their lodging in Prague, while instructors employed by the company received paid leave for practices and were reimbursed for travel expenses.[691] The trade unions also bought its members tickets to the Strahov performances.[692]

---

předsednictva vlády, 16. července 1987. Ibid, Stanovisko k materiálům pro jednání finančně-hospodářského úseku komise pro přípravu ČSS 1990, 3. 6. 1986.

[688] "Milióny do trvalých hodnôt". *Šport*, vol. 43, 25. 10. 1989, p. 3.

[689] AČOS, f. Československá spartakiáda 1985, Usnesení vlády ČSSR ze dne 17. 11. 1983 n. 287.

[690] Krupička, J.: "Prvé poznatky z II. celostátní spartakiády", pp. 136–137.

[691] Svatoň, Vratislav: "Zabezpečení cvičitelů ZRTV v přípravě spartakiádních skladeb". In: *Sborník ze semináře FTVS UK Praha*, pp. 22–26.

[692] For instance, total trade union expenses for the 1985 Spartakiad were estimated at nearly 50 million crowns. NA, f. ÚV ČSTV, k. 288, Materiál pro schůzi předsednictva ÚV ČSTV dne 21. 1. 1986, Návrh ekonomického a materiálního zabezpečení ČSS 1990.

Some Spartakiad costs were covered by ticket sales. Unlike the Slets, for which this was a main source of income covering, except for the final Slet in 1948, most of the (Sokol) expenses, in the case of the Spartakiads this was only a tiny fraction of the total costs. In the budget for the 1980 Czechoslovak Spartakiad, for instance, ticket proceeds from the usually sold out Strahov performances could be expected to exceed sixteen million crowns. The ticket price for seating was around 60 crowns, 20 crowns for standing-room only.[693]

The costs for Czechoslovak Spartakiads were (with the exception of the 1st All-State Spartakiad in 1955) relatively stable and consisted of three main items: modifications to Strahov Stadium, reimbursement for overtime to teachers and the costs related to the organization of performances at Strahov. Strahov stadium consumed vast funds not only due to the costly construction projects (the completion of the east grandstand cost hundreds of millions),[694] but also due to routine maintenance that grew in expense partly because of the stadium's massive size and partly because it was practically unused during the period between Spartakiads. The amount of 48 million crowns was, for instance, calculated for the routine maintenance which included an inspection of the light and strong current, insulation of the grandstands and renovations to the field for the 1985 Spartakiad .[695] The financing of stadium modifications also came from multiple sources. According to one report, a total of nine ministries and other institutions were involved in renovations for the 1965 Spartakiad.[696] The renovations of stadiums in district

---

693 AČOS, f. Československá spartakiáda 1985, Důvodová zpráva k návrhu rozpočtu Československé spartakiády 1980.
694 Other large investments were tied to the Spartakiads; for instance, a swimming pool stadium was quickly completed in Podolí for the 2nd All-State Spartakiad. See NA, ÚV ČSR/ČR-RŽP, Úřad vlády ČSR/ČR, Praha – Usnesení vlády.
695 AČOS, f. Československá spartakiáda 1985, Zpráva k návrhu usnesení vlády ČSSR o opatřeních pro zajištění příprav Československé spartakiády 1985.
696 AČOS, f. III. celostátní spartakiáda 1965, Průvodní zpráva ke generelu III. CS, Krajský projektový ústav.

towns before the district Spartakiads also required investments in the tens of millions.[697] Another major cost exceeding a hundred million crowns was overtime remuneration for teachers practicing Spartakiad pieces as non-obligatory physical education classes. The increased involvement of teachers in practicing led not only to higher costs during the "normalization" Spartakiads in particular, but also to tension between the teachers and club instructors who had always led practices for free.[698]

Another significant item in the Spartakiad budget was the preparations for Spartakiad performances. Above all, there were the wages and other expenses related to the Spartakiad staff of several hundred members, which planned coordinated and monitored practices, transportation, accommodations and food services, as well as the Strahov performances themselves. The large cost of temporary work was covered separately. This had previously been performed for free by Sokol volunteers, but now became a welcomed additional source of money for Prague students in particular.[699] Not even the work performed at local Spartakiads was for free: the Czechoslovak Physical Education Association had to e.g. pay eight thousand crowns for four brass bands that played during the parade of the district Spartakiad in Jihlava.[700] Separate contracts were signed for the creation of the individual pieces whose average rate was twenty

697 AČOS, f. Československá spartakiáda 1980, Zpráva k návrhu usnesení vlády ČSR o opatřeních pro zajištění příprav Československé spartakiády 1980 v České socialistické republice.

698 Drdácká, B.: "Podíl svazu ZRTV na čs. spartakiádě v r. 1990", pp. 27–32; Svatoň, V.: "Zabezpečení cvičitelů ZRTV v přípravě spartakiádních skladeb". In 1984 the Ministry of Education stated that the number of gymnasts is directly proportional to the amount of money for teacher salaries and warned that if wages did not increase then it could not be expected that the number of gymnasts would increase. NA, f. ÚV ČSTV, k. 268, Materiál pro schůzi českého štábu ČSS 1985 dne 17. ledna 1984. See also Přerovský, J.: "Podíl školství na přípravě Československé spartakiády 1985", p. 20.

699 The post 1989 Slets also could not rely on unpaid volunteers and, to the dismay of older Sokol members, the organizers had to pay considerable sums for temporary workers. See Waldauf, J.: *Sokol. Malé dějiny velké myšlenky*, vol. 3, p. 651.

700 AČOS, f. Československá spartakiáda 1975, Vyúčtování ČSS 75 – KV, MV, OV ČSTV.

thousand crowns in royalties (the rate was based on the number of minutes a piece ran, which is apparently one of the reasons why the Spartakiad pieces were so long[701]).

The 1st All-State Spartakiad of 1955, which still was not organized by the Czechoslovak Physical Education Association, represents a separate chapter. Though there does not exist any overall budget for the event, it is clear that excessive costs were incurred due to the delayed and chaotic preparations. As the organizers themselves admitted, the centralization of management increased the cost of Spartakiads compared to Sokol Slets. For the Sokols, inspections of the practices were made "by bike to the neighboring village and not by Tatraplan car from Prague."[702] The party's direct involvement meant that the issue of whether costs were adequate or not now played a secondary role. Expenses included e.g. a budget for the closing ceremony of two million post-reform crowns including 10,000 crowns for a silk portrait of comrades Stalin and Gottwald.[703] This closing ceremony was performed only once at Strahov, as the Spartakiad staff forbade it from being reprised on the ensuing days of the Spartakiad due to its utter inappropriateness.[704]

Taking, for instance, the official, clearly undervalued figure of 670 million crowns spent on the 1980 Spartakiad, we can speculate what the communist regime could have spent that amount on. The average wage in Czechoslovakia in 1980 stood at nearly 2,700 crowns per month, which means that the budget for a single Spartakiad was equal to more than twenty thousand annual salaries. Converted to five-year Spartakiad cycles, one could say that, instead of Spartakiads, the Czechoslovak state could have employed over four

701 Fuchs, Jan: "Diskusní příspěvek". In: Sborník ze semináře FTVS UK Praha, p. 88.
702 Appelt, K.: "Poznámky k dotazníkové akci", p. 121.
703 NA, f. SVTVS, k. 64, inv. n. 190, Podklady pro schůze štábu I. celostátní spartakiády (leden–duben 1955), Předběžný rozpočet závěrečného obrazu I. CS.
704 See AČOS, f. I. celostátní spartakiáda 1955 – Politické materiály, Zápis z 8. porady komise ÚV KSČ pro zajištění I. celostátní spartakiády, konané dne 27. června 1955 v 17.00 hod. na strahovském stadionu.

thousand people full time.[705] Yet the question is whether the state apparatus was capable of efficiently making use of hundreds of millions of crowns in another way. The discussions at that time about Spartakiads included criticism of the "call to arms" and inefficient costs linked to it, yet it seems that, given the cumbersome mechanisms of the communist economy, it was in these urgent appeals that the system worked relatively efficiently. Accepting Hayek's theory that a fundamental problem of a communist economy is the inability to compensate for the information flow that a market "normally" provides, then the clear priority assigned to Spartakiads, the mobilization of all involved entities for this purpose and the stress from risk of possible failure ensured that, compared to other areas of production, the Spartakiad machine was quite efficient. Though the communist regime certainly could not rely as much as Sokol on the volunteer work of its members, the success of Spartakiads largely depended on the willingness of its participants and instructors, as well as on many other people linked to Spartakiad preparations. The daily *Rudé právo* quite accurately wrote that no such event would have been possible in the West. If there had been the need to motivate all Spartakiad participants economically, then Spartakiads would have been at least one notch costlier. The Communist Party got relatively "cheaply" a spectacle by which it demonstrated its ability to effectively control the socialist society.

Yet the larger question of whether the Spartakiads "paid off" for the communist regime depends on the notion of market mechanisms. Nevertheless, principles of the moral economy, in which precise economic calculations are neither possible nor desired, governed the communist political economy. Spartakiads were part of a complex symbolic exchange in the state-socialist moral economy.

---

705 For comparison: due to coal reserves valued at 2.5 billion crowns (other estimates put this figure at 1.9 billion) the medieval town of Most was razed and a new city was built in its place with 60,000 inhabitants. See Spurný, Matěj: *Most do budoucnosti. Laboratoř socialistické moderny na severu Čech.* Karolinum, Prague 2016.

They became a gift from the party to the people. The people gratefully accepted this gift and, in return, sacrificed their own time to prepare it. And in this moral economy, no work was completely "free." The participants and instructors expected a reciprocal gift from the regime, even if they usually did not have the opportunity to demand it (another typical feature of a moral economy). They asked that the regime acknowledge their social engagedness, or at least expected the state to leave them alone for some time. The moral economy exchange was also binding in the sense that the party leaders could not simply cancel Spartakiads, even if they did not pay off for the party. Loss of prestige from failure in the role as the Spartakiad ritual's sponsor was hardly reparable.

✕✕✕

At first glance, the Spartakiads were an overwhelming organizational success of state socialism. Despite the chaos accompanying the first Spartakiad, a relatively effective management system was gradually put into place that was able to make use of vast state resources to create a mass spectacle that was internationally unique in its size and scope (for comparison's sake: the opening ceremonies of the 1980 Olympic games in Moscow saw the performance of 16,000 active participants in front of 103,000 spectators[706]). Yet in addition to the massive state investments (which, however, also diminished the legitimacy of state socialism in many public eyes), this success was based on an organisational paradox. The organizational paradox of the Spartakiads consisted of a more general and wholly fundamental problem of the communist regime: how to take away a society's

---

706   Riordan, James: "Moscow 1980. The Games of the XXIInd Olympiad". In: John F. Findling – Kimberly D. Pelle (eds.): *Historical Dictionary of the Modern Olympic Movement*, Greenwood Press, London 1996, pp. 161–168.

autonomy, while at the same time mobilizing it. In order to achieve the image of a perfectly disciplined mass of participants (i.e. of "the people"), the communist party had to create a considerable autonomous space for former Sokol officials and for the creators of Slet choreographies. Only in allowing Spartakiads to become "Slets in a different form," was it able to mobilize not only professional cadres, but, above all, tens of thousands of trainers that did most of the organizational work, usually voluntarily and free of charge.

Society and Spartakiads

Though the question of whether most of society accepted the Spartakiads is central to our discussion, it is largely unanswerable. An honest answer would have to navigate numerous methodological and theoretical obstacles exceeding the scope of this book and the abilities of its author, and would essentially represent the response to the question of what kind of relationship society had to state socialism in general. Society during the communist regime was characterized by a low degree of self-organization and the almost complete absence of a free public space. This is essentially an ahistorical question since society under communism lacked the means to form an opinion on Spartakiads or to communicate this opinion.[707] Different social groups as well as individuals reacted to Spartakiads in different ways; regional (Prague vs. villages, traditional Sokol areas of Bohemia and Moravia vs. Slovakia, Silesia and Sudetenland), generational (pre-war generation socialized in Sokol vs. post-war which had only heard about Sokol and the Slets) and gender (distinct feminization of gymnastics over the course of four decades of state socialism) differences played an important role in this. The response to the initial question of whether people accepted Spartakiads will certainly disappoint: Some did some of the time.

The sources available to us reveal a broad range of reactions: from the dark shades of open resistance to the light tones of enthusiastic reception. We find (even if marginally) those who tried to prevent Spartakiads from taking place, who cut power lines or made bomb threats. There were also those who tried to ignore or ridicule the event. Most common was the attempt to "appropriate" the Spartakiads, to take advantage of a unique moment, in which official places try to accommodate society as much as possible, as a welcomed chance to step out of the grey of the everyday routine. Last but not least, we can find the "unselfish" enthusiasm for mass gymnastic

---

707 See Corner, Paul (ed.): *Popular Opinion in Totalitarian Regimes. Fascism, Nazism, Communism.* Oxford University Press, Oxford 2009.

45. The arrangement of junior women and women for a performance at Strahov Stadium during the 1980 Spartakiad (photo Pavel Štecha).

performances, especially among former Sokol members and their offspring.

Surprisingly, society's relationship to Spartakiads changed little over time. If we disregard the first Spartakiad, the Strahov grandstands were always full and the number of exercise participants always exceeded the capacity of Strahov's field. It was not rare for both individual spectators and participants to have taken part in all six communist Spartakiads (and one or two Slets before that). What's more, the lack of interest among participants and spectators in the first Spartakiad did not stem from an aversion to mass gymnastic performances under communism, but to the Stalinist policy of "sportification of Sokol" The Communist Party first dissolved the former Sokol clubs in the early 1950s only to change its mind and decide on organizing something similar to a Sokol Slet in just a few months. This led to often indiscriminate pressure on people who did not belong to the original Sokol subculture, which understandably caused resistance. Yet it can be said in general that communism created a relatively unchanging habitus that protected mass gymnastic performances as a cultural form of the late 19th century from the erosive power of modernizing changes in postwar Europe.

OPEN RESISTANCE

Within the typology of public reactions to Spartakiads, open resistance was a relatively marginal phenomenon. It is also difficult to determine its actual extent, since the only source systematically providing testimony on this are secret police briefings. The secret police undoubtedly exaggerated, if not directly generated active resistance. Its *raison d'être* was the fight against the class enemy, the absence of which put the very existence of the secret police in doubt. It therefore could not report that nothing was happening.

Secret police reports clearly show that a considerable obstacle for Spartakiad organizers was the ethnic makeup of the state. According to these reports – and the organizers themselves confirmed this – Slovaks and national minorities were not exactly enthusiastic about the Spartakiad. Indeed, unlike the Czech lands, the eastern part of the republic lacked the tradition of mass gymnastic performances. During the period between the wars there were only a few dozen Sokol clubs in Slovakia, and even these were linked with the unpopular idea of Czechoslovakism. Consequently, in introducing the concept of a Spartakiad here, the organizers were going up against not only an aversion to the communist regime, but also disdain for what mass gymnastic performances represented in the period between the wars: namely, Czech paternalism, progressiveness and anticlericalism. Preparations for the first Spartakiad in 1955 thus encountered in Slovakia considerable resistance. Internal reports by the organizers mention incidents of arson, posters being torn down and power lines being cut. In the town of Galanta, a local Spartakiad was interrupted by a confirmation ceremony that lured away some participants and spectators. Yet, all in all, the report concluded that the influence of the "disruptive activity" was kept to a minimum thanks to "solid cooperation with the police."[708] During

---

708 AČOS. f. I. celostátní spartakiáda 1955 – Základní dokumenty, Situační zprávy I. CS, Třetí zpráva zvláštních instruktorů SVTVS o stavu příprav okresních a krajských spartakiád.

the preparations, the StB was also carefully monitoring the behavior of the Hungarian minority there, though it did not report any distinct protests.[709] The popularity of Spartakiads gradually increased in Slovakia, especially in larger towns and cities, and the resistance faded. Indeed, at the close of 1989 a discussion was held on the fate of the prepared 1990 Spartakiad with many Slovak instructors and participants protesting its cancellation.

Organizers' reports indicated that the Polish minority also held a reluctant stance toward Spartakiads. An internal report focused on the participation of different nationalities in Spartakiad practices stated: "The issue of nationalities is a very thorny matter in the Ostrava region. Czechoslovak citizens of Polish nationality are usually active in their own sporting organization [...] These citizens are not active in trade union or Sokol clubs, and this results in a lack of members, especially officials. Citizens of Polish nationality have a negative view of the Spartakiad. One Polish citizen was even prosecuted for outright sedition and for encouraging members practicing for the first Spartakiad not to take part in the event and not to practice their calisthenics."[710]

Personal testimony and secret police reports both indicate that there was even unrest in Prague. The director Jiří Menzel recalls, for instance, seeing in 1955 that someone had scrawled on the imposing and not easily accessed front wall of the Josef Stalin Secondary School in Prague the message "Slet = Freedom, Spartakiad = Terror."[711] The secret police claimed at that time that they had prevented even graver threats of "enemy elements," such as the plan of an 8-member group to assassinate president Zápotecký during the

---

709 ABS, f. Historický fond StB, H-190 (Spartakiáda), Vyhodnocení poznatků k I. celostátní spartakiádě, Zpráva o nepřátelských projevech vůči I. celostátní spartakiádě a o závadách zjištěných v průběhu okresních a krajských spartakiád ze dne 23. června 1955.
710 AČOS. f. I. celostátní spartakiáda 1955 – Základní dokumenty, Situační zprávy I. CS, Souhrnná zpráva o průzkumu stavu příprav na I. CS v krajích, ve dnech 29. 11. až 2. 12. 1954.
711 Menzel, Jiří: *Rozmarná léta*. Slovart, Prague 2013, p. 43.

Spartakiad and to set the Strahov dressing room facilities on fire.[712] The secret police counterintelligence division's reports on the 1985 Czechoslovak Spartakiads tell of later protests against Spartakiads. These reports lead us to believe that the situation was similar during previous Spartakiads.[713] The secret police reported that Ladislav Lis allegedly attempted to agitate Prague dissent to take advantage of the presence of foreign guests at the event and garner their support for Charter 77.[714] A few "anti-socialist" fliers appeared around Prague, as did graffiti celebrating Charter 77, Alexander Dubček, but also National Socialism.[715] Some of this graffiti was allegedly written by the gymnasts themselves. The StB reported that Jehovah's Witnesses carried out their "annunciation activities" among the participants[716] while the punks insulted the gymnasts.[717] Ten years earlier during the 1975 Spartakiad, "hooligans" had allegedly tried to prevent participants of the north Moravian region from entering the bus on the way back from Strahov Stadium. "They were using inappropriate language and provocative chants and were belittling their history."[718]

712   ABS, f. Historický fond StB, H-190 (Spartakiáda), Vyhodnocení poznatků k I. celostátní spartakiádě, Zpráva o nepřátelských projevech vůči I. celostátní spartakiádě a o závadách zjištěných v průběhu okresních a krajských spartakiád ze dne 23. června 1955. See Lenčéšová, M: *Prvá celoštátna spartakiáda 1955.*
713   ABS, f. X. správa SNB (A 36), inv. j. 704, Informace z 3. odboru X. S., leden–říjen 1985.
714   ABS, f. X. správa SNB (A 36), inv. j. 702, Československá spartakiáda 1985 – informace ze dne 21. 6. 1985, p. 2.
715   ABS, f. X. správa SNB (A 36), inv. j. 702, Československá spartakiáda 1985 – svodná informace ze dne 30. 6. 1985, p. 2. See also AČOS, f. Československá spartakiáda 1975, Denní hlášení pro politicko-výchovný odbor Ústředního štábu Československé spartakiády 1975 (further PVO ÚŠ ČSS 1975), 28. 6. 1975.
716   ABS, f. X. správa SNB (A 36), inv. j. 702, Československá spartakiáda 1985 – informace ze dne 21. 6. 1985, p. 3.
717   ABS, f. X. správa SNB (A 36), inv. j. 702, Československá spartakiáda 1985 – svodná informace ze dne 26. 6.1985, p. 2.
718   AČOS, f. Československá spartakiáda 1975, Denní hlášení pro PVO ÚŠ ČSS 1975, 27. 6. 1975. Similarly, some 150 Sparta soccer fans tried on their return from Banská Bystrica to take over a special Spartakiad train and were prevented from doing so only after the police intervened.

The StB investigated dozens of anonymous letters and phone calls threatening to kidnap participating children, to release nerve gas at Strahov Stadium, or to blow up train tracks so that participants could not reach Prague. While these threats were made under the cover of anonymity (although the anonymous writer threatening a nerve gas attack was eventually apprehended), a number of Spartakiad participants dared to protest publicly. The junior women from the South Moravian Region refused "for [...] unknown reasons" to form the image of a Soviet flag in the Spartakiad parade.[719] Several soldiers and even officers were also punished for refusing to practice.[720]

It is also clear that many Prague inhabitants were not thrilled with how the Spartakiads disturbed the everyday run of the city.[721] The Secret Police e.g. reported "inappropriate behavior" of the driver of bus no. 217 who "in passing through the Strahov complex on 22 June 1985 between 9:00–9:15 a.m. coarsely insulted, in plain view of his passengers, police officers helping to direct traffic at the 1985 Spartakiad, vulgarly insulted participants in the 1985 Spartakiad, etc. Some of his passengers joined in this unacceptable behavior."[722]

Some of those in open opposition also appeared in official organizations. One of the cameramen for Czechoslovak Television often spread "distorted views of the 1985 Spartakiad" among his colleagues. He compared the exercises of men and soldiers to fascist

See ABS, f. X. správa SNB (A 36), inv. j. 702, Československá spartakiáda 1985 – informace ze dne 21. 6. 1985, p. 2.
719 ABS, f. X. správa SNB (A 36), inv. j. 702, Československá spartakiáda 1985 – svodná informace ze dne 25. 6.1985, p. 7.
720 Ibid.
721 A report based on the inspection of allegedly 48 million correspondence letters during 1960 also attested to the dissatisfaction of much of the population. The most frequent criticism of Spartakiads concerned the overburdening of school children, especially during the regional Spartakiads. According to the report, a change of view occurred when the main Spartakiad event was being held and most letter writers, including former Sokol members, highly praised the 1960 Spartakiad as the most successful gymnastic performance ever. NA, f. KSČ – Ústřední výbor 1945–1989, 02/2–299–283, Zpráva II. zvl. odboru MV, Zpráva PB ÚV KSČ, 7. 3. 1961.
722 ABS, f. X. správa SNB (A 36), inv. j. 702, Československá spartakiáda 1985 – svodná informace ze dne 23. 6. 1985. Ibid, p. 4.

parades, saying that Spartakiads were only missing the "drums and whistles." The Spartakiad was in his view a completely superfluous event, "a national pilgrimage, in which for at least one week all scarce goods were available; the working people could once every five years taste in peace the fruits of their labor and not have to seek them under the counter."[723] During a Spartakiad performance a certain editor of the daily *Československý sport* (Czechoslovak Sports) seated in the press section of the grandstands "insulted members of the Communist Party and vilified the Czechoslovak state system," though in his case it was probably the result of overdoing it at the press refreshment center, from where he had to be carried out after falling several times.[724]

723 ABS, f. X. správa SNB (A 36), inv. j. 702, Československá spartakiáda 1985 – svodná informace ze dne 27. 6. 1985, p. 5.
724 ABS, f. X. správa SNB (A 36), inv. j. 702, Československá spartakiáda 1985 – svodná informace ze dne 30. 6. 1985, p. 4.

WEAPONS OF THE WEAK

Although there were instances of open resistance to Spartakiads, the organizers themselves were much more concerned about passive resistance. The public utilized hundreds of different tactics to weaken the effect of the regime's strategy, or even used it to its own benefit.[725] The public at large, the spectators and even the participants had a wide range of passive-resistance methods at their disposal that James C. Scott calls "weapons of the weak".[726]

Perhaps the most popular of these was ridicule. In spite of all their seriousness, the Slets and Spartakiads inherently possessed a certain comic charge. Miroslav Tyrš had long ago warned that "we need to get rid of everything, such as push-ups, that may cause laughter."[727] The comic element consisted mainly in the conflict between the metropolitan and Sokol *habitus*, i.e. in the disruption of established social norms, such as the exposure of scantily clad bodies of both sexes in the urban setting, the close proximity of these bodies and their mutual contact.[728] A host of quasi-Spartakiads made use of this, whether it was exercises with beer bottles instead of conical batons or men swapping their exercise outfits for women's. Popular folk singer Jaromír Nohavica composed the lewd song "Spartakiad" during the 1985 Spartakiad in which, to the melody of "Ode to Joy," he presented the Spartakiads as a mass sex orgy. Artist Jan Švankmajer

---

[725] For the contrast of strategy and tactics, see Certeau, Michel de: *The Practice of Everyday Life*. University of California Press, Berkeley 1984.

[726] Scott, James C.: *Weapons of the Weak. Everyday Forms of Peasant Resistance*. Yale University Press, New Haven 1985.

[727] Tyrš, Miroslav: "Cvičení veřejná a závodnická". *Sokolský archiv*, vol. 5. Československá obec sokolská, Prague 1932, p. 266; quoted from Serbus, L. – Kos, B. – Mihule, J.: *Historický vývoj a základy tělovýchovných vystoupení v ČSSR*, p. 52.

[728] The Spartakiad organizers were aware of this cultural conflict and e.g. in 1965 warned the participants: "The scant exercise outfit is appropriate for Strahov, but certainly not for the Prague streets. Girls and women should not walk around in overly revealing sportswear or only in shorts, and neither should men go around with their shirts off. It is neither aesthetically or hygienically appropriate." Viz "Nelíbí se nám". *Život spartakiády*, vol. 1, n. 4, 1. 7. 1965, p. 1.

used the subliminal homo-erotic tension of the military performances in his work *Fizkultura in the Services of Eroticism and Militarism: Play of Analogies* (1976), in which he combined photographs from 1975 military performances at Spartakiads with illustrations from the works of the Marquis de Sade.[729] Švankmajer then employed the same motif in the short documentary film *The End of Stalinism in the Czech Lands* from 1990. In this surrealistic historical narrative in which, for instance, dough rollers represent Soviet tanks from 1968, Švankmajer analyzed the relationship between "baser instincts" and a totalitarian political regime. The rapid alternating of Spartakiad photographs with Marquis de Sade illustrations gives the impression of a continuous flow of mass orgies intensified by the movement of the camera passing analogously back and forth between the two types of visual material. Unlike the aforementioned picture, Švankmajer uses here a larger number of Spartakiad photographs arranged roughly in chronological order and representing various phases of a Spartakiad exercise.

Along with laughter, the weak's arsenal also included silence.[730] Communist leadership had seen this form of resistance before during the 1948 Slet when Sokol members had marched around the grandstand where newly anointed president Klement Gottwald was standing, their heads turned away from him in silence. In 1975, when the first Spartakiad since the Soviet intervention in 1968 was held, political-education workers from the West Bohemia Region complained of a lack of enthusiasm during the parade: "Yet we must admit that there was very little use of the prepared chants. It was interesting that at the start of the parade and then from Vodičkova Street on, the

---

729   Reprented for instance in: *Analogon*, 1990, vol. 2, n. 2, p. 73.
730   There were many ways to avoid the event. According to eyewitness Michal Horáček, army recruits took advantage of the desire of Spartakiad organizers to show off the tanned bodies of muscular soldiers and during organized sunbathing they intentionally let themselves become sunburned. Apparently motor oil was used as suntan oil to facilitate this. Interview with the author, Fakulta humanitních věd Univerzity Karlovy, 5. 4. 2006.

mood and engagedness was much better than on Wenceslas Square itself where the public was very reserved and the participants reacted stiffly. The atmosphere during the parade was far from ideal. Although many discussions had been held, the organization of chants largely failed."[731] Their Prague colleagues concurred and pointed out that the "political-educational work should be even more intense and effective. (You can tell, for instance, that chants about friendship with the USSR are less enthusiastically received in the parade.)"[732]

Attempts at coaxing people outside the realm of the traditional Sokol community to work towards the success of Spartakiads met with even worse results. Sokol Slets had traditionally relied on a vast amount of volunteer work by the individual instructors and officials. This volunteer participation was essential for the Spartakiads' success from both a practical and symbolic perspective. The communist regime lost a great many volunteers in the process of unification of physical education, and still more in their inherent drive to meticulously control any spontaneous activity. In 1985, for instance, the Spartakiad staff received the report that the renovations to Strahov Stadium were running behind schedule since the planned number of temporary workers could not be attained. Instead of the expected three hundred volunteers, fewer than eighty showed up. According to the same report, those who came did not stay long: "The head of the Municipal Committee of the Czechoslovak Physical Education Association in Prague needs to be informed that the temporary workers are arriving to the job late and that most do not observe the work hours; some show their faces in the morning and then leave the workplace within a few minutes, often with tools borrowed from the Sports Construction Works company."[733]

---

731 AČOS, f. Československá spartakiáda 1975, Denní hlášení pro PVO ÚŠ ČSS 1975, 29. 6. 1975.

732 Ibid.

733 AČOS, f. Československá spartakiáda 1985, Informace o účasti brigádníků na Strahově, Materiál pro schůzi vedení Ústředního štábu CS 85, 25. 4. 1985. For volunteer work cf. Jana

A similar unwillingness to take part in preparations beyond the obligatory point is attested to by a somewhat curious report from secret police files on the same Spartakiad.[734] A teachers' committee of one elementary school in Prague 10 opposed the decision of the district national committee, which had assigned it with the daily task of monitoring the streets around the hotels in the school's area, especially the Solidarita hotel, to ensure that no contact occurred between the students and foreign guests of the Spartakiad. According to the StB, pupils of the elementary school there "are in undesirable contact with visa-permitted foreigners, from whom they are requesting foreign currency and are photographed doing so, looking like 'begging' children." The teachers' committee protested that this was the job of the StB and that if the teachers were to follow the orders, "not only would the foreigners be able to photograph 'begging' children, they would also be able to photograph female teachers on the streets making some money on the side."

Another telling example was the attempt by the organizers of the first Spartakiads to lodge some of the participants in private Prague homes. The organizers had relied on the experience from the first workers' Spartakiad in 1921 when workers were housed in the poor dwellings of their comrades in Prague and from similar practices of Sokol Slets. The Accommodations Department of the Spartakiad Staff thus optimistically declared in 1955: "We believe that during the 1st All-State Spartakiad every single household in Prague will provide at least one visitor from outside the city with accommodations."[735]

Ratajová's article in which she shows that there occurred starting in the late 1950s a significant shift from temporary work on large industrial projects to caring for one's own city, street or even home, often not exceeding ordinary maintenance. Ratajová, Jana: "Pražské májové oslavy 1948–1989. Příspěvek k dějinám komunistické propagandy". *Kuděj. Časopis pro kulturní dějiny*, 2000, vol. 2, n. 1, p. 54.

734 ABS, f. X. správa SNB (A 36), inv. j. 702, Československá spartakiáda 1985 – svodná informace ze dne 26. 6. 1985, p. 6.

735 NA, f. SVTVS, k. 64, inv. n. 190, Podklady pro schůze štábu I. celostátní spartakiády (leden–duben 1955), Zpráva ubytovacího odboru I. CS 1955.

In such a request, the Spartakiad organizers overstepped the barrier between the public and private spheres, which – as Ladislav Holý pointed out – paradoxically developed as the result of the regime's pressure on "nationalizing" all spheres of human life.[736] The Accommodations Department was then forced to disappointedly state that, despite the efforts of those working to promote the scheme, the campaign "did not meet with success" and fewer than five thousand participants were lodged in private homes.[737] According to the testimony of *Mladý svět* (Young World) magazine, the situation at the following Spartakiad in 1960 was even worse:

"Even though [...] residents of Prague offered Spartakiad visitors 2,000 beds, it was not enough. So the accommodations service has arranged for a night showing at the Sevastopol cinema, after which the visitors can sleep in comfortable leather seats until eight in the morning. If the Sevastopol cinema does not suffice, other cinemas are available."[738] Not only did Spartakiad organizers no longer try to lodge participants in private homes during the "normalization" period, they were prohibited from doing so in order to facilitate the organization of the participants' daily program.[739] Both an improvement in organizational procedures and a resignation to the mobilization of the Prague public at large were behind this telling shift in policy.

We saw in the first part of this chapter that the popularity of Spartakiads had a limited geographic scope roughly corresponding to the expansion of Sokol between the wars. The Spartakiads also did not

736   Holý, L.: *The Little Czech and the Great Czech Nation*.
737   NA, f. SVTVS, k. 69, inv. n. 204, Informační bulletin štábu I. celostátní spartakiády ze dne 12. dubna 1955. Nevertheless, after the Spartakiad had ended *Rudé právo* thanked Prague's citizens for hosting "ten thousand visitors" in their homes. In: "Poděkování Pražanům za pohostinnost ve spartakiádních dnech". *Rudé právo*, vol. 35, 8. 7. 1955, p. 1.
738   "Za oponou CS". *Mladý svět*, 1960, vol. 2, n. 27, p. 7.
739   "Regarding the accommodations for gymnasts from outside of Prague, we cannot allow them to stay in private, with friends or relatives." Viz NA, f. ÚV ČSTV, k. 268, Zásady pro další řešení ubytování aktivních účastníků Československé spartakiády 1985.

appeal to all social groups. This is well illustrated by the *Mladý svět* survey taken among twelve celebrities on the Spartakiad in 1965.[740] The magazine asked them all what they hoped for or expected from the 3rd All-State Spartakiad and whether they would rather be a participant or a spectator at the Spartakiad. Except for Olympic gymnast Věra Čáslavská, who confirmed that she herself would be participating in the Spartakiad at Strahov and wished that there were more Spartakiads, none of the "stars" expressed even a hint of enthusiasm. A clear feeling of social superiority is apparent from most of their responses. Actor Jan Tříska felt sorry for the sweaty Spartakiad crowd: "You know, I feel quite sorry when I see so many people together without the chance to properly shower, to eat and drink in peace. That's what I would really hope that all involved in the 3rd Spartakiad could have." Actress Jiřina Bohdalová was mostly looking forward to not having to participate in the Spartakiad herself. Writer Josef Škvorecký explained that his "unjustified biases" concerning mass gymnastic performances stemmed from childhood experiences. As a small child he apparently had to take part in Sokol Slets and at one of them he had accidentally wedged his foot in an underground speaker. Singer Hana Hegerová confessed that she was not fond of "things involving masses" and preferred peace and calm. Other famous figures looked forward to the Spartakiad bringing things that were completely unrelated to mass performances. The artist Jan Zrzavý hoped that the participants would help boost the attendance at his exhibition taking place at that time and also that the streetcars would run on time, the sidewalks would be clean and that the "cornices on building wouldn't fall off." Interestingly, the second question concerning their possible participation was in the conditional tense and did not assume that these "stars" would be performing with the others. Most of the respondents did not take the question seriously at all. The singer Waldemar Matuška said

---

740 "Dvanáct dostižených". *Mladý svět*, 1965, vol. 7, n. 26, pp. 8–9.

that he would like to be an ice-cream vendor at Strahov Stadium. The jazz musician Karel Velebný responded that he would like to be a female gymnast since "the world would be far more beautiful for me if I could brazenly wear a purple t-shirt." Yet as a supporter of the Slavia football club, the main rival of the Sparta football club, he rejected the entire Spartakiad until they renamed it "Slaviakiad." Director Miloš Forman said that he could not decide whether he would rather be a night watchman on Petřín Hill (a popular place for lovers not far from Strahov) during the Spartakiad or a "beautiful, tan, muscular gymnast" with his "place marker as close as possible to the main grandstands," while the remaining part of his response focused mainly on the junior women's "youthful bloom."

State authorities also made sure that people from the other end of the social ladder would not take part in Spartakiads. At the suggestion of Jindřich Kotal, the deputy of all six ministers of national security during the period of 1951–1968, "preventative measures against asocial elements" were already in place for the first Spartakiad.[741] The order received by directors from the regional administration of the Secret Police demonstrates that this practice was maintained until the end of state socialism:

"to prevent the arrival of problematic individuals to the 1985 Spartakiad in Prague," to ensure the thorough monitoring of "groups of problematic youth" and, in cooperation with medical personnel, the "temporary isolation" of alcoholics, drug addicts and "dangerous psychopaths."[742]

---

[741] AČOS, f. I. celostátní spartakiáda, Politické materiály, Zápis ze 6. porady komise ÚV KSČ pro zajištění I. celostátní spartakiády, konané 25. června 1955 v 9.00 hod. na strahovském stadionu.

[742] ABS, f. X. správa SNB (A 36), inv. j. 704, Informace z 3. odboru X. S., leden–říjen 1985, p. 3; See also ABS, f. X. správa SNB (A 36), inv. j. 702, Československá spartakiáda 1985 – svodná informace ze dne 27. 6. 1985, p. 1. As Malte Rolf pointed out, the "cleaning" of cities before state holidays was a practice well known in the Soviet Union as well. Rolf noticed a Boris Ignatovich photograph from 1927 in which the children of the city's poor walked in torn clothes along with Pioneers in the May Day Parade. Such a photograph could not have been taken a few years later during Stalinist rituals. Rolf, M.: *Das sowjetische Massenfest*, p. 210.

It is clear then that the various tactics of passive resistance posed a much greater threat to Spartakiads than open resistance. The organizers and sponsors of Spartakiads did not hesitate, as we shall now see, to make far-reaching concessions in matters of ideological content and social control, and also to invest considerable funds into avoiding this resistance.

SPARTAKIAD POTLATCH

With their immense budgets, regularity and predictability, the Spartakiads created the field for a broad range of cultural practices that always involved a certain trade-off with the regime. Karen Petrone, who examined rituals in Stalinist Russia, pointed out that, despite the attempts to have these festivities bear the mark of modernity and technical advancement, they actually remained in a pre-modern, pesant logic.[743] In releasing vast funds during the Spartakiads for private consumption, the organizers copied the agricultural yearly rhythm of scarcity and surplus. Rituals played an important role in that they regularly, even for just a few days, validated the "rhetoric of mythical abundance." Of course, the funds accumulated for the celebrations were lacking before and after the festivity, or outside of Prague. The communist rituals were thus well adapted to the established rhythm of fasts and feasts and became one of the many aspects of the communist moral economy.

The most visible and easiest way of consuming the Spartakiad ritual was the simple consumption of the food and drink that the regime generously offered. The Party's policy resembled the potlatch ritual of Native American Indians, in which profligacy and waste is a symbol of power, prestige and favor of the gods.[744] In the 1950s and 1960s in particular, the Spartakiads were an occasion to give the people, during a period of relative scarcity, the chance "to taste" the coming communist paradise. This is perhaps why the press and film documentaries of that day placed such an emphasis on the supply of exotic fruit, symbolizing the exceptionality of the Spartakiad days

---

[743] Petrone, Karen: *Life Has Become More Joyous, Comrades. Celebrations in the Time of Stalin.* Indiana University Press, Bloomington – Indianapolis 2000, p. 16. The author points out that rituals similarly affected the distribution of work. Economic plans were often linked to important holidays and led to a "call to arms" right before them. The holidays themselves stopped work, evoking the agricultural economy with its unequal distribution of work and leisure.

[744] See in particular Mauss, Marcel: *The Gift. The Form and Reason for Exchange in Archaic Societies.* Routledge, London (1925) 1990.

46. Refreshments at Strahov Stadium during the 1960 Spartakiad (photo Václav Chochola).

and their "heavenly" aspect. Also playing an important role along with exotic fruit was meat, especially smoked meats. *Rudé právo* emphasized that in order to enrich the Prague market during the 1st All-State Spartakiad, the state-owned foreign trade company Koospol had imported eighty tons of genuine winter salami and "a new type of Italian salami from Romania." A special type of salami was even produced for the 1960 Spartakiad with "Best of luck to the Spartakiad" printed on the package. This cult of meat and smoked meats endured until the "normalization" period, even though it clashed with the notion of a healthy diet at that time.[745] During the 1975 Spartakiad, *Rudé právo* proudly published photographs of a number of female participants "making short work of delicious sausages" following a Spartakiad rehearsal.[746]

The amount of food consumed during Spartakiads was a favorite theme for journalists covering the event. The commentary to Jaroslav Papoušek's film on the 1960 Spartakiad (the main camera work was by renowned cinematographer Jan Špáta) enthusiastically reported that a "whole city of temporary shops" had been erected at Strahov, selling five million oranges and nearly the same number of cigarettes. Two thousand hectoliters of beer had been drunk at the stands and restaurants at Strahov and twelve million eggs had been consumed (according to the commentary, an omelet from so many eggs would "cover the Sahara and part of the Gobi Desert," and if this amount were a single egg, "the hen laying it would have to be the size of the Queen Mary ocean liner.")[747]

The abundant supply of the Spartakiad also resembled a potlatch ritual in that the offer of "gifts" from the "patron" was binding and a failure to fulfill it had serious consequences. The participants deciding to take part in the event were certainly not mere props with which the organizers could do what they liked even though the photographs from the Strahov performances give that very impression. The participants could quite vocally let it be known whenever they felt that the social contract on which the Spartakiads were based had not been upheld. Supply shortages led to emphatic protests that overshadowed all other forms of dissent with Spartakiads. It is

---

745 See Franc, Martin: Socialism and the Overweight Nation: Questions of Ideology, Science and Obesity in Czechoslovakia, 1950–70. In: Oddy, Derek J. – Atkins, Peter J. – Amilien, Virginie (eds.): *The Rise of Obesity in Europe. A Twentieth Century Food History.* Farnham – Burlington, Ashgate 2009, pp. 193–205.

746 *Rudé právo*, vol. 55, 26. 6. 1975, p. 8.

747 Papoušek, Jaroslav: *II. celostátní spartakiáda.* II: *Mládí a krása.* Krátký film, Prague 1960, 44 mins.

significant that the largest protests during Spartakiads did not come from outside the ritual framework, but from within.

Professor Josef Charvát, the founder of Czech endocrinology, recorded in his diary a telling incident from the 1st All-State Spartakiad. Apparently President Antonín Zápotocký arrived at Strahov before the end of a morning rehearsal for a children's performance. The organizers decided to repeat the rehearsal for the president without giving the children who were extremely hungry, anything to eat or drink. Instead of expressing the "obligatory enthusiasm" during the line-up, the youngsters chanted "We're hungry, we want to eat, we want to go home." Then during the rehearsal the children ignored the president and did whatever they wanted. When the president visited the dressing rooms afterwards "not only did nobody notice him, the children were fighting and screaming so much that the president remarked 'I can't help but think that Czech youth act like cattle.'"[748]

Charvát's testimony is confirmed by the fact that the *Rudé právo* article on the president's visit to the rehearsal is surprisingly brief.[749] In her dissertation on mass gymnastic performances, Jana Berdychová also mentioned this incident as proof that it was not always possible to achieve the "expected morally, political and culturally educated effect on the participants."[750]

Such incidents often occurred during Spartakiads.[751] The secret police were quite concerned with the situation as apparent in their report on the 1985 Spartakiad:

748 Charvát, J.: *Můj labyrint světa*, p. 398. My gratitude to Martin Franc for bringing this episode to my attention.
749 "Představitelé strany a vlády zhlédli přípravy na Strahově". *Rudé právo*, vol. 35, 23. 6. 1955, p. 1.
750 Berdychová, J.: *Funkce tělovýchovných skladeb pro hromadná vystoupení mládeže*, p. 8. This was not an exceptional case. In the days that followed there also were also incidents in which there was "a lack of discipline" among the children and adolescent participants, as well as problems in logistics.
751 For instance, during the 1975 Spartakiad political education worker Jiří Hroza reported that "the men are becoming extremely critical due to problems in supplying food; they are, however,

"Nearly all regional reports tell of insufficient meal portions [...] In leaving the Spartakiad stadium the participants spontalneously [sic!] expressed their dissatisfaction by chanting "WE ARE HUNGRY". Our operatives report that foreign participants and tourists from capitalist countries took advantage of this situation by throwing cookies into the passing crowd of participants, offering them fruit, chocolate and popsicles, while photographing it all."[752]

The State Police immediately discussed the matter with the head of the Czechoslovak Physical Education Association, which promised that the situation would be "immediately rectified regardless of the funds spent."[753]

While the consumption of food – if properly handled logistically – could support the image of the party as a caring guardian, the consumption of alcohol was much more controversial. On the one hand, alcohol and the ritual were inseparably linked in Czech culture. Yet on the other hand, its excessive consumption (later also the smoking of tobacco products) was inconsistent with the model of the ideal Spartakiad gymnast. Nevertheless, unrestrained drinking was a permanent feature of Czechoslovak Spartakiads and was far from limited to adult men as we can read in one of the reports:

"Women and junior women have begun to frequent pubs. As for the men, this can be expected to occur as soon as the program provides them with free time."[754] There were frequent complaints that drunk participants were destroying the furnishings of the trains arranged specially for the Spartakiad and disrupting the carefully prepared transportation schedule (especially trains carrying mining apprentices

doing their job, though not without complaint." AČOS, f. Československá spartakiáda 1975, Denní hlášení pro PVO ÚŠ ČSS 1975, 25. 6. 1975.

752   ABS, f. X. správa SNB (A 36), inv. j. 702, Československá spartakiáda 1985 – svodná informace ze dne 27. 6. 1985, p. 2.

753   Ibid.

754   AČOS, f. Československá spartakiáda 1975, Denní hlášení pro PVO ÚŠ ČSS 1975, 23. 6. 1975.

from North Moravia and Silesia).[755] There was also drinking in the lodgings where alcohol-induced fights occurred and "socialist property" was destroyed.[756] The reports reveal that the organizers did not at all attempt to rigidly curb excessive alcohol consumption and usually tried to deal with such transgressions by police warning. That the Strahov complex was abundantly supplied with alcohol only contributed to its consumption. Political-educational workers were shocked by the fact that the "beer was sold by distributors right at the assembly point"[757] – meaning that it was sold right where the participants were lined up before the performances, i.e. in front of the entrance to Strahov Stadium.[758] The organizers also tried in vain to limit smoking. For instance, a political-educational worker for the Parents and Children piece encountered a typical example of socialist *Eigensinn*: "Numerous mothers were smoking in their Spartakiad outfits at the assembly point while their children were running around. Some of them did not respond overly politely to tactful warnings." The importance of the abundance of food and drink gradually diminished with the rise in living standard and was replaced by the more sophisticated consumption of metropolitan experiences. The Spartakiad organizers knew better than to leave the decision about how free time was spent to the people themselves: "[…] only an absolute minimum amount of personal free time should be left up to the participants."[759]

---

755   See for instance ABS, f. X. správa SNB (A 36), inv. j. 702, Československá spartakiáda 1985 – svodná informace ze dne 22. 6. 1985, p. 2.

756   See for instance ABS, f. X. správa SNB (A 36), inv. j. 702, Československá spartakiáda 1985 – svodná informace ze dne 23. 6. 1985.

757   AČOS, f. Československá spartakiáda 1975, Denní hlášení pro PVO ÚŠ ČSS 1975, 25. 6. 1975.

758   The consumption of alcohol during Spartakiads and other socialist rituals wholly correspond to the traditional model of village festivals. Malte Rolf, who examined provincial Soviet festivals in particular, describes how Soviet officials quickly eased up in their attempt to organize "dry" holidays and instead showed the moderate consumption of alcohol to be a sign of the new Soviet "kulturnost." Rolf, M.: *Das sowjetische Massenfest*, p. 245. See also Petrone, K.: *Life Has Become More Joyous, Comrades*, p. 19.

759   AČOS, f. Československá spartakiáda 1975, Denní hlášení pro PVO ÚŠ ČSS 1975, 23. 6. 1975.

Yet it was soon realized that the participants would modify the program of their stay in Prague to suit themselves. "The juniors are much more interested in invigorating activities and less in those of political-education. The teachers and trainers are aware of this fact and are trying to guide the juniors' interest in the required educational direction."[760]

They therefore organized for the participants quite costly "entertainment programs," particularly at the Julius Fučík Park of Culture and Relaxation where all the big stars of the Czech "normalization" pop-culture performed. In 1975, the Spartakiad Carousel, a "diverse program of music and humor" was, for instance, held here on twelve outdoor stages.[761] Some pop stars took this role very seriously. In 1985, Czech pop-singer Michal David told *Rudé právo*: "We perform four times day to help create the best Spartakiad atmosphere possible."[762] Shopping was also a high priority for the participants. The generally better-stocked capital became even more so during the Spartakiads, naturally to the detriment of the other parts of the country. We know from the daily reports that Strahov Stadium itself became the center of vibrant and often not exactly legal trade. In addition to overpricing,[763] the organizers came across ideological impropriety of some of the sold goods. "Even stands at Strahov," complained eastern Slovak political-educational workers "are selling t-shirts with inappropriate messages and names of capitalist countries and companies."[764]

760   AČOS, f. Československá spartakiáda 1975, Denní hlášení pro PVO ÚŠ ČSS 1975, 24. 6. 1975.

761   "Hlavní město omládlo". *Rudé právo*, vol. 55, 26. 6. 1975, p. 1.

762   "Nechť rostou do krásy. S Michalem Davidem a Františkem Janečkem o ‚poupatech'". *Rudé právo*, vol. 65, 28. 6. 1985, p. 8.

763   E.g., ABS, f. X. správa SNB (A 36), inv. j. 702, Československá spartakiáda 1985 – informace ze dne 24. 6. 1985, p. 3. See also "Trestuhodné chytračení". *Rudé právo*, vol. 60, 27. 6. 1980, p. 2.

764   AČOS, f. Československá spartakiáda 1975, Denní hlášení pro PVO ÚŠ ČSS 1975, 25. 6. 1975. With their massive means of mobilization, Spartakiads were also a good opportunity for theft. A "refrigerator and four upholstered chairs were stolen" right from the instructors'

47. The Spartakiad parade at Wenceslas Square in Prague in 1955 (photo Václav Chochola).

Consumption activities in Prague went further than merely watching light entertainment and shopping. The city itself became a spectacle in which the crowds of participants played a leading part, though in a completely different role than what the Spartakiad

platform on the roof of the western grandstands of Strahov Stadium from where the entry of tens of thousands of participants was orchestrated. AČOS, f. Československá spartakiáda 1975, Letter from Jaroslav Novák, ÚŠ ČSS economic committee chairman, to the local police department in Prague-Břevnov from 29. 7. 1975.

organizers had planned for. In interviews or testimony, many participants spoke of a carnival-like atmosphere, of a city in which people from all over the country were chaotically mingling, as were soldiers, foreigners (black people in particular attracted the attention of the many villagers), the western cars of diplomats, medieval architecture and several neon signs ("They're unfamiliar with Prague, and yet / they're turning the metropolis inside out," wrote poet Miroslav Florian[765]). It all had a profound effect on the participants and created, beyond the Spartakiad ritual at the stadium, a truly impressive festive atmosphere. It is by no means simple to reconstruct this experience since much more dynamic and deeper experiences of traveling abroad and opening oneself to a global culture following the 1989 revolution have often trumped the Spartakiad memories in their minds. Yet preserved in archives are numerous letters from participants and spectators that attest to the power of the Spartakiad experience. Junior women from the Secondary Medical School in Slovak Rožňava described in detail their trip to the Prague subway, or rather their search for it: "We had already agreed in our room that we would first head for the subway. We were looking forward to riding it, and free of charge." An even greater experience for them was the number of foreigners in Prague, which they described as a second Babylon: "We were laughing, surprised that we were in Prague and hadn't encountered a single Czech."[766]

The feeling from the city – surprising, "liminal" and dangerous – where anything seemed possible was further solidified by a range of sexual myths linked to the Spartakiad.[767] In addition to the macabre panics caused by the case of the "Spartakiad killer"[768]

765 Florian, Miroslav: "Cvičenci". In: Florian, Miroslav: *Óda na mladost*. Olympia, Prague 1988.
766 AČOS, f. Československá spartakiáda 1975, Letter from junior female of SZŠ Rožňava to Spartakiad organisers 26. 6. 1975.
767 For more on liminality, see the seminal work Turner, Victor W.: "Betwixt and Between. The Liminal Period in Rites de Passage". In: Turner, V. W: *The Forest of Symbols*, pp. 93–111.
768 The "Spartakiad killer," a sixteen-year-old apprentice named Jiří Straka attacked eleven women on separate occasions in Prague and its vicinity, murdering three of them. His attacks had

it was also rumored at the time that Spartakiads were accompanied by a wave of extramarital affairs that led to a five-year demographic cycle corresponding to the Spartakiads (statistics of births and abortions show that this was merely a myth[769]). Nevertheless, Spartakiad organizers and the police had to go to lengths to separate the two sexes (there is no mention in source documents of same-sex contact). The secret police reported many attempts, often quite sophisticated, at entering the lodgings of the female participants (e.g., one unknown man succeeded in passing himself off as an official of the Central Committee of Socialist Youth Association), and commanded the accommodations committee to tighten its supervision of the entrance to the lodgings and to warn the female participants of the "impropriety of receiving male visitors."[770]

The secret police were most concerned with the contact made between foreign students and the female participants: "Based on the warning from the inteligence network, measures have been taken to prevent female gymnasts lodged at the VOLHA and VLTAVA dormitories from attending dance parties organized by foreign students at the SÁZAVA dormitory [...] These measures have been taken to prevent this activity, which is a gross violation of the Spartakiad rules for female participants and disrupts the peace and order among junior women and women lodged in dormitories."[771]

Although it is clear that, owing to strict social control, the Spartakiads did not turn into an opportunity for loose morals on a massive scale, the fact that tens of thousands of young people were freed from

---

nothing to do with Spartakiad, nevertheless the police were under great pressure to apprehend the killer before the Spartakiad began. They finally did so on May 22, 1985. See "Nebezpečný pachatel dopaden". *Rudé právo*, vol. 65, 24. 5. 1985, p. 2.

769 See for instance příslušné ročníky *Statistické ročenky Československé socialistické republiky*. SNTL, Prague.

770 ABS, f. X. správa SNB (A 36), inv. j. 702, Československá spartakiáda 1985 – informace ze dne 24. 6. 1985, pp. 2–3.

771 ABS, f. X. správa SNB (A 36), inv. j. 702, Československá spartakiáda 1985 – informace ze dne 24. 6. 1985, pp. 2–3.

their usual social bonds contributed to the creation of new relationships. Though there is no proof of a demographically significant group of "Spartakiad kids" conceived during the Spartakiads, there are quite a few "Spartakiad marriages," i.e. relationships begun during the Spartakiad practices or performances in Prague.[772]

---

772 This social aspect of the Spartakiads was examined in the press of that period. Co-ed performances were appreciated for providing the "possibility to teach the necessary interpersonal, social and working relations between girls and boys." Šiktanc and Šotola praised Spartakiads for preparing "the youth without the tremor of sexual secrecy." The magazine *Mladý svět* (Young World) published a comic entitled "Exercising in Pairs" that shows rows of amorous couples on benches at the exercising field of the Strahov Stadium. Seliger, V. a spol.: "Výzkum fyziologické a pedagogické náročnosti skladeb hromadných vystoupení", p. 672; Šotola, Jiří – Šiktanc, Karel: "Člověk v zástupech". In: C. Rybár – J. Novotný (eds.): *V rytmu krásy a radosti; Mladý svět*, 1960, vol. 2, n. 28, p. 16.

AN ENTHUSIASTIC RECEPTION

In examining the full spectrum of reactions to Spartakiads, perhaps the most interesting is the last one – their enthusiastic reception. Until now we have adhered to a model of a socialist festivity known from previous studies: of a communist celebration characterized by the concept of appropriation in which the ruling power was able to create a ritual framework, but was unable to mediate the ritual's content. Yet this model does not capture Czechoslovak Spartakiads in their entirety. Besides the various strategies of resistance (mostly very moderate), the appropriation of a ritual and its use for their own enjoyment, there was also sincere enthusiasm for the idea of Spartakiads which had virtually nothing to do with the material benefits (accommodations in Prague, a potlatch of food and drink, ogling the female participants). While the concept of appropriation would explain why spectators came to Strahov, it does not answer the question why the participants, especially of the adult performances, devoted so much of their free time to Spartakiad practices (nine months, once or even twice a week). In this, the Spartakiads differed considerably from e.g. the May Day festivities, in which the time commitment was limited to a single lost morning. The participation of those exercising in the Spartakiad performances cannot be fully explained unless we believe that the idea of Spartakiad at least partially resonated with them. The core of the instructors and the vast majority of adult participants belonged to the Sokol subculture not motivated to participate by material interests, but by their own convictions. Many Spartakiad participants simply felt that the Spartakiads were not only fun, but also the right thing to do.

The main reason we rarely come across authentic enthusiasm for socialist rituals in publications on the subject is because this intuitive assumption is not easy to prove in sources. One of the possibilities is the use of propaganda during the period, for which the individual's personal experience represented an important part of the overall narrative. Individual testimony confirmed the general proclamations on the success of Spartakiads and the people's enthusiasm, but also served as an important way to support official statements about Spartakiads. Another role of individual testimony was to suppress the oppressive impression of the anonymous crowd that the performances could have on some readers and spectators. In 1975, for instance, *Rudé právo* published a regular column entitled "The View of One in a Million," which clearly aimed at variety in terms of both the writer's origin as well as the style of language used. The participants wrote in this column about their profound experience in the Spartakiad performance and about the "adversities" that they had to overcome to get to Strahov and perform in front of "our comrade president." One instructor from Plzeň described her impressions from the rehearsal: "[…] on Thursday I wept from the very first beat, I had goose bumps from the excitement and stage fright. What can you expect from a woman, from a schoolteacher, who as an instructor brought with her to Prague twenty future carpenters and varnishers."[773] A female apprentice from Prievidza, who had come to Prague for the first time in her life, had similar recollections: "When the Gate of Athletes opened and we ran onto the field, I was seized by stage fright and anxiety. I didn't feel the coldness of my rain-soaked t-shirt. Instead, a feverish excitement coursed through my body."[774] Obviously, these testimonies were generated by official propaganda, as the participants were encouraged to send their impressions to the editors, who chose those which were ideologically suitable, undoubtedly often deleting and embellishing to serve the purpose.[775]

---

773 Macháčková, Dana: "Mrazilo mne v zádech". *Rudé právo*, vol. 55, 28. 6. 1975, p. 8
774 Martinik, Jozef: "Na shledanou za pět let". *Rudé právo*, vol. 55, 30. 6. 1975, p. 8. See also e.g., Žáček, Miloslav: "Tělocvična, nebo bačkory". *Rudé právo*, 26. 6. 1975, p. 8; Hlavatá, Iveta: "O nejmladší cvičence". *Rudé právo*, 27. 6. 1975, p. 8.
775 For instance one of the letters by a female university student from Brno, written in a very light and informal tone throughout ("practicing is really a bore"), was undoubtedly edited to include a penultimate paragraph about "the happy and sunny May days thirty years ago." See Kalabisová, Jiřina: "Přijďte, zamáváme". *Rudé právo*, vol. 55, 25. 6. 1975, p. 8.

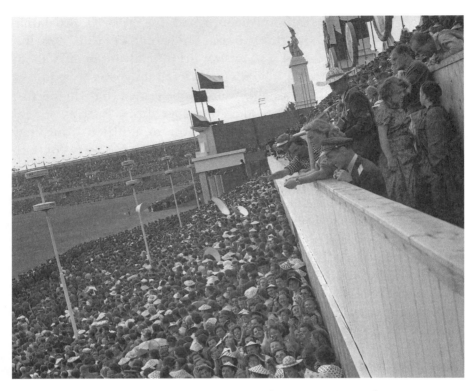

48. Strahov Stadium stands during the 1955 Spartakiad (photo Václav Chochola).

In the 1950s we also come across the letter writers' curious need to emphasize that they were participating voluntarily.[776] Hundreds of these testimonies can therefore be dismissed as the product of propagandistic machinery, just as the enthusiastic faces of participants and spectators in film footage can be ignored as the result of a highly selective editing process. Yet in doing so we are depriving ourselves of important insight into the workings of a socialist society.

[776] "Z naší přípravy na spartakiádu". *Československý voják*, 1955, vol. 4, n. 12, p. 27.

Indeed, many other sources confirm that the Spartakiad were a truly profound experience for part of the public. The Spartakiad Staff received, for example, hundreds of enthusiastic letters whose authenticity can hardly be doubted. Some used an official style of language, such as Olga Ralousová from the city of Most: "Dear Comrades, I am hereby writing to all of you who took part in organizing the Czechoslovak Spartakiad to express my gratitude. I'm certainly not the only one who needed to fight back tears in watching it. [...] I am overcome by a wonderful feeling that I belong to a nation that is able to create such beauty. [...] The Spartakiad is simply an enormous song of peace."[777] Others ignored the official socialist lingo altogether. "Grandmother M. from Brno," went the furthest in this sense in her letter to the organizers: "Dear Sir or Madam, I am praying that it does not rain in Prague. I feel sorry for the participants and you. Try praying yourselves, the Good Lord might listen to you, but we do not know His will. If you do not know the Lord's Prayer, pray in your own words or ask Madonna of Turzovka to intercede."[778]

The enthusiasm of some of the participants for the Spartakiad was such that it repeatedly disrupted the event. On a number of occasions the participants (sometimes even with their trainers) forced their way into the stands to watch the performances of their colleagues.[779] For organizational reasons, but also due to the great demand for tickets, no seats had been allotted to the participants as spectators. Another incident demonstrates that the participants were not indifferent to the success of their performance. A Secret Police report reveals that the older pupils protested the mistakes made by the chairman of the director's committee, Jiří Žižka, who repeatedly botched the timing of the start of the performance and musical accompaniment.

777   AČOS, f. Československá spartakiáda 1985, Letter from Olga Rousalová to ÚV ČSTV 28. 6. 1985.

778   Ibid, Letter to Spartakiad organisers 29. 6. 1985.

779   AČOS, f. Československá spartakiáda 1975, Denní hlášení pro PVO ÚŠ ČSS 1975, 28. 6. 1975. Similar indcidents occured at the previous Spartakiads as well.

The participants had agreed that if there were repeated errors they would stop performing and all whistle.[780] The authors of the students' piece also joined the protest.

There are even public opinion surveys on the popularity of Spartakiads, though their testimonial value is certainly limited. Researchers of the Department of Physical Culture Theory of the Faculty of Physical Education and Sports took in June 1985, for instance, a survey of nearly seven hundred adult participants.[781] The most important finding was that 90 percent of the men and 92 percent of the women expressed an interest in taking part in the next Spartakiad.[782] The research also revealed some sociological data about this group of people. Above all, there was a large age discrepancy between the men and women: while the average age of the male respondent was 44 years, the average age of the female respondent was not even 33 years. This difference is even greater if we do not take into account the male Slovak participants, since a quarter of the male participants from the Czech lands were over 50 years of age. Most of the male respondents also stated that they had been exercising in

---

780   ABS, f. X. správa SNB (A 36), inv. j. 702, Československá spartakiáda 1985 – svodná informace ze dne 29. 6. 1985, p. 3. Jiří Žižka's failure could be one of the reasons why there were generational changes made in the leadership of the Spartakiad staff with Pavel Belšan replacing Žižka. (Interview with Pavel Belšan on 10 February 2006 in Prague conducted by Petr Roubal, author's archive.) Peter Flamík recalls this incident in his blog: "We ran out to the metal markers positioned on the stadium's sandy field and waited. For the music and the command. We were supposed to start moving on the command of some bigwig, who would give the sign with the wave of his hand. Well, maybe he was tone deaf, or under too much stress or otherwise indisposed, but he waved when he shouldn't have. A national embarrassment occured right at Strahov stadium! He finally got the wave right and we were grinning as we performed the piece." Flamík, Peter: *Spomienka na Spartakiádu 1985 – tú poslednú*. Dostupné na: http://peterflamik.blog.sme.sk/c/176979/Spomienka-na-Spartakiadu-1985-tu-poslednu.html [retrieved 13. 11. 2013].

781   Drdácká, Božena – Falcmanová, Vlasta: "Tělesná kultura v hodnotové orientaci žen a mužů vystupujících v hromadných tělovýchovných skladbách Svazu ZRTV na Čs. spartakiádě 1985". In: *Sborník ze semináře FTVS UK Praha, p.* 92–107. Also see Drdácká, Božena – Falcmanová, Vlasta: "Tělesná kultura v hodnotové orientaci žen a mužů vystupujících v Československé spartakiádě 1985". *Teorie a praxe tělesné výchovy*, 1987, vol. 35, n. 7, pp. 407–411.

782   An anonymous survey conducted by the military among its gymnasts during the 1965 Spartakiad reached the same conclusion. See AČOS, f. Výběr skladeb 1960–1975, Záznam diskuse k předvedení ukázky skladby armády.

gymnastics clubs since they were young. We can infer then that many of the men performing at the final Spartakiad were former members of Sokol clubs. Over 40 percent of the men were blue-collar workers, while fewer than 20 percent of the women were. While in the Czech part of the federation, the distribution of rural and urban habitation corresponded to the general distribution between cities and villages, almost all the Slovak participants were from towns and cities. For instance, only three percent of the men practiced in Slovak towns of up to two thousand residents, while 30 percent did so in Czech towns of the same size. The surveys also explored the motives that led the participants to become involved in the practices. Even though the participants were to officially express their involvement as loyalty to the communist party and gratitude to the Soviet Union, ideological motivation did not at all figure among the offered choices as evidenced by the following chart:[783]

Motives for participation	Women	Men
health and better condition	38%	38%
good collective	36%	33%
recruited for exercises and no regrets	8%	13%
recruited for exercises with regrets	X	3%
improving natural movements	5%	X
desire to perform at Strahov	5%	5%
other reason	4%	5%
nicer figure	3%	X
a member of the Sport-for-All Association club which practiced a Spartakiad piece	1%	3%

783 Drdácká, B. – Falcmanová, V.: "Tělesná kultura v hodnotové orientaci žen a mužů vystupujících v hromadných tělovýchovných skladbách", p. 102 The chart is slightly modified. It isn't clear from the text whether both sexes received the same options to choose from or if some (such as "nice figure") were gender specific. However, ideological motivation was assumed in a similar 1960 survey. The terms "optimism," "joy from collective work," and "social consciousness" were used here. ATVS NM, f. Spartakiády (1953–1990), k. 3, Dotazník ÚV ČSTV pro cvičence.

The press of that period also openly conceded the absence of ideological motives. This is well illustrated by an interview by the well-known sports journalist Václav Pacina with Eva Bémová, one of the authors of a women's piece at the last Spartakiad of 1985.

Pacina: If I ask why women are most interested in Spartakiad performances, you will probably tell me they want to be found attractive.
Bémová: That wouldn't be my answer at all. Tell me something, if there is going to be fourteen thousand of them at Strahov and then another fourteen thousand, how could someone find one of the women attractive?
Pacina: Right then, so…
Bémová: And you know what? I have no idea why women are so eager to take part in the Spartakiad.
Pacina: Come on now! Eva Bémová, one of the authors of the Spartakiad piece for women, […] doesn't know?! […]
Bémová: I'm around them, I've been exercising with them for dozens of years, they write me, I travel from one practice to another, and when I think about it […] They have an attractive outfit and certainly the feeling that they look nice, that they look good doing the routines, that perhaps they'll get to go to Prague, but is that the real reason? They're also glad to be in a collective. […] The fact that they exercise to music is certainly psychologically pleasing and lets them forget about their worries. A woman might come to the gym and say: "I didn't even want to come today, girls. I have so much ironing to do at home! And then after the exercises she'll say: I'm really glad that I came! You see, she was able to get off the everyday carousal and enter a different world – this is certainly a reason too. Another reason is that in other sports clubs they demand from her difficult movements and exceptional performances, but in our gymnastics clubs she is only expected to make natural movements for recreational purposes.[784]

784 Pacina, Václav: "Ženy útočí na Strahov". *Mladá fronta*, vol. 41, 9. 2. 1985, p. 8.

As we will see later in the text, the ideological timidity of the sociological surveyors and the press was perhaps exaggerated. If they had found the right key words such as "Sokol idea," "national tradition," "show themselves to the world," "shared work," they probably would have been surprised to what extent the participants themselves "ideologically" understood their involvement.

From the very beginning it was clear that some former Sokol members perceived the Spartakiads as a continuation of the Sokol's Slet tradition. Their participation in Spartakiads was then seen as an obligation to society, country and, paradoxically, to their former movement. We even find a number of such positions in a survey following the 1st All-State Spartakiad in 1955. In response to the question of their strongest impression from the Spartakiad, Ladislav Mach, a clerk from the town of Studená answered: "Since it was already my fifth time at Strahov, I had no uncertainty, just a feeling of responsibility and national pride in passing through the Gate of Athletes. This moment, even for an old participant, is the main impression."[785] Albin Patzák, a cashier, saw his participation at the Spartakiad in similar terms: "Even though I am an old Sokol member, I never took part in any Slet except for a 1933 regional Slet in Ústí nad Labem. But what I witnessed today in Prague left an indelible impression on me; especially the feeling of personal gratification that my work as an instructor was not in vain. I wish the very best to the next Spartakiad!"

A unique document has been preserved in the archives offering us at least a partial glimpse into the mindset of the participants immediately following the fall of communism. Shortly after the Velvet Revolution in November 1989 the discussion arose of whether to hold the planned 1990 Spartakiad. In a newly discovered passion for

785 Appelt, K.: "Poznámky k dotazníkové akci", p. 123. See also Stránský, Antonín: "Odraz ideje hromadných cvičení u cvičence a u diváka". In: *Vědecká konference o teoretických a metodických základech masových tělovýchovných vystoupení*, p. 52.

democratic decision-making, the heads of the Czechoslovak Physical Education Association appealed to the "Spartakiad public," i.e. the participants and instructors, to express their views on whether to continue with the practices or cancel the event.

The response was enormous. By January 3, 1990 the Czechoslovak Physical Education Association, Czechoslovak State Television and several dailies, which were also taking part in the survey, had received three thousand letters, of which two thousand were from gymnastics clubs consisting of nearly 200,000 participants. Support for preserving Spartakiads clearly prevailed: 78 percent of respondents were for continuing the event while only 22 percent opposed it.[786] Even more important is the content of these letters revealing the importance that people ascribed to Spartakiads. With its thousands of petitions, proclamations and demonstrations, the Velvet Revolution brought a temporary politicization of society in which ordinary people considered it proper and necessary to publicly express their views.[787] The revolutionary fervor was also partially reflected in the language of these letters in which the official lingo of state socialism vies with the traditional nationalistic discourse of the Sokols.

Certainly not all of the hundreds of letters found in the archives expressed the genuine views of participants. Some people had clearly been coaxed by their instructors or sports officials to write letters of protest, as attested to by the postcard written by a woman from Prague: "Greetings, Dear Television! I attend Spartakiad exercises at the club TJ Spoje Balkán in Prague 3. They told us there that we should write to the State Television so that we can exercise in various places of Prague [sic!] – at least I understood it that way. I am

---

786 AČOS, f. Československá spartakiáda 1990, Vyhodnocení dotazníkové ankety ke konání Československé spartakiády 1990.

787 See Krapfl, James: *Revolution with a Human Face: Politics, Culture, and Community in Czechoslovakia, 1989–1992.* Cornell University Press, Ithaca 2013.

letting you know that I want to do the Spartakiad exercises."[788] The frequent repetition of certain motives also demonstrates that the media had a considerable share in forming the participants' views, with a television debate on the fate of the Spartakiad having perhaps the strongest influence on this discussion.[789]

Such topos included drawing a parallel between the Spartakiads and the Olympics, both of which are the final goal striven for by both the athletes and the mass exercise participants. ("Just as the Olympics are the final goal for athletes, so is the Spartakiad for us."[790]) Yet most of the letters attest to a deep relationship to Spartakiads and the intensive personal and even physical experience that this event meant for the participants.

The chairman of a small gymnastics group, who had taken part in Slets in 1938 and 1948 and in all Spartakiads after that, recounted in his letter an unforgettable experience from Strahov Stadium:

> It's hard to describe the experience to someone who's never experienced and never passed through the Gate of Athletes, especially for a young person to have 150,000 pairs of hands applauding you; it's hot and it gives you goose bumps, your eyes tear up, as you take a step when entering, your shoulders back, head up, your fingers and entire body strain – you don't speak – then all the weight falls from you and you perform flawlessly – perhaps like never before.[791]

According to another collective letter, passionately headed "We won't give up!", it was precisely the absence of this experience that

788 AČOS, f. Československá spartakiáda 1990, Letter of a gymnast of club Spoje Balkán (signature unlegible) to Czechoslovak Television, 19. 12. 1989.
789 The television debate entitled "Spartakiad: Yes, or No" took place on 17 December 1989.
790 AČOS, f. Československá spartakiáda 1990, Letter of gymnasts of club ZRTV TJ Lokomotiva Zvolen to Spartakiad Staff 4. 1. 1990.
791 AČOS, f. Československá spartakiáda 1990, Letter of Josef Fiala, the head of gymnastic club Sokol Jinočany to Spartakiad Staff 26. 12. 1989.

would lead some people to "campaign against the Spartakiad."[792] Their opponents apparently lacked the experience of "passing through the Gate of Athletes, standing on a place marker, being a small but necessary link in a massive collective of participants and hearing the applause," and therefore they now do not understand the significance of this event, which is the "pride of the nations of our republic."

The most frequently expressed argument for preserving the Spartakiads was that it was embedded in the national tradition of mass gymnastic performances. It is noteworthy that in this point the letter writers did not deviate from the hitherto strategy of the Spartakiad organizers, who had always, especially during the "normalization" period, presented this argument as justification for holding the Spartakiads in the first place.[793] The participation of many of the letter writers in the Sokol Slets was an important strategy intended to provide them with the authority in deciding the fate of Spartakiads. They often blurred any distinction between communist and pre-communist mass gymnastic performances demonstrating the fact that the continuity between Spartakiads and Slets did not reside only in the external form of the ritual or organizational structure, but also in the heads of the participants. Such letters described the Spartakiad as an integral part of the "century-long"[794] tradition of gymnastic performances that embody the best traditions of the Czech nation, and their authors understood their involvement in Spartakiads as a contribution (and often as a sacrifice) to this tradition. Those letters written by Czechs largely ignored the state's dual

---

792   AČOS, f. Československá spartakiáda 1990, Letter of gymnastic trainers of club TJ Sokol Bolevec Plzeň to the Civic Forum of Instructors and Creators of Mass Gymnastic Performances 17. 1. 1990.

793   Cf. the basic ideological guidelines published with few changes for each Spartakiad. Marek, J. et al.: *Politickovýchovné působení funkcionářů, cvičitelů, trenérů a učitelů tělesné výchovy při přípravě Československé spartakiády 1985*.

794   AČOS, f. Československá spartakiáda 1990, Letter of Eva Janovcová to Czechoslovak Television 12. 12. 1989.

nation reality at that time and spoke of "a nation" in the singular as a non-problematic category: they either left the Slovaks out altogether or returned to the First Republic idea of a Czechoslovak nation. They were very willing to get rid of the "Spartakiad" title and other "Byzantine bombastic features"[795] and offered to exercise in the new democratic conditions at mass gymnastic performances, "no matter what we call it."[796] They often suggested that the event go back to being named a "Slet," e.g. as the "Czechoslovak Slet" in combining the Spartakiad and Slet names (the same letter proposed organizing the traditional final Slet scene on the theme of "the 1989 revival").[797] The authors of these letters felt most strongly about preserving the tradition of mass gymnastics performances and not allowing for an interruption that would lead to a loss of the special skills needed for such performances and to the end of the Sokol movement as such: "Losing the Sokol," wrote a former Prague Sokol member, "would for the nation be as when we lost Bohemian Brethren in the past."[798]

The letters also often completely denied the link between Spartakiads and communism, while emphasizing their deep meaning for people. This is strongly conveyed in e.g., a letter from one female participant from the town of Sokolov: "I feel that most participants of the Czechoslovak Spartakiad were not interested in the slogan under which it was held; the importance for us consisted of the essence and idea of the Czechoslovak Spartakiad [...] The Spartakiad gives us a wonderful feeling of belonging to a group of people; it is actually the only chance we have to realize that we are part of a

---

795   AČOS, f. Československá spartakiáda 1990, Letter of JUDr. Karel Loula to the Spartakiad Staff 19. 12. 1989.

796   AČOS, f. Československá spartakiáda 1990, Letter of club ZRTV TJ ZKL – Klášterec n/Ohří to the Spartakiad Staff 15. 1. 1990.

797   AČOS, f. Československá spartakiáda 1990, Letter of JUDr. Karel Loula to the Spartakiad Staff 19. 12. 1989.

798   AČOS, f. Československá spartakiáda 1990, Letter of a gymnast from Prague (signature unlegible) to the Spartakiad Staff 29. 12. 1989.

broader society."[799] One participant from the town of Karlovy Vary actively taking part in the events since the 11th All-Sokol Slet in 1948 was baffled by the opposition to the Spartakiads:

"It never occurred to me that these mass gymnastic exercises would glorify anything other than the healthy bodies of the participants and of the entire nation." Canceling the Spartakiad would in his view be like "destroying the Palace of Culture" or "the subway" merely because they were built during a "criticized period."[800]

There was then only a small step from understanding the Spartakiads as the direct descendent of Sokol Slets without significant influence of the communist party to their integration into the ongoing "democratization process."[801] This corresponded to the efforts of the Spartakiad Staff to transform the Spartakiads into a "Gymnastics Festival of National Understanding"[802] that was to be held "to support the ongoing society-wide revitalizing process of democracy, freedom, humanism and national understanding." While the sudden revelation of the Spartakiad staff was largely a pragmatic maneuver by which the staff sought a new sponsor for the Spartakiad ritual, the protest letters expressed true joy in the political changes and the active involvement of the letter writers in anti-communist activities. Some of the female participants revealed that they had attended protests right after their Spartakiad practice: "For there is nothing more beautiful than exercising in a free state and conveying in our Spartakiad exercises the enthusiasm that we are living

---

799   Ibid, Letter of V. Latislavová of Sokolov to the Spartakiad Staff 28. 12. 1989.
800   AČOS, f. Československá spartakiáda 1990, Letter of a gymnasts of Karlovy Vary (signature unlegible) to the Spartakiad Staff 22. 12. 1989. The Palace of Culture, a major building of the normalisation era, which hosted Communist Party congresses. Presently called the Prague Congress Centre.
801   AČOS, f. Československá spartakiáda 1990, Petition of trainers and participants of 3rd training meeting of the spartakiad performance of men, Prostějov 9. 12. 1989.
802   AČOS, f. Československá spartakiáda 1990, Komuniké z jednání ÚŠ ČSS 1990 ze dne 14. 12. 1989.

through."[803] Not only did the participants feel no contradiction between the anti-communist protests and the Spartakiad performances, they actually viewed them as being logically connected. The link between them was to be provided by the very basis of gymnastic performances, i.e. district discipline and "voluntary" subordination to the whole. A letter by Eva Janovcová, a lecturer at Charles University's Faculty of Arts, who had participated as a student in the 1938 Slet (and who equated the atmosphere at that time with that of November 1989), can serve as an example:

I will remind you of one instance when the unity of the nation, voluntary discipline and an incredible sense for spontaneous organization appeared in tangible form, and in my view it was the tradition of the Slets and Spartakiads somewhere deep in us which had a decisive impact: it was the first large demonstration on Wenceslas Square on Monday, November 20th. The enormous crowd [...] moved up the square to the statue of St. Wenceslas and to the highway, ending any possible further movement. Then the crowd gave the command starting with those at the top of square to those down below: "Everyone face Můstek." Before I realized what this meant [...], all the demonstrators had turned around like one person, including all their signs, and those who had been last – down at the bottom of the square at Můstek – became the front of the march and smoothly led the march back the other way and down National Avenue. It was wonderful and also had deep democratic import – it wasn't a leader, but the people led by their own conviction, by their truth [...]. I truly believe that "strength in unity" lies behind this, that deep feeling and voluntary discipline cultivated – without our awareness of it – that very tradition (no longer decades old, but a century old) of the Sokol Slets and later Spartakiads.[804]

803 AČOS, f. Československá spartakiáda 1990, Letter of Prague female gymnasts to the Spartakiad Staff 19. 12. 1989.
804 AČOS, f. Československá spartakiáda 1990, Letter of Eva Janovcová to Czechoslovak Television 12. 12. 1989.

This excerpt is merely a better articulated version of the motive we find in many other letters. Variations on the theme of "how Spartakiads contributed to the fall of communism" may seem strained or even absurd at first glance. Yet they demonstrate how discipline became in the ideological world of the Sokol subculture a leading value, "the nation's school," which constituted its unified "collective body." At the same time there is a strong element of "sharing the fate of the nation." According to this logic, it was the duty of the Sokols to head the movement of the nation's collective body and it was not their fault if this movement was not always straightforward. Sokol was not only supposed to stand "above all parties," as Tyrš had claimed, but also above all regimes.

✕✕✕

The enthusiastic and conscious acceptance of Spartakiads described in this chapter only represents one of the many types of society's reactions to the Spartakiads. It was largely limited to participants coming from the Sokol subculture for whom Spartakiads resonated with their collective Sokol memory and identity.[805] There appeared along with this attitude many other tactics for dealing with the regime's longing to create the image of a united body. In other words, there was no uniform reaction to Spartakiads (or, for that matter, to communism as such), just like there was no single uniform society. The notion of such a society that constantly crops up in current discussions on "coming to terms with the past" is a myth standing in stark contradiction with the social reality of the complexly structured modern Czechoslovak post-war society. It is certainly a paradox that the myth of a homogenous socialist society "collaborating

---

805 See Mayer, Françoise: *Les Tchéques et leur communisme. Mémoire et identités politiques,* Paris 2003.

with" or "fighting against" the communist regime copies the logic of a social festivity, especially of Spartakiads, which persistently (and futilely) attempted to create the image of a united socialist people.

The popularity of Spartakiads attests to the abilities of the communist leadership to impose its own ritualized framework, to determine the event's basic parameters and to coax society to take part in it. Yet as a didactic project that was to create a "new socialist society" and a "new socialist person," the Spartakiads were a flop.[806] Not even the most complex political anatomy or social geometry were able to transform the people's behavior and rupture existing bonds, not even for the two Spartakiad days. Instead, the party leadership had to pay dearly for the participation of "the people" – not only through the Spartakiads' massive budget, but also in tolerating behavior not at all conducive to their aims. It almost seems as if it was in fact the communist regime that lost in this strange game of "tit for tat " – a game in which it had to continue at all costs so as not to risk an irrecoverable loss of prestige.

---

[806] The organizers of Nazi Nuremberg rallies also had to deal with a similar discrepancy between the official image of perfect discipline and the actual behavior of the ritual's participants. Richard Grunberger e.g. writes that in 1936 nine hundred members of the Association of German Girls aged fifteen to eighteen years of age returned from Nuremberg pregnant. In four hundred cases the ensuing investigation failed to determine paternity. Grunberger, Richard: *Social History of the Third Reich*. Penguin Books, London 1991, p. 356.

CONCLUSION

A new collective body appeared in the late 1980s in Prague's public spaces; this time it was not made up of "perfectly legible and obedient" exercise participants in stadiums, but revolutionary crowds in city squares. Using simple mass choreography the protest demonstrations formed a very similar political symbolism.[807] As with the mass gymnastic performances, this was an attempt to embody the political collective, people or nation and its will. The protest demonstrations, in which never more than a tenth of the population participated, took up the task of embodying the "collective us" by physically occupying the symbolic centers of the country (while chanting "We're already here!"). The main element of the mass choreography of the demonstrations and their key political symbol was the density of the crowd. The impression of a single body and single will of this compact mass was created by the synchronization of the crowd through uniform chanting, singing and other physical acts such as the clinking of keys, waving, jumping (the famous shots of the jumping lines from Letná Plain are not of a spontaneous act, but a reaction to a "command" by the speaker Václav Malý). The protestors were able to convince the hesitant public, political elite and themselves that they actually represented the people of Czechoslovakia. Song writer Michal Horáček wrote at that time in his journal his impressions of Wenceslas Square crammed full of people: "Today the mother of cities stands here, proud and determined to once again decide a key moment in our history. The nation stands here."[808] The protestors created that which Victor Turner calls the *communitas*, an intensive, transcendental and temporary

---

807 See Holý, L.: *The Little Czech and the Great Czech Nation*; Stehlíková, Eva: "Listopadová katarze". *Theatralia*, 2009, vol. 12, n. 1–2, pp. 19–33; Roubal, Petr: "Jak se dělá lid? Listopadové demonstrace jako vizuální politická strategie". *Dějiny a současnost*, 2009, vol. 31, special issue to commemorate the 20th anniversary of November 17, 1989, pp. 40–43.
808 Horáček, Michal. *Jak pukaly ledy*. Ex libris, Prague 1990, p. 88.

collective experience in which formal social structures give way to an authentic community. That the highly individualized consumer society of the 1990s emerged from this deeply collective experience is indeed a paradox.

Spartakiads did not politically survive the Velvet Revolution. Many of the participants ceased to practice the Spartakiad pieces. The most drastic dropout occurred in the male juniors category, traditionally the most problematic demographic group, as well as university students of both sexes who had been on strike. Those involved in revolutionary Prague, largely students and people from the alternative culture, had little interest in synchronized exercises at Strahov. Despite the protests of Spartakiad organizers, who had rapidly formed the Civic Forum of Instructors and Creators of Mass Gymnastic Performances, and of the vast majority of exercise participants, the new federal government and particularly the Czech Ministry of Education refused to continue to support the preparations and financing of Spartakiads (especially in the key issue of ending the school year prematurely). It turned out that, without the support of state and municipal authorities and public financing for the organization of such a massive gymnastics event, "spontaneous enthusiasm" was not enough. The proverbial final nail in the coffin of Spartakiads was struck by the renewed Sokol movement, which after a certain amount of wavering, refused the courtship of Spartakiad organizers and the renaming of the 1990 Czechoslovak Spartakiad to the 12th All-Sokol Slet. As in 1970 (the disappointed instructors and participants did not forget to emphasize this historical parallel), mass gymnastic performances were only held on a district level and with absolutely no media coverage under the title of the Czechoslovak Gymnastics Festivals.

The renewed Sokol, supported by a massive restitution of property, hoped that it would be able to overcome the Spartakiad tradition by linking itself to the tradition of its own Slets. It commenced preparations for the first post-communist Slet, scheduled for 1994, but soon discovered that practically no "new Sokol members" were joining the movement and that, if the event were to be held, they would have to cooperate with the former Spartakiad organizers and involve former Spartakiad instructors and participants. Responsible for the preparation of the Slet were post-1989 Sokol gymnastic directors, Jiří Žižka and Jarina Žitná, both long-time Spartakiad organizers and both also original Sokol members.[809] Žitná, co-author of the Spartakiad choreography "Poupata" (Buds), stated at that time: "Forty years later we have returned to the stadium that has become a symbol. After forty years of forced silence, Sokol has re-entered the sandy field of Strahov Stadium to show a slightly astonished nation that it is once again here, that it wants to and will live."[810] Many of the performances of the first post-communist Slet were revamped versions of the Spartakiad prepared for 1990. Yet in comparison with Spartakiads, the 1994 Slet was ultimately a flop. Though prominent guests led by Václav Havel were present in the government boxes, the spectators were sparse. There were so few participants that only every other place marker was occupied, though even so a large part of the stadium's field remained empty. After this experience, which drained significant funds, the Sokol abandoned Strahov Stadium and moved to the neighboring Rošický stadium with roughly a tenth of the capacity. Strahov Stadium then began to dilapidate and became overgrown with vegetation until 2002 when – in a resounding gesture ending the century-long dispute between gymnastics and sports – it was leased by the Sparta soccer club which built eight practice soccer fields and an administrative building on its original field.[811]

---

809 After Žižka, Vratislav Svatoň, whose father was a Sokol instructor, took over the leadership of the younger generation of Spartakiad organizers.

810 Žitná, Jarina: "Cestou sokolskou". In: *XII. všesokolský slet. Praha 1994*. Česká obec sokolská, Prague – Litomyšl 1995, pp. 8–9.

811 The fate of the other communist central stadiums is also telling: The 10th-Anniversary Stadium in Warsaw, where the annual Dozynki (harvest) festivals were held (in 1968 this was the site of Ryszard Siwiec's self immolation), began to deteriorate in the 1980s and was leased

The failure of the post-1989 Slets shows that the Velvet Revolution resulted in not only the political death of communist Spartakiads, but that it also brought an end to mass gymnastic performances as a cultural form. In its economic backwardness and conservative values, state socialism had created a kind of open-air museum of economics and, with it, of gymnastics. In his essay *The Mass Ornament* written between the wars on the mass choreography of the Tiller Girls dance performances, which strongly resembled gymnastic drills, Siegfried Kracauer wrote that these performances are "superstructural expressions" of the prevailing mode of production based on alienation and subjugation of the worker's body.[812] In the author's view, the dancers' perfectly synchronized legs corresponded as a cultural superstructure to the workers' arms in assembly-line production. Kracauer's theory partially explains the prevalence of the genre of mass gymnastic exercises under communism and its rapid end following its demise. Indeed, the dictatorship of the communist party merely changed the ownership of the means of production, not only preserving the dominant mode of production, but prolonging its lifespan by several decades. While mass production and mass society met with crisis in the West, leading to the creation of new technological-power-economic relations, the policy of the Czechoslovak Communist Party froze a certain developmental level of capitalist production as well as its "superstructural" expression in the form of mass gymnastic performances. After 1989, we see a radical transformation of the "superstructure:" the aesthetics of

to a private company in 1989 that turned the stadium into a massive and quite dubious outdoor market known as Jarmark Europa. The Leipzig stadium also underwent a phase of dilapidation and transformation into an open market (like the Soviet's Luzhniki Stadium), but it was renovated around the turn of the millenium in hopes of winning the right to host the Olympic Games.

A smaller stadium with a seating capacity of 25,000 was built within the communist stadium with its original 100,000 seating capacity. After a fifteen-year interval, the 2002 Deutsches Turnfest, marked by bad weather and the revelation that the main organizer had cooperated with the Stasi, was held here.

812 Kracauer, Siegfried: *The Mass Ornament,* Harvard University Press, Cambridge, Ma. 1995, pp. 75–86.

a perfectly disciplined, uniformed and asexual mass of the bodies of mass gymnastic performances is replaced by the aesthetics of a single, idealized, free and erotic body of the advertising world.

We can still discern from the recollections of Spartakiad participants a strong nostalgic tone regarding these events, and there are many reasons for this. One of these is the general disappointment in the course of the post-1989 socio-economic transformation and the disturbing discovery that communism did not hold a monopoly on ineffective and corrupt rule. Spartakiad nostalgia is also undoubtedly an expression of individual longing for a period of one's life long past when those reminiscing and their partners and friends were still young, beautiful and able to do headstands. Yet in addition to this feeling of purely personal loss, Spartakiad nostalgia also resonates with regret for the lost capacity for a collective action ("nobody will ever again do this kind of thing"), fear of an eroded public space and of the atomization and individualization of society, in which each individual is figuratively and literally enclosed in his or her own "privatized" rhythm. This is nostalgia for the experience of the "mighty we," of a collective self-experience. The Velvet Revolution was the last such experience in which the people once again presented themselves as the people, i.e. the highest authority and the architects of their own history. The later political rituals of liberal democracy could hardly fill this gap. The act of voting, which often remains the only expression of political activity, points to the emotional deficit of the new regime. Dropping a ballot in a ballot box is a convenient and effective way of taking part in political process, but it does not provide the experience of a political community; the collective act only occurs *ex post* in the exit-poll television coverage. Finally, nostalgia is also an expression of fear of the erosion of that which is actually meant to be symbolized through collective movement – whether it is the people or the nation. Collective identity is threatened not only by the individualization of society from within, but also by the loss of the clear image of an enemy from without.

The writer Ludvík Vaculík, a former Sokol member and Spartakiad participant, summed up these fears in a newspaper column upon the occasion of the third post-1989 Slet in 2006 (Sokol members returned to the six-year cycle of mass gymnastic performances). "A young Czech journalist of the European type," complained Vaculík regarding the media's lack of interest in the Slet, "is a nihilist and cynic towards noble concepts" and "a spokesperson for indolent idlers who reject the collective, common step and discipline." Vaculík placed Spartakiads and Slets on equal footing and defended Spartakiad participants: "I recall people despising participants of socialist Spartakiads who allegedly served this regime. Nonsense! They too served it simply by eating! People have different needs – lower and higher, narrower and broader. The desire of an ordinary, unknown and inconspicuous person is to distinguish himself by participating in a significant event." At a time in which, in Vaculík's view, it is not clear what "country" means and who its enemies are, Sokol and its tradition of collective exercises as "one of few fortunate legacies" is placing before society a new task: "[…] to define the dangers threatening the country and to dare to annunciate them."[813]

Yet the Sokol Slets can only satisfy the longing for a collective experience through collective movement with an ever-shrinking group of former Sokol and Spartakiad participants. New compensatory efforts (though much more primitive ones) to synchronize the "national body" appeared soon after 1989. In addition to the various anti-Roma marches, this phenomenon is perhaps best visible in celebrations of sports victories and the support of national sports representation. Since the mid 1990s Czech stadiums have echoed with the telling chant: "Whoever doesn't hop is not Czech! Hop! Hop! Hop!")[814] We once again see here the well known technique

813 Vaculík, Ludvík: "Paže tuž, vlasti služ!". *Lidové noviny,* vol. 19, 11. 7. 2006, p. 12.
814 This chant along with the hopping that accompanies it did not arise spontaneously, but was thought up and instilled in the crowd by sports personality Petr Salava, who has a wealth

of creating the nation's collective body through the synchronized movement of individuals. Movement thus determines whether one belongs or does not belong to the national community, but instead of the deadly serious frame of a political ritual, the figure of the collective Leviathan mentioned in the foreword is formed within the realm of mass entertainment.

of experience with crowd choreography: he also introduced "the wave" in Czech stadiums. Interview with Petr Salava, 9. 9. 2011, Prague, author's archive.

Appendix

I. Alfons Mucha-designed poster for the 6th All-Sokol Slet in 1912 (National Museum).

II. Max Švabinský-designed poster for the 9th All-Sokol Slet in 1932 (National Museum). The avant-garde magazine *Žijeme* criticized the conservatitve concept of the poster that did not utilize the possibilities of modernist design and "instead added yet another altar image to the gymnasiums, framed it, in time branches and a number of banners will be added and life around will once again crawl around so lifelessly and dully, just as Tyrš had never intended."

III. Ladislav Sutnar-designed poster for the 3ʳᵈ Workers' Olympiad 1934 (National Museum).

IV. The main poster for the 1955 Spartakiad (National Museum). The military gymnast Vladimír Kejř was the model for the poster. The wreath indicates the individual organizations that took part in the event.

V. Recruitment poster for the 1960 Spartakiad (National Museum).

VI. Promotional poster for the military piece at the 1965 Spartakiad.

VII. Zdeněk Filip-designed poster for the 1975 Spartakiad.

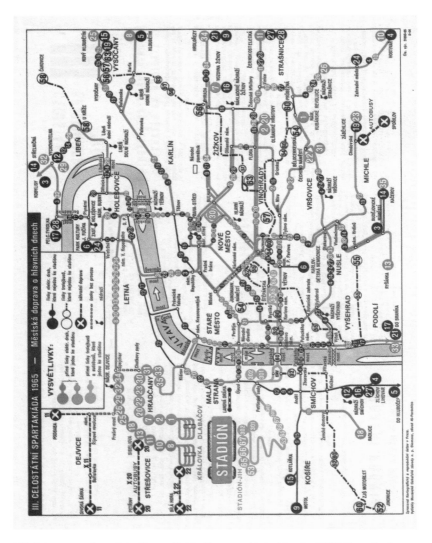

VIII. Information flyer of the Prague Public Transit published for the 1965 Spartakiad.

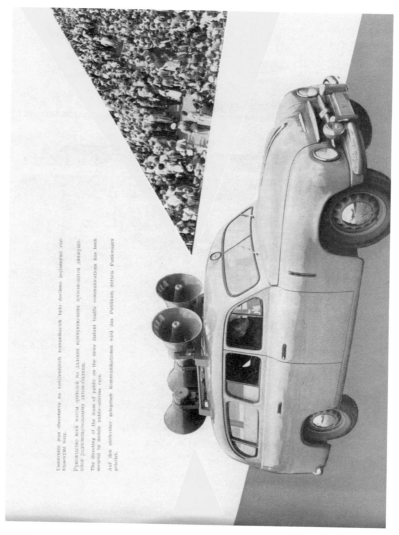

Usměrňění mas obecenstva na vzdálenějších komunikacích bylo docíleno pojízdnými rozhlasovými vozy.

Руководство всей массой зрителей на дальних коммуникациях производится движущимися радиовещательными автомобилями.

The directing of the mass of public on the more distant traffic communications has been secured to mobile public-address cars.

Auf den entfernter gelegenen Kommunikationen wird das Publikum mittels Funkwagen geleitet.

IX. Promotional brochure published by the Tesla company for the 1955 Spartakiad.

X. The final scene of the juniors' piece "To New Tomorrows" by Marie Rejhonová at the 1960 Czechoslovak Spartakiad at Strahov Stadium in Prague, which was meant to be an "allegory of an atomic chain reaction". We can see in the middle of the photograph the launched model of a rocket with the word "Peace".

XI. A piece for the women and junior women at the 1985 Spartakiad at Strahov Stadium in Prague.

XII. A piece for the junior women at the 1985 Spartakiad at Strahov Stadium in Prague.

XIII. A military piece at the 1985 Spartakiad at Strahov Stadium in Prague.

XIV. An opening part of the women's performance at the 1985 Spartakiad.

BIBLIOGRAPHY

Archives

Národní archiv – NA (National Archives):
coll. Státní výbor pro tělesnou výchovu a sport 1949–1956 (SVTVS)
coll. KSČ – Ústřední výbor 1945–1989
coll. KSČ – Byro ÚV KSČ pro řízení stranické práce v českých zemích
coll. Ústřední výbor Československého svazu tělesné výchovy a sportu
    (ÚV ČSTV)
coll. Ústřední akční výbor Národní fronty 1948–1955 (ÚAV NF)
coll. Úřad vlády ČSR/ČR, Praha – Usnesení vlády (ÚV ČSR/ ČR-RŽP)
Archiv tělesné výchovy a sportu Národního muzea – ATVS NM (National
    Museum Archives of Physical Education and Sport):
coll. Spartakiády (1953–1990)
Archiv bezpečnostních složek – ABS (Security Services Archives):
coll. E-6 Ministerstvo vnitra – Správa internačních, sběrných
    a pracovních středisek Praha
coll. Historický fond StB fond X. správa SNB (A 36) fond Agenturní svazky
Archiv České obce sokolské – AČOS (Archives of the Česká obec sokolská):
coll. Spartakiáda 1955–1990 (unprocessed)
Vojenský historický archiv – VHA (Military History Archives):
coll. MNO – 1955
coll. MNO – 1958
coll. MNO – 1965
Prague City Archive
coll. 119 Internační tábory Němců

Abbreviations used in archival sources:
inv./arch. j./č. (inventární/archivní jednotka/číslo) = inventory/archival
    unit/number; k. (karton) = box

Periodicals
Československý sport
Literární noviny
Mladá fronta
Obrana lidu
Rudé právo
Svobodné slovo
Večerní Praha
Zemědělské noviny

Primary printed sources

Adamus, Milan et al.: "Vliv nácviku spartakiádní skladby 'Jeden za všechny' na morální, pohybový a funkční rozvoj chlapců ve věku 11 až 13 let". *Teorie a praxe tělesné výchovy*, 1966, vol. 14, nr. 4, pp. 226–232.

Appelt, Karel: "Poznámky k dotazníkové akci". In: *Vědecká konference o teoretických a metodických základech masových* tělovýchovných vystoupení (19.–20. 2. 1956). Institut tělesné výchovy a sportu, Prague 1956, pp. 120–124.

Banzet, Jaroslav: "Sletiště". In: *Památník XI. sletu všesokolského v Praze 1948*. Československá obec sokolská, Prgue 1949, pp. 30–32.

Bartůňková, Staša et al. "Funkční a energetická náročnost skladeb ČSS 1980". *Teorie a praxe tělesné výchovy*. 1981, vol. 29, pp. 145–152.

Belšan, Pavel: "Choreografie a funkce náčiní, nářadí a režijních prostředků ve skladbách ČSS". In: *Sborník ze semináře FTVS UK Praha k problematice hromadných vystoupení Československé spartakiády*. Metasport, Ostrava 1986, pp. 48–57.

Berdychová, Jana: *Funkce tělovýchovných skladeb pro hromadná vystoupení mládeže v systému socialistické tělesné výchovy*. Habilitační práce. Fakulta tělesné výchovy a sportu Univerzity Karlovy, Prague 1960.

Berdychová, Jana: "Problematika dětských tělovýchovných skladeb pro hromadná vystoupení". *Teorie a praxe tělesné výchovy*, 1978, vol. 26, nr. 11, pp. 678–684.

Berdychová, Jana: "Příspěvek k problematice tělovýchovných vystoupení dětí s hlediska pedagogického". In: *Vědecká konference o teoretických a metodických základech masových tělovýchovných vystoupení* (19.–20. 2. 1956). Institut tělesné výchovy a sportu, Prague 1956, pp. 59–69.

Berdychová, Jana: *Skladba pro rodiče a děti*. Olympia, Prague 1974.

Berdychová, Jana: "Vývojové tendence skladeb pro rodiče a děti na čsl. spartakiádách". In: *Sborník ze semináře FTVS UK Praha k problematice hromadných vystoupení Československé spartakiády*. Metasport, Ostrava 1986, pp. 83–87.

Berdychová, Jana – Georgieva-Chaloupková, Marie: *Tance sovětských národů*. Popis s obrázky a hudebním doprovodem. Nakladatelství Československé obce sokolské, Prague 1951.

Blablová, Jarmila: "Radostná jar. skladba mladšího žactva 9–11letého", *Teorie a praxe tělesné výchovy*, 1961, vol. 9, special issue: Výsledky výzkumu II. celostátní spartakiády 1960, pp. 11–12.

Bláha, Arnošt: "Na dobré cestě". *Sokolský věstník*, vol. 41, nr. 26, 28. 6. 1939, pp. 318–319.

Bláha, František: "O sokolský národ". In: *Památník XI. sletu všesokolského v Praze 1948*. Československá obec sokolská, Prague 1949, pp. 21–22.

Bláha, František – Martínková, Blažena: "Sletová premiéra". In: *Památník XI. sletu všesokolského v Praze 1948*. Československá obec sokolská, Prague 1949, pp. 128–136.

Bláha, Pavel: "Antropologický výzkum konaný v souvislosti s ČSS 1985". *Teorie a praxe tělesné výchovy*, 1986, vol. 34, pp. 502–504.

Bláha, Pavel et al.: *Antropometrie československé populace od 6 do 35 let*. Československá spartakiáda 1980, 1–2. ÚNZ hl. m. – ÚV ČSTV, Prague 1982, 1984.

Bláha, Pavel et al.: *Antropometrie československé populace od 6 do 55 let*. Československá spartakiáda 1985, 4 vols. Ústřední štáb Československé spartakiády, Prague 1985–1987.

Brdíčková, Miroslava: "Nástupy a odchody při tělovýchovných vystoupeních". In: *Vědecká konference o teoretických a metodických základech masových tělovýchovných vystoupení* (19.–20. 2. 1956). Institut tělesné výchovy a sportu, Prague 1956, pp. 153–155.

Břicháček, Josef – Petrák, Bořivoj – Syrůčková, Drahomíra: "Ideově výchovné působení II. CS na diváky Strahovského stadiónu". *Teorie a praxe tělesné výchovy*, 1961, vol. 9, special issue: Výsledky výzkumu II. celostátní spartakiády 1960, pp. 38–40.

Budský, František (ed.): *Vilém Mucha*. Olympia, Prague 1976.

Cubr, František – Hrubý, Josef: "Architektonické úpravy a výzdoba strahovského areálu pro II. celostátní spartakiádu 1960". *Architektura ČSSR*, 1960, vol. 19, nr. 10, pp. 703–706.

Čapek, Karel: "Cesta květů a slávy". *Lidové noviny*, vol. 46, 7. 7. 1938, p. 1.

Čapek, Karel: "Den slávy". In: *Vendelín Josef Krýsa: X. všesokolský slet*. Prague 1938, pp. 72–73.

Čapek, Karel: *Hovory s T. G. Masarykem*. Československý spisovatel, Prague 1990.

Čejka, Jaroslav: "Sen o stadiónu". In: Otakar Mohyla – Karel Procházka (eds.): *Verše ze Strahova*. Olympia, Prague 1985, unpag.

Černý, Václav: *Paměti* II. *Křik Koruny české: 1938-1945*. Náš kulturní odboj za války. Atlantis, Brno 1992.

Československá spartakiáda 75. Program hromadných tělovýchovných vystoupení Praha-Strahov. Olympia, Prague 1975.

Československá spartakiáda 1980. 100 otázek a 100 odpovědí. Mladá fronta, Prague 1980.

Čížek, Ludvík: "Sletiště VII. sletu všesokolského v Praze na Letné". In: Jan Hiller (ed.): *Památník VII. sletu všesokolského v Praze 1920*. Československá obec sokolská, Prague 1923, pp. 59–82.

Disman, Miloslav: "Duha z Prahy do Košic". In: *Památník XI. sletu všesokolského v Praze 1948*. Československá obec sokolská, Prague 1949, p. 160.

Disman, Miloslav: "Praha IV na všech vlnách, ve zvuku i v obraze". In: *Památník XI. sletu všesokolského v Praze 1948*. Československá obec sokolská, Prague 1949, pp. 148–149.

Disman, Miloslav: "První takt sletové symfonie". In: *Památník XI. sletu všesokolského v Praze 1948*. Československá obec sokolská, Prague 1949, pp. 66–68.

Disman, Miloslav: "Sovětští fyskulturníci mezi námi". In: *Památník XI. sletu všesokolského v Praze 1948*. Československá obec sokolská, Prague 1949, p. 139.

Dolanský, Julius et al.: *Sto deset let Sokola, 1862-1972*. Olympia, Prague 1973.

Domorázek, Karel: "Po stopách díla". In: Miroslav Tyrš: *Tělocvik v ohledu esthetickém*. Karel Novák, Prague 1926, pp. 83–101.

Dostál, Jiří: "Živel organizující množství". In: *Památník XI. sletu všesokolského v Praze 1948*. Československá obec sokolská, Prague 1949, pp. 154–156.

Drdácká, Božena: "Podíl svazu ZRTV na čs. spartakiádě v r. 1990 (východiska)". In: *Sborník ze semináře FTVS UK Praha k problematice hromadných vystoupení Československé spartakiády*. Metasport, Ostrava 1986, pp. 27–32.

Drdácká, Božena – Falcmanová, Vlasta: "Tělesná kultura v hodnotové orientaci žen a mužů vystupujících na Československé spartakiádě 1985". *Teorie a praxe tělesné výchovy*, 1987, vol. 35, nr. 7, pp. 407–411.

Drdácká, Božena – Falcmanová, Vlasta: "Tělesná kultura v hodnotové orientaci žen a mužů vystupujících v hromadných tělovýchovných skladbách Svazu ZRTV na Čs. spartakiádě 1985". In: *Sborník ze semináře FTVS UK Praha k problematice hromadných vystoupení Československé spartakiády*. Metasport, Ostrava 1986, pp. 92–107.

Dryje, František: "Sen o spartakiádě, 26. 8. 80". *Analogon*, 1996, vol. 8, nr. 16, p. 44.

Dvořáková, Zora: *Miroslav Tyrš. Prohry a vítězství*. Olympia, Prague 1989.

Fetter, Vojtěch – Suchý, Jaroslav: "Základní tělesné rozměry cvičenců III. CS ve srovnání s rozměry cvičenců I. a II. CS". *Teorie a praxe tělesné výchovy*, 1966, vol. 14, nr. 6, pp. 348–360.

Fialová, Milka – Rejhonová, Marie: *Skladba pre dorastenky*. Šport, Bratislava 1974.

Florian, Miroslav: "Cvičenci". In: Miroslav Florian: *Óda na mladost*. Olympia, Prague 1988.

Frýd, Norbert: "Jsme bohatší". *Literární noviny*, 1955, vol. 4, nr. 28, p. 1.

Fuchs, Jan: "Diskusní příspěvek". In: *Sborník ze semináře FTVS UK Praha k problematice hromadných vystoupení Československé spartakiády*. Metasport, Ostrava 1986.

Gottwald, Klement: "Drazí bratři!". In: *Památník XI. sletu všesokolského v Praze 1948*. Československá obec sokolská, Prague 1949, pp. 142–143.

Hanzlíková, Míla: "Spartakiáda není jen akce". *Náš domov*, vol. 35, 31. 8. 1984, pp. 1–3.

Heller, Viktor: "Na Staroměstské radnici". In: *Památník XI. sletu všesokolského v Praze 1948*. Československá obec sokolská, Prague 1949, pp. 156–157.

Hintnaus, Ladislav: "Pohádka. Cvičení nejmladšího žactva 6–8letého". *Teorie a praxe tělesné výchovy*, 1961, vol. 9, special issue: Výsledky výzkumu II. celostátní spartakiády 1960, pp. 9–10.

Hitler, Adolf: *Mein Kampf*. Zentralverlag der NSDAP, München 1942.

Hlaváč, František: "Zájmy pubescentních dívek a jejich postoje k tělesné kultuře", *Teorie a praxe tělesné výchovy*. 1988, vol. 36, nr. 7, pp. 423–427.

Hlaváček, Karel: "Když jsme táhli ulicemi…". In: Jan Hiller (ed.): *Památník VII. sletu všesokolského v Praze 1920*. Československá obec sokolská, Prague 1923, p. 25.

"Hlediska pro hodnocení II. celostátní spartakiády". *Teorie a praxe tělesné výchovy*, 1961, vol. 9, special issue: Výsledky výzkumu II. celostátní spartakiády 1960, pp. 2–5.

Hock, Jaromír: "Problematika stravování při II. CS". *Výživa lidu*, 1960, vol. 15, nr. 6, pp. 88–89.

Hohler, Vilém: "Výzkum II. CS z hlediska estetického". *Teorie a praxe tělesné výchovy*, 1961, vol. 9, special issue: Výsledky výzkumu II. celostátní spartakiády 1960, pp. 41–64.

Hohler, Vilém: "Základní estetické aspekty skladeb III. CS". *Teorie a praxe tělesné výchovy, 1966*, vol. 14, nr. 4, pp. 251–254.

Holub, Miroslav: "O příštích spartakiádách". *Plamen*, 1960, vol. 2, nr. 8, pp. 150–151.

Honke-Houfek, Olivier – Kuna, Zdeněk – Stupka, Zdeněk: "Spartakiádní stadion na Strahově – východní tribuna", *Architektura ČSR*, 1975, vol. 34, nr. 7, pp. 301–306.

Hošek, Zdeněk – Kašpar, Jiří (eds.): *Gymnastika vojáků. Masová gymnastická skladba*. Olympia, Prague 1974.

Hrčka, Jozef: "Celoštátna spartakiáda 1980 a výskum". *Teorie a praxe tělesné výchovy*, 1979, vol. 27, nr. 11, pp. 699–701.

Hrčka, Jozef: "O niektorých problémoch športovo-rekreačnej aktivity občanov a voľného času". In: Jozef Hrčka a kol.: *Voľný čas a športovo rekreačná aktivita občanov*. Príspevky zo seminára Vedeckej rady SÚV ČSZTV. Šport, Bratislava 1974, pp. 5–32.

Charvát, Josef: *Můj labyrint světa. Vzpomínky, zápisky z deníku*. Galén, Prague 2005.

Chvalný, Július: *Československá spartakiáda 1975*. Olympia, Prague 1976.

Chvalný, Július a kol.: *Československá spartakiáda 1980*. Olympia – Šport, Prague – Bratislava 1981.

Janoušek, Vladimír: "Scény při tělovýchovných slavnostech". In: *Vědecká konference o teoretických a metodických základech masových tělovýchovných vystoupení (19.–20. 2. 1956)*. Institut tělesné výchovy a sportu, Prague 1956, pp. 159–162.

Jesenská, Milena: "Pověz, kam utíkáš – povím ti, kdo jsi". *Přítomnost*, vol. 15, n. 38 (21 September 1938), pp. 594–595.

Jesenská, Milena: "Nad naše síly". *Přítomnost*, vol. 15, nr. 41 (12 October 1938), pp. 650–651.

Jiráček, Karel: *El Car vzpomíná. Z historie dělnického Agitpropu*. Orbis, Prague 1971.

Kainar, Josef: Český sen. Československý spisovatel, Prague 1953.

Kavalír, Miroslav: "Před sjednocením". *Sokolský věstník*, vol. 41, 10. 5. 1939, p. 1.

Klímová-Fügnerová, Miroslava: "Zdravotnickou osvětou k úspěchu spartakiády". *Výživa lidu*, 1960, vol. 15, nr. 4, pp. 49–50.

Kolář, Jiří: *Sedm kantát*. Družstvo Dílo, Prague 1945.

Konečný, Robert: "Slety po stránce jejich psychologického působení". In: *Deset sletů. Přednášky z mimořádné vzdělávací školy Československé obce sokolské o první desítce všesokolských sletů ve dnech 17. a 18. ledna 1948*. Nakladatelství Československé obce sokolské, Prague 1948, pp. 18–24.

Konrád, Edmond: "Duchový Tábor". In: *Památník XI. sletu všesokolského v Praze 1948*. Československá obec sokolská, Prague 1949, pp. 119–120.

Köppl, Evžen: "Organizace sletu". In: *Památník XI. sletu všesokolského v Praze 1948*. Československá obec sokolská, Prague 1949, pp. 24–27.

Köppl, Evžen: "Slet v číslech". In: *Památník XI. sletu všesokolského v Praze 1948*. Československá obec sokolská, Prague 1949, pp. 198–199.

Kos, Bohumil: "Vývojové tendence v tvorbě a režii pohybových skladeb". In: *Sborník ze semináře FTVS UK Praha k problematice hromadných vystoupení Československé spartakiády*. Metasport, Ostrava 1986, pp. 46–48.

Kössl, Jiří: "Profesor Jaroslav Marek šedesátiletý". *Teorie a praxe tělesné výchovy*, 1989, vol. 37, nr. 12, p. 767.

Kössl, Jiří: "Za univ. prof. PhDr. Ladislavem Serbusem". *Teorie a praxe tělesné výchovy*, 1987, vol. 35, nr. 11, p. 704.

Kössl, Jiří – Krátký, František – Marek, Jaroslav: *Dějiny tělesné výchovy II. Od roku 1848 do současnosti*. Olympia, Prague 1986.

Kostková, Jarmila: "Některé poznatky ke zlepšení postupu při hodnocení a výběru skladeb pro větší tělovýchovné slavnosti." *Vědecká konference o teoretických a metodických základech masových tělovýchovných vystoupení* (19. – 20. 2. 1956). Institut tělesné výchovy a sportu, Prague 1956, pp. 111–114.

Kostková, Jarmila: "Podmínky vzniku Svazu ZTV – ZRTV". In: Jarmila Kostková (ed.): *Svaz základní a rekreační tělesné výchovy*. Česká asociace Sport pro všechny, Prague 2005, pp. 8–12.

Kouřimský, Gustav: *Spartakiádní areál Strahov*. Olympia, Prague 1982.

Kozlík, Jaroslav: "Jak v podmínkách příprav na II. CS se plnily zákl. úkoly tělesné výchovy ve školách". *Teorie a praxe tělesné výchovy*, 1961, vol. 9, special issue: Výsledky výzkumu II. celostátní spartakiády 1960, pp. 24–25.

Kožík, František: "Jeden a půl miliónu". In: Ctibor Rybár – Jan Novotný (eds.): *V rytmu krásy a radosti. 15 let československé tělovýchovy*. Státní tělovýchovné nakladatelství, Prague 1960.

Kožík, František: "Komu patří dík". In: *Památník XI. sletu všesokolského v Praze 1948*. Československá obec sokolská, Prague 1949, p. 94.

Kožík, František: "Myšlenka Tyršova". In: *XII. všesokolský slet*. Prague 1994. Česká obec sokolská, Prague – Litomyšl 1995, p. 7.

Kožík, František: "Sokolátka se sjíždějí". In: Rudolf Procházka (ed.), *Památník X. všesokolského sletu v Praze 1938*. Československá obec sokolská, Prague 1939, p. 83.

Kožík, František: "Ve jménu vzpomínky". In: *Památník XI. sletu všesokolského v Praze 1948*. Československá obec sokolská, Prague 1949, pp. 17–19.

Kožík, František: *Věnec vavřínový*. Československý spisovatel, Prague 1987.

Kožík, František: *Vzpomínky*. Orbis, Prague 1995.

Král, Antonín: "IV. ČSS – Světová gymnastická slavnost". *Teorie a praxe tělesné výchovy*, 1969, vol. 17, nr. 9, pp. 513–514.

Král, Antonín: "Československá spartakiáda 1980". *Teorie a praxe tělesné výchovy*, 1981, vol. 29, nr. 3.

Král, Antonín: "Funkce OHV z hlediska příprav skladeb a koordinace činnosti složek tělovýchovného hnutí". In: *Sborník ze semináře FTVS UK Praha k problematice hromadných vystoupení Československé spartakiády*. Metasport, Ostrava 1986, pp. 12–17.

Král, Jiří – Mathé, Ervín: "Zdravotnický průzkum II. CS". *Teorie a praxe tělesné výchovy*, 1961, vol. 9, special issue: Výsledky výzkumu II. celostátní spartakiády 1960, pp. 52–53.

Kramář, Karel: "Sokolům!". *Národní listy*, vol. 66, 4. 7. 1926, p. 1.

Krejčí, Jan: "Za sjednocením". *Sokolský věstník*, vol. 41, 8. 2. 1939, p. 1.

Kroha, Jiří: "Státní stadion na Strahově – úprava pro I. celostátní spartakiádu". *Architektura ČSR*, 1956, vol. 15, nr. 1–2, pp. 136–138.

Krupička, Jiří: "Organisace stravovací služby při I. celostátní spartakiádě". *Výživa lidu*, 1955, vol. 10, nr. 4, pp. 53–54.

Krupička, Jiří: "Prvé poznatky z II. celostátní spartakiády". *Výživa lidu*, 1960, vol. 15, nr. 9, pp. 136–137.

Kříž, Václav: "Slavnosti Svazu a Federace D.T.J.". *Věstník sokolský*, 1921, vol. 23, nr. 17, pp. 439–449.

Kundera, Milan: Člověk zahrada širá. Verše. Československý spisovatel, Prague 1953.

Lhoták, Zdeněk: "Model Society". *Aperture*, 1998, vol. 47, nr. 152.

Libenský, Jan – Martínková, Blažena: "Sletová vystoupení dorostu". In: *Památník XI. sletu všesokolského v Praze 1948*. Československá obec sokolská, Prague 1949, pp. 99–102.

Luhanová, Zdeňka: "Jedeme na spartakiádu". *Výživa lidu*, 1960, vol. 15, nr. 4, p. 52.

Lustig, Arnošt – Ota, Pavel: "Úvod, k němuž jsme nechtěli hledat název". In: Vladimír Dobrovodský (ed.): *III. celostátní spartakiáda 1965*. Sportovní a turistické nakladatelství, Prague 1966.

Lví silou. Pocta a dík Sokolstvu. Nakladatelské družstvo Máje, Prague 1948.

Majerová, Marie: "Chvála spartakiády". In: Vilém Mucha (ed.): *První celostátní spartakiáda 1955*. Státní tělovýchovné nakladatelství, Prague 1956, pp. 7–8.

Marek, Jaroslav: "Politickovýchovná práce při přípravě ČSS". In: *Sborník ze semináře FTVS UK Praha k problematice hromadných vystoupení Československé spartakiády*. Metasport, Ostrava 1986, pp. 75–80.

Marek, Jaroslav: *Politickovýchovné působení funkcionářů, cvičitelů, učitelů tělesné výchovy a trenérů při přípravě Československé spartakiády 1980*. Olympia, Prague 1980.

Marek, Jaroslav: "Vývoj a obsah tělovýchovné činnosti Sokola v letech 1862–1871". *Acta Universitatis Carolinae. Gymnica*, 1967, vol. 2, nr. 2, pp. 85–115.

Marek, Jaroslav (ed.): *Za socialistický systém tělesné výchovy. Dokumenty od nár. a demokratické revoluce po XV. sjezd KSČ*. Olympia, Prague 1978.

Marek, Jaroslav a kol.: *Politickovýchovné působení funkcionářů, cvičitelů, trenérů a učitelů tělesné výchovy při přípravě Československé spartakiády 1985*. Olympia, Prague 1985.

Marek, Jaroslav – Málinka, Ján: *Zpráva o činnosti Československého svazu tělesné výchovy za období 1967-1972*. Olympia, Prague 1973.

Marek, Jaroslav – Svatoň, Vratislav: *Politickovýchovné působení funkcionářů, cvičitelů, trenérů a učitelů tělesné výchovy při přípravě Československé spartakiády 1990*. Olympia, Prague 1989.

Masaryk, Jan: *Mezinárodní význam všesokolských sletů*. Nakladatelství Československé obce sokolské, Prague 1948.

Matějcová, Anna: "Orientační průzkum podmínek cvičenců na III. CS v Praze z hlediska zdravotního". *Teorie a praxe tělesné výchovy*, 1966, vol. 14, nr. 4, pp. 249–250.

Matějovcová, Božena: "Rej pro třicet tisíc cvičenek". In: *Památník XI. sletu všesokolského v Praze 1948*. Československá obec sokolská, Prague 1949, pp. 55–56.

Maxa, Prokop: "Slety po stránce slovanské". In: *Deset sletů*. Přednášky z mimořádné vzdělávací školy Československé obce sokolské o první desítce všesokolských sletů ve dnech 17. a 18. ledna 1948. Nakladatelství Československé obce sokolské, Prague 1948, pp. 9–17.

Mayer, Stanislav: "Zpráva sletového finančního odboru". In: Rudolf Procházka (ed.), *Památník X. všesokolského sletu v Praze 1938*. Československá obec sokolská, Prague 1939, pp. 299–300.

Mináč, Vladimír: "Tíha folklóru". *Literární noviny*, 1958, vol. 7, nr. 12, p. 1.

Moos, Jindřich: "Do Prahy!". In: *Památník XI. sletu všesokolského v Praze 1948*. Československá obec sokolská, Prague 1949, pp. 195–197.

Mucha, Vilém: *Dějiny dělnické tělovýchovy v Československu*. Olympia, Prague 1975.

Mucha, Vilém (ed.): *První celostátní spartakiáda 1955*. Státní tělovýchovné nakladatelství, Prague 1956.

Mucha, Vilém: *První celostátní spartakiáda 1955: věcí všeho pracujícího lidu Československa*. SVTVS, Prague 1955.

Nárožník, Karel: "Hospodářský zdar sletu". In: *Památník XI. sletu všesokolského v Praze 1948*. Československá obec sokolská, Prague 1949, pp. 213–214.

Neuendorff, Edmund: "Die Deutsche Turnersschaft ihr Wesen und Wollen". In: *Führer und Turnfestordnung zum 15. Deutschen Turnfest Stuttgart 1933*. Union, Stuttgart 1933, p. 8.

Neumann, Stanislav: *Píseň o lásce a nenávisti*. Mladá fronta, Prague 1952.

Nezval, Vítězslav: *Křídla. Básně z let 1949-1952*. Československý spisovatel, Prague 1952.

Nezval, Vítězslav: "Sborový zpěv". *Nový život*, vol. 1955, nr. 9, pp. 893–896.

Očenášek, Augustin: "Doslov". In: Miroslav Tyrš: *Tělocvik v ohledu esthetickém*. Karel Novák, Prague 1926, pp. 102–109.

Očenášek, Augustin (ed.): *Památník sletu slovanského Sokolstva roku 1912 v Praze*. Česká obec sokolská, Prague 1912.

Památník V. sletu všesokolského v Praze 1907. Česká obec sokolská, Prague 1908.

Památník XI. sletu všesokolského v Praze 1948. Československá obec sokolská, Prague 1949.

Památník XI. sletu všesokolského v Praze 1948. Sokolský pomocný výbor, New York 1967 (reprint).

Penniger, Evžen: "Po sletu". In: *Památník XI. sletu všesokolského v Praze 1948*. Československá obec sokolská, Prague 1949, pp. 214–215.

Pergl, Václav: "Prvý den dorostu 26. VI.". In: Rudolf Procházka (ed.): *Památník X. všesokolského sletu v Praze 1938*. Československá obec sokolská, Prague 1939, pp. 125–126.

Petrák, Bořivoj: "Výzkum III. CS z pozic sociologie". *Sociologický časopis*, 1965, vol. 1, nr. 5, pp. 628–629.

Pilař, Jan: "Ženám na Strahově". In: Otakar Mohyla – Karel Procházka (eds.): *Verše ze Strahova*. Olympia, Prague 1985.

Pinkava, Jindřich: "Estetika a sport". *Teorie a praxe tělesné výchovy*, 1967, vol. 15, nr. 11, pp. 667–671.

Pluhař, Jan: "O činnosti dozorčího sboru". In: Rudolf Procházka (ed.), *Památník X. všesokolského sletu v Praze 1938*. Československá obec sokolská, Prague 1939, pp. 288–290. *Program I. celostátní spartakiády 1955*. Státní tělovýchovné nakladatelství, Prague 1955.

"Poučení z hodnocení vývoje tělovýchovné organizace v uplynulém období schválené XII. plenárním zasedáním ÚV ČSTV dne 25. září 1971". In: Jaroslav Marek (ed.): *Za socialistický systém tělesné výchovy. Dokumenty od nár. a demokratické revoluce po 15. sjezd KSČ*. Olympia, Prague 1978, pp. 200–215.

Procházka, Rudolf: "29. června". In: Rudolf Procházka (ed.): *Památník X. všesokolského sletu v Praze 1938*. Československá obec sokolská, Prague 1939, p. 144.

Procházka, Zdeněk Horymír: "Hudba jako nedílná součást hromadného vystoupení". In: *Vědecká konference o teoretických a metodických*

základech masových tělovýchovných vystoupení (19.–20. 2. 1956).
Institut tělesné výchovy a sportu, Prague 1956, pp. 98–101.

Prokešová, Hana: "Jsme pro název Sokol". *Základní tělesná výchova,*
1968, vol. 13, nr. 7, pp. 1–2.

Provazníková, Marie: "Láska k vlasti". *Sokolský věstník,* vol. 41, nr. 29,
19. 7. 1939, p. 365.

Provazníková, Marie: "Vývoj sletových společných cvičení žen". In: *Deset
sletů.* Přednášky z mimořádné vzdělávací školy Československé obce
sokolské o první desítce všesokolských sletů ve dnech 17. a 18. ledna
1948. Nakladatelství Československé obce sokolské, Prague 1948,
pp. 42–47.

Provazníková, Marie: "Ženský tělocvik sokolský za Tyrše a dnes". In:
Rudolf Procházka (ed.): *Památník IX. sletu všesokolského pořádaného
na oslavu stých narozenin Dr. Miroslava Tyrše za účasti svazu
"Slovanské Sokolstvo".* Československá obec sokolská, Prague 1933,
pp. 24–27.

První dělnická olympiáda v Praze 1921. Česká grafická unie a.s., Prague
1921.

Průkazky a pásky pro činovníky, ostatní pracovníky a pořadatelský sbor
ČSS 1975. Sportpropag, Prague 1975.

Přerovský, Jan: "Podíl školství na přípravě Československé spartakiády
1985". In: *Sborník ze semináře FTVS UK Praha k problematice
hromadných vystoupení Československé spartakiády.* Metasport,
Ostrava 1986, pp. 18–21.

Přibáň, Vilém: "Nastal čas rozhodujících činů!" *Tělovýchovný pracovník,*
1969, vol. 15, nr. 20, p. 220.

Riedlová, Ludmila: "Život vítězí nad smrtí". *Teorie a praxe tělesné
výchovy,* 1961, vol. 9, zvláštní číslo: Výsledky výzkumu II. celostátní
spartakiády 1960, pp. 31–33.

Riefenstahl, Leni: *Hinter den Kulissen des Reichsparteitag-Films.* Eher,
München 1935. *Richtlinien für die Leibeserziehung in Jungenschulen.*
Weidmannsche Verlagsbuchhandlung, Berlin 1937.

Rjumin, Jevgenij: *Massovye prazdnestva.* GIZ, Moscow – Leningrad
1927.

Romains, Jules: "Krok svobody". *Lidové noviny,* vol. 46, 3. 7. 1938, p. 1.

Rutte, Miroslav: "Sokolská prostná". In: *Památník XI. sletu všesokolského
v Praze 1948.* Československá obec sokolská, Prague 1949, pp. 137–138.

Sedlmayerová, Anna: "Matky". In: *Památník XI. sletu všesokolského v Praze 1948*. Československá obec sokolská, Prague 1949, pp. 102–103.

Segal, Michail D.: *Fizkuľturnoje prazdniki i zrelišča*. Fizkuľtura i sport, Moscow 1977.

Seifert, Jaroslav: "My chceme nový, lepší svět. Verše k sletovým dožínkám". In: *Památník XI. sletu všesokolského v Praze 1948*. Československá obec sokolská, Prague 1949, pp. 162–166.

Seliger, Václav a spol.: "Energetický výdej u skladeb hromadného vystoupení na III. CS". *Teorie a praxe tělesné výchovy*, 1966, vol. 14, nr. 3, pp. 137–153.

Seliger, Václav a spol.: "Výzkum fyziologické a pedagogické náročnosti skladeb hromadných vystoupení na Československé spartakiádě 1975". *Teorie a praxe tělesné výchovy*, 1976, vol. 24, nr. 11, pp. 644–685.

Serbus, Ladislav: "Historický vývoj masových tělovýchovných vystoupení u nás". In: *Vědecká konference o teoretických a metodických základech masových* tělovýchovných vystoupení (19.–20. 2. 1956). Institut tělesné výchovy a sportu, Prague 1956, pp. 1–29.

Serbus, Ladislav: *Tělesná kultura v podmínkách socialistické alternativy vědeckotechnické revoluce*. Plán věd. práce Univ. Karlovy v Praze "Socialistické Československo dnes a v roce 2000". Fakulta tělesné výchovy a sportu Univerzity Karlovy, Prague 1973.

Serbus, Ladislav – Kos, Bohumil – Mihule, Jaroslav: *Historický vývoj a základy tělovýchovných vystoupení v ČSSR*. STNP, Prague 1962. Společná cvičení pro veřejné vystoupení části I. divize v Irkutsku v měsíci červnu 1919. S.n., s.l.

Stavěl, Jiří: "Co dala sletu Praha". In: Rudolf Procházka (ed.), *Památník X. všesokolského sletu v Praze 1938*. Československá obec sokolská, Prague 1939, pp. 306–308.

Stránský, Antonín: "Odraz ideje hromadných cvičení u cvičence a u diváka". In: *Vědecká konference o teoretických a metodických základech masových tělovýchovných vystoupení* (19. – 20. 2. 1956). Institut tělesné výchovy a sportu, Prague 1956, pp. 49–52.

Strnad, Miloš: "Životní jubileum doc. dr. Boženy Drdácké, CSc.". *Teorie a praxe tělesné výchovy*, 1987, vol. 35, nr. 3, p. 192.

Svatoň, Vratislav: "Zabezpečení cvičitelů ZRTV v přípravě spartakiádních skladeb". In: *Sborník ze semináře FTVS UK Praha k problematice hromadných vystoupení Československé spartakiády*. Metasport, Ostrava 1986, pp. 22–26.

Šaršeová, Jožka: *Tak to jsem já...*. Mladá fronta, Prague 1981.

Škrobánková, Zora – Kroupa, Jaroslav: "Vliv nácviku skladby 'Jaro země mé' na rozvoj pohybové paměti a kultury pohybu cvičenek". *Teorie a praxe tělesné výchovy*, 1966, vol. 14, nr. 4, pp. 245–247.

Šotola, Jiří – Šiktanc, Karel: *II. celostátní spartakiáda*. Státní tělovýchovné nakladatelství, Prague 1961.

Šotola, Jiří – Šiktanc, Karel: "Člověk v zástupech". In: Ctibor Rybár – Jan Novotný (eds.): *V rytmu krásy a radosti. 15 let československé tělovýchovy*. Státní tělovýchovné nakladatelství, Prague 1960.

Šourek, Otakar: "Slety a umění hudební". In: *Deset sletů*. Přednášky z mimořádné vzdělávací školy Československé obce sokolské o první desítce všesokolských sletů ve dnech 17. a 18. ledna 1948. Nakladatelství Československé obce sokolské, Praguea 1948, pp. 35–41.

Štech, Václav Vilém: "Slety a výtvarné umění". In: *Deset sletů*. Přednášky z mimořádné vzdělávací školy Československé obce sokolské o první desítce všesokolských sletů ve dnech 17. a 18. ledna 1948. Nakladatelství Československé obce sokolské, Prague 1948, pp. 28–34.

Šterc, Jaroslav: Československé spartakiády. Nejmasovější projev naší tělesné výchovy. Olympia, Prague 1975.

Šterc, Jaroslav: "Řízení tělovýchovných podniků". In: *Vědecká konference o teoretických a metodických základech masových tělovýchovných vystoupení* (19.–20. 2. 1956). Institut tělesné výchovy a sportu, Prague 1956, pp. 108–110.

Štoll, Ladislav: *Politický smysl sokolství*. Karel Borecký, Prague 1932.

Šverma, Jan: "Nedáme se!". *Rudé právo*, vol. 18, 3. 7. 1938, p. 1.

Thiele, Vladimír: "Sletové město". In: *Památník XI. sletu všesokolského v Praze 1948*. Československá obec sokolská, Prague 1949, p. 28.

Träger, Josef: "Sokolstvo a divadlo". Žijeme, 1932, vol. 2, nr. 3–4, pp. 76–77.

Třešňáková, Vlasta: "Úloha cvičebních úborů při hromadném vystoupení". In: *Vědecká konference o teoretických a metodických základech masových tělovýchovných vystoupení* (19.–20. 2. 1956). Institut tělesné výchovy a sportu, Prague 1956, pp. 150–152.

Tvrdík, František: "Povětrnostní služba na sletišti". In: Památník XI. Sletu Všesokolského V Praze 1948. Československá obec sokolská, Prague 1949, pp. 208–209.

Tyrš, Miroslav: *Cvičení veřejná a závodnická.* Československá obec sokolská, Prague 1932.

Tyrš, Miroslav: *Náš úkol, směr a cíl.* Vzlet, Prague 1992.

Tyrš, Miroslav: "Řeč o veřejném cvičení Sokola Pražského dne 26. března 1865". In: Josef Scheiner (ed.): Úvahy a řeči Dr. Miroslava Tyrše. Nákladem tělocvičné jednoty Sokol, Prague 1894.

Tyrš, Miroslav: *Tělocvik v ohledu esthetickém.* Karel Novák, Prgue 1926.

Tyršová, Renáta: *Miroslav Tyrš, jeho osobnost a dílo.* Podle zápisků, korespondence, rukopisné pozůstalosti a mých vzpomínek. Český čtenář, Prague 1932.

Vaculík, Ludvík: "Paže tuž, vlasti služ!". *Lidové noviny*, vol. 19, 11. 7. 2006, p. 12.

Vaníček, Karel: *Sokolstvo, jeho směr a cíl.* Edv. Grégr, Prague 1891.

Veselý, Josef (ed.): *Směr Strahov.* Sborník nejdůležitějších informací, metodických návodů, námětů, básní a písní k rozvíjení kulturně výchovné a sportovní činnosti v průběhu přípravy a konání Čs. spartakiády 1990. Naše vojsko, Prague 1989.

Vorel, Miroslav: "Hygienicko-technický průzkum III. CS". *Teorie a praxe tělesné výchovy*, 1966, vol. 14, nr. 8, pp. 483–487.

Wallhausen, Johann Jacobi von: *Kriegskunst zu Fuss.* Oppenheim 1615.

Weigner, Karel: "Zdravím k síle národa a ke kráse života". In: Jan Hiller (ed.): *Památník VII. sletu všesokolského v Praze 1920.* Československá obec sokolská, Prague 1923, pp. 30–33.

Weiss, Jiří: "Natáčíme sletový film". In: *Památník XI. sletu všesokolského v Praze 1948.* Československá obec sokolská, Prague 1949, p. 182–183.

Wolf, Augustin: "Hygiena stravování na spartakiádě". *Výživa lidu*, 1955, vol. 10, nr. 6, pp. 1–2.

Záhořík, Karel: "Pohled dopředu i zpět". *Sokolský věstník*, vol. 43, 12. 3. 1941.

Zápotocký, Antonín: *Rudá záře nad Kladnem.* Práce, Prague 1951.

Zedník, František: "Orientace cvičenců na cvičišti při II. CS". *Teorie a praxe tělesné výchovy*, 1960, vol. 8, pp. 153–156.

Zeman, Miloš: "Komplexní prognostický model československé tělovýchovy". *Teorie a praxe tělesné výchovy*, 1973, vol. 21, nr. 5, pp. 263–271.

Zich, Otakar: "Estetické dojmy sletové". In: Jan Hiller (ed.): *Památník VII. sletu všesokolského v Praze 1920.* Československá obec sokolská, Prague 1923, pp. 265–267.

Zich, Otakar: *Sokolstvo s hlediska estetického*. Československá obec sokolská, Prague 1920.

Žáček, Rudolf: "Závěry z orientačního průzkumu organizačního provozu východní části strahovského areálu v době III. ČS". *Teorie a praxe tělesné výchovy*, 1966, vol. 14, nr. 4, pp. 247–249.

Žáček, Rudolf: "Několik metodických závěrů pro tělovýchovnou praxi ze zkušeností z I. celostátní spartakiády". In: *Vědecká konference o teoretických a metodických základech masových tělovýchovných vystoupení* (19.–20. 2. 1956). Institut tělesné výchovy a sportu, Prague 1956.

Žitná, Jarina: "Cestou sokolskou". In: *XII. všesokolský slet*. Prague 1994. Česká obec sokolská, Prague – Litomyšl 1995, pp. 8–9.

Žižka, Jiří: "Dramaturgie hromadných tělovýchovných vystoupení ČSS 75". *Teorie a praxe tělesné výchovy*, 1975, vol. 23, nr. 6, pp. 321–327.

Žižka, Jiří: *Pořadová cvičení*. Sportovní a turistické nakladatelství, Prague 1957.

Žižka, Jiří: "Tělovýchovná vystoupení ve svazu ZRTV". In: Jarmila Kostková (ed.): *Svaz základní a rekreační tělesné výchovy*. Česká asociace Sport pro všechny, Prague 2005, pp. 92–104.

Secondary sources

Adorno, Theodor W. – Horkheimer, Max: *Dialectic of Enlightenment: Philosophic Fragments*, trans. Edmund Jephcott, Stanford University Press, Stanford 2002.

Anderson, Benedict: *Imagined Communities. Reflections on the Origin and Spread of Nationalism*. Verso, London 1993.

Bakhtin, Mikhail M.: *Rabelais and his World*. Indiana University Press, Bloomington, IN. 2009.

Balcárek, Ferdinand – Kopp, Karel: "Masarykův státní stadion na Strahově". *Architekt SIA*, 1938, vol. 37, nr. 7, pp. 109–121.

Bale, John: "The Spatial Development of the Modern Stadium". *International Review for the Sociology of Sport*, 1993, vol. 28, nr. 2–3, pp. 121–133.

Bell, Catherine: *Ritual. Perspectives and Dimensions*. Oxford University Press, Oxford 2009.

Berezin, Mabel: *Making the fascist self. The political culture of interwar Italy*. Cornell University Press, Ithaca 1997.

Berlant, Lauren: *The Queen of America Goes to Washington City. Essays on Sex and Citizenship*. Duke University Press, Durham 1997.

Berlin, Isaiah: *Der Nationalismus*. Hain, Bodenheim 1990.

Binns, Christopher A. P.: "The changing Face of Power. Revolution and Accommodation in the Development of the Soviet Ceremonial System I., II.". *Man* (New Series), 1979, vol. 14, nr. 4, pp. 585–606; 1980, vol. 15, nr. 1, pp. 170–187.

Borák, Mečislav: "Zločin v Katyni a jeho české a slovenské souvislosti". In: Miroslav Šesták – Emil Voráček (eds.): *Evropa mezi Německem a Ruskem. Sborník prací k sedmdesátinám Jaroslava Valenty*. Historický ústav Akademie věd České republiky, Prague 2000, pp. 505–522.

Bredekamp, Horst: *Thomas Hobbes Der Leviathan. Das Urbild des modernen Staates und seine Gegenbilder. 1651-2001*. Akademie Verlag, Berlin 2003.

Bren, Paulina: *The Greengrocer and his TV: The Culture of Communism After the 1968 Prague Spring*. Cornell University Press, Ithaca 2010.

Bröckling, Ulrich: *Disziplin. Soziologie und Geschichte militärischer Gehorsamsproduktion*. Wilhelm Fink Verlag, München 1997.

Burian, Michal: *Sudetoněmecké nacionalistické tělovýchovné organizace a československý stát v letech 1918 až 1938*. Karolinum, Prague 2012.

Canetti, Elias: *Crowds and Power*. The Viking Press, New York 1962.

Certeau, Michel de: *The Practice of Everyday Life*. University of California Press, Berkeley 1984.

Cohen, Jean-Louis: "Le Corbusier's and Pierre Jeanneret's 1936 Stadium for The People's Front". *Arqtexto*, 2010, vol. 10, pp. 17, pp. 6–15.

Corner, Paul (ed.): *Popular Opinion in Totalitarian Regimes. Fascism, Nazism, Communism*. Oxford University Press, Oxford 2009.

Day, Andrew: "The Rise and Fall of Stalinist Architecture". In: James Cracraft – Daniel B. Rowland (eds.): *Architectures of Russian Identity. 1500 to the Present*. Cornell University Press, Ithaca 2003, pp. 172–192.

Deak, Frantisek: "'Blue Blouse' (1923–1928)". *The Drama Review*, 1973, vol. 17, nr. 1, pp. 35–46.

Dedijer, Vladimir: *Tito Speaks. His Self Portrait and Struggle with Stalin*. Weidenfeld & Nicolson, London 1953.

Doorn, Jacques van: "Militärische und industrielle Organisation". In: Joachim Matthes (ed.): *Soziologie und Gesellschaft in den Niederlanden*. Neuwied, Berlin 1965, pp. 276–300.

Douglas, Mary: *Purity and Danger. An Analysis of Concepts of Pollution and Taboo*. Routledge & Kegan Paul, London 1978.

Düding, Dieter – Friedemann, Peter – Münch, Paul (eds.): *Öffentliche Festkultur. Politische Feste in Deutschland von der Aufklärung bis zum Ersten Weltkrieg*. Rowohlt, Hamburg 1988.

Edelman, Robert: *Serious fun. A history of spectator sports in the USSR*. Oxford University Press, New York 1993.

Eichberg, Henning: *Bodily democracy. Towards a philosophy of sport for all*. Routledge, London 2011.

Eichberg, Henning: "Body culture and democratic nationalism. 'Popular gymnastics' in nineteenth-century Denmark". *The International Journal of the History of Sport*, 1995, vol. 12, nr. 2, pp. 108–124.

Eichberg, Henning: *Body Cultures. Essays on Sport, Space and Identity*. Routledge, London – New York 1998.

Eichberg, Henning: "Stadium, Pyramid, Labyrinth. Eye and Body on the Move". In: John Bale – Olof Moen (eds.): *The Stadium and the City*. Keele University Press, Stafordshire 1995, pp. 323–347.

Eisen, George: "Zionism, Nationalism and the Emergence of the Jüdische Turnerschaft". *Leo Baeck Institute Yearbook*, 1983, vol. 28, nr. 1, pp. 247–262.

Eisenberg, Christiane: "Charismatic National Leader. Turnvater Jahn". *The International Journal of the History of Sport*, 1996, vol. 13, nr. 1, pp. 14–27.

Elias, Norbert: *The Germans*. Polity Press, Cambridge 1994.

Fidelius, Petr: *Řeč komunistické moci*. Triáda, Prague 1998.

Fierzová, Olga: *Dětské osudy z doby poválečné. Záznamy ze záchranné akce přátel Milíčova domu v Praze*. Spolek přátel mládeže a družstva Milíčův dům, Prague 1992.

Fišerová, Eva (ed.): *XIII. všesokolský slet*, Praha 2000. Česká obec sokolská, Prague 2001.

Fitzpatrick, Sheila: "Ascribing Class. The Construction of Social Identity in Soviet Russia". In: Sheila Fitzpatrick: *Stalinism. New Directions*. Routledge, London 2000, pp. 20–46.

404

Fitzpatrick, Sheila: *Everyday Stalinism. Ordinary Life in Extraordinary Times. Soviet Russia in the 1930s.* Oxford University Press, Oxford – New York 2000.

Fitzpatrick, Sheila (ed.): *Stalinism.* New Directions. Routledge, London 1999.

Fojtík, Pavel: *Po kolejích na Petřín.* Dopravní podnik hl. m. Prahy, Prague 2001.

Foucault, Michel: *Discipline and Punish: The Birth of the Prison.* Penguin Books, Harmondsworth 1985.

Franc, Martin: "Socialism and the Overweight Nation: Questions of Ideology, Science and Obesity in Czechoslovakia, 1950–70". In: Oddy, Derek J. – Atkins, Peter J. – Amilien, Virginie (eds.): *The Rise of Obesity in Europe. A Twentieth Century Food History.* Ashgate, Farnham – Burlington 2009, pp. 193–205.

Franc, Martin – Knapík, Jiří (eds.): *Průvodce kulturním děním a životním stylem v českých zemích 1948–1967.* Academia, Prague 2011.

Frie, Ewald: "Militärische Massenrituale". In: Michael Krüger (ed.): *Der deutsche Sport auf dem Weg in die Moderne. Carl Diem und seine Zeit.* LIT, Berlin 2009, pp. 59–74.

Frommer, Benjamin: *National Cleansing: Retribution against Nazi Collaborators in Postwar Czechoslovakia.* Cambridge University Press, New York 2005.

Fulbrook, Mary. "The Concept of 'Normalisation' and the GDR in Comparative Perspective". In: Mary Fulbrook (ed.) *Power and Society in the GDR, 1961–1979. The "Normalisation of Rule"?.* Berghahn Books, New York – Oxford 2009.

Geertz, Clifford: *Negara. The Theatre State in Nineteenth-Century Bali.* Princeton University Press, Princeton 1983.

Geldern, James von: *Bolshevik Festivals, 1917–1920.* University of California Press, Berkeley 1993.

Gentile, Emilio: *The Sacralization of Politics in Fascist Italy.* Harvard University Press, Cambridge, MA 1996.

Goldman, Wendy: *Women at the Gates. Gender and Industry in Stalin's Russia.* Cambridge University Press, Cambridge 2001.

Grebeníčková, Růžena: *Tělo a tělesnost v novověkém myšlení.* Prostor, Prague 1997.

Griffin, Roger: *The Nature of Fascism.* Pinter Publishers, London 1991.

Grigorov, Dimitar: "'Druže Tito, mi ti se kunemo.' Ritual and Political Power in Yugoslavia. Tito's Birthday Celebrations (1945–1987)". In: Joaquim Carvalho (ed.): *Religion, Ritual and Mythology. Aspects of Identity Formation in Europe*. Pisa University Press, Pisa 2006, pp. 275–292.

Boris Groys, *The Total Art of Stalinism, Avant-Garde, Aesthetic Dictatorship, and Beyond*.: Princeton University Press, Princeton 1992.

Grunberger, Richard: *Social History of the Third Reich*. Penguin Books, London 1991.

Gudeman, Stephen: *Economics as Culture*. Routledge, London 1986.

Hajo, Bernett: *Der Weg des Sports in die nationalsozialistische Diktatur*. Hofmann, Schorndorf 1983.

Hartmann, Grit: "Der verleugnete Architekt. Die Planungen des Werner March". In: Grit Hartmann – Cornelia Jeske – Daniel Sturm (eds.): *Stadiongeschichten 1863-2012. Leipzig zwischen Turnfest, Traumarena und Olympia*. Forum Verlag, Leipzig 2002, pp. 21–38.

Hartmann, Grit: "Drei Hepp-hepps und drei Hurras. Turnfeste in Leipzig 1863–1987". In: Grit Hartmann – Cornelia Jeske – Daniel Sturm (eds.): *Stadiongeschichten 1863-2012. Leipzig zwischen Turnfest, Traumarena und Olympia*. Forum Verlag, Leipzig 2002, pp. 66–82.

Havelková, Hana – Oates-Indruchová, Libora: *The Politics of Gender Culture under State Socialism. An Expropriated Voice*. Routledge, New York 2014.

Havlíček, Věnceslav: *Tyršovy snahy vojenské - Tyrš či Hanuš? - Vliv Darwinovy nauky na Tyrše*. Československá obec sokolská, Prague 1923.

Heczková, Libuše: "Tělo v pohybu. Národní sokolské tělo od daltonismu k rytmice". In: Taťána Petrasová – Pavla Machalíková (eds.): *Tělo a tělesnost v české kultuře 19. století*. Academia, Prague 2010, pp. 157–166.

Hermann, Tomáš: "Antropologie, evoluční teorie, život národa". In: Taťána Petrasová – Pavla Machalíková (eds.): *Tělo a tělesnost v české kultuře 19. století*. Academia, Prague 2010, pp. 15–26.

Hoberman, John M.: *Sport and Political Ideology*. University of Texas, Austin 1984.

Holý, Ladislav: *The Little Czech and the Great Czech Nation. National Identity and the Post-Communist Transformation of Society*. Cambridge University Press, Cambridge 1996.

Horáček, Michal: *Jak pukaly ledy*. Ex libris, Prague 1990.

Janáček, Pavel: "Listopad ve znamení Théty". *Tvar*, 2001, vol. 12, nr. 1, p. 1 and 4.

Jančář, Josef: "Dokonalost prostého života. Lidová kultura, folklor a folklorismus". *Dějiny a současnost*, 2004, vol. 26, nr. 6, pp. 27–31.

Jandásek, Ladislav: *Dr. Miroslav Tyrš*. Moravský legionář, Brno 1924.

Janke, Pia: *Politische Massenfestspiele in Österreich zwischen 1918 und 1938*. Böhlau Verlag, Wien 2010.

Jarausch, Konrad (ed.): *Dictatorship as Experience. Toward a Socio-Cultural History of the GDR*. Berghahn Books, New York – Oxford 1999.

Jerome, K. Jerome: *Tři muži na toulkách*. XYZ, Prague 2008.

Johnson, Molly Wilkinson: *Training Socialist Citizens. Sports and the State in East Germany*. Brill Academic Publishers, Leiden 2008.

Kalinová, Lenka: *Společenské proměny v čase socialistického experimentu. K sociálním dějinám v letech 1945-1969*. Academia, Prague 2007.

Kaplan, Karel: *Národní fronta 1948-1960*. Academia, Prague 2012.

Klimó, Árpád – Rolf, Malte: "Rausch und Diktatur". *Zeitschrift für Geschichtswissenschaft*, 2003, vol. 51, nr. 10, pp. 877–895.

Kocka, Jürgen: "German History before Hitler. The Debate about the German 'Sonderweg'". *Journal of Contemporary History*, 1988, vol. 23, nr. 1, pp. 3–16.

Kolářová, Kateřina (ed.): *Jinakost - postižení - kritika. Společenské konstrukty nezpůsobilosti a hendikepu*. SLON, Prague 2012.

Kopeček, Michal: *Hledání ztraceného smyslu revoluce. Zrod a počátky marxistického revizionismu ve střední Evropě 1953-1960*. Argo, Prague 2009.

Kozáková, Zlata: *Sokolské slety 1882-1948*. Orbis, Prague 1994.

Kracauer, Siegfried: *The Mass Ornament*, Cambridge, Ma.: Harvard University Press, 1955.

Krakovský, Roman: *Rituel du 1er mai en Tchécoslovaquie: 1948-1989*. L'Harmattan, Paris – Budapest –Torino 2004.

Kramerová, Daniela (ed.): *Bruselský sen. Československá účast na světové výstavě EXPO 58 v Bruselu a životní styl 1. poloviny 60. let*. Arbor vitae, Prague 2008.

Krapfl, James: *Revolution with a Human Face: Politics, Culture, and Community in Czechoslovakia, 1989-1992*. Cornell University Press, Ithaca 2013.

Krejčí, Antonín: *Dr. Josef Scheiner*. Moravský Legionář, Brno 1932.

Krejčí, Jaroslav: *Miroslav Tyrš. Filozof, pedagog a estetik českého tělocviku*. Index, Köln 1986.

Krüger, Arnd: "There Goes This Art of Manliness. Naturism and Racial Hygiene in Germany". *Journal of Sport History*, 1991, vol. 18, nr. 1, pp. 135–158.

Krüger, Michael: "Die Bedeutung der Deutschen Turnfeste des Reichsgründungsjahrzehnts für die kulturelle Nationsbildung in Deutschland". *Sozial- und Zeitgeschichte des Sports*, 1995, vol. 9, nr. 1, pp. 7–21.

Krüger, Michael: "Turnfeste als politische Massenrituale des 19. und frühen 20. Jahrhunderts". In: Michael Krüger (ed.): *Der deutsche Sport auf dem Weg in die Moderne. Carl Diem und seine Zeit*. LIT, Berlin 2009, pp. 75–91.

Lane, Christel: The Rites of Rulers. Ritual in Industrial Society – the Soviet Case. Cambridge University Press, Cambridge 1981.

Lavrentiev, Aleksandr Nikolajevich: Aleksander Rodchenko. Fotografi. Planeta, Moscow 1987.

Le Corbusier – Jeanneret, Pierre: *Oeuvre Complete, 1934-1938*. Girsberger, Zurich 1939.

Lenčéšová, Michaela: *Prvá celoštátna spartakiáda 1955*. MA Thesis, FF UKF, Nitra 2015.

Lévi-Strauss, Claude: *The savage mind*. Weidenfeld & Nicholson, London 1972.

Lissinna, Hartmut E.: *Nationale Sportfeste im nationalsozialistischen Deutschland*. Palatium-Verlag, Mannheim 1997.

Ljunggren, Jens: "The Masculine Road through Modernity. Ling Gymnastics and Male Socialization in Nineteenth-Century Sweden". In: James A. Mangan (ed.): *Making European Masculinities. Sport, Europe, Gender*. Routledge, London 2013, pp. 86–111.

Lüdtke, Alf: "'… den Menschen vergessen'? – oder: Das Maß der Sicherheit. Arbeiterverhalten der 1950er Jahre im Blick von MfS, SED, FDGB und staatlichen Leitungen". In: Alf Lüdtke – Peter Becker (eds.): *Akten, Eingaben, Schaufenster - Die DDR und ihre Texte. Erkundungen zu Herrschaft und Alltag*. Akademie Verlag, Berlin 1997, pp. 189–222.

Lüdtke, Alf: *Eigen-Sinn. Fabrikalltag, Arbeitererfahrungen und Politik vom Kaiserreich bis in den Faschismus*. Ergebnisse, Hamburg 1993.

Lüdtke, Alf: "The Role of State Violence in the Period of Transition to Industrial Capitalism. The Example of Prussia from 1815 to 1848". *Social History*, 1979, vol. 4, nr. 2, pp. 175–221.

Luh, Andreas: *Der Deutsche Turnverband in der Ersten Tschechoslowakischen Republik. Vom völkischen Vereinsbetrieb zur volkspolitischen Bewegung.* Verlag Oldenbourg, München 2006.

Macura, Vladimír: *Masarykovy boty.* Pražská imaginace, Prague 1993.

Macura, Vladimír: "Souvislosti Štollovy marxistické analýzy sokolství. O odborné práci Ladislava Štolla Politický smysl sokolství (1932)". *Česká literatura*, 1982, vol. 30, nr. 6, pp. 547–550.

Macura, Vladimír: *Šťastný věk a jiné studie o socialistické kultuře.* Academia, Prague 2008.

Macura, Vladimír: *Znamení zrodu. České národní obrození jako kulturní typ.* H & H, Jinočany 1995.

Magdalinski, Tara: "Beyond Hitler. Alfred Baeumler, Ideology and Physical Education in the Third Reich". *Sporting Traditions*, 1995, vol. 11, nr. 2, pp. 61–79.

Mangan, J. A.: "The Potent Image and the Permanent Prometheus". In: Mangan, J. A (ed.): *Shaping the Superman. Fascist Body as Political Icon - Aryan Fascism.* Frank Cass, London 1999, pp. 11–22.

Masaryk, Tomáš Garrigue: *Česká otázka - Naše nynější krize - Jan Hus.* Ústav T. G. Masaryka, Prague 2000.

Mauss, Marcel: "Les techniques du corps". *Journal de Psychologie*, 1936, vol. 32, nr. 3–4, pp. 271–293.

Mauss, Marcel: *The Gift. The Form and Reason for Exchange in Archaic Societies.* Routledge, London (1925) 1990.

Mayer, Françoise: *Les Tchéques et leur communisme. Mémoire et identités politiques*, Paris 2003.

Messner, Michael A.: "Sports and Male Domination. The Female Athlete as Contested Ideological Terrain". In: Michael A. Messner – Donald F. Sabo (eds.): *Sport, men and the gender order. Critical Feminist Perspetives.* Human Kinetics Books, Champagne, Il. 1990, pp. 31–44.

Mojsejev, Igor A.: "Úvod". In: Milan Horák – Bohumil Kos – Miroslav Kremlík (eds.): *Sborové písně a tance Sovětské armády.* Naše vojsko, Prague 1952.

Moravia, Sergio: "From Homme machine to Homme Sensible. Changing Eighteenth-Century Models of Man's Image". *Journal of the History of Ideas*, 1978, vol. 39, nr. 1, pp. 45–60.

Mosse, George L.: *Nationalism and Sexuality. Middle Class Morality and Sexual Norms in Modern Europe.* Howard Fertig, New York 1985.

Mosse, George L.: *Nazi Culture. Intellectual, Cultural and Social Life in the Third Reich.* University of Wisconsin Press, Madison 2003.

Mosse, George L.: *The Image of Man. The Creation of Modern Masculinity.* Oxford University Press, Oxford 1996.

Mosse, George L.: *The Nationalisation of the Masses. Political Symbolism and Mass Movements in Germany from the Napoleonic Wars through the Third Reich.* Cornell University Press, New York 1975.

Možný, Ivo: *Moderní rodina. Mýty a skutečnosti.* Blok, Brno 1990.

Nabert, Thomas: "Stadionpläne – von der Grosskampfbahn am Völkerschlachtdenkmal zum Adolf-Hitler-Sportfeld". In: Thomas Nabert – Nannette Jackowski – Wolf-Dietrich Rost (eds.): *Sportforum Leipzig. Geschichte und Zukunft.* Pro Leipzig, Leipzig 2004, pp. 58–81.

Neumann, Herbert: *Deutsche Turnfeste, Spiegelbild der deutschen Turnbewegung.* Limpert, Wiesbaden 1987.

Nolte, Claire E.: "All For One! One For All! The Federation of Slavic Sokols and the Failure of Neo-Slavism". In: Pieter M. Judson – Marsha L. Rozenblit (eds.): *Constructing Nationalities in East Central Europe.* Berghahn Press, New York 2005, pp. 126–140.

Nolte, Claire E.: "Every Czech a Sokol! Feminism and Nationalism in the Czech Sokol Movement". *Austrian History Yearbook*, 1993, vol. 24, nr. 24, pp. 79–100.

Nolte, Claire E.: *The Sokol in the Czech Lands to 1914. Training for the Nation.* Palgrave Macmillan, New York 2002.

Nolte, Claire. "Celebrating Slavic Prague: Festivals and the Urban Environment," *Bohemia: Zeitschrift für Geschichte und Kultur der böhmischen Länder*, vol. 52 (2012), nr. 1, pp. 37–54.

Novotná, Viléma: "Ženské složky v ZRTV". In: Jarmila Kostková (ed.): *Svaz základní a rekreační tělesné výchovy.* Česká asociace Sport pro všechny, Prague 2005, pp. 84–90.

Oates-Indruchová, Libora: 'The Ideology of the Genderless Sporting Body: Reflections on the Czech State-Socialist Concept of Physical Culture'. In: Naomi Segal, Roger Cook, Carl Stychin and Lib Taylor (eds.): *In/determinate Bodies*, Macmillan, London 2002, pp. 48–66.

Ozouf, Mona: *Festivals and the French Revolution.* Harvard University Press, Cambridge, Ma. 1988.

Pasák, Tomáš: "Přemysl Pitter – zachránce německých a židovských dětí v roce 1945". In: *Přemysl Pitter. Život a dílo*. Pedagogické muzeum Jana Amose Komenského, Prague 1994.

Pažout, Jaroslav: "'Chceme světlo! Chceme studovat!' Demonstrace studentů z vysokoškolských kolejí v Praze na Strahově 31. října 1967". *Paměť a dějiny*, 2008, vol. 2, nr. 1, pp. 4–13.

Perútka, Jaromír – Grexa, Ján: *Dejiny telesnej kultúry na Slovensku*. Univerzita Komenského, Bratislava 1995.

Petrone, Karen: *Life Has Become More Joyous, Comrades. Celebrations in the Time of Stalin*. Indiana University Press, Bloomington – Indianapolis 2000.

Pfister, Gertrud: "Frauen bei deutschen Turnfesten. Zum Wandel der Geschlechterordnung in der Turnbewegung". *Sportwissenschaft*, 2000, vol. 30, nr. 2, pp. 156–179.

Pfister Gertrud: "Militarismus in der kollektiven Symbolik der Deutschen Turnerschaft am Beispiel des Leipziger Turnfestes 1913". In: Heinrich Becker (ed.): *Sport im Spannungsfeld von Krieg und Frieden*. DVS, Clausthal-Zellerfeld 1985, pp. 64–79.

Phillips, Sarah D.: "'There Are No Invalids in the USSR!' A Missing Soviet Chapter in the New Disability History". *Disabilities Studies Quartely*, 2009, vol. 29, nr. 3, pp. 1–35.

Pokludová, Andrea – Svatošová, Hana: "Turneři, sokolové a obecní samospráva. Opava, Olomouc, Praha". In: Taťána Petrasová – Pavla Machalíková (eds.): *Tělo a tělesnost v české kultuře 19. století*. Academia, Prague 2010, pp. 59–69.

Pokorný, Jiří: "Sokol". In: Kristina Kaiserová – Jiří Rak (eds.): *Nacionalizace společnosti v Čechách 1848-1914*. Univerzita Jana Evangelisty Purkyně, Ústí nad Labem 2008, pp. 375–396.

Provazníková, Marie: *To byl Sokol*. České slovo, Munich 1988.

Randák, Jan – Nečasová, Denisa: "Genderové aspekty konstrukce reálného a symbolického těla". In: Taťána Petrasová – Pavla Machalíková (eds.): *Tělo a tělesnost v české kultuře 19. století*. Academia, Prague 2010, pp. 139–147.

Ratajová, Jana: "Pražské májové oslavy 1948–1989. Příspěvek k dějinám komunistické propagandy". *Kuděj. Časopis pro kulturní dějiny*, 2000, vol. 2, nr. 1, pp. 51–64.

Reifová, Irena: "Kryty moci a úkryty před mocí". In: Jakub Končelík – Barbara Köpplová – Irena Prázová (eds.). *Konsolidace podnikání a vládnutí v České republice a Evropské unii. II. Sociologie, prognostika a správa.* Matfyzpress, Prague 2002, pp. 354–371.

Riordan, James: "Moscow 1980. The Games of the XXIInd Olympiad". In: John F. Findling – Kimberly D. Pelle (eds.): *Historical Dictionary of the Modern Olympic Movement*, Greenwood Press, London 1996, pp. 161–168.

Riordan, James: *Sport in Soviet Society*. Cambridge University Press, Cambridge 1977.

Roček, Antonín: *Analýza vývoje turnerské tělovýchovy v českých zemích a Československu 1810-1965*, 2. Národní muzeum, Prague 2000 (unpublished).

Rodekamp, Volker (ed.): *Sport: Schau. Deutsche Turnfeste 1860-2002*. Stadtgeschichtliches Museum Leipzig, Leipzig 2002.

Rolf, Malte: *Das sowjetische Massenfest*. Hamburger Edition, Hamburg 2006.

Roubal, Petr: "Jak se dělá lid? Listopadové demonstrace jako vizuální politická strategie". *Dějiny a současnost*, 2009, vol. 31, special issue to the 20. anniversary of November 17, 1989, pp. 40–43.

Roubal, Petr: "Visual Representation of the Czech/Czechoslovak State, 1945–2000. A Survey of the Literature". *European Review of History - Revue européenne d'Histoire*, 2006, vol. 13, nr. 1, pp. 83–113.

Sak, Robert: *Miroslav Tyrš*. Vyšehrad, Prague 2012.

Scott, James C.: *Weapons of the Weak. Everyday Forms of Peasant Resistance*. Yale University Press, New Haven 1985.

Sedlák, Prokop: *Historie golfu v českých zemích a na Slovensku*. Svojtka & Co, Prague 2004.

Schieder, Theodor (ed.): *Dokumentation der Vertreibung der Deutschen aus Ost-Mitteleuropa. Die Vertreibung der deutschen Bevölkerung aus der Tschechoslowakei*, 4/2. Deutscher Taschenbuch Verlag, München 1984.

Schmidt, Thomas: *Werner March. Architekt des Olympia-Stadions: 1894-1976*. Birkhäuser, Basel – Berlin 1992.

Schnapp, Jeffrey T.: *Staging Fascism. 18 BL and the Theater of Masses for Masses*. Stanford University Press, Stanford 1996.

Schovánek, Radek (ed.): *Svazek Dialog. Stb Versus Pavel Kohout. Dokumenty StB z operativních svazků Dialog a Kopa*. Paseka, Prague – Litomyšl 2006.

Slezkine, Yuri: "The USSR as a Communal Apartment, or How a Socialist State Promoted Ethnic Particularism". In: Sheila Fitzpatrick (ed.): *Stalinism. New Directions*. Routledge, London – New York 2000, pp. 313–347.

Sontag, Susan: *Under the Sign of Saturn*. Vintage Books, New York 1991.

Spurný, Matěj: *Most do budoucnosti. Laboratoř socialistické moderny na severu Čech*. Karolinum, Prague 2015.

Staněk, Tomáš: *Poválečné "excesy" v českých zemích v roce 1945 a jejich vyšetřování*. Ústav pro soudobé dějiny Akademie věd České republiky, Prague 2005.

Staněk, Tomáš: *Tábory v českých zemích 1945-1948*. Tilia, Šenov u Ostravy 1996.

Stehlík, Michal: "Spisovatel František Kožík a Státní bezpečnost. Cesta ke konci spolupráce 1968–1982". In: Pavel Andrš – Jana Čechurová – Luboš Velek a kol.: *Posláním historik. Pocta prof. Robertu Kvačkovi k 80. narozeninám*. Nakladatelství Lidové noviny, Prague 2012, pp. 455–466.

Stehlíková, Eva: "Listopadová katarze". *Theatralia*, 2009, vol. 12, nr. 1–2, pp. 19–33.

Stehlíková, Eva: "Obřadní a divadelní prvky v sokolském hnutí". In: *Divadlo v české kultuře 19. století*. Národní galerie, Prague 1985, pp. 161–166.

Strakoš, Martin: "Na cestě k socialistickému realismus – architektura Jiřího Krohy 40. let". In: Marcela Macharáčková (ed.): *Jiří Kroha (1893-1974). Architekt, malíř, designér, teoretik v proměnách umění 20. století*. Muzeum města Brna, Brno 2007, pp. 292–327.

Svobodová, Markéta: "Státní stadion v Praze". In: Rostislav Švácha (ed.): *Naprej! Česká sportovní architektura 1567-2012. Prostor - architektura, interiér, design*, Prague 2012, p. 154.

Svobodová, Markéta: "Věčný ruch a věčná nespokojenost nad Strahovským stadionem". *Stavba*, 2004, vol. 11, nr. 2, pp. 14–19.

Synnott, Anthony: *The Body Social. Symbolism, Self and Society*. Routledge, London – New York 1993.

Šikula, Martin: "Tři poznámky k násilné transformaci Sokola. Regionální sondy do postupné likvidace tradiční spolkové organizace v letech 1948–1952". Časopis Matice moravské, 2012, vol. 131, nr. 1, pp. 89–116.

Šinkovský, Roman: "Vývoj XV. turnerského kraje Deutschösterreich v letech 1886–1904. Přeměna liberálního tělocvičného svazu v antisemitskou organizaci". *Česká kinantropologie*, 2005, vol. 9, nr. 1, pp. 101–110.

Štěpánová, Irena: "Formování a funkce sokolského kroje v české společnosti v šedesátých a sedmdesátých letech 19. století". *Český lid*, 1997, vol. 84, nr. 2, pp. 137–147.

Štichová, Helena (ed.): *Retro spartakiáda 1955-1985*. Popron Music, Prague 2013.

Thamer, Hans-Ulrich: "The Orchestration of the National Community. The Nuremberg Party Rallies of the NSDAP". In: Gunter Berghaus (ed.): *Fascism and Theatre. Comparative Studies on the Aesthetics and Politics of Performance in Europe 1925-1945*. Berghahn, Oxford 1996, pp. 172–190.

Tolleneer, Jan: "The dual meaning of 'Fatherland' and Catholic gymnasts in Belgium, 1892–1914". *International Journal of the History of Sport*, 1995, vol. 8, nr. 12, pp. 94–107.

Turner, Victor W.: *The Forest of Symbols. Aspects of Ndembu Ritual.* Cornell University Press, Ithaca 1967.

Ueberhorst, Horst: *Friedrich Ludwig Jahn and His Time: 1778-1852*. Moos, München 1982.

Ueberhorst, Horst: *Turner unterm Sternenbanner. Der Kampf der deutsch--amerikanischen Turner für Einheit, Freiheit und soziale Gerechtigkeit 1848 bis 1918*. Heinz Moos Verlag, München 1978.

Uhlíř, Jan B. – Waic, Marek: *Sokol proti totalitě*. Univerzita Karlova, Fakulta tělesné výchovy a sportu, Prague 2001.

Verspohl, Franz-Joachim: *Stadionbauten von der Antike bis zur Gegenwart. Regie und Selbsterfahrung der Massen*. Anabas-Verlag, Giessen 1976.

Veyne, Paul: *Bread and Circuses. Historical Sociology and Political Pluralism*. Penguin Books, London 1992.

Vodochodský, Ivan: "Patriarchát na socialistický způsob. K genderovému řádu státního socialismu". *Gender - rovné příležitosti - výzkum*, 2007, vol. 8, nr. 2, pp. 34–42.

Waic, Marek: *Byli jsme a budem*. Agentura Leman, Prague 2012.

Waic, Marek: "Rej těl v rytmu vlastenectví. Sokolské slety 1882–1938". In: Taťána Petrasová – Pavla Machalíková (eds.): *Tělo a tělesnost v české kultuře 19. století*. Academia, Prague 2010, pp. 51–58.

Waic, Marek: "Sokol Josef Scheiner". *Střed. Časopis pro mezioborová studia*, 2011, special issue: Muži října 1918, pp. 81–94.

Waic, Marek et al.: *Sokol v české společnosti 1862–1938*. Univerzita Karlova, Fakulta tělesné výchovy a sportu, Prague 1997.

Waic, Marek: "Sokolská organizace a pokus o sjednocení tělesné výchovy po mnichovském diktátu". In: Václav Hošek – Petr Jansa (eds.): *Psychosociální funkce pohybových aktivit v životním stylu člověka.* Univerzita Karlova, Fakulta tělesné výchovy a sportu, Prague 2000, pp. 116–118.

Waic, Marek (ed.): *Tělovýchova a sport ve službách české národní emancipace*. Karolinum, Prague 2013.

Waldauf, Jan: *Sokol. Malé dějiny velké myšlenky*, 1–3. Atelier IM, Luhačovice 2007–2010.

Weber, Wolfgang – Black, Paula: "Muscular Anschluss. German Bodies and Austrian Imitators". In: James A. Mangan (ed.): *Superman supreme. Fascist body as political icon - global fascism*. Frank Cass, London 2000, pp. 62–81.

Wheeler, Robert F.: "Organized Sport and Organized Labour. The Workers 'Sports Movement'". *Journal of Contemporary History*, 1978, vol. 13, nr. 2, pp. 191–210.

Wilk, Christopher (ed.): *Modernism. Designing a New World, 1914–1939*. Victoria & Albert Museum, London 2006.

Zakharov, Alexander V.: "Mass Celebrations in a Totalitarian System". In: Alla Efimova – Lev Manovich (eds.): *Tekstura. Russian Essays on Visual Culture*. University of Chicago Press, Chicago 1993.

Zarecor, Kimberly Elman. *Manufacturing a Socialist Modernity: Housing in Czechoslovakia, 1945–1960*. University of Pittsburgh Press, Pittsburgh 2011.

Zarecor, Kimberly Elman: "Jiří Kroha Reconsidered". *Umění*, 2004, vol. 52, nr. 5, pp. 435–444.

Zarecor, Kimberly Elman: "Stavoprojekt and the Atelier of National Artist Jiří Kroha in the 1950s/ Stavoprojekt a atelier národního umělce Jiřího Krohy v 50. letech.". In: Marcela Macharáčková (ed.): *Jiří Kroha (1893–1974) –Architect, Painter, Designer, Theorist: A 20th-century Metamorphosis/ Jiří Kroha (1893–1974) - architekt, malíř, designér, teoretik v proměnách umění 20. století*. Brno: ERA; Muzeum města Brna, pp. 103–140.

Zídek, Petr: "Soudružky a soudruzi, tužme se". *Lidové noviny*, příloha Orientace, vol. 18, 25. 6. 2005, pp. I–II.

Documentary films

Frič, Martin – Kádár Ján et al.: *Spartaki*áda. Studio uměleckých hraných filmů Praha, 1955, 88 min.

Frič, Martin – Kádár Ján et al.: *Mladé dny*. Studio uměleckých hraných filmů Praha, 1955, 83 min.

Frič, Martin: *X. všesokolský slet*. Československá obec sokolská, 1939, 12 min.

Krejčík, Rudolf. *Českoslove*nská *spartakiáda 1975*. Krátký film, Prague 1975, 64 min.

Krejčík, Rudolf: *Symfonie psané pohybem. Tradice hromadných tělovýchovných vystoupení I, II, III*. Krátký film, Prague 1987–1988, 88 min.

Krejčík, Rudolf: *Českoslove*nská *spartakiáda 1980*. Krátký film, Prague 1980, 63 min.

Mihle, Rudolf: *Zelená pro Strahov*. Amateur documentary film, 1980, 14 min.

Papoušek, Jaroslav: *II. celostátní spartakiáda*. II: *Mládí a krása*. Krátký film, Prague 1960, 44 min.

Střecha, Jiří: *Českoslove*nská *spartakiáda 1985*. Krátký film, Prague 1985, 12 min.

Weiss, Jiří: *Píseň o sletu I, II*. Československý státní film, 1948, 171 min.

LIST OF ILLUSTRATIONS

Cover photo: Performance of the army at the 1985 Czechoslovak Spartakiad (ČTK)

1. A poster for the 1938 Turnfest in Breslau (Wrocław) (National Museum).
2. A team of Prague Sokol Gymnastic Trainers at the 1st All-Sokol Slet in 1882. (National Museum).
3. A study by Josef Mánes for an illustration of the forged Dvůr Králové Manuscript.
4. Nude of Tyrš by Antonín Waldhauser.
5. Tyrš's own illustration to his article on the first Sokol Slet published in *Sokol* magazine in 1882.
6. Rehearsal of the ceremonial scene "Marathon" for the VI. All-Sokol Slet in 1912 on Letná Plain (National Museum).
7. Men taking the field at the 6th All-Sokol Slet in 1912 on Letná Plain (National Museum).
8. Exercises by female members of the Žižkov Sokol at Rieger Gardens in June 1914. (František Drtikol photograph National Museum).
9. Men performing a piece entitled the "An Oath to the Republic" at the 10th Slet at Strahov Stadium in 1938 (National Museum).
10. The construction of one of the corner entrances to Strahov Stadium in preparation for the 9th All-Sokol Slet of 1932.
11. Josef Sudek's photograph of the parade of Sokols during the 1932 Slet, published in the avantgard journal *Žijeme*.
12. A recruitment poster for exercises at the 1948 Slet (National Museum).
13. Women's entrace at the 1948 All-Sokol Slet (photo Václav Chochola).
14. Sokol parade in 1948 on Charles Bridge (photo Václav Chochola).
15. Illustration of a synchronized step drill in the book by Jiří Žižka: *Pořadová cvičení*. Prague 1957.
16. Performance of students with paper cubes at the 1st Czechoslovak Spartakiad of 1955 (photo Václav Chochola).
17. A performance by the apprentices of the work reserves entitled "A New Shift Begins" for the 1955 Spartakiad at Strahov Stadium.

18. Conclusion of the "A New Shift Begins" performance by the apprentices of the work reserves during the 1955 Spartakiad (National Museum).
19. A performance by Revolutionary Trade Union men for the 1955 Spartakiad (photo Václav Chochola).
20. Detail of a performance by the Revolutionary Trade Union women for the 1955 Spartakiad (photo Václav Chochola).
21. A performance by the Revolutionary Trade Union women for the 1955 Spartakiad (photo Václav Chochola).
22. An illustration from an instruction manual of the women's performances for the cancelled 1970 Spartakiad.
23. A performance by older female students entitled "My Country Is a Blossoming Meadow" during the 1965 Spartakiad (National Museum).
24. Parents and children exiting Strahov Stadium after performing at the 1975 Spartakiad (National Museum).
25. A women's performance during the 1975 Spartakiad. (photo Marie Hlušičková).
26. Performance of the older female students during the last Spartakiad in 1985 (National Museum).
27. Zdeněk Lhoták photograph from the *Spartakiad* series documenting the military's performance at a district Spartakiad in Prague in 1985.
28. Zdeněk Lhoták photograph from the *Spartakiad* series documenting the military's performance at a district Spartakiad in Prague in 1985.
29. Shooting Martin Fryč's film on the 1955 Spartakiad (photo Václav Chochola).
30. Communication diagram of position heads at Strahov Stadium during the 1975 Spartakiad.
31. Choreography plan of Spartakiad composition based on Piet Mondrian's *Tableau I: Composition with Black, Red, Grey, Yellow and Blue* from 1921 that Spartakiad organizer Pavel Belšan submitted at a 1986 seminar.
32. Manufacturing batons for women's performances at the 1975 Czechoslovak Spartakiad.
33. "Principles of Size System" from the brochure *Information on the Sizes of Gymnastics Attire*, published by several textile companies for the needs of 1975 Spartakiad participants.

34. Rehearsal for the 1955 Spartakiad in the gym of a Prague elementary school (photo Václav Chochola).
35. Rehearsal for the 1955 Spartakiad. Performance of Revolutionary Trade Union members at the Municipal Library in Prague (photo Václav Chochola).
36. A special Slet and Spartakiad tram circuit at Břevnov during the 1960 Spartakiad (photo Václav Chochola).
37. Pictogram from the brochure *Health Tips for Participants of the 1980 Czechoslovak Spartakiad.*
38. Departing the stadium during the 1960 Spartakiad (photo Václav Chochola).
39. The eastern stands of the Strahov Stadium remodelled in the international style by architects Josef Hrubý and František Cubra.
40. Linear perspective of Strahov Stadium's eastern grandstands from a northern view created in March 1968 by the architect Honke-Houfek as part of the 1970 Spartakiad preparations.
41. Layout of Strahov Stadium and dressing-room town prepared for the 1980 Spartakiad.
42. Arrangement of gymnasts for a performance at the 1st Czechoslovak Spartakiad in 1955 (photo Václav Chochola).
43. Choreography plan for the 1975 Spartakiad military performance documenting the "social geometry" that every Spartakiad piece was based on.
44. Chart of choreographic changes in the military piece for the 1975 Spartakiad.
45 The arrangement of junior women and women for a performance at Strahov Stadium during the 1980 Spartakiad (photo Pavel Štecha).
46. Refreshments at Strahov Stadium during the 1960 Spartakiad (photo Václav Chochola).
47. The Spartakiad parade at Wenceslas Square in Prague in 1955 (photo Václav Chochola).
48. Strahov Stadium stands during the 1955 Spartakiad (photo Václav Chochola).

Appendix

I.   Alfons Mucha-designed poster for the 6th All-Sokol Slet in 1912 (National Museum).

II.   Max Švabinský-designed poster for the 9th All-Sokol Slet in 1932 (National Museum).

III.   Ladislav Sutnar-designed poster for the 3rd Workers' Olympiad 1934 (National Museum).

IV.   The main poster for the 1955 Spartakiad (National Museum).

V.   Recruitment poster for the 1960 Spartakiad (National Museum).

VI.   Promotional poster for the military piece at the 1965 Spartakiad.

VII.   Zdeněk Filip-designed poster for the 1975 Spartakiad.

VIII.   Information flyer of the Prague Public Transit published for the 1965 Spartakiad.

IX.   Promotional brochure published by the Tesla company for the 1955 Spartakiad.

X.   The final scene of the juniors' piece "To New Tomorrows" by Marie Rejhonová.

XI.   A piece for the women and junior women at the 1985 Spartakiad.

XII.   A piece for the junior women at the 1985 Spartakiad.

XIII.   A military piece at the 1985 Spartakiad.

XIV.   An opening part of the women's performance at the 1985 Spartakiad.

INDEX